P9-DHT-465

AN INTRODUCTION
TO THE
LAW OF EVIDENCE

By

GRAHAM C. LILLY
Professor of Law
University of Virginia

ST. PAUL, MINN.
WEST PUBLISHING CO.
1978

COPYRIGHT © 1978 By WEST PUBLISHING CO.
Printed in the United States of America
Library of Congress Cataloging in Publication Data

Lilly, Graham C   1938–
    An introduction to the law of evidence.

    Includes index.
    1. Evidence (Law)—United States. I. Title.
KF8935.L54   347'.73'6   78–15868

ISBN 0–8299–2013–7

Lilly Law of Evld. MTB

2nd Reprint—1981

To Margaret Kemper Lilly

*

III

PREFACE AND ACKNOWLEDGEMENTS

My reader deserves a brief explanation why, in a field abundant with fine texts and treatises, I add yet another volume devoted to the law of evidence. I have long felt that students of evidence —broadly including all of those who inquire into the rules and principles of judicial proof—need a comparatively concise treatment of the subject, one that presupposes little or no prior knowledge in the field. Even practicing professionals often seek recourse to an introductory text, either to refresh their memories or to learn for the first time a subject not formally studied in law school; for this reason, I have endeavored to include within these pages adequate citations to primary and secondary sources.

But how will this book serve the law student who enrolls in a basic evidence course? Presumably, he or she has a coursebook and ready access to the great works in the field of evidence. My hope that this text may have at least a supplementary role in the formal educational process is based in part upon conversations with my own students. They find the law of evidence relatively simple in its separate parts, but elusive and difficult to grasp as a whole. They also affirm the widespread recognition among educators that the demands imposed by important new areas of law curtail the time available for the traditional legal subjects. The old ground must be covered more efficiently and quickly than in the past. Finally, I sense among my colleagues who teach evidence a restive attitude, a growing conviction that new pedagogic techniques must be developed both to engage the students' interest and to free the teacher from the arid repetition of the evidential basics.* Perhaps a book of this kind will have utility for those seeking a fresh approach in the classroom.

My debts to those who have encouraged and assisted me in writing this book are too numerous fully to recount here. I particularly want to thank Dean Monrad G. Paulsen and his suc-

---

* A coursebook that breaks new ground by abandoning the traditional case method of study is Lempert & Saltzburg, A Modern Approach to Evidence, West Publishing Co. (1977).

PREFACE AND ACKNOWLEDGEMENTS

cessor Dean Emerson G. Spies for their support, and to gratefully acknowledge that officials of the University of Virginia made available to me a grant under the Sesquicentennial Associateship Program of the Center for Advanced Studies, enabling me to devote a semester to writing and research. I am especially indebted, also, to my colleague, Professor Stephen A. Saltzburg who patiently read each page of the manuscript and made many valuable suggestions, and to the following of my student assistants who by laboring far beyond the limits imposed by their meager financial compensation contributed immeasurably to the final product: Robert Cave, David Hunt, Christopher Farley, Andrew Merdek, Ann Mische, Russell Pollack, Michael Ross, and Daniel Rowley. I could not close these acknowledgements without expressing special gratitude to Madeline Branch, my typist, whose stenographic skill and fortitude played a significant role in production of this book.

GRAHAM C. LILLY

Charlottesville, Virginia
August, 1978

AUTHOR'S NOTE ON COVERAGE, STYLE, AND CITATIONS

The coverage of this text typifies that of a basic three- or four-hour course in Evidence. All of the major evidentiary rules and principles are discussed, except for those constitutionally based rules of exclusion—principally grounded on the Fourth Amendment—that usually are included in the course in Criminal Procedure. Ideally, this book should be read sequentially from beginning to end, at least it was so designed. But the format and an ample index permit selective reference. To accommodate the user who will not read the book in its entirety, the footnotes contain many cross-references; as a further convenience, there is occasional repetition in the textual discussion.

The use of the masculine gender throughout this book should not suggest that the author is indifferent either to the growing number of women in the legal profession or to the significance of their contribution. This usage, which accords with accepted grammatical practice, is simply to spare the reader the distraction of alternating pronouns.

The citations to certain references have been abbreviated in accordance with the illustrations below. These sources, especially the standard works of Wigmore and McCormick, appear frequently throughout the text and footnotes. Professor McCormick's splendid treatise was revised and updated in 1972 under the general editorship of Professor Edward W. Cleary. It remains the most comprehensive and scholarly single-volume treatment of the field of evidence.

ABBREVIATED CITATIONS

1. Ladd & Carlson at 281.

M. Ladd & R. Carlson, Cases and Materials on Evidence 281 (1972).

2. Lempert & Saltzburg at 108.

R. Lempert & S. Saltzburg, A Modern Approach to Evidence 108 (1977).

3. Louisell et al. at 132.

D. Louisell, J. Kaplan & J. Waltz, Cases and Materials on Evidence 45 (3rd ed. 1976).

4. Maguire et al. at 257.

J. Maguire, J. Weinstein, J. Chadbourn & J. Mansfield, Cases and Materials on Evidence 257 (6th ed. 1973).

5. McCormick, § 47, at 98.

C. McCormick's Handbook of the Law of Evidence, § 47, at 98 (2d ed. Cleary 1972).

6. Morgan at 103.*

E. Morgan, Basic Problems of State and Federal Evidence 103 (5th ed. Weinstein 1976).

7. Weinstein & Berger, ¶ 408[03], at 20.

J. Weinstein & M. Berger, Weinstein's Evidence, ¶ 408[03], at 20 (1977).

8. II Wigmore, § 376, at 305.**

J. Wigmore, A Treatise on the Anglo-American System of Evidence in Trials at Common Law, § 376, at 305 (3rd ed. 1940).

---

* Citations to the fourth edition (E. Morgan, Basic Problems of Evidence) are noted by date: Morgan at 103 (1963).

** Revised volumes are noted by author: III Wigmore, § 761, at 133 (Chadbourn).

TABLE OF CONTENTS

CHAPTER IV. COMPETENCY OF WITNESSES AND THE PROCESS OF TRIAL

CHAPTER V. RELEVANCE: RECURRING PROBLEMS OF CIRCUMSTANTIAL PROOF

TABLE OF CONTENTS

CHAPTER VI. THE HEARSAY RULE: ITS NATURE AND RATIONALE

CHAPTER VII. THE HEARSAY RULE: SELECTED EXCEPTIONS

PART A. PARTY ADMISSIONS

PART B. SPONTANEOUS DECLARATIONS

TABLE OF CONTENTS

PART C. PHYSICAL OR MENTAL CONDITION

PART D. RECORDED RECOLLECTION

PART E. RECORDS OF BUSINESS AND RELATED ENTERPRISES

PART F. PUBLIC RECORDS

PART G. FORMER TESTIMONY

PART H. DYING DECLARATIONS

PART I. DECLARATIONS AGAINST INTEREST

PART J. HEARSAY AND EXCEPTIONS: PAST AND FUTURE

TABLE OF CONTENTS

CHAPTER VIII. IMPEACHMENT

CHAPTER IX. PRIVILEGE

CHAPTER X. THE ROLE OF JUDGE AND JURY: A SUMMARY

TABLE OF CONTENTS

TABLE OF CASES

References are to Pages

TABLE OF CASES

TABLE OF CASES

TABLE OF CASES

TABLE OF CASES

TABLE OF CASES

TABLE OF CASES

TABLE OF CASES

TABLE OF CASES

†

AN INTRODUCTION
TO THE
LAW OF EVIDENCE

CHAPTER I

EVIDENCE IN CONTEXT *

§ 1. The Role of Evidence in the Process of Adjudication

The introduction and use of evidence is but one part of the complex process of litigation. This process formally begins with the filing of a complaint and terminates with the entry and satisfaction of a final judgment or decree. During the course of the various judicial proceedings, the parties' lawyers participate in a variety of matters: pleadings and motions, investigation and discovery, settlement negotiations, the presentation of evidence, closing argument, and (where appeal takes place) the preparation of the appellate brief and the delivery of oral argument.

Two concerns are central to all phases of litigation: first, a concern with establishing facts; and, second, a concern with the choice and application of legal rules. The formal study of law emphasizes the choice, construction, and impact of legal rules and principles. This academic preference has pedagogic advan-

---

* This chapter is designed to set out some of the fundamental characteristics of the adversarial system, especially those that bear upon the factual component of a case. At various points, some knowledge of civil procedure is assumed. The reader may wish to consult F. James & G. Hazard, Civil Procedure (2d ed. 1977), especially pp. 1–8, 262–303, 318–346; 2 F. Harper and F. James, The Law of Torts §§ 15.1–15.5 (1956).

tages, but it obscures a basic reality: the outcome of most cases is determined by counsel's success in establishing *facts* favorable to his client. The governing rules of law are contested with much less frequency than is suggested by a study of the reported cases. Furthermore, the factual posture of a controversy often has a decisive effect upon extra-judicial disposition such as voluntary dismissal or settlement. Thus, facts, and consequently *evidence of facts*, can have a profound influence upon the resolution of disputes. Understandably, lawyers spend a substantial part of their professional lives developing and analyzing evidence in an effort to establish facts favorable to their client.

§ 2.   Evidence: Definition and Professional Evaluation

It no doubt is a questionable simplification to define evidence as any matter, verbal or physical, that can be used to support the existence of a factual proposition.[1] For present purposes, however, this definition is useful because it emphasizes the perspective of the legal profession, which associates evidence with the facts of a case.

Another aspect of "evidence," unique to the legal profession, is not directly related to the definition or inherent qualities of evidence but rather consists of the criteria by which lawyers assess the usefulness or probative worth of evidence. When attorneys contemplate litigation, their evaluation of prospective evidential materials departs sharply from that of other professionals or lay persons:[2] lawyers must anticipate the impact the rules of evidence will have upon the *admissibility* of these materials should a judicial trial be necessary.[3] At trial, the rules of evi-

---

1. For a different and more comprehensive definition of the term, see I Wigmore, § 1, at 3; see also Hart and McNaughton, Evidence and Inference in the Law, in Evidence & Inference 48 (Lerner, ed. 1958).

2. Cf. Hart and McNaughton, supra note 1, at 52–53.

3. The rules of evidence that bar admissibility usually are not enforced in hearings before administrative agencies. McCormick, § 348, at 837. Of course, evidence that would be rejected as untrustworthy in a judicial proceeding may not be given much weight by the hearing officer. For a complete discussion of the reasons underlying the admissibility and use

dence may operate to exclude all or part of the proffered testimony or tangible items; evidence so rejected will not be considered in the decisional process of the tribunal.[4] As a consequence, these materials are diminished in importance even before trial, despite their apparent relevance.

§ 3. The Bases of Evidentiary Restriction: A Prefatory View

There is no simple answer to the question of why the law
should turn its face against evidentiary materials that investiga-
tors and factfinders generally would deem useful. The purpose
of this book is to provide the reader with a framework that will
facilitate analysis of this issue. For the moment, it suffices to
note that judicial trials are different from other investigations.
The evidence is presented by adversaries, each one offering evidence favorable to himself and each demanding a fair chance to
challenge the reliability of the other's proof. As a consequence,
evidence (such as hearsay) that may be plausible, but that can
not be tested adequately by the adversary's cross-examination,
often is rejected. Trials are distinctive, also, in that the fact-

---

of evidence in administrative proceedings, see K. Davis, Administrative Law Treatise, §§ 14.01–14.17
(1952 & Supp.1970); K. Davis, Administrative Law of the Seventies,
§§ 14.00–14.17 (1976). As a practical matter, administrative tribu-
nals may have to adhere to the evidentiary rules established by the
courts that review administrative
findings. See, e. g., cases cited in
S. Saltzburg and K. Redden, Federal Rules of Evidence Manual 714–
15 (2d ed. 1977).

4. In trials held before a judge sitting without a jury, there is a decided tendency to relax the exclusionary rules and admit evidence
that might be rejected in a jury
trial. See McCormick, § 60, at 137.
If incompetent evidence is *admitted*
in a nonjury case, a reviewing appellate court is likely to sustain
the judgment below if, within the
trial record, competent evidence
can be found that is sufficient to
support the judge's findings.
Builders Steel Co. v. Commissioner,
179 F.2d 377, 379 (8th Cir. 1950)
(dictum). The trial judge is presumed to have ignored or discount-
ed the evidence that was wrongly
admitted. Conversely, erroneous
exclusion by the judge will result in
reversal in those cases where the
rejected evidence is likely to have
a significant impact on the outcome. See Builders Steel Co. v.
Commissioner, 179 F.2d 377 (8th
Cir. 1950). Note the usual necessity
for the judge to acquaint himself
with the evidence *before* he intelligently can rule upon its formal
admissibility. Thus, in non-jury
trials the factfinder, by reason of
practical necessity, usually is exposed to inadmissible evidence.

finders often are lay persons (the jury), not trained experts. This suggests a need to exclude evidentiary materials that pose a substantial risk of misuse by the jury. Finally, trials are public affairs; the evidence often reveals to the community and media confidential information. Instances arise in which the interests served by the preservation of confidentiality should take precedence over those interests advanced by the utilization of evidentiary material. In these circumstances, the evidence is said to be privileged and is deemed inadmissible.

There are other distinctive features of judicial trials,[5] but the foregoing characteristics—partisan presentation, the lay jury, and the public nature of the proceedings—provide an introduction to the reasons for rules that limit or exclude evidence. Note that at least one of the characteristics of judicial trials, the use of a jury, might be accommodated by a control device other than exclusion. In some instances, for example, the judge provides guidance to the jury through cautionary instructions; this serves as an alternative to exclusion where the risk of the jury's misuse of evidentiary material is not great. Arguably, similar guidance also could suffice where apparently reliable evidence can not be tested fully by the adversary of the party offering the evidence. In any event, it is important to emphasize that the framework of trial and the nature of the adversary system yield rules that restrict the admissibility (input) of evidence or circumscribe its use in some way.

§ 4. Building an Evidentiary Record: Allocation of Responsibility for Input and Exclusion

We have seen that a lawyer's development of facts often critically affects the outcome of litigation, and that at trial facts are established by an adversarial presentation of evidence. It is the responsibility of each party to gather and present his own evidence, either in the form of witnesses (testimonial evidence) or tangible things (real evidence) such as documents or chattels. This principle of party presentation is a fundamental tenet of

---

5. See Hart and McNaughton, supra
    note 1, at 56.

Anglo-American adjudication.[6] The operative effect of this principle is to leave the development of a case largely in the hands of the adverse parties, whose interests usually are represented by counsel.[7] Only such evidence as the parties present will be considered by the trier. The assumption is that each partisan will proffer the evidence that he deems most advantageous. This mode of presentation is thought to encourage a full evidentiary record. But the theory does not require a full record in fact. The proceedings satisfy the public interest if each party has been afforded a fair *opportunity* to present evidence and to test the evidence offered by his adversary, even in cases where the resulting evidentiary record is meager or incomplete.[8] Generally, the Anglo-American adversarial trial has not embraced a policy that the judge [9] or some representative of the public supply

---

6. See Millar, The Formative Principles of Civil Procedure, 18 Ill.L. Rev. 1, 9 (1923); F. James & G. Hazard, Civil Procedure, § 1.2, at 6 (2d ed. 1977).

7. Professor Millar distinguishes party presentation, which makes it incumbent upon the parties to define the scope and content of a case, from party-prosecution, which makes the parties responsible for moving a case forward. See Millar, supra note 6, at 9, 19. The adversary system embraces both of these characteristics.

Currently gaining support is a proposal to make lawyers advocates for truth as well as for their clients. See, e. g., Frankel, The Search for Truth: An Umpireal View, 123 U.Pa.L.Rev. 1031 (1975); Uviller, The Advocate, The Truth and Judicial Hackles: A Reaction to Judge Frankel's Idea, 123 U.Pa. L.Rev. 1067 (1975). But see Freedman, Judge Frankel's Search for Truth, 123 U.Pa.L.Rev. 1060 (1975).

8. Increasingly, however, certain kinds of litigation, such as those dealing with welfare, the environment, or racial and sexual discrimination, are being perceived as quasi-public in nature. Participation (intervention) by interested parties has been frequent. For an interesting article that makes a convincing argument that the model of civil litigation is changing from one dominated by private interests to one in which public concerns are paramount, see Chayes, The Role of the Judge in Public Law Litigation, 89 Harv.L.Rev. 1281 (1976). See also 28 U.S.C.A. § 2403 (government intervention of right in private action "wherein the Constitutionality of any Act of Congress affecting the public interest is drawn in question"); Fed.R.Civ.P. 24 (conditions of intervention, both "of right" and "permissive", set out).

9. There is little doubt that the judge can call and (or) examine witnesses, although he is under no duty to do so. Fed.R.Evid. 614,

evidence that the parties, through error or by design, withhold from the tribunal.

In addition to controlling evidentiary presentation, a party can exert another influence upon the evidentiary record: by making a timely objection, he can sometimes block the admission of evidence offered by his adversary. The success of such an objection depends upon whether the judge determines that an exclusionary rule dictates exclusion of the proffered evidence. A party, however, is not required to object, even though an exclusionary rule is available to prevent the admission of the evidence. If, by careless omission or deliberate inaction, a party makes no objection,[10] the evidence against him is admitted and becomes part of the material available to the trier of fact. Only in extreme cases, usually involving a criminal charge, will the judge intervene and exclude the evidence on his own motion. Again, the Anglo-American judicial system places primary reliance upon the partisan interests of the opposing parties, acting through counsel, to shape the factual basis of the dispute.

§ 5. Use and Evaluation of the Admitted Evidence: Allocation of Responsibility

The trier of fact (or factfinder) has the responsibility of evaluating the evidence and deciding what occurred, that is, the trier determines the adjudicative or historical facts. In cases where there is no right to a jury (such as those formerly entertained in equity courts) the judge is the factfinder. In other cases the jury acts as the trier of fact, unless the parties have failed to assert or agreed to waive their right to trial by jury.

706; McCormick § 8. Judges sometimes exercise this power, especially in cases where each side has presented expert testimony and the experts' conclusions (opinions) are conflicting. The judge may appoint and call to the stand an impartial expert. Fed.R.Evid. 706. Nevertheless, primary responsibility for evidentiary presentation remains with the parties. IX Wigmore § 2484. As to the wisdom of appointing experts to testify for the court, see Diamond, The Fallacy of the Impartial Expert, 3 Archives of Crim. Psychodynamics 221 (1959), reprinted in part in Lempert & Saltzburg at 108.

10. The rules governing objections are set out in Chapter XI.

After the presentation of all of the evidence in the case, each party has an opportunity to make a closing argument. In this forensic presentation, counsel for each litigant attempts to convince the trier to accept certain evidence as reliable and to draw inferences favorable to his client. Thus, the parties can influence the factfinder's conclusions by debate and persuasion. Closing argument is the one phase of the trial that is directed to the meaning and weight of evidence, rather than to establishing what evidence should be considered.

In a jury case, the parties also may attempt to affect the trier's evaluation of the evidence by persuading the judge to give certain instructions that guide the jury in its use of the evidence. These instructions are of three general kinds: a *cautionary* instruction, advising that certain evidence should be weighed with care because of a risk that it is untrustworthy; a *limiting* instruction, restricting the use of designated evidence to one or more stated purposes; and a *peremptory* (finding) instruction, directing that if certain evidence is believed, then specified consequences (such as a verdict for the plaintiff) must ensue.

When appropriate, the judge may give instructions even where none have been requested by the parties. It generally is regarded as the judge's responsibility to charge the jury correctly on the basic aspects of the case. However, if the judge charges the jury with regard to the applicable substantive law, he usually is not required to go further and give evidentiary instructions. To ensure that the judge's charge includes evidentiary instructions, the interested party must make a specific request that identifies the instruction(s) he desires. His failure to do so is dispositive in a subsequent appeal.[11] Once again party activity, or lack of it, can be a determinant in the factfinding process.[12]

---

11. See Fed.R.Civ.P. 51; Ostapenko v. American Bridge Div. of U.S. Steel Corp., 267 F.2d 204, 205–206 (2d Cir. 1959); Turner Const. Co. v. Houlihan, 240 F.2d 435, 439 (1st Cir. 1957); Hatfield v. Levy Bros., 18 Cal.2d 798, 810, 117 P.2d 841, 847 (1941); State ex rel. State Highway Comm'n v. Yackel, 445 S.W.2d 389, 393 (Mo.App.1969).

12. In an non-jury trial, the parties can request that the judge in his evaluation of the evidence apply

§ 6.   The Role of Judge and Jury: A General View *

Lawyers sometimes use the expression that the jury decides questions of fact, and the judge resolves questions of law. This description of function loosely accords with prevailing practice. The rationale for such a division is obvious: the judge, through training and experience, is particularly qualified to resolve legal questions, while the jury, which brings to the courtroom the common experience of the community, is better equipped to settle factual disputes. As we shall see, however, it is not as easy to make the division between judge-jury responsibility as this lawyers' colloquialism suggests.

The first qualification to this general statement of function is that the jury can discharge its factfinding role only in those cases where the state of the evidence reasonably justifies a finding in favor of either party. If from the evidence there is no *reasonable* dispute as to the historical (adjudicative) facts, the judge prevents the jury (by the use of an instruction, directed verdict, or other appropriate device) from making any finding that is contrary to the preponderating evidence. Thus, the function of adjudicating historical facts, a function that normally belongs to the jury, is assumed by the judge in cases where the evidence reasonably supports only one factual resolution.[13]

A second qualification to the general statement of judge-jury function arises where, by giving a general verdict, the jury applies the substantive law (as described in the judge's charge) to

---

the same principles that would, in a jury trial, be expressed in instructions to the jury. However, there is no way of ascertaining the judge's mental evaluative processes unless he reveals his thoughts in his findings of fact and conclusions of law. See Fed.R.Civ.P. 52.

* Chapter X discusses in detail the role of judge and jury. This section provides a general, prefatory statement of the division of function between judge and jury in the adjudicatory process.

13. In criminal cases, by uniform tradition if not constitutional compulsion, the jury always applies the law to the facts unless the defendant waives his right to jury trial. Annot., 72 A.L.R. 899 (1931). See Fed.R.Crim.P. 29(a) (abolishing motions for directed verdicts in criminal cases). Of course, the judge can take the case from the jury and render a judgment in the *defendant's* favor by granting the defendant's motion for acquittal. See Fed.R.Crim.P. 29(a).

the particular facts of the case. In some instances, notably where community values and standards are thought to be particularly important, the standard contained in the applicable law is expressed by a very general phrase. A defendant is negligent, for example, if he fails to "act reasonably" or does not exercise "due care." In these cases involving a broadly stated legal rule, the jury's application of law to fact involves a *characterization* of the adjudicative facts in the light of the jury's collective experience and in terms of the indeterminate language that constitutes the legal standard.[14] In a sense, the jury is giving the legal principles involved the necessary precision to resolve the case before them.[15]

The judge, too, assumes functions that vary from his more familiar task of deciding questions of law. He does, as we have seen, determine which rules of substantive law will apply in a particular case. But there are numerous occasions when the judge makes factual determinations. In the pre-trial process, he resolves factual questions pertaining to the jurisdiction of the court over the subject matter or over the parties. He also settles factual disputes that may arise in connection with discovery proceedings. Even after a trial by jury is commenced, the judge assumes important roles in the determination of facts. He monitors the evidence and, as already noted, removes from jury consideration any factual determinations that by reason of the state of the evidence could be resolved in only one way. The judge

---

14. See 2 F. Harper and F. James, Law of Torts, § 15.3, at 880–83 (1956); Hart and McNaughton, supra note 1, at 60–61.

15. There are control devices, including summary judgment, instructions, and directed verdict, that can be used to limit the jury's characterization. These devises ensure that the jury is not allowed to reach an irrational characterization of the conduct. See F. James & G. Hazard, Civil Procedure, § 7.-11, at 275–79, §§ 7.12–7.22 (2d ed. 1977). For example, it would be irrational to characterize as negligent a hazardous, but correctly performed, surgical procedure if it were the only known means of saving the patient's life. But substantial latitude is inherent in such imprecise terms as "reasonable," and if the facts as well as the issue of reasonableness or due care are disputed, the jury's verdict normally is decisive. See F. Harper and F. James, Law of Torts, § 15.2, at 872–80 (1956); Weiner, The Civil Jury Trial and the Law-Fact Distinction, 54 Cal.L.Rev. 1867, 1872–74 (1966).

also decides preliminary factual questions that accompany the application of the exclusionary rules of evidence.[16] The rules of evidence often are stated by a formula that includes a reference to the attending factual circumstances; the judge determines the existence or nonexistence of these circumstances. For example, a rule states that in proving the terms of a writing the original document must be produced unless it is destroyed or otherwise unavailable.[17] Suppose the proponent claims that the original was destroyed or lost, but the opponent disputes this assertion.[18] In order to avoid prolonging the trial and overburdening or confusing the jury, the judge makes the preliminary factual determination necessary to apply the rule.

§ 7.   Factfinding Outside of the Record: Judicial Notice

An interesting accommodation of the roles of judge, counsel, and jury occurs when an adjudicative fact [19] has the degree of certainty that justifies the invocation of judicial notice. The device of judicial notice allows certain, specified facts to be established without the introduction into the record of supportive evidence. Modern authority holds that a "judicially noticed fact must be one not subject to reasonable dispute in that it is either (1) generally known within the territorial jurisdiction of the trial court or (2) capable of accurate and ready determination by resort to sources whose accuracy cannot reasonably be questioned." [20] The fact that Mission Street is a place of business activity is generally known to those in San Francisco, California; the time of sunrise or sunset can be ascertained by refer-

---

16. Chapter X explores his role in this regard. See, e. g., Fed.R.Evid. 104(a).

17. This rule is discussed in Chapter XIII, § 116.

18. This example appears in McCormick, § 53, at 121.

19. See note 28 infra for a discussion of the difference between adjudicative and legislative facts.

20. Fed.R.Evid. 201. See McCormick, §§ 329–30. Older cases tend to use a more limited formula, restricting judicial notice to indisputable facts of common knowledge within the jurisdiction. See, e. g., Varcoe v. Lee, 180 Cal. 338, 345, 181 P. 223, 226 (1919).

ence to reliable sources, as can many historical, geographical, or scientific facts.[21]

The judge may take judicial notice on his own motion. Under the preferable view, he must do so (assuming it is appropriate) if requested by counsel and provided with such information as may be necessary to facilitate the process.[22] There is vigorous debate, however, over whether the noticed fact must be accepted by the jury as conclusively established or whether the opponent may attempt to secure a contrary finding.[23] If judicial notice of adjudicative fact is limited to indisputable facts, it is incongruous to permit a contrary finding by the jury.[24] Thus, most jurisdictions hold that, at least in civil cases, judicial notice is conclusive, and disproof by contrary evidence and argument is impermissible.[25] In criminal cases, however, there is a decided tendency to let the jury refuse to find any fact alleged against the accused;[26] the rationale is that the accused's right to jury

---

21. Varcoe v. Lee, 180 Cal. 338, 347, 181 P. 223, 227 (1919) (character of Mission Street); Beardsley v. Irving, 81 Conn. 489, 491, 71 A. 580, 581 (1909) (whether June 3, 1906, fell on a Sunday). See McCormick, §§ 328–29, at 758, 763–65. With the *Varcoe* case, compare Russo v. Russo, 21 Cal.App.3d 72, 90, 98 Cal.Rptr. 501, 541 (1971) (not common knowledge that Haight-Ashbury district unsafe for children). For a recent federal case in which judicial notice was taken of a series of increases in oil prices, see Mainline Investment Corp. v. Gaines, 407 F.Supp. 423, 426–27 (N.D.Tex.1976). See also United States v. Blunt, 558 F.2d 1245 (6th Cir. 1977) (federal prison on federal land). But see Clark v. South Central Bell Tel. Co., 419 F.Supp. 697, 704 (W.D.La.1976) (refusal to notice population of parish 30% black).

22. Fed.R.Evid. 201(c), (d). In some jurisdictions, it apparently is the rule that the judge *must* take judicial notice of those facts that are commonly known and indisputable. See Morgan at 4–5, 9.

23. See, e. g., McNaughton, Judicial Notice—Excerpts Relating to the Morgan-Wigmore Controversy, 14 Vand.L.Rev. 779 (1961).

24. The recently enacted Federal Rules of Evidence provide that in civil actions any fact judicially noticed must be accepted by the jury as conclusively established. Fed. R.Evid. 201(g).

25. Fed.R.Evid. 201(g); McCormick, Judicial Notice, 5 Vand.L.Rev. 296, 321–22 (1952). For a collection of representative cases, see Morgan at 9 n. 32.

26. See State v. Main, 94 R.I. 338, 180 A.2d 814 (1962); State v. Lawrence, 120 Utah 323, 234 P.2d 600 (1951). Fed.R.Evid. 201(g) provides that in criminal cases the

trial, which prevents the judge from directing a verdict against him, makes it similarly inappropriate to bind the jury by judicial notice.[27]

This text will not consider the entire scope of judicial notice.[28] The foregoing sketch provides a condensed description of one as-

judge "shall instruct the jury that it may, but is not required to, accept as conclusive any fact judicially noticed." But see Fla.Stat. Ann. § 90.206.

27. See House Judiciary Comm. Report on H.Res. 5463, H.R.No.650, 93rd Cong., 2nd Sess. (1974), reprinted at 28 U.S.C.A. 823, 828 (1975); Adv.Comm. Note to Fed.R. Evid. 201(g); Preliminary Draft of Proposed Rules of Evidence, 46 F. R.D. 161, 205. If judicial notice is limited to matters beyond reasonable dispute, it appears illogical in any case, civil or criminal, to sanction what purports to be counter-vailing evidence and to permit a finding at odds with certainty. Why should there be a right to trial by jury as to a fact that reasonably can not be disputed?

28. The text mentions only judicial notice of adjudicative fact—meaning the facts of the particular case or, simply stated, when, where, and what the parties did. Adjudicative facts usually are decided by a jury.

Judicial notice of legislative facts involves a different concept. See the leading articles by Professor Kenneth Davis: An Approach to Problems of Evidence in the Administrative Process, 55 Harv.L.Rev. 365, 404–07 (1942), and Judicial Notice, 55 Colum.L.Rev. 945, 952–59 (1955). Legislative facts are those which compose the setting or condition in which a rule of law oper-

ates. Thus, a court might consider social data indicating the probable effect of integrated schools upon the students, Brown v. Board of Educ., 347 U.S. 483, 494 n. 11 (1954), or psychiatric information pertinent to when an accused should be relieved of criminal responsibility because of insanity. Durham v. United States, 214 F.2d 862, 870–74 (D.C.Cir. 1954), overruled, United States v. Brawner, 471 F.2d 969 (D.C.Cir. 1972). Courts also engage in assumptions about legislative facts as the Supreme Court did in Hawkins v. United States, 358 U.S. 74, 77 (1958), when it concluded that adverse testimony given by one spouse against the other in a criminal proceeding would be likely to destroy their marriage. See generally McCormick § 331.

It generally is considered undesirable and impractical to restrict courts to only those legislative facts beyond reasonable dispute. Indeed, in cases where a statute is attacked as unconstitutional, it may be necessary only to conclude that data about existing conditions were sufficient to cause a reasonable legislature to act as it did. Even where legislative facts are used to fashion a rule of law, as in the case of *Brown* and *Durham*, supra, courts often are forced to settle for the probable. See McCormick, § 331, at 768–69. The standard of indisputability, while appealing in the abstract, seldom can be met on the basis of available information.

pect of the subject and yields at least two points. First, judicial notice is a substitute for formal proof, that is, it relieves counsel from the obligation formally to introduce evidence to support a noticed fact. His obligation does not extend beyond supplying the judge with such information as may be necessary to demonstrate that the proposition in question is beyond reasonable dispute. Second, judicial notice is a device that both expedites the trial of a case and serves as a method by which the judge can prevent highly improbable findings of fact by the jury.

Considerations of judicial control and trial expedition should influence a judge to take the initiative and declare as settled all of those facts that he finds are indisputable. But the adversary system has not always contained procedures that secure the rights of the parties to participate in this process. Counsel at least should have the opportunity to present argument as to why a particular fact does not meet the criteria of judicial notice. This opportunity to be heard had not gained wide recognition [29] until recently, when it was adopted as part of the rule governing judicial notice in federal courts: Rule 201(e) of the Federal Rules of Evidence entitles a party, upon request, to the opportunity of showing the impropriety of taking judicial notice.[30]

NOTES

1. *Bases of Evidentiary Rules.* It has been said that the law of evidence is a "product of the jury system . . . where ordinary un-

Because any rule of law declared by the court (whether an affirmation of the old one or the announcement of a new one) presupposes certain underlying conditions, the ideal of certainty is unaffordable. If legislative facts can be used even though their existence is less than certain, should not the parties have an opportunity to argue about the likelihood of the existence of these facts? See S. Saltzburg & K. Redden, Federal Rules of Evidence Manual 59–60 (2d ed. 1977): "We do not claim that Judges cannot rely on a broad range of facts to force the law for-

ward. We suggest only that the parties should be permitted to participate in the march."

29. See McCormick, § 333, at 771–72.

30. Compare the opportunity to be heard regarding judicial notice of legislative fact, see supra note 28, which remains an acute problem. As McCormick states, "[l]egislative facts . . . have not fitted easily into any effort to propound a formalized set of rules applicable to judicial notice." McCormick, § 333, at 772.

trained citizens are acting as judges of fact." Thayer, A Preliminary
Treatise on Evidence 509 (1898). However, not all of the evidentiary
rules reflect a concern for the jury's lack of expertise. Certainly the
protection of confidential information, which is conferred by the various rules prohibiting the evidential disclosure of "privileged" communications, is not grounded in concerns about the lay jury. In any
event, subject to the qualifications set out supra in footnote 4, the rules
of evidence apply in trials without a jury. An article that traces the evolution of the jury's role, explores the nature of legal evidence, and
proposes that the exclusionary rules be relaxed is Forkosch, The Nature of Legal Evidence, 59 Cal.L.Rev. 1356 (1971).

2. *Judge's Comment on the Evidence.* In some jurisdictions, including the federal judiciary, the judge, after the close of the evidence
and the final arguments of counsel to the jury, can sum up the evidence and comment upon its weight. Other jurisdictions allow only an
impartial summary, while many others forbid any kind of evidentiary
review by the judge. See Vanderbilt, Minimum Standards of Judicial
Administration 224–29 (1949).

3. *Civil Law System.* The system of trials used on the continent
of Europe differs significantly from the Anglo-American approach:

> [T]he continental law . . . recognizes the inquisitorial
> system. We misunderstand what is meant by the phrase "the
> inquisitorial system" if we think that it is necessarily asso-
> ciated with torture. It means that it is the judge's function
> to take an active part in establishing the truth; to do so, he
> must himself question the parties and the other witnesses,
> and, if necessary, he may direct that additional witnesses
> who he believes can give relevant evidence, shall be sum-
> moned. . . . Counsel may suggest questions that they
> think ought to be asked . . . .

Goodhart, A Changing Approach to the Law of Evidence, 51 Va.L.Rev.
759, 764 (1965). Generalizations about the various systems of adjudication extant on the European continent can be misleading in at least
two respects. First, there are significant differences among the various civil law countries both in the theory underlying the adjudicative
process and in the implementing provisions declared in statutes and
other official sources. Second, the actual adjudicative practices may
depart sharply from what one would expect from examining the official sources. For example, a court may have extensive powers to take
the initiative, ex officio, in controlling the scope of a judicial action or
in developing the evidence, but in practice these powers may be utilized only partially or infrequently.

Subject to these cautions, it can be said that the general pattern in civil law countries is for a private party to initiate a civil suit and, with some notable exceptions, for a public minister to institute criminal prosecutions. Typically, the judge in a continental country is more active than his English-American counterpart in the following areas: controlling the progress of the litigation; shaping the alleged claims and defenses; dismissing and adding parties; and developing the proof. In the last regard, the judge may order additional documentary evidence or (in some countries) call for witnesses who were not presented by the parties. A notable feature of civil law adjudication is that the judge, not the lawyers, primarily is responsible for examining the witnesses. The examination typically permits the witness a wide latitude to give a narrative account, following which the judge will ask questions. Counsel may suggest topics for inquiry and, in some countries, ask questions or submit a list of questions to the judge.

Because in most civil law countries there is no jury, the introduction of evidence is not limited because of apprehension about jury misuse; there are, however, some rules of exclusion and some prescriptions concerning the use of evidence, that is, some evidence may not be considered suitable legal proof. For an interesting and concise description of many of the existing continental judicial systems, see M. Cappelletti & J. Jolowicz, Public Interest Parties and the Active Role of the Judge in Civil Litigation 197–235 (1975).

Criminal trials on the continent are somewhat different from civil trials because the former may involve a jury (used in a few countries for serious crimes) or, if not, will probably involve lay assessors who sit with the judges. Continental judges generally are more active in criminal than in civil trials. For an insightful comparison between adversarial and non-adversarial criminal trials, with special emphasis upon the admissibility and use of evidence, see Damaska, Evidentiary Barriers to Conviction and Two Models of Criminal Procedure: A Comparative Study, 121 U.Pa.L.Rev. 506 (1973).

4. *Judicial Notice of Law.* The term "judicial notice" often is applied to the process by which a judge, usually with the assistance of counsel, determines or discovers the procedural or substantive law in his or some other jurisdiction. Usually there is recourse to statutes, court rules, or cases that are referenced by citation without any need to introduce into evidence the original (or copies) of the pertinent material. Where there is no widely available source, however, such as a code or a system of case reports, it may be necessary formally to provide evidence of the alleged rule of law. See Johnson v. City of Tulsa, 258 P.2d 695, 700 (Okl.Cr.App.1953) where the court refuses to judicially notice a municipal ordinance and indicates that a certified copy

or some substantive device must be used to enter the provisions of the ordinance into the record. Foreign law, the content of which may pose difficulties of discovery and interpretation, is subject to judicial notice only if a statute so provides. See McCormick, § 335, at 779.

CHAPTER II

RELEVANCE: AN INTRODUCTION

§ 8. Basic Concepts

Relevance is the basic and unifying principle underlying the evidentiary rules. First, it connotes the probative relationship between the testimonial or real evidence proffered by a party and the factual proposition to which the evidence is addressed. For example, evidence that A consumed six highballs is relevant to show that he was intoxicated when, two hours later, he was involved in an automobile accident. Second, it involves analysis of the relationship, often termed "materiality" or "consequentialness," between the factual proposition toward which the evidence points and the substantive law. Thus if A, a passenger in a bus, sues B, the driver of another vehicle, for injuries sustained when B negligently collided with the bus in which A was riding, evidence of A's drinking may be irrelevant. No doubt evidence that he consumed excessive amounts of intoxicating liquor is probative to show that he was intoxicated at the time of the accident. But if, under the substantive law, the intoxication of a passenger does not affect his right of recovery or the damages to which he is entitled, evidence of A's drinking would be excluded on objection as immaterial or inconsequential.

Because the concept of relevance applies to all proffered evidence, it pervades the entire course of trial. All admissible evidence must satisfy the test of relevance—at least when the opponent of the evidence challenges its admissibility by proper objection. The two distinct components of relevance both must be present: evidence is relevant only if it (1) tends to prove or disprove a proposition of fact (2) that is of consequence (or "material") to a charge, claim, or defense. In subsequent sections we shall explore more fully the degree of probative force necessary to satisfy the requirement that the evidence tend to "prove or disprove" a factual proposition. It is important at the outset, however, to establish clearly the origin and importance of the

17

requirement that evidence is relevant only if it supports a proposition of fact that is "of consequence" to the outcome of the suit.

Determining what facts are consequential involves an analysis of the controlling substantive law which will be found in statutes, judicial opinions, and other primary sources. These substantive provisions specify the legal consequence that will attach to the establishment of certain propositions of fact. It is these propositions which are sometimes referred to as the elements of a criminal charge, a civil claim, or a defense.[1] Evidence is material or consequential, therefore, whenever it tends to establish the existence or non-existence of an element (of a charge, claim, or defense) that is derived from the controlling substantive law. Indeed, this conclusion is often expressed by use of the terminology "material element" to describe those propositions which constitute an essential part of a plaintiff's or defendant's case. Suppose in a suit for assault and battery initiated by *A* against *B*, the latter offers evidence that he mistakenly thought that *A* was another person, *C*. This evidence should be rejected if the proposition to which it is directed—mistaken identity—is of no legal consequence under the substantive law. That is, if the law of intentional torts imposes liability notwithstanding this kind of mistake, the evidence should be deemed irrelevant.[2]

It has been suggested [3] that the word "materiality" should be used discriminately, in preference to the broader term "rele-

---

1. See Ch. III, § 15.

2. Of course, if mistaken identity were a factor that under the law of damages could be considered in determining the amount of the award, evidence of mistake would be relevant (material) not to excuse liability, but to ascertain the appropriate damages.

Evidence could be immaterial because the pleadings dictate that the proposition supported by the evidence is not properly provable in the case. In a contracts case in which the defense of forgery must be specially pleaded, evidence that the plain-

tiff planned to forge the defendant's name would be relevant to show a false signature, but would be immaterial unless the defendant's pleading asserted (or was amended to allege) the defense of forgery. Other actions by the adversaries, such as stipulations or admissions during the discovery process, may render evidence immaterial or, to use the terminology of the Federal Rules of Evidence, inconsequential. See text accompanying note 5 infra.

3. See James, Relevancy, Probability and the Law, 29 Cal.L.Rev. 689, 691 n. 6 (1941).

vance," in those situations involving only the relationship between the factual proposition toward which evidence points and the elements of a charge, claim or defense. Federal Rule of Evidence 401, which governs proceedings in United States' courts,[4] contains the following definition:

> "Relevant evidence" means evidence having any tendency to make the existence of any fact that is of consequence to the determination of the action more probable or less probable than it would be without the evidence.

In this concise provision, the rulemakers have embodied the dual aspects of relevance, even though they did not use the word "materiality" (preferring instead the phrase "of consequence").[5] Evidence is relevant if it (1) increases the probability [the first relationship] of (2) a consequential fact [the second relationship]. In practice, courts often use the terms materiality and relevance loosely and interchangeably, neglecting to differentiate between them. Perhaps the word "consequence," used in the Federal Rule, will add precision to the vocabulary. In any event, careful attention to issues of relevance quickly will lead to a recognition of which aspect of this basic requirement is in question.

Although the requirement of consequentialness always involves analysis of the relationship between the substantive law and the factual proposition supported by the evidence, the effect of pleadings or other procedural devices such as stipulations should not be ignored. These may serve to narrow the dispute and, hence, confine the range of materiality, for if a party has stipulated or otherwise conclusively admitted a fact of consequence, there is no reason to receive evidence bearing upon the established proposition.[6] Thus, evidence is consequential only if it relates to a *contested* element of a claim or defense.

---

4. Fed.R.Evid. 101.

5. Adv.Comm.Note to Fed.R.Evid. 401.

6. See supra note 2.

§ 9. Circumstantial and Direct Evidence

Whether evidence is characterized as circumstantial or as direct turns upon whether or not the evidence requires the trier to reach the ultimate factual proposition to which the evidence is addressed by a process of inference. Testimony that the accused was seen in possession of the instrument used in a criminal assault is circumstantial evidence that he was the assailant; testimony that he was seen making the attack is direct evidence that he was the assailant. Observe that even though testimony relating to the defendant's possession of an instrument is *direct* evidence of the proposition that he possessed the object, it is *circumstantial* evidence of the ultimate proposition that he was the assailant. The relationship of the evidence to the *ultimate* factual proposition it supports determines its character; that is, if the evidence ultimately is directed toward an inferred fact it is circumstantial, even though it is directly supportive of the initial proposition from which inferences are to be drawn.

When direct evidence of a consequential proposition is presented (as, for example, when a witness testifies that he saw B attack A), the trier is concerned solely with whether to believe the witness. But when circumstantial evidence is introduced (as, for example, when a witness testifies that B fled the scene of the assault), the trier not only must be concerned with whether to believe the witness, but also with whether the evidence increases the probability of the proposition to which it is directed (that B was the assailant). It will also be observed that whether evidence is direct or circumstantial determines the degree of analysis necessary for the judge to resolve issues of relevance. Where direct evidence is offered, the judge need only inquire whether the factual proposition to which the evidence relates is consequential. When circumstantial evidence is offered, the judge must determine whether the ultimate proposition to which the evidence is directed is consequential *and* whether the evidence affects the probability of the existence of that proposition.

§ 10. The Test of Probative Value

We have seen that relevance involves a probative relationship between evidence and a factual proposition. Suppose that in April a prison guard, *A*, is murdered and that in May another guard, *B*, is murdered. The investigation by authorities intensifies and, in late May, *D*, a prisoner, tries to escape from prison. In a subsequent trial for the murder of *A* in which *D* is named the accused, is *D*'s attempted escape relevant? [7]

Persons responding to this question may disagree. Clearly the evidence does not establish the accused's guilt, but this is not the point. Only the total evidence introduced need be sufficient to justify a finding of guilt. A single item of evidence is relevant if it has any tendency to increase the probabilities of a consequential factual proposition. It is not even necessary to demonstrate that it is *more probable* that escape was motivated by the fear of detection in connection with *A*'s murder than by other possible motives such as feared detection in connection with *B*'s murder or simply the desire to gain freedom.[8] The question is whether the probability that the accused committed the murder for which he is on trial is to some degree increased by evidence that he attempted to escape. So put, it may be argued that the evidence is relevant and hence it should be considered along with other circumstantial evidence (such as fingerprints, blood stains, and so forth) in the determination of guilt beyond a reasonable doubt.

The examples discussed thus far in this chapter suggest that the test of probative value is derived from commonplace experience. That is, the test usually involves no more than a common-sense determination, made in the light of human observation and experience, that certain events or conditions either are causally connected or normally associated with other events or

---

7. This problem, with some variation, is posed in McCormick, § 185, at 438.

8. McCormick, § 185, at 437, 439. But see Standafer v. First Nat'l Bank, 236 Minn. 123, 52 N.W.2d 718 (1952) (circumstantial evidence must, to be admissible, make the desired proposition more likely than other propositions that are contrary to the proponent's position).

conditions. In the words of Professor Thayer, relevance is an "affair of experience and logic, and not at all of law." [9] Common observation teaches that if one fled the scene of a robbery, his guilt thereby is made somewhat more probable than it would be in the absence of the flight. Similarly, human experience indicates that if one had a motive for murder, it is more probable that he murdered than it would be if no motive existed. The touchstone of relevance, at least in the first sense—probative value—is the presence of a logical relationship between the evidence and the ultimate proposition [10] that the evidence is offered to support.

A recent case vividly illustrates both the kind of inquiry typically undertaken in resolving questions of relevance and the strength of the probative relationship that must exist between the evidence and the related proposition. In United States v. Robinson,[11] the accused was prosecuted for a bank robbery committed by four persons. Only one person (who admittedly was involved in the robbery and who was cooperating with the government at the time of trial) could identify the accused as one of the participants. To strengthen the government's evidence bearing on identification, the prosecutor introduced evidence that when the accused was arrested ten weeks after the robbery, he had in his possession a .38 caliber revolver. There was evi-

---

9. Thayer, A Preliminary Treatise on Evidence 269 (1898).

10. See also, S. Saltzburg & K. Redden, Federal Rules of Evidence Manual 102 (2d ed. 1977):

There is no litmus paper test or simple formula for applying the general definition [of relevance]. Logic and experience together must supply the Judge with skills in determining whether a given piece of evidence tends to prove a material proposition. It may be helpful, however, for the Trial Judge to focus on two factors: (1) the likelihood the evidence would exist if the proposition at issue is true; (2) the likelihood that the evidence would exist if the material proposition is false. If the evidence is as likely to exist when the proposition is known to be true as in cases where the proposition is known to be false, it tends to prove nothing. The greater the likelihood that evidence exists in cases where the proposition is true as compared to cases where it is not true, the greater the importance [probative value] of the evidence and the more significant it seems to be.

11. 544 F.2d 611 (2d Cir. 1976) rev'd en banc 560 F.2d 507 (1977).

dence that at least one (and perhaps two) of the pistols used in the robbery were of this caliber. Aside from a similarity in caliber, however, there was no evidence that the gun in the accused's possession was used in committing the offense. The government argued, first, that from possession at the time of arrest it could be inferred that the accused possessed the gun at the time of the robbery, and, second, that the fact that the accused had a weapon of the same caliber as one that allegedly was used in the commission of the offense increased the likelihood that he was a participant. The trial judge admitted evidence of the accused's possession of the gun and instructed the jury that they could consider this evidence for such probative value as it might have on the issue of identity.

On appeal, the defense did not contest the relevance of the evidence, but argued that its probative value was substantially outweighed by its prejudicial effect—an argument we shall examine later in this chapter. The Court of Appeals, on rehearing en banc, reversed its initial panel decision, held the contested evidence admissible, and affirmed the conviction. It is significant, however, that with only a brief discussion both the panel and the full court concluded that the evidence was relevant because it tended to make the accused's participation in the offense more probable than it would be without the evidence.[12] For present purposes, it is enough to note that even though the probative force of the evidence was attenuated by the several inferential steps necessary and by the rather modest probabilities associated with each step, the court concluded that the basic test of relevance had been satisfied.

Professor Edmund Morgan has provided a revealing illustration of the process involved in drawing the inferences essential to the use of circumstantial proof.[13] Suppose that in the prosecution of D for the premeditated murder of V, the government offers in evidence a love letter written by D to V's wife. The

---

12. Evidence of the possession of the gun may have been a decisive factor in the conviction. See the further discussion of this case that begins infra at note 29.

13. See Morgan at 168–71.

trier is asked to infer from the letter than D loved V's wife, that his love caused him to desire her exclusive attention and affection, that this desire led to a concommitant desire to "get rid" of V, which in turn led to a plan [14] to accomplish the murder, which, finally, led to the execution of the plan. For each inferential step, one can construct an unarticulated premise: for example, "A man who writes a love letter to a woman is probably in love with her [premise one]; . . . A man who loves a woman probably desires her for himself alone [two]; . . . A man who loves a married woman and desires her for himself alone desires to get rid of her husband [three]; . . . A man who desires to get rid of the husband of the woman he loves probably plans to do so [four]; . . . and . . . A man who plans to get rid of the husband of the woman he loves is probably the man who killed him [five]." [15]

In assessing the probative force of the love letters to establish the ultimate proposition (that D killed V), it becomes apparent that two major determinants are involved: the first is the number of inferential steps and the second is the degree of probability that exists between the inferential links.[16] The *more inferences* one must draw to reach the desired conclusion, the weaker the probative force. The *weaker each inferential link* (that is, the less likely each sequential inference derived from the basic fact), the less the probative force. In the foregoing example, there were five inferential steps. Note that some of the inferential links are comparatively strong (e. g., from love letters to deep affection), yet others are comparatively weak (e. g., from the desire to possess to a plan to kill). Does the love letter still pass the test of relevance? It does because it increases somewhat the likelihood that D committed the murder. Of course, whether the prosecution can establish beyond a reasonable doubt

---

14. In circumstances where the killing appeared to be the result of sudden passion, the premise concerning a plan would be inappropriate, as would several of the other premises and their associated inferences.

15. Morgan at 169.

16. Id. at 169. For a more comprehensive analysis of the illustrative problem, see id. at 169–71.

that the accused committed the offense charged is an entirely different matter which depends upon the combined probative effect of all of the inculpatory evidence introduced at trial.

§ 11. Assessing Probative Value

Questions of relevance, which arise constantly in the course of litigation, ordinarily are not resolved by the explication of assumed premises, nor even by detailing all of the serial inferences. In the illustrative case of the love letter, the prosecutor might assert merely that the proffered love letter was relevant because it demonstrated D's love of V's wife, and that this affection was the motive for the murder. However, careful consideration of the nexus between proffered evidence and the ultimate proposition to which it is directed is useful in planning trial strategy, in the formulation of evidential argument to the jury, and in advocacy before trial and appellate judges. Different items of circumstantial evidence that support a single proposition normally will vary in probative value. If the issue in an action for property damage is whether the defendant's blasting operation caused the damage to plaintiff's property or whether, as defendant asserts, the damage resulted from faulty construction, it would be relevant to show that neighboring structures also were damaged at the time of the explosions in question.[17] Evidence of damage simultaneously occurring to a house adjacent to that of the plaintiff and constructed of similar materials has considerable probative value indicating that the explosion caused the damage to plaintiff's house. Quite obviously, evidence of damage to a structure composed of less substantial materials and located nearer to the site of the explosion is less convincing.

A further example: suppose A makes an oral lease with B in which the latter grants to A grazing rights for A's livestock during the summer. Subsequently, a dispute develops regarding whether B reserved the right to graze a certain number of his

---

17. See Poston v. Clarkson Const.
Co., 401 S.W.2d 522 (Mo.App.1966);
Annot., 45 A.L.R.2d 112 (1956).

cattle on the leased land.[18] The following evidence might be available:

(a) The parties had a similar lease during the two preceding summers for the same land, and B had reserved grazing rights.

(b) The parties had a lease the preceding summer involving different acreage and different terms (e. g., rent, watering rights, fence repair, etc.), but B had reserved grazing rights.

(c) B had, several years before, leased the same acreage to X and, in a lease similar to the present one with A, reserved grazing rights.

(d) B had seven leases (covering various tracts of land) during the present summer with a number of persons, including A. These leases varied in their terms, but in five of the lease arrangements, B had reserved grazing rights.

It is apparent that some of these evidentiary offerings are more persuasive than others. In the circumstances given, the degree of relevance increases roughly in proportion to the similarity of conditions between the lease in question and the other executed leases. Other factors being equal, it is arguable that prior arrangements between A and B are more probative than arrangements that B may have made with third parties. A past agreement between the immediate parties is probative, to some extent, to show A's willingness (or lack thereof) to agree to joint use of the property. Thus, evidence that the principal parties had entered into similar oral leases for the same land over a period of several years and that each lease contained a reservation of grazing rights clearly is probative that there was a reservation during the summer in question. Conversely, evidence indicating dissimilar circumstances (different land, different parties, different terms) has little or no tendency to persuade the trier that grazing rights were reserved. The point to be stressed is that an important aspect of proving one's case involves careful selection of the most probative evidence that can be offered to support a desired factual proposition.

---

18. See Firlotte v. Jessee, 76 Cal.
App.2d 207, 172 P.2d 710 (1946).

Thus far, we have assumed that probative force depends upon variations in the evidential material used to support inferentially a desired proposition. It should be apparent, however, that the probative value of the *same* evidence may be stronger or weaker depending upon the proposition to which it is directed. Consider, for example, the exhibition of an infant to the jury in a paternity case, where the plaintiff seeks to display the infant to the trier for the purpose of establishing, by comparison of facial features, that the defendant is the father. If the child is quite young, this evidence is of doubtful probative force, at least in the absence of some distinctive inherited trait possessed by both the putative father and the infant. Suppose, however, that an issue in the case were the race of the infant. Directed toward the question of race, the exhibition of the child would be more persuasive.[19]

A leading evidence casebook [20] recites the Biblical story [21] of two women, who each claimed the same infant as her son. The king directed that the child be severed and that each claimant be given a half. One claimant assented to this solution, but the other pleaded with the king to spare the child and give it to her rival. Is the evidence (the reaction of the claimants) directed at the proposition that the litigant willing to give up the baby was the biological mother? Or is it directed at the proposition that the forfeiting claimant would be the "better parent," regardless of whether she was the biological mother? Arguably it is more probative of the latter proposition than the former.

To summarize, probative value can be increased or decreased by changing the evidence offered to establish a particular proposition; similarly, as the last examples show, probative force can be altered by changing the proposition to which the evidence is directed. Because evidence frequently supports more than one proposition of consequence, the proponent may have the opportunity to select the proposition for which the evidence is offered. Thus, careful assessment of probative value involves scrutiny

---

19. See White v. Holderby, 192 F.2d 722 (5th Cir. 1951) (involving school segregation).

20. Louisell et al. at 45.

21. I Kings 3:16–28 (King James).

both of the available evidence and of the related consequential factual propositions.

§ 12.   The Assumptive * Admissibility of Relevant Evidence

Because by definition relevant evidence helps to prove a fact of consequence to the case, it could, but need not necessarily, follow "that unless excluded by some rule or principle of law, all [evidence] that is logically probative is admissible." [22]   There are, as we have seen,[23] rules of exclusion, such as hearsay and privilege, that operate to disallow evidence that has probative value.   These exclusionary rules rest upon grounds that are thought to justify exclusion even though the resulting cost is to deny to the factfinder any use of the evidence.   Unless, however, there is some reason of policy or fairness that justifies excluding relevant evidence, a basic principle—the assumptive admissibility of relevant evidence—dictates that the evidence should be received.[24]   For example, the Federal Rules of Evidence state:

> All relevant evidence is admissible, except as otherwise provided by the Constitution . . . by act of Congress [or] by these rules. . . . Evidence which is not relevant is not admissible.[25]

This provision makes clear that as a general rule relevant evidence is admissible, subject to such exceptions as may be declared by specific rules or provisions.

In the chapters ahead, many of these reasons for exclusion will be considered in detail.   We then shall see that certain exclusionary rules, such as hearsay and privilege, apply to speci-

---

* The word "assumptive" is used in place of the commonly encountered term "presumptive" because the latter term, when carefully used, refers to a prescribed effect that is accorded to evidence which already is admitted. See Ch. III, § 16.

22.   Thayer, Preliminary Treatise on Evidence 265 (1898).

23.   Ch. 1, § 3.

24.   McCormick, § 184, at 433–34 (quoting the influential passage of Professor Thayer, supra note 22, at 434).

25.   Fed.R.Evid. 402.

fied classes of evidence. There is, however, an exclusionary principle of general application that is applied to every item of relevant evidence. We shall examine this principle in the following section.

§ 13. Discretionary Exclusion Based on Considerations of Practical Policy

Every item of relevant evidence must be measured against several practical bases of exclusion. Thus, relevant evidence which assumptively is admissible will be rejected by the trial judge if he determines that the probative value of the evidence is outweighed by considerations of prejudice, confusion of the issues, misleading the jury, undue consumption of time, or, possibly, unfair surprise. These considerations [26] of policy are counterweights to relevance, justifying exclusion in instances where the probative benefit of the evidence fails to outweigh the practical burdens of its admission.

The decision whether the probative value of the evidence outweighs one or more of the counterweights is made by the trial judge, usually after objection by counsel.[27] Appellate courts wisely have reposed in the trial court considerable discretion in applying this balancing test. Unless there is a clear abuse of this discretion, no error is committed.[28]

Chapter V deals with some specific recurring situations in which appellate courts, after an assessment of relevance and the applicable counterweights, have directed the trial court either to admit or to exclude particular items or types of evidence. These appellate pronouncements, which have hardened into absolute rules, govern the trial judge's action in resolving certain recurring evidentiary issues. Nonetheless, many issues of relevance are not governed by the foregoing rules. These issues often arise in circumstances peculiar to the case being tried. Hence, questions involving evidence claimed by the proponent to

---

26. The same considerations underlie some of the specific exclusionary rules. See, e. g., Ch. V, §§ 33, 34, 36, 43.

27. See Ch. 1, § 4.

28. See McCormick, § 185, at 440.

be relevant and admissible are often resolved by the trial judge on an ad hoc basis. He first determines if the proffered evidence is relevant, and he then measures the probative value of the evidence against the practical reasons for exclusion.

The *Robinson* [29] case, discussed earlier,[30] illustrates the process. The case involved a federal prosecution in which the accused was charged with bank robbery. Part of the evidence against the accused consisted of testimony that when arrested ten weeks after the offense, he possessed a revolver of the same caliber as one of the weapons that, according to the testimony of an accomplice, had been used in the bank robbery. In the first trial, the trial judge excluded evidence of possession of the pistol and the jury "hung," with eight of twelve jurors favoring conviction. In the second trial, the judge admitted evidence of the accused's possession of the gun and, after long deliberation, the jury convicted Robinson. The issue on appeal was whether the trial judge had abused his discretion in admitting this evidence; the focus of the appellate court was upon whether the probative value of the evidence was overcome by its prejudicial effect. Federal Rule of Evidence 403 states:

> Although relevant, evidence may be excluded if its probative value is substantially outweighed by the danger of unfair prejudice, confusion of the issues, or misleading the jury, or by considerations of undue delay, waste of time, or needless presentation of cumulative evidence.

Acknowledging that the trial judge has wide discretion in the application of this balancing process,[31] a panel of the Court of Appeals nonetheless held that the admission of the contested evidence was reversible error. The panel, which later was reversed on rehearing en banc, characterized as weak the required inferences: (1) that possession of a .38 caliber weapon at the time of arrest is probative that there also was possession at the time of

---

29. United States v. Robinson, 544 F.2d 611 (2d Cir. 1976), rev'd en banc 560 F.2d 507 (1977).

30. See supra § 10 at note 11 and accompanying text.

31. 544 F.2d at 616.

the offense, and (2) that possession of a pistol having in common with the weapon used by the bank robber only the caliber is probative that the possessor was the robber. In weighing the probative force of the evidence against its prejudicial effect, the panel noted a serious risk that the evidence might cause the jury to rest its decision on an improper basis. An armed arrestee, singled out by the authorities for apprehension and, subsequently, for prosecution, is likely to be viewed by the jury as a person who would use his weapon for an illegal purpose. Thus, said the panel, there was a substantial risk that the trier would "conclude that the possessor of the gun is a dangerous person who ought to be segregated from society." [32] Because, in the panel's view, the evidence had little probative force toward a legitimate proposition (the identification of the accused) and a high potential for prejudice, it held that the trial judge erred in admitting it.[33]

In a subsequent opinion (following an en banc rehearing), the full court, with two judges dissenting, took a different view.[34] Emphasizing the broad discretion reposed in the trial judge, the

---

32. Id. at 618–19.

33. The *Robinson* case should be contrasted with an earlier case in the same Circuit, also involving a bank robbery. In United States v. Ravich, 421 F.2d 1196, 1203–05 (2d Cir. 1967), the accused and his co-defendants were found in possession of six .38 caliber pistols, a box of .38 ammunition, and more than $95,000. The court upheld the admission of the guns as a proper exercise of the trial judge's discretion, even though the only evidence that any of these weapons were used in the robbery was "attenuated" and served to connect only three of the six weapons. The basis for sustaining the trial judge's exercise of discretion was that possession of the guns was "relevant to establish opportunity or preparation to commit the crime charged, and thus . . . tended to prove the identity of the robbers, the only real issue in this trial." Id. at 1204. See also United States v. McMillian, 535 F.2d 1035 (8th Cir. 1976); Walker v. United States, 490 F.2d 683 (8th Cir. 1974); United States v. McKinley, 485 F.2d 1059 (D.C.Cir. 1973); United States v. Cunningham, 423 F.2d 1269 (4th Cir. 1970).

The reader may wish to reconsider the hypothetical posed at the outset of the chapter with a view to weighing the probative value of evidence of an attempted escape from prison against its prejudicial impact.

34. United States v. Robinson, 560 F.2d 507 (2d Cir. 1977) (en banc).

court declared that when the trial judge has measured probative value against prejudice and the other practical counterweights, his decision on admissibility will not be disturbed absent a showing that he acted arbitrarily or irrationally. The court found that the evidence of possession at the time of arrest increased the probabilities that Robinson possessed the weapon on the day of the bank robbery—a factual proposition supported by the co-felon who testified against the accused. Further, if Robinson possessed a .38 caliber revolver at the time of the offense, this possession added to the probabilities that he was a participant in the robbery: it made it more likely than it would be without the evidence that he was engaged in criminal activity involving the same type of weapon. The court reinforced its conclusion that the contested evidence was relevant on the issue of identity by declaring that the evidence both corroborated the government's principal witness and, independently of that use, "tended to show that [Robinson] had the 'opportunity' to commit the bank robbery, since he had access to an instrument similar to that used to commit it." [35]

Note, however, that the corroborative effect of the evidence is dependent upon its probative value to establish identity. Furthermore, citing opportunity as an independent reason for admitting the evidence adds little to the relevance argument, at least under the facts of this case. The showing that Robinson had the opportunity to commit the crime simply increases the likelihood that he (as opposed to someone who did not possess a .38 caliber revolver) participated in its commission—a proposition that admittedly bears upon identity but is not separable from it.[36] In any event, the en banc court, noting that the trial judge had carefully assessed the possible prejudicial effect of the disputed evidence and had cautioned the jury not to draw unwarranted or prejudicial inferences, held that the lower court did not abuse its discretion.

Although the full court's narrow holding probably is justified, its opinion offers little guidance for future cases. First, doubt is

---

35. Id. at 513.

36. Id. at 520–21 (Oakes, J., dissenting).

left as to the degree of convincing force necessary to sustain the inference that Robinson possessed a .38 caliber revolver on the day of the robbery. Suppose, for example, the arrest had been made one year after the offense. Should the court admit evidence that the arrestee-accused possessed a revolver of similar caliber? Second, the court is somewhat equivocal as to the effect, if any, that might come from other evidence (aside from the gun) of participation in the offense charged.[37] For example, if bank photographs taken during the robbery and eyewitnesses to the offense convincingly showed that Robinson was a participant, would evidence of the gun still be admitted? Here the degree to which evidence of possession would alter the jury's conclusion about the probability of Robinson's participation is slight; the potential for prejudicial influences, however, is not abated. Hence, the existence of other evidence strengthens the argument for rejecting evidence that the accused possessed a weapon similar to that used by one of the robbers.

Although the *Robinson* court was concerned with the prejudicial effect of relevant evidence, other reported cases contain many examples of the application of the various practical reasons for the exclusion of relevant evidence.[38] In an action against a manufacturer for damages to plaintiff's farm resulting from fumes, considerations of time consumption and jury confusion justified the rejection of evidence concerning the condition of other agricultural lands twenty miles away;[39] in a prosecution for tax evasion, distraction and confusion of the jury were sufficient reasons to reject complicated exhibits from civil litiga-

---

37. Id.

38. See generally McCormick, § 185, at 438–41; I Wigmore, § 29a, at 412–15, and additional sections cited therein (note, however, that Wigmore also discusses situations in which a fixed rule dictates exclusion). For a recent federal case that applies the balancing test, see United States v. Cook, 538 F.2d 1000 (3d Cir. 1976).

39. Thompson v. American Steel & Wire Co., 317 Pa. 7, 175 A. 541 (1934). See also Skogen v. Dow Chemical Co., 375 F.2d 692, 705–06 (8th Cir. 1967) (products liability trial was long, and testimony of another expert witness in rebuttal would have been cumulative); Bunn v. Caterpillar Tractor Co., 415 F.Supp. 286 (W.D.Pa.1976) (judge finds that to admit all of P's evidence would be too time consuming).

tion relating to the funds in question;[40] and finally, unfair prejudice was a valid reason to reject evidence of a wife's infidelity (offered to show her ill will toward the husband-victim in the murder prosecution of the wife) when the infidelities occurred months before the offense.[41]

Federal Rule of Evidence 403, set forth above, generally accords with the common-law rule as developed in most federal and state cases.[42] Two points, however, should be noted. If the balance is close between probative force and one or more counterweights, the federal rule favors admissibility. That is, it provides for exclusion only if one or more practical reasons for rejection "substantially" outweigh probative value. Further, the rule does not include, as some cases have,[43] unfair surprise as a basis for rejecting relevant evidence. This omission represents a judgment that in cases where surprise occurs, a continuance, rather than exclusion of the evidence, is the preferred remedy.[44]

§ 14. Conditional Relevancy

It now should be apparent that the test of relevancy is infinitely less stringent than the tests to determine whether the totality of the evidence is *sufficient* to justify a finding for the party who must prove the affirmative—ordinarily the government in a criminal case and the plaintiff in a civil case. The measures of sufficiency are, in a criminal prosecution, proof beyond a reasonable doubt and, in a typical civil trial, proof by a preponderance[45] of the evidence. These standards mean that

---

40. United States v. Pollock, 394 F. 2d 922 (7th Cir.), cert. denied 393 U.S. 924 (1968).

41. State v. Flett, 234 Or. 124, 127–28, 380 P.2d 634, 636 (1963) (however, evidence of illicit sexual acts nearer in time to the alleged killing was held properly admitted).

42. Adv.Comm.Note to Fed.R.Evid. 403. Exclusion of relevant evidence under Federal Rule 403 on the ground of prejudice is consid-

ered extensively in Dolan, Rule 403: The Prejudice Rule in Evidence, 49 S.Cal.L.Rev. 220 (1976).

43. McCormick, § 185, at 440.

44. Adv.Comm.Note to Fed.R.Evid. 403.

45. The word "preponderance" does not mean the greater quantity of evidence, but refers rather to the probative (convincing) force of the evidence. In general, the prepon-

the total evidence must be sufficiently probative to permit a rational trier to find that the party bringing the action (or, specifically, the party with the burden of persuasion) has established his facts to the required degree of probability. If he were required to show that every item of evidence makes the proposition to which it is directed more likely than not (or likely beyond a reasonable doubt), the introduction of evidence would be restricted severely. As McCormick notes, "a brick is not a wall"; [46] the question at the conclusion of the case is whether the evidence *taken together* meets the applicable standard.

Sometimes, however, the preponderance test, which involves a "more-probable-than-not" standard,[47] applies to a *single* item of evidence. This more demanding standard applies whenever the existence of one fact, *A*, conditions (is necessary for) the relevance of evidence of an allied fact, *B*. Put conversely, the relevance of allied fact *B* is dependent (conditioned) upon the existence of underlying fact *A*. In this circumstance, it is necessary to provide sufficient evidence of fact *A* to enable the trier to use the evidence of fact *B* for a consequential (material) purpose.

Relevancy is conditioned upon the existence of an underlying fact in the following illustrative situations: (1) On the issue whether *X* committed suicide, the proponent offers a page from a diary, which reflects that the writer was mentally depressed (fact *B*). Mental depression is probative of suicide, but the trier can not consider the diary as evidence of depression (and hence, by further inference, of suicide) unless it finds that *X* wrote the diary entry (fact *A*); [48] (2) On the issue whether *X* drove negli-

---

derance standard is met if the evidence would reasonably justify a finding that the existence of the facts necessary to sustain the party with the affirmative burden of persuasion is more likely than their nonexistence. F. James & G. Hazard, Civil Procedure, § 7.6, at 243–44 (2d ed. 1977). A more demanding standard of proof is required in certain civil cases. For example, some jurisdictions require that fraud must be established by clear and convincing evidence.

46. McCormick, § 185, at 436.

47. See supra note 38.

48. For a recent federal case applying the conditional relevance rule to a document, see In re James E. Long Const. Co., 557 F.2d 1039 (4th Cir. 1977).

gently at the point of an automobile collision (a curve in the highway), the proponent offers evidence that a black sedan of American manufacture was traveling at a high rate of speed one half mile from the curve (fact B). This increases the likelihood that the car was speeding at the curve, but the trier can not consider the evidence unless it finds that X was the driver of the black sedan (fact A); (3) On the issue whether X assumed the risk of flying a private plane with a mechanical defect, the proponent offers evidence that an aircraft mechanic stated to several persons that the defect existed (fact B). The trier can not use this evidence to find that X assumed the risk unless it finds that X overheard or had knowledge of the mechanic's statement (fact A).

In all of the foregoing situations, the application of the basic test of relevance, which inquires whether the evidence has some probative force, is dependent or conditioned upon a conclusion that an underlying fact exists. The judge must ensure that there is sufficient evidence upon which the jury can find that the existence of the underlying fact is more probable than its nonexistence. Federal Rule 104 states in part:

> (b) Relevancy conditioned on fact—When the relevancy of evidence depends upon the fulfillment of a condition of fact, the court shall admit it upon, or subject to, the introduction of evidence sufficient to support a finding of the fulfillment of the condition.

The rule recognizes the practical accommodation that must accompany the receipt of evidence conditioned upon the existence of an underlying fact. In the strict sense, evidence of the underlying fact (e. g., that X inscribed the diary page) is not relevant without the associated conditioned evidence (that the writer was depressed) and vice-versa.[49] The judge determines whether the

49. Morgan at 39. For a recent federal case presenting a problem of conditional relevance, see United States v. Campion, 560 F.2d 751 (6th Cir. 1977) (papers reflecting payment to some person for relaying results of races can not be used to implicate accused in illegal gambling because evidence is insufficient that accused was the person designated in the papers). The court in *Campion* cites only Fed.R. Evid. 402, but Rule 104(b) is also apposite. See supra note 25.

proponent's order of presentation is satisfactory and, under the Federal Rule as well as common-law practice, he may permit the proponent first to introduce either evidence of the underlying (conditioning) fact or evidence of the conditioned fact. However, unless circumstances make it clear that the connecting evidence will be forthcoming, the judge should seek assurances from the proponent that he has the linking evidence and that it is in an admissible form. The proponent's subsequent failure to connect the admitted evidence with sufficient evidence of the underlying fact dictates that the judge strike evidence of the conditioned fact from the record and instruct the jury to disregard it. Because the possible relevance of the conditioned fact often is apparent to the jury, there is a risk of improper influence from exposure to the stricken evidence. For example, if the jury hears evidence that a black sedan was speeding, it may be influenced by this evidence even though the evidence subsequently is struck because the judge concludes that the evidence that X was driving is insufficient to support a finding that he was the operator. This risk of improper influence is most acute when there is *some* properly admitted evidence to suggest that X drove the speeding black sedan; despite the proponent's failure satisfactorily to "connect up" his evidence, the jury may conclude that X was driving the speeding vehicle.

NOTES

1. *The Counterweight of Time Consumption.* Although undue time consumption may warrant the trial judge's rejection of relevant evidence, there is little point in making an appellate issue of his admission of time-consuming evidence. The time lost obviously cannot be recaptured, and appellate argument on the point represents an additional drain on judicial resources.

2. *Judge's Role: Evidentiary Issues.* Note that with regard to questions of relevance, the judge is acting as a monitor of the evidence. He ensures that a reasonable trier could find the evidence probative and, in the case of conditional relevance, that the trier could find the existence of the underlying fact. However, where the application of an exclusionary rule of evidence (including the competence of a witness) requires a factual resolution, the judge actually determines the facts. His role in this regard is treated in detail in Chapter X. Major disadvantages would attend the practice of having the jury

decide the facts pertinent to the application of an exclusionary rule of evidence. Such a practice would unduly burden the jury with numerous "subsets" of factfinding determinations that involve the admissibility of evidence. Further, many of the exclusionary rules are founded in whole or in part on policy considerations that would not be understood or appreciated by the jury. This unappreciated policy basis adds to the risk that the jury would be influenced improperly by exposure to evidence that, in accordance with the judge's instructions, it later determined was inadmissible. Federal Rule of Evidence 104 provides in part:

> (a) Questions of admissibility generally—Preliminary questions concerning the qualification of a person to be a witness, the existence of a privilege, or the admissibility of evidence shall be determined by the court . . . .

3. *Relevance; Materiality.* Examine the following passage, noting particularly the sense in which "relevance" is used:

> Unfortunately, . . . theoretical and practical difficulties surround the very concept of the "facts of the case" and these blur any distinctions that may be drawn between the material truth on the one hand, and the truth according to the allegations of the parties, on the other. It is common for lawyers and others to speak and write of "the facts of a case" as if this phrase conveyed a simple meaning, but as soon as it is qualified by the addition of the essential word "relevant," so as to make the phrase read "the relevant facts of the case," its apparent simplicity disappears. In the context of civil litigation, "relevant" must mean relevant for the resolution of the dispute in accordance with the law, and the test of relevancy is thus the law itself. It is, however, impossible to know what principles of law are applicable in a given case unless the relevant facts are known, and the argument thus proceeds in a circle.

M. Cappelletti & J. Jolowicz, Public Interest Parties and the Active Role of the Judge in Civil Litigation 254 (1975). How, as a practical matter, can one deal with the dilemma posed by the authors? Consider Rule 15 of the Federal Rules of Civil Procedure that provides for amendments to the pleadings. With leave of court, amendments may be made late in the trial, even after judgment has been entered.

The reader who is familiar with trials probably will agree that many disputes about relevance center upon the materiality or consequentialness of the proponent's proposition of fact. It is quite likely that he has correctly perceived the existence of a probative relationship between his evidence and the proposition of fact that it is offered to support. Often, the problem is how that proposition relates to the governing substantive law.

4. *The Distracting Charm of Irrelevance.* Trials, which are practical affairs, often do not strictly adhere to admissibility (or exclusion) as prescribed by the rules of evidence. For example, experienced practitioners often refrain from objecting to irrelevant evidence for fear of appearing obstructive to the jury. As a result, juries, while attempting to apply complicated instructions from the judge, may find themselves swayed by reactions to details wholly irrelevant to any legal issue. Consider Judge Bok's example:

> Irrelevance can be highly enlightening. The witness who starts with what she ate for breakfast and remembers it was Thursday because her husband's sister came down with the measles when she shouldn't if she had only gone to the doctor, the one with glasses—should be a delight to the judge's heart and make the jury feel at home. Behind this leisurely sweep of incident they can follow her as they please, and it will give them at least her barometric pressure at the time when she signed the note at the bank without reading it. After listening to enough of it, any idiot would know that she was an accommodation endorser who had done it to help her husband and had got nothing out of it herself .   .   .   .

Bok, I Too, Nicodemus 322 (1946).

5. *Conditional Relevance.* Does United States v. Robinson, discussed in § 13, involve a problem of conditional relevance?

CHAPTER III

PROCEDURAL CONCEPTS AND CONSEQUENCES

§ 15. Burdens of Persuasion and Production

We have seen that a judicial trial employs the principles of party presentation and persuasion, but places the responsibility for dispute resolution in the hands of neutral participants—the judge and jury. In a jury trial, the judge instructs or "charges" the jury concerning the elements of a claim or defense and directs them, first, to ascertain the historical (adjudicative) facts from the evidence, and, then, by applying the law as described in the charge, to determine whether the claim or defense is established. For example, the judge may instruct the jury that slander consists of a defamatory statement [which would be further defined], that was communicated or "published" to one other than the person allegedly defamed, and that caused the defamed person to sustain pecuniary damage or harm to reputation. Depending upon what defenses are asserted, the judge also may instruct the jury that if they find that the statement is true or that it is privileged [which would be further explained], there is no liability. Of course, in a non-jury trial, the judge alone determines the historical facts and applies the governing legal principles—that is, he alone determines the existence or nonexistence of the elements.

In both judge and jury trials, there is a need to specify the consequences of a determination that all (or alternatively only some) of the elements of a claim or defense are present. This specification takes the form of allocating to the plaintiff and defendant their respective obligations with regard to establishing the elements of a claim or defense. Thus, in a civil trial for slander the judge should make it clear to the jury that the plaintiff, if he is to recover, must establish the existence of all of the elements of slander: the defamatory statement, its publication, and the resulting damage or harm. The assertion of certain defenses (called "affirmative" defenses) requires additional in-

40

structions that make it clear that as to these defenses the defendant has the responsibility of proof. For example, if the defendant claims the affirmative defense of truth, the judge will charge the jury that *if the defendant* establishes the truth of the defamatory statement, he is not liable.

This allocation of the responsibility for proof is made not on an ad hoc basis, but in accordance with precedent or statutory provisions. A number of considerations influence the rules of allocation, such as which party seeks to have the court alter the status quo, whether one party alleges an event that appears improbable, whether any social or public policy militates for or against recovery, and whether certain evidence is available more readily to one party than to the other.[1] It is no simple matter to predict which of these factors may be dominant, but it is relatively easy to ascertain from statute or precedent the allocative rules of a particular jurisdiction. The rules loosely are spoken of as governing the "burden of proof"; the more precise phrase is "burden of persuasion" (or, alternatively, "the risk of nonpersuasion"), because it connotes that the party with the responsibility for particular elements has the burden of persuading (or bears the risk of not persuading) the trier that each of these particular elements exists.[2] The burdened party must persuade the trier of the existence of these elements according to a standard or degree of certainty mandated by the type of proceeding: in a criminal trial, the government must prove the elements of an offense beyond a reasonable doubt; in a typical civil case, a party must prove the elements of his claim by a preponderance of the evidence (sometimes expressed by the phrases "greater weight of the evidence" or "more probable than not").[3] There

---

1. For a discussion of these and other factors, see F. James & G. Hazard, Civil Procedure, § 7.8, at 249–53 (2d ed. 1977).

2. The phrase "burden of proof" often has been used to refer to two separate and distinct responsibilities of the parties: the "burden of persuasion" and the "burden of production." Id., § 7.5, at 240.

The distinction between these two responsibilities is discussed in this section.

3. McCormick, § 339, at 793–94. In criminal cases, an accused may have the burden of persuading the trier of the existence of certain affirmative defenses by a preponderance of the evidence. See Patterson v. New York, 432 U.S. 197

also are intermediate standards, such as "clear and convincing" proof,[4] that apply in particular kinds of civil cases or to particular elements within them. For example, where a party claims that his opponent engaged in fraudulent conduct, he may be required to prove the elements of fraud by clear and convincing evidence.[5]

These standards are intended to indicate the convincing force of the evidence required to meet the burden of persuasion, not quantitatively to measure the evidence.[6] A defendant who presents five witnesses will not always prevail over a plaintiff who presents one. What is important is the factfinder's belief in the existence or nonexistence of the disputed elements. Believability is not necessarily a function of the number of witnesses or quantity of evidence presented.[7]

The diagrammatic framework below illustrates an allocation of the burdens of persuasion to the respective parties for the various elements of the foregoing defamation case. To establish the framework for a particular case, one must know or assume the elements of the claims or defenses asserted. Here, assume the plaintiff must prove three elements by a preponderance of the evidence: the existence of the defamatory statement [A], the communication or publication to a third party [B], and the resulting damage (or harm) [C]. Assume that the defendant denies that he made the statement and asserts, as a second defense [D], that the alleged defamatory statement is true. The latter defense usually is an affirmative one,[8] so the defendant has

---

(1977). However, there are limits to the state's power to allocate a burden of persuasion to the accused in a criminal case. See Mullaney v. Wilbur, 421 U.S. 684 (1975).

4. The phrasing of an intermediate standard varies from state to state, but it generally includes the terms "clear" and "convincing." See McCormick, § 340, at 796.

5. The clear and convincing standard also applies to the impeach-

ment (contradiction) of a notary's seal of acknowledgment. For other examples, see IX Wigmore, § 2498, at 329–34.

6. F. James & G. Hazard, Civil Procedure, § 7.6, at 243 (2d ed. 1977).

7. Id.

8. A defendant generally must *plead* such a defense affirmatively. F. James & G. Hazard, Civil Procedure, § 4.9, at 143 (2d ed. 1977).

the burden of persuasion.[9] Thus, each party has an affirmative responsibility of proof, although the defendant will prevail if either the plaintiff fails to persuade the trier of the existence of elements A, B and C or the defendant does persuade the trier that the alleged statement was true (element D).

For the plaintiff to discharge his burden of persuasion, the evidence underlying the various elements *at least* must be such that a jury, viewing the evidence most favorably to the plaintiff, reasonably could find that the existence of the elements is more probable than their nonexistence. Because the jury resolves only those questions that reasonably can be disputed, the plaintiff, as a first step, must offer evidence sufficient to allow jury consideration of the existence of each element.[10] In the diagram below, the evidence at a minimum must justify the jury resolution signified by block II. If evidence pertaining to one or more elements is insufficient to raise a jury question (that is, insufficient to move all elements in the plaintiff's case to block II), the judge, on proper motion, will direct a verdict against the plaintiff. Put otherwise, if plaintiff's evidence has failed to create a *reasonable* dispute as to one or more elements, the case is resolved by the judge (block I).

Plaintiff's Elements	Existence of Element Reasonably Disputable	Defendant's Element
I	II	III
[Judge Resolution in Favor of D]	[Jury Resolution Based on the Evidence]	[Judge Resolution in Favor of P]
A (defamatory statement)		
B (publication)		
C (damage or harm)		D (truth)

[B9103]

Thus, to meet his burden of persuasion, the plaintiff must satisfy the essential preliminary step of producing evidence sufficient to move all the elements necessary to his recovery from block I (resolution by the judge) to block II (resolution by the jury). Unless his opponent has conceded the existence of one or

---

9. Id., §§ 4.7–4.8, at 138–43.   10. See Ch. I, § 6.

more elements,[11] the plaintiff begins this process of proof by producing evidence to support each element. This burden of coming forward with the evidence needed to avoid an adverse resolution by the judge is called the *burden of producing evidence* (or "burden of production"). It is a responsibility distinct from the burden of persuasion—the *ultimate* burden of *convincing* the factfinder of the existence of the essential elements of a claim or defense. However, by meeting the immediate responsibility imposed by the burden of production, the plaintiff avoids a directed verdict and moves the dispute at least as far as block II.

Of course, the plaintiff, if he can, will present evidence so convincing on one or more elements that no reasonable jury could find against him. Absent persuasive rebuttal evidence by defendant on elements so established, there would be a judge resolution (block III) *in favor* of the plaintiff. The judge either would enter a directed verdict for the plaintiff (if all elements indisputably were present) or would take from jury consideration, through a peremptory instruction, those elements that indisputably were proven. If the plaintiff, during his case in chief, were able to produce evidence of such convincing force that the existence of all the necessary elements was indisputable, the state of the evidence would be reflected as follows:

Plaintiff's Elements	Existence of Element Reasonably Disputable	Defendant's Element(s)
I [Judge Resolution]	II [Jury Resolution]	III [Judge Resolution]
A (defamatory statement) ———————————————————		➤ A
B (publication) ———————————————————		➤ B
C (damage or harm) ———————————————————		➤ C
		D (Truth)

[B9101]

---

11. The element might be conceded, for example, in the pleadings, by stipulation, or by an admission made during discovery. Furthermore, if the facts constituting a particular element were judically noticed, no production of evidence would be necessary. See Ch. I, § 7.

Before the judge resolves the presence of any or all elements in plaintiff's favor, however, he must give the defendant the opportunity to rebut plaintiff's evidence. The depicted state of the evidence, therefore, requires that the defendant take steps in rebuttal or else face a directed verdict. The burden of *producing evidence now has shifted to the defendant,* although the burden of persuasion has remained fixed upon the plaintiff. Because the plaintiff must show the existence of all three elements in order to recover, the defendant can avoid a directed verdict (that is, he can meet the shifted burden of production) by rebutting at least one element so that he raises a jury question as to that element.[12]

Ideally, of course, the defendant would like to present evidence of such convincing force that one or more elements would be resolved in his favor by the judge (block I of diagram), thus entitling him to a directed verdict. If the defendant were thus successful, the burden of production on the element(s) in block I would shift to the plaintiff, who would attempt to produce sufficient rebuttal evidence to move the issue of the existence of the element(s) back into block II. As a practical matter, however, multiple shifts in the burden of production are unusual because it is not often that the state of the evidence fluctuates back and forth between the extremes represented by blocks I and III; more frequently the determination of whether an element exists depends upon a jury assessment of credibility (block II).

But the defendant is not limited to evidence that negates the plaintiff's evidence concerning elements A, B, and C. He also can avoid liability by establishing the affirmative defense of truth. To do so, he must first meet his burden of production by providing sufficient evidence of the truth of his statement to raise a jury question (that is, to move element D into block II). If the evidence of truth were highly convincing (block I), the defendant could shift to the plaintiff the burden of production for the affirmative defense of truth. Note, however, that the

---

12. As to those elements not rebutted (i. e., not moved out of block III by defendant), the judge will give a peremptory instruction that these elements shall be taken as established.

burden of *persuasion* on the element of truth would not shift to the plaintiff, but would remain fixed upon the defendant where it was originally allocated.

Various assumptions about the state of the evidence, including the allocation of the burdens of production and persuasion, can be depicted in the diagram. Suppose, for example, *at the conclusion* of the case, the following state of the evidence existed:

Plaintiff's Elements	Existence of Element Reasonably Disputable	Defendant's Element(s)
I [Judge Resolution]	II [Jury Resolution]	III [Judge Resolution]
A (defamatory statement) ————————————————		——▶ A
B (publication) ————————		——▶ B
C (damage or harm) ———————▶ C		
	D ◀————————	——— D (Truth)

[B9102]

The judge would instruct the jury that it shall take as an established fact that the defendant uttered (published) a slanderous statement to a third person (elements A and B). Jury questions exist, however, as to whether damage or harm was incurred (element C) and as to whether the statement was true (element D). Regarding these reasonably disputed elements, both plaintiff and defendant have discharged their respective *burdens of production* and must now meet their *burdens of persuasion*. Accordingly, it is necessary to instruct the jury that the plaintiff has the burden of persuasion on the element of damage or harm and the defendant has the burden of persuasion on the element of truth. If the jury does not believe that damage or harm occurred, it will render a defendant's verdict. If it finds (by a preponderance of the evidence) that there was damage or harm and if it is unconvinced that the statement was true, it will return a verdict for the plaintiff. On the other hand, if the jury is persuaded that the statement was true, it will return a defendant's verdict regardless of whether the plaintiff sustained damage or harm.

Suppose, however, that the jury is in a state of indecision or equipoise regarding the issue of damage (harm) or truth.[13] When the jury agrees that the probabilities of the existence or nonexistence of an element are equal, the *allocation of the burden of persuasion becomes decisive in determining who prevails.* Because the party to whom that burden is allocated has failed to convince the jury affirmatively of the existence of the element(s) for which he is responsible, that party has not discharged his burden of persuasion and the jury, in obedience to proper instructions from the court, should find against him. Thus, if the jury concludes that it is equally likely that plaintiff did or did not suffer damage (or harm) from the alleged defamatory statement, the plaintiff loses. He has failed to meet his burden of persuading the jury that it is more likely than not that he sustained a loss. Correspondingly, if the jury believes that the probabilities of the truth or falsity of the defamatory statement are equal, the defendant has failed to carry his burden of persuasion on the affirmative defense.

The section that follows will examine the effects of a presumption upon the burden of persuasion and the burden of production. A true presumption always affects the burden of production, but in most jurisdictions a presumption does not affect the burden of persuasion.

§ 16. Presumptions: General Nature and Effect

A trial involves many instances in which the trier of fact makes a factual determination by a process of inference. The factfinder first accepts the existence of a certain fact or set of

---

13. The problem of a jury in a state of decisional balance can arise regarding the existence of any element of a claim or defense that, because of the state of the evidence, is the proper subject of jury resolution. As to any element in block II, the jury may conclude that the probabilities of the existence of the element are equal to the probabilities of its nonexistence. Of course, if the judge is the factfinder—that is, there is no jury—the judge also resolves disputed issues of fact in accordance with the allocation of the burden of persuasion. Note again that in the illustration in the text, the defendant prevails if either the plaintiff fails to carry his burden of persuasion on all essential elements or the defendant carries his burden of persuasion on the element of truth.

facts and then infers the existence of a related fact or facts. Human experience yields countless situations in which a fact or group of facts, if believed to exist, can by the process of inferential reasoning lead to a related factual conclusion. For example, if there is evidence that a letter was addressed properly and thereafter posted, it may be inferred that the addressee received the letter. As further examples: if a vehicle is labeled with the name of a person or company, it may be inferred that the name is that of the owner; if a person can not be found and neither family nor acquaintances have heard from him for a long period of years, it may be inferred that he is dead.[14] In each of these situations certain *basic* facts (proper mailing, name on vehicle, absence without word) support a finding of the *inferred* facts (receipt, ownership, death).

Although the number and variety of basic facts that can lead to an inferential conclusion are countless, certain patterns, such as those found in the foregoing illustrations, frequently recur. The courts and legislatures have singled out many sets of basic and inferred facts such as mailing-receipt, absence-death, labeling-ownership, and have given to them the status of presumptions. In many of these recurring instances, there appears to be a strong likelihood of the existence of the inferred or, more accurately, *presumed* conclusion. In other instances, the probative force of the basic facts may not be so convincing, yet some policy rationale or procedural convenience may make the presumed conclusion desirable. Thus, when an article is found to be damaged after having been transported by more than one carrier, a presumption is raised that the last carrier caused the damage.[15] Here, as among several carriers, the probative value of the presumption that the damage occurred while the property was in the custody of the last carrier may appear weak. Absent any evidence that pinpoints the cause of damage, it could be argued that it is no more probable that damage occurred while the goods were on the terminal carrier than it is that the damage occurred on one of the prior carriers. On the other hand, if the

---

14. For further examples, see infra § 17.

15. Chicago & N.W. Ry. v. C.C. Whitnack Produce Co., 258 U.S. 369 (1922).

goods already were damaged at the time the last carrier took custody, it perhaps is probable that the last carrier would have noted or recorded the damaged condition. More important, the presumption here serves as a procedural device that gives to the plaintiff (who in the setting just described is disadvantaged in ascertaining the facts) a fair chance to recover by tentatively placing the damage with the last carrier.

At this point, a presumption must be distinguished from an inference. Although the language used with reference to presumptions is exasperatingly indiscriminate, a genuine presumption is raised by a basic fact or facts that, when accepted as true by the trier,[16] give rise to a *mandatory* inference, properly called a presumed fact. Once the basic facts are believed, the resulting presumed fact must be accepted by the trier *unless* it is rebutted by contravening evidence. An inference never has such a compulsory effect. The trier always is at liberty either to accept or reject an inferred fact. Note further that because a presumption creates a compulsory finding that remains obligatory until the presumed fact is rebutted, the raising of a presumption always shifts to the opposing party the *burden of producing evidence.* This is not true of an inference, which results only in creating a jury question whether the inferred fact exists.

Although the terms "presumption" and "inference" as defined above have gained general usage, terminology in this area is not uniform. For example, judges and lawyers sometimes speak of "permissive presumptions" or "presumptions of facts," by which terms they usually mean an inference. The cases also contain the term "presumption of law," which usually means a rebuttable presumption [17] of the kind herein denominated simply a

---

16. The existence of the basic fact could be proved at the trial or established by the pleadings, stipulation, or judicial notice.

17. IX Wigmore, § 2491, at 288. The slippery language that permeates the area of presumptions should make the cautious reader or practitioner reserve judgment on what is meant by a particular

term until a careful inquiry is made. For the varying meaning of the word "presumption," either standing alone or with various modifiers, see Morgan at 25–26; Ladd and Carlson at 1216–17; Laughlin, In Support of the Thayer Theory of Presumptions, 52 Mich.L.Rev. 195, 196–207 (1953); Louisell, Construing Rule 301: Instructing the Jury on Presumptions

presumption.   Finally, a "conclusive presumption," often encountered in statutes, is not really a presumption at all, but rather is a rule of substantive law.   This "presumption" declares that certain basic facts, once established, give rise to an *irrebuttable* conclusion.   For example, it may be presumed conclusively that a child under the age of seven years cannot commit a felony.   This rule, although stated in presumptive language, is merely a substantive principle that serious criminal responsibility may not be imposed upon one under the age of seven.[18]

In criminal cases, special considerations limit the effect of presumptions.   To begin with, a directed verdict against the accused is never permitted in a criminal case; in a jury trial, a conviction must rest upon a jury finding that each element of the offense was present.   Accordingly, despite the common use of the term "presumption" in criminal cases, the establishment of basic facts in a criminal case only creates an inference.   In criminal cases, a "presumption" still leaves the trier at all times free to reject the presumed fact.   This comports with the basic principle that the trier has the sole and unfettered responsibility of determining guilt, which must be established beyond a reasonable doubt.[19]   Consequently, the judge does not instruct the jury

---

in Civil Actions and Proceedings, 63 Va.L.Rev. 281, 289–291 (1976).

18.   Morgan   at   25;   Louisell, Construing Rule 301, supra note 17, at 289–90.   As substantive rules, "conclusive   presumptions"   must comport with due process and equal protection tests.   Weinberger v. Salfi, 422 U.S. 749 (1975) (upholding a conclusive statutory definition of "widow" for Social Security eligibility requirements); Cleveland Bd. of Educ. v. LaFleur, 414 U.S. 632 (1974) (invalidating a conclusive school board regulation on maternity leave); Vlandis v. Kline, 412 U.S. 441 (1973) (invalidating a conclusive statutory definition of "residents" for university tuition);   Stanley v. Illinois, 405 U.S. 645 (1972) (invalidating a conclusive presumption against parental fitness of unwed father).

19.   See McCormick, § 341, at 798–99. The "presumption of innocence" that applies to the accused in a criminal case is not really a presumption consisting of a basic and a presumed fact; it is a statement that the prosecutor has the burden of showing guilt.   The "presumption of innocence," through loose but common usage, has come to connote the prosecution's burden of producing evidence and of persuading the jury beyond a reasonable doubt.   McCormick, § 342, at 806. The "presumption of sanity" is not really a presumption, but a statement that the defendant has the

that upon finding certain basic facts, they must accept as true the related presumed fact. Rather, the judge instructs the jury that they *may* find the existence of the presumed fact from the basic facts.

It is probable that in a criminal case the United States Constitution forbids the use against the accused of a presumption that has a mandatory effect until sufficient rebuttal evidence is presented.[20] Furthermore, the Constitution has been interpreted to require, in criminal cases, a strong probative connection between the basic facts and the "presumed" fact.[21] This connection must be supported by human experience such that it is *at least* more likely than not that the basic fact will be accompanied by the presumed fact.[22] Moreover, recent cases strongly indicate that if a presumed fact is an element of an offense or operates to negate a defense, the basic facts must render the existence of the presumed fact certain beyond a reasonable doubt.[23]

---

burden of producing evidence and, in some jurisdictions, the burden of persuasion on his lack of mental capacity. Id., § 346, at 830.

20. A good discussion is contained in McCormick, §§ 344, 346, at 817, 829–33.

21. Barnes v. United States, 412 U. S. 837 (1973) (prior cases cited and reviewed); United States v. Gainey, 380 U.S. 63, 65–68 (1965); United States v. Romano, 382 U.S. 136, 139–44 (1965); Tot v. United States, 319 U.S. 463, 467–68 (1943). For criticism of the rational connection test, see McCormick, § 344, at 814–15. For a recent decision striking down a presumption that a gun found in an automobile is presumed to be possessed by all of the car's occupants, see Allen v. Ulster County Court, 568 F.2d 998 (2d Cir. 1978).

22. Leary v. United States, 395 U.S. 6, 36 (1969). McCormick, § 344, at 814–15. It is clear, however, that the connection will be assessed not only in terms of what is in the record of trial, but also with regard to such information as can be gleaned from other reliable sources such as documentation available to Congress, court records in other cases, etc. See Turner v. United States, 396 U.S. 398, 408–16 (1970); McCormick, § 344, at 816.

23. McCormick, § 344, at 815–16. Christie and Pye, Presumptions and Assumptions in the Criminal Law: Another View, 1970 Duke L. J. 919, 923 n. 24.

The various tests, "rational connection," "more likely than not" and "reasonable doubt" are reviewed, and the ambiguous relationship of one to the other is recognized in Barnes v. United States, 412 U.S.

The emerging principle that apparently requires in criminal cases a "reasonable doubt" connection between the basic and presumed fact has a nice consonance with traditional ideas about the state's burden of persuasion; it also has a logical flaw. Assuming the state has the power to redefine a crime so that the presumed fact no longer is an element of the offense, the state should have the lesser included authority of keeping the presumed fact as an element but providing that its existence (absent rebuttal) will be presumed if certain basic facts are established. Because the state, under the assumption here made, could eliminate the presumed element entirely, it should be able to provide a statutory presumption that connects the basic facts and the presumed fact by a nexus of lesser certainty than a reasonable doubt. Nevertheless, the United States Supreme Court has, so far at least, rejected this analysis.[24]

The discussion that follows, unless otherwise noted, is limited to presumptions and inferences in civil cases. These terms will be used consistently with the foregoing discussion.

§ 17. Some Sample Presumptions

Although presumptions are found in all jurisdictions, what one jurisdiction considers a presumption, another may classify as an inference. Since there are dozens if not hundreds of presumptions, the illustrative list that follows is but a small sample.[25]

There is a measure of probative force in each of the correlative groupings below.[26] Other considerations, however, including superior knowledge or easier access to the evidence (numbers 1, 2, 6, 7, 8) and policies favoring the settlement of estates

837 (1973). The Court avoided the question of a mandatory "reasonable doubt" standard, but noted that a statutory inference that satisfies that standard "clearly accords with due process." 412 U.S. at 843.

24. See Leary v. United States, 395 U.S. 6, 34–35 (1969); Tot v. United States, 319 U.S. 463, 472 (1943).

25. For a more comprehensive list see McCormick, § 343, at 807–11; Ladd & Carlson at 1218–19; West's Ann.Cal.Evid. Code §§ 600 et seq.

26. As to the last presumption, see the textual discussion supra at note 15.

Basic Fact(s)	Presumed Fact
1. Letter regularly addressed and mailed	Received by addressee
2. Vehicle lawfully stopped is struck from rear by second vehicle	Driver of second vehicle negligent
3. Violent death from external means	Death was an accident (not a suicide)
4. Absence for 7 years without explanation or any communication to family or friends; inquiries unavailing	Absentee deceased
5. Will can not be found	Revoked by testator
6. Employee in accident while driving vehicle owned by employer	Employee was acting within scope of employment
7. Goods delivered to bailee in good condition, but damaged upon return	Bailee negligent
8. Goods damaged during transit provided by more than one carrier	Last carrier caused damage

[B9104]

(4, 5), the protection of survivors (3, 4), or the recovery of damages in cases of accident (2, 6), appear to be operative.[27] The next section will examine whether the considerations behind a particular presumption support a departure from the usual rule that a presumption shifts the burden of producing evidence, but does not disturb the burden of persuasion, which remains fixed upon the party to whom it originally was assigned.

§ 18.   Presumptions: Impact Upon Opponent and Effect of Rebuttal Evidence

It will be recalled that the effect of a presumption always may be avoided by proving the nonexistence of the basic facts that support the presumed fact. However, the probative force of the rebutting evidence showing the nonexistence of the basic facts often is not so compelling as to cause the judge, by instructions or otherwise, to remove from the case altogether any consideration of a presumption. If the evidence against the existence of

---

27. See McCormick, § 343, at 806–
11; Louisell, Construing Rule 301,
supra note 17, at 292–93.

the basic facts is not so persuasive as to cause the judge to resolve the question of their existence, he will instruct the jury that the presumed fact arises only if the jury first finds the existence of the basic facts. For example, where the evidence conflicts on whether a letter was regularly addressed and mailed, the judge will charge the jury that no presumption of receipt will arise unless the jury finds these basic facts.

The foregoing discussion does not consider what general effect is to be given to a presumption after the basic fact is found to exist, nor does it address the related issue of the measure of rebuttal evidence necessary to negate the presumed fact. The jurisdictions lack uniformity in their approach to these fundamental aspects of presumptions. There are two dominant views regarding the general effect of a presumption. One view, which prevails in a majority of jurisdictions, holds that when a presumption arises after the establishment of the basic facts, its only procedural effect is to shift the burden of producing evidence to the opponent.[28] The opponent must meet the shifted burden of producing evidence, but he does not bear the ultimate burden of convincing the trier of fact of the nonexistence of the presumed fact. The second view, a minority one, holds that for most (but usually not all) presumptions, the procedural effect is to shift the burden of persuasion.[29] This position, sometimes called the Morgan view because of its advocacy by the late Professor Edmund Morgan,[30] places great weight both on the probative link between basic and presumed facts and on the supposed utility of presumptions in advancing desirable social policy.[31] The minority approach gives maximum effect to most presumptions: a shift in the burden of persuasion results in placing upon the opponent the burden of convincing the trier that the nonexistence of the presumed fact is more probable than its existence.

---

28. McCormick, § 345, at 821; Morgan at 28–29; IX Wigmore § 2491.

29. See, e. g., Maine R.Evid. 30; Wis.Stat.Ann. § 903.01; West's Ann.Cal.Evid.Code §§ 603–06.

30. Morgan, Some Problems of Proof, 74–81 (1956).

31. McCormick, § 345, at 826–28. There is no consensus as to exactly what considerations (policy, probative force, or both) dictate which presumptions should have the effect of relocating the burden of persuasion.

Whether it is desirable to modify the usual rule that permanently fixes upon a party the burden of persuasion is debatable. It generally is conceded that in some cases a shift in the burden of persuasion accords too much advantage to the proponent of the presumption, resulting in unfairness to the opponent. Thus, few if any jurisdictions adhere to the view that all presumptions result in shifting the burden of persuasion in civil cases. The problem becomes one of determining which presumptions should be accorded the significant impact of reallocating the burden of persuasion. One minority approach is to shift the burden of persuasion only when there is a substantial probative relationship between the basic facts and the presumed fact.[32] Another minority approach, adopted by California, is to shift the burden of persuasion for those presumptions identified by the legislature or the courts as based upon "public policy." [33] Because many presumptions have some public policy underpinnings, the determination of which presumptions fit into this category is not easy.[34] Under the California approach, presumptions outside this public-policy category shift only the burden of producing evidence.[35]

In the majority of jurisdictions, which limit the role of presumptions to that of shifting the burden of producing evidence,[36] there nonetheless are variations in approach. These variations largely are found in the measure of rebuttal evidence that is considered sufficient to negate the presumed fact. Most courts in the majority column have been influenced by the apparent view of James Bradley Thayer, an evidence authority whose influential treatise on evidence was published near the end of the

---

32. Kan.Stat.Ann. § 60–414.

33. West's Ann.Cal.Evid.Code § 605.

34. For discussion of the difficulties inherent in the California approach, see Note, 53 Cal.L.Rev. 1439, 1445–50 (1965).

35. West's Ann.Cal.Evid.Code § 603.

36. Even in these jurisdictions, one or two presumptions, notably the presumption governing the legitimacy of children born during wedlock and (less frequently) that which favors accidental death, may be deemed to change the burden of persuasion. See McCormick, § 344, at 810; § 345, at 822.

19th Century.[37]   His view, later endorsed by Wigmore, was that a presumption disappears after rebuttal evidence is produced that is sufficiently probative to *make it reasonable for the jury to find the nonexistence of the presumed fact.*[38]   Whether the jury believes the rebuttal evidence is immaterial.[39]   Once sufficient rebuttal evidence is presented, the jury determines the existence or nonexistence of the presumed fact as if no presumption ever were in the case, thus eliminating any need to give one or more instructions on the subject of presumptions.

Critics complain, however, that the majority (Thayer) view gives insufficient effect to presumptions.[40]   They point out that the policy reasons that underlie many presumptions are the same, or at least similar to, the policy justifications that dictate the initial allocation of the burden of persuasion.   Furthermore, they argue that because most presumptions exhibit a strong probative link between the basic facts and the presumed fact, judicial policy should give full recognition to this probative force by placing upon the opponent of the presumption the burden of disproving the presumed fact.   These policy considerations and their concomitant objectives, they conclude, are frustrated by the Thayer (majority) view, which enables the opponent to negate a presumption with only a minimal effort in rebuttal.[41]

---

37.   Thayer, Preliminary Treatise on Evidence (1898). See especially pp. 314, 336–37. There is some doubt as to precisely what Thayer's view was concerning the extent to which a presumption should persist in the face of rebuttal evidence. See McCormick, § 345, at 821 n. 36.

38.   IX Wigmore, § 2491(2), at 289 ; Morgan at 28–29.   The Thayer view has been adopted by the American Law Institute in its Model Code of Evidence, Rule 704 (1942).

39.   Morgan at 28 ; Louisell, Construing Rule 301, supra note 17, at 301.

40.   These critics have given the Thayer approach such unappealing names as the "bursting bubble theory" and have analogized it to Maeterlinck's male bee, which "having functioned" disappears. McCormick, § 345, at 821 n. 35.

41.   McCormick, § 345, at 822. Professor Morgan has been the leading critic of the Thayer approach. E. g., E. Morgan, Some Problems of Proof 81 (1956) ; Morgan and Maguire, Looking Backward and Forward at Evidence, 50 Harv.L.Rev. 909, 913 (1937) ; Morgan, Presumptions, 12 Wash.L.Rev. 255 (1937).

Critics of the majority view are correct in their assertion that it is comparatively easy to rebut a Thayer presumption. The opponent need only present enough rebuttal evidence to permit a reasonable trier to find the nonexistence of the presumed fact. On the other hand, the Thayer view is easy to understand and administer. Additionally, because almost all presumptions are supported by a logical relationship between the basic and presumed fact,[42] the destruction of the presumption does not negate the probative force yielded by the basic facts. That is, the disappearance of a presumption only removes its compulsory effect; after a presumption vanishes, there still remains the inference that arises from the basic facts. In most jurisdictions, the judge may instruct the jury concerning the existence of this residual inference;[43] it seems especially desirable to give such an instruction in cases where either the probative relationship between the basic and presumed fact is very strong or the rebuttal evidence barely is sufficient to eliminate the presumption. Such a practice makes the Thayer view more acceptable, and may represent the best compromise in an area marked by severe disagreement and by the practical difficulties of trial administration.

A small number of jurisdictions, while adhering to the majority view that a presumption does not alter the burden of persuasion, have modified the Thayer view that a presumption vanishes in the face of only enough rebuttal evidence to make it reasonable to find the nonexistence of the presumed fact. These jurisdictions have hybrid rules that take a middle ground between the majority (Thayer) and minority (Morgan) positions.

---

42. Even some presumptions commonly thought to originate only in procedural convenience or fairness (e. g., goods damaged during transit: damage caused by last carrier in the series) may be regarded as based upon logical inferences. See In re Woods Estate, 374 Mich. 278, 288–89 n. 3, 132 N.W.2d 35, 42 (1965). See supra note 15 and accompanying text.

43. See Louisell, Construing Rule 301, supra note 17, at 303–04 n.82, quoting McCormick, § 345, at 821; H.Rep.No.1597, 93d Cong., 2d Sess. 5–6 (1974) (Conference Report on H.R. 5463) reprinted in 1974 U.S. Code Cong. & Admin. News 7099. But see McCormick, § 345, at 825–26.

A few jurisdictions allow a presumption to disappear only when the rebuttal evidence is substantial. In other of these "hybrid" jurisdictions, the presumption persists unless the rebuttal evidence makes the nonexistence of the presumed fact at least as probable as its existence.[44] Although these compromise positions appear to avoid some of the asserted shortcomings of both the majority and minority approaches, they often cause confusion and practical difficulties, especially in jury trials. For example, what constitutes substantial or equal evidence defies definition and, often, recognition as well. Further, it is not always clear whether the judge or jury makes the determination of the sufficiency of the rebuttal evidence. When the determination is left to the jury and the rebuttal evidence reasonably could be considered substantial, but is not indisputably so, the jury may be instructed concerning the existence of a presumption, but told that the presumption is to be disregarded if in their view the rebuttal evidence is substantial. Such an instruction invariably is difficult to follow. Finally, if the rebuttal evidence is of sufficient strength to create a jury question, yet falls below the persuasive effect necessary to cause the judge (or perhaps the jury) to find that the presumption has disappeared, it is the practice of some courts to give the case to the jury under an instruction that permits them to consider the presumption along with other evidence.[45] This confusing procedure appears to transform a presumption, which is a rule about how evidence is evaluated, into a part of the evidence itself.[46]

§ 19. Presumptions: Instructing the Jury

Under both the predominant Thayer view of presumptions and the minority Morgan view, it is not necessary to use the term

---

44. Various intermediate formulations are set out in Morgan at 28–30. For a case reviewing these formulations, their rationale, and the decisions implementing them, see Hinds v. John Hancock Mutual Life Ins. Co., 155 Me. 349, 155 A.2d 721 (1959).

45. Hinds v. John Hancock Mutual Life Ins. Co., 155 Me. 349, 355, 155 A.2d 721, 726 (1959).

46. For a criticism of this metamorphosis, see S.Rep.No.93–1277, 93d Cong., 2d Sess. (1974) reprinted in 1974 U.S. Code Cong. & Admin. News 7051, 7056.

"presumption" in instructing the jury. Avoidance of this term is desirable because the jury may misunderstand its function and effect. Under the Thayer view, if there is no rebuttal evidence and the existence of the basic fact is undisputed, the judge either directs a verdict (if the presumed fact is dispositive) or instructs the jury that they shall consider the presumed fact as proven. In the latter instance, use of the term presumption is unnecessary.[47] The judge simply describes the presumed fact: "You shall find that the letter in question, written by *A* and addressed to *B*, was received." If the basic fact is contested, but there is no evidence rebutting the presumed fact,[48] it still is unnecessary to mention the term presumption: the judge simply instructs the jury that "If from the evidence you believe that the letter in question was regularly addressed and mailed, you shall find that it was received." Finally, if there is sufficient rebuttal evidence directed at the presumed fact so as to entitle a reasonable jury to find the nonexistence of that fact, the presumption disappears from the case in a Thayer jurisdiction. In recognition of any residual inference, however, the judge should direct the jury that if they conclude that the letter was properly addressed and mailed, they *may* find that it was received.[49] Despite the simplicity and seeming appeal of the foregoing, the cases reveal inconsistent practices.[50]

In jurisdictions that hold that presumptions (or at least certain designated presumptions) shift the burden of persuasion, the jury also may receive the case without mention of the term presumption. If, for example, the basic facts are admitted or indisputably established and the opponent of the presumption at-

---

47. See Morgan at 33.

48. As a practical matter, this is unlikely to occur because the opponent will probably also offer evidence rebutting the presumed fact. But it could occur (as, for example, where the addressee is not available as a witness) that there is no evidence available to rebut the presumed fact.

49. See supra note 43 and accompanying text. McCormick warns that some jurisdictions may consider this instruction an opinion on the facts. McCormick, § 345, at 826.

50. See McCormick, § 345, at 822–23; IX Wigmore, § 2491, at 290.

tacks only the presumed fact, the judge should instruct the jury [to continue the example] that "you will find that the letter in question was received, unless from the evidence you believe its nonreceipt is more probable than its receipt." This instruction gives the maximum effect to the presumption by shifting the burden of persuasion on the issue of receipt to the party against whom the presumption operates. If the opponent attacks both the basic facts and the presumed fact, the judge should instruct "that if from the evidence you believe that the letter in question was addressed properly and thereafter mailed, then you also shall find that it was received, unless you believe that its nonreceipt is more probable than its receipt."

Other variations could be described, but it is sufficient to re-emphasize that the minority approach, which shifts the burden of persuasion, shares with the majority approach, which shifts the burden of production, the advantage of avoiding complicated, confusing instructions that entwine the jury in a difficult analysis of the legal effect of presumptions.[51] Conversely, the intermediate approaches that seek to invest presumptions with a somewhat greater effect than the Thayer view, but which do not go as far as to shift the burden of persuasion, often involve the jury in complex determinations. Frequently, the judge's instructions set out the meaning of presumptions and explain their allowable impact. For example, the jury may be directed to measure the probative strength of rebuttal evidence or to consider and weigh a presumption along with other evidence.[52]

§ 20. Presumptions Under the Federal Rules of Evidence

Rules 301 and 302 of the Federal Rules of Evidence deal with presumptions. No provision is made for presumptions in criminal cases, largely because at the time of the passage of the Federal Rules these presumptions were being considered in connection with a revision of the federal criminal code. The Federal

---

51. However, courts often do not seize the opportunity to avoid a charge that contains language about presumptions. McCormick, § 345, at 824–26.

52. See supra notes 44–46 and accompanying text.

Rules neither define nor enumerate presumptions, but only state their function and probative effect.[53] In proceedings where federal substantive law governs the claim or defense, Rule 301 adopts the Thayer view, specifying that "a presumption imposes on the party against whom it is directed the burden of going forward with the evidence to rebut or meet the presumption, but does not shift to such party the burden of proof in the sense of the risk of nonpersuasion .   .   .   ." [54]

The Rules also contain an accommodation to the varying state approaches to presumptions. Rule 302 specifies that "the effect of a presumption respecting a fact which is an element of a claim or defense as to which State law supplies the rule of decision is determined in accordance with State law." [55] Students of civil procedure will recognize that this accommodation accords with the policy, if not the command, of Erie Railroad Co. v. Tompkins.[56] The Rule defers to state law only as to those presumed facts that constitute an element of a claim or defense; presumptions of lesser impact are governed by the Thayer approach of Federal Rule 301—even in diversity cases where state

---

53. Fed.R.Evid. 301 & 302 and accompanying Report, Senate Committee on the Judiciary, supra note 46.

54. Fed.R.Evid. 301. See Usery v. Turner Elkhorn Mining Co., 428 U. S. 1, 27–31 (1976); United States v. Ahrens, 530 F.2d 781 (8th Cir. 1976); Lora v. Board of Educ., 74 F.R.D. 565 (E.D.N.Y.1977). The phrase "risk of nonpersuasion" is synonymous with "burden of persuasion." As previously noted in the text, the party with the burden of persuasion bears the risk that he will lose his case if he is unable to persuade the trier. For a discussion of the measure of rebuttal evidence that will negate the presumption, see S. Saltzburg & K. Redden, Federal Rules of Evidence

Manual 81 (2d ed. 1977). Professor Louisell argues that an intermediate approach may be taken in the implementation of Rule 301, rather than a pure Thayer approach. Louisell, Construing 301, supra note 17, at 312–20.

55. Fed.R.Evid. 302 and accompanying Adv.Comm. Note. See, e. g., United States v. Wilson, 433 F. Supp. 57 (N.D. Iowa 1977).

56. 304 U.S. 64 (1938). See Dick v. New York Life Ins. Co., 359 U.S. 437 (1959). For an incisive analysis of the impact of the Federal Rules of Evidence on state law, with special attention to privileges, see C. Wright, Law of Federal Courts 458–63 (3d ed. 1976).

law is applicable.[57] Of course, the Thayer approach, embodied in Rule 301, governs with regard to facts underlying a federal claim or defense, even if these are joined with state claims or defenses. Thus, in a case involving both federal and state claims, as well as in cases involving state claims supported by a presumption and an incidental matter also supported by a presumption, the judge and jury may have to deal with several presumptions of differing force and effect. When this occurs, it may be difficult to instruct the jury in understandable terms as to the proper effect of the various presumptions.[58]

NOTES

1. *Presumptions Against the Burdened Party.* There is little point in raising a presumption if it operates on an element of a claim or defense upon which the opponent of the presumption already has the burden of persuasion. In discharging his burden, the opponent will negate the effect of a presumption under either the majority or the minority view. The only utility in raising a presumption *against* the party who already has the burden of persuasion on the matter to which the presumption applies arises where the effect is to cause the burdened party to have to disprove the presumed fact by a greater showing than simply a preponderance.

2. *Conflicting Presumptions.* It is possible for evidence in a case to establish two sets of basic facts which then give rise to conflicting presumptions. For example, when there is evidence of a legal marriage between H and W, there often is a presumption that the marital status continues. Another presumption often arises when the basic fact of a ceremonial marriage between H and W–2 is shown: Any prior marriage is presumed to have been dissolved. Suppose in a given case both of these presumptions arise. According to the Thayer approach, "there never can be conflicting presumptions; one necessarily will prevent the creation of the other or destroy it if created." Morgan at 32. Most courts, however, have not applied the Thayer view strictly. The usual approach is to give effect to the presumption supported by the stronger reason. McCormick, § 345, at 823–824; Morgan at 32. However, it often occurs that neither presumption appears to have a dominant basis in public policy; when this occurs, neither presumption is given effect. See Uniform R.Evid. 301(b); Legille v. Dann, 544 F.2d 1 (D.C. Cir. 1976).

---

57. Weinstein & Berger, ¶ 302, at 3–4.

58. For a suggested approach to the problem of conflicting federal and state presumptions, see S. Saltzburg & K. Redden, Federal Rules of Evidence Manual 95 (2d ed. 1977).

CHAPTER IV

COMPETENCY OF WITNESSES AND THE PROCESS OF TRIAL

§ 21. Introduction: Scope

This chapter examines the competency of witnesses, the format of a trial, and certain procedures applicable to eliciting testimonial evidence. Competency, once a major consideration in the law of evidence, has been reduced in importance by modern statutory reform. This subject is given only brief attention in the following materials, which are largely devoted to trial format and the procedures of interrogation. Understanding the trial format will promote a contextual understanding of the exclusionary rules that serve to screen out some relevant evidence; knowledge of the constraints imposed upon interrogating counsel by the evidentiary rules provides a further indication of the impact of the adversarial system on the process of proof.[1] Offers of proof and objections to evidence, although fundamental aspects of evidentiary procedure, are reserved for a later chapter,[2] at which point we will have encountered most of the exclusionary rules which demonstrate the practical impact of these procedures.[3]

---

1. The basic principles underlying the adversarial system are discussed in Ch. I.

2. See Ch. XI. The study of expert opinion also is postponed (Ch. XII); the materials contained in Ch. VI and VII will lay the groundwork for understanding the hearsay problems that arise in connection with expert testimony. Finally, the admission of tangible evidence, including writings, is covered late in the text (Ch. XIII). Documents often raise many of the evidentiary problems (such as those associated with hearsay and privilege) that are encountered in earlier chapters.

3. Perhaps the order in which one studies the law of evidence is a matter of indifference. It appears, however, that evidence teachers struggle more than their brethren with the problems of how to present seemingly unruly and overlapping materials. See Preface to Sullivan & Hardin, Evidence, Cases and Materials (1968). Two major themes have influenced the order of presentation in this text: the materials that generally are applicable to problems of proof such as relevance, burdens of proof, and trial process are collected in the early chapters of the

§ 22. Competency: In General

The word "competent" is often used to describe evidence that is admissible to prove a consequential proposition. So used, the term signifies that the evidence is not only relevant, but also is outside the reach of the various exclusionary rules. As applied to a witness, "competent" denotes that a person called to testify has the necessary testimonial qualifications. This latter application of the term is the concern of this chapter.

At early common law, rigid and, often, illogical rules of incompetency precluded many potentially helpful witnesses from testifying. The rules of preclusion were based largely upon apprehensions about inaccurate or perjured testimony. A major basis of disqualification was interest in the outcome of the litigation, and this ground served to disqualify even the parties to an action from taking the witness stand. Other disabilities resulting in incompetence were the witness's infancy, insanity, disbelief in a supreme being, conviction of a crime, and marriage to a party.

Over the course of the last century, statutory reform has largely abolished these objections to competency.[4] In some instances the statutes provide that the disability which formerly resulted in incompetency may still support the claim of a privilege not to testify. This transformation from incompetency to privilege occurred, for example, with regard to the disability arising from marriage to a party. In most jurisdictions a marital partner has a privilege which can be claimed so as to prevent one spouse from testifying against an accused spouse in a criminal proceeding.[5]

Not all grounds of incompetency, however, have been transformed or removed by statute. Vestiges of the common-law

book; materials that are either comparatively difficult or that require a substantial understanding of related parts of the law of evidence are deferred, insofar as possible, to the middle and latter portions of the text.

4. Morgan at 86–88.

5. E. g., 22 Okl.Stat.Ann. § 702; Va. Code § 8–288. In some jurisdictions the privilege is given to the accused, in others to the testifying spouse, and in still others to both spouses. See Ch. IX, § 89 for a discussion of the privilege.

proscriptions may still be found.[6] Furthermore, all jurisdictions have rules designed to ensure the neutrality of the judicial tribunal. Typically, such rules govern (and usually forbid) testimony by judges and jurors in cases in which they are officially participating.[7] With regard to witnesses generally, however, the modern approach is to disqualify a witness only when he is shown to be incapable of perceiving, remembering, or describing the event in question, or when he is deemed unable to appreciate his duty to testify truthfully.[8] The application by the trial judge of these general criteria can result in a ruling of incompetency in instances where the proffered witness is extremely youthful[9] or suffers from a certain kind (or degree) of mental illness.[10] Even where statutory reform prevents disqualification of a witness on grounds of incompetency, the disability formerly asserted as the basis of the claim of incompetence often bears upon credibility, and for this latter purpose evidence of the disability is admissible.[11] Thus, evidence that the witness has been convicted of a felony or has a financial interest in the outcome

---

6. E. g., Code of Ala. tit. 7, § 434 (conviction of perjury disqualifies). But in Washington v. Texas, 388 U.S. 14 (1967), the Supreme Court declared unconstitutional a state statute which prohibited co-participants in the same crime from testifying for each other.

7. E. g., Fed.R.Evid. 605, 606; West's Ann.Cal.Evid.Code §§ 703, 704.

8. See, e. g., West's Ann.Cal.Evid. Code §§ 700–702; Fed.R.Evid. 601–04 (generally limiting incompetency to lack of personal knowledge and failure to declare that he will testify truthfully). See infra note 26.

9. State v. Noble, 90 N.M. 360, 563 P.2d 1153 (1977); Hollaris v. Jankowski, 315 Ill.App. 154, 42 N.E.2d 859 (1942).

10. Truttmann v. Truttmann, 328 Ill. 338, 159 N.E. 775 (1927) (test for incompetency because of mental infirmity held to be whether derangement or feeblemindedness is such as to make the proffered witness untrustworthy). Few witnesses, however, are disqualified because of a lack of mental capacity. See Weihofen, Testimonial Competence and Credibility, 34 Geo. Wash.L.Rev. 53 (1965); Adv.Comm. Note to Fed.R.Evid. 601. See generally United States v. Van Meerbeke, 548 F.2d 415 (2d Cir. 1976) (witness allowed to continue testifying even though under the influence of opium).

11. See, e. g., Conn.Gen.Stat.Ann. § 52–145; N.Mex.Comp.Laws § 20–1–8.

of the suit may be admitted to discredit or impeach his testimony.[12]

The trial judge rules upon an issue regarding the competency of a proffered witness. In making his decision, he may find it necessary to hear and enter formally into the record evidence bearing upon competency. If such a hearing is required, the judge must decide whether a risk of prejudice, embarrassment, or some other consideration, dictates that he receive this evidence out of the jury's presence.[13]

§ 23. Competency: The Dead Man's Statutes

In some jurisdictions, there is one aspect of contemporary litigation where the legacy of the common-law rules governing incompetency still has a disquietingly sharp effect. The common law rejected the testimony of parties and other persons who had a direct pecuniary or proprietary interest in the outcome of the trial. This rule of exclusion assumed that testimony given by an interested party would be biased and, very likely, perjured. Whatever the incidence of these supposed abuses, the cost of the prohibition became increasingly apparent. The rules of incompetency frequently barred from the witness stand the persons who had the most knowledge about the event in question. Thus, statutory reform was inevitable. Reform is seldom achieved, however, without compromise. Those with allegiance to the common-law rule barring parties and other interested persons from testifying urged its retention in a civil suit between two parties, one of whom is deceased (or otherwise incapacitated). Their argument was appealing: if the surviving party is allowed to testify, an adversarial imbalance will result because the deceased party, whose interests are represented by a fiduciary, will usually suffer a disadvantage in rebutting the survivor's testimony. Since death or some other disability (such as severe mental

---

12. See Ch. VIII, §§ 81–82. See also Adv.Comm.Note to Fed.R.Evid. 601.

13. See, e. g., People v. Coca, —— Colo.App. ——, 564 P.2d 431 (1977). See Fed.R.Evid. 104(c). "Voir dire" is the name sometimes given to such a hearing held outside the jury's presence, although the term more frequently applies to the examination of prospective jurors.

incapacity) precludes the testimony of one of the individuals most apt to have knowledge of the event in question, special rules of competence should apply to equalize the adversaries' opportunities to produce evidence.

This argument was sufficiently persuasive to produce a host of statutes designed to equalize the adversarial posture of litigants in cases where one party, deceased or otherwise incapacitated, has his interests represented by a fiduciary. In their most extreme form, these "dead man's statutes" simply prohibit the surviving party from testifying—a solution which one commentator described as "blind and brainless." [14] The injustice that results from this rule is apparent in cases where the survivor has a valid claim stemming from an oral agreement with the deceased or from a personal injury caused by the decedent. The living party is unable to substantiate his claim by his own testimony, which may be the best and, perhaps, only available evidence to support his recovery.

In recent years, there has been general recognition of the injustices produced by the dead man's statutes, and amendments negating or ameliorating their effect have gained widespread support. However, there is still no uniform approach. Differences among the statutes as originally passed have been compounded by variations resulting from the amending process. The only feature common to the present statutes is that each still is designed to equalize the opportunities of proof in litigation between a decedent and survivor where the subject matter of the suit is a transaction or event that occurred when both were living.[15] Even today, some of the statutes bar the survivor from testifying to any conversation with the deceased,[16] while others also prohibit the survivor's testimony about any transac-

---

14. See McCormick, § 65, at 143, attributing this description to Jeremy Bentham.

15. Good introductory materials are collected in Maguire et al. at 236–48. See also the comprehensive discussion in Jones on Evidence §§ 20:20–20:46 (6th ed. Gard 1972).

16. E. g., Minn.Stat.Ann. § 595.04. But an exception or waiver may operate in certain circumstances as, for example, where the interested survivor is called to the stand by the adversary. McCormick, § 65, at 143.

tion with or act done by the deceased.[17] A liberalizing statutory provision which has gained favor in recent years permits the survivor to testify, but balances this supposed advantage with the counterpoise that relevant hearsay statements of the decedent shall be admissible.[18] Some states which have abandoned the absolute prohibition nonetheless require that the survivor's testimony will not sustain a judgment in his favor unless his interested testimony is corroborated by other evidence.[19] Other approaches include raising the standard of proof that the survivor must meet [20] or vesting the trial judge with a discretionary power to admit the survivor's testimony where exclusion would cause hardship or injustice.[21]

Significantly, an increasing number of states do not prohibit a survivor from testifying,[22] although it is common for these jurisdictions to admit the deceased's hearsay statements or otherwise try to equalize opportunities of proof; this approach probably points the way of the future. The Federal Rules of Evidence accommodate the policy of those states which have dead man's statutes by providing that in "civil actions and proceedings, with respect to an element of a claim or defense as to which State law supplies the rule of decision, the competency of a witness shall be determined in accordance with State law." [23] This def-

---

17. E. g., Ky.Rev.Stat.Ann. § 421.-210(2).

18. E. g., Conn.Gen.Stat.Ann. § 52–172; Va. Code Ann. § 8.01–397. Illustrative statutes are collected in Maguire et al. at 246.

19. E. g., Va. Code Ann. § 8.01–397. Cases are collected in Annot., 21 A.L.R.2d 1009 (1952). This approach raises difficulties when the survivor is not a claimant, but rather a defendant. Maguire et al. at 246. The usual approach is to strike the defendant's uncorroborated testimony and to instruct the jury to disregard it. Annot., 21 A. L.R.2d 1009, 1030–43 (1952).

20. E. g., N.J.Stat.Ann. 2A:81–2.

21. See Ariz.Rev.Stat. § 12–2251; Mont.Rev.Code Ann. § 93–701–3 (Cum.Supp.1977). Recent state cases also have confined the reach of dead man's statutes. See e. g., Deaton, Gassaway, & Davidson, Inc. v. Thomas, 564 P.2d 236 (Okl.1977).

22. See Cal.Evid.Code § 700 et seq., 1261. N.J.Stat.Ann. § 2A:81–2; N. Mex.Comp.Laws § 20–2–5; R.I.Gen. Laws § 9–17–12.

23. Fed.R.Evid. 601. Presumably, where state law provides the claim or defense, the federal court will

erence to state rules of competence has the general effect of incorporating into the Federal Rules of Evidence a state dead man's statute in cases founded upon diversity of citizenship, although the language of the federal rule encompasses any other state rules that restrict competency.[24]   However, in federal criminal proceedings and in federal civil proceedings not dependent upon a state claim or defense "[e]very person is competent to be a witness except as otherwise provided" [25] by the Federal Rules of Evidence.   Aside from the general command of Rule 602 that a witness should have personal knowledge about the matter to which he testifies, the only specific rules that would disqualify a witness are 603 (requiring oath or affirmation), 605 (barring the presiding judge), and 606 (barring jurors).   However, the trial judge still has authority to exclude the testimony of a witness if reasonable men could not believe that he observed, remembers, and is able to relate the event in question.[26]

§ 24. The Components of Trial: Opening Statement

At the commencement of trial, the plaintiff's counsel or, in a criminal case, the prosecutor, customarily makes an opening statement. These opening remarks are simply to acquaint the trier with the case and to set out, usually in a general way,[27]

---

apply a state dead man's statute even if it provides that the survivor can testify, but contains protections or offsetting provisions such as corroboration or admissibility of the decedent's hearsay statements. It should not matter that the state may not characterize its statute as one of "competence." S. Saltzburg & K. Redden, Federal Rules of Evidence Manual 268 (2d ed. 1977).

24. Weinstein & Berger, ¶ 601[02] contains a survey of possible grounds of incompetency under state law. As noted in the text, however, most jurisdictions now have abolished the various grounds of incompetency that existed at

common law. See supra notes 7–11 and accompanying text. Congress recognized that the provision incorporating state rules of competency would apply primarily to dead man's statutes.   H.Rep.No.93–650, 93d Cong., 2d Sess. 9, (1973), reprinted in 1974 U.S. Code Cong. & Admin. News 7075, 7083.

25. Fed.R.Evid. 601.

26. Weinstein & Berger, ¶ 601[01], at 10. This exclusion could be based upon lack of relevancy.

27. There is a tactical risk in detailing exactly what the forthcoming evidence will show. If some of the witnesses testify otherwise than what counsel expects to prove. Although counsel tries to outline his case in an appealing, persuasive way, an opening statement (in contrast to a closing statement) is not, strictly speaking, an argument. Rather, it is an introduction to the case and to the contentions that counsel expects to support with the forthcoming evidence.

In most cases, the plaintiff's or prosecutor's opening statement is followed immediately by the defendant's opening statement. However, in some jurisdictions the defendant may reserve his opening statement until later in the case. When this postponement occurs, the defense counsel delivers his opening statement after the plaintiff has completed his principal evidential presentation and just before the defendant presents his main evidence.[28]

§ 25. The Components of Trial: Format and Order of Proof

The party initiating a legal action—whether it is criminal or civil—presents his real and testimonial evidence first. Since, in order to secure a conviction or recovery, he must establish the existence of the factual elements which the substantive criminal or civil law prescribes, he has the burden of persuasion, meaning that he must ultimately persuade the trier.[29] This burdened party also has, initially at least, a second burden: that of producing evidence.[30] He must produce sufficient evidence supporting his claims to avoid a directed verdict. This initial presentation of evidence is usually called the plaintiff's (or government's) case in chief. The plaintiff calls in turn each of his wit-

---

expected, the opposing counsel can point to this discrepancy in his closing argument. The availability of modern discovery, however, has enabled counsel to make more detailed statements about the forthcoming evidence.

28. See infra § 25 for a description of the order of proof.

29. If after deliberation by a jury in a civil trial their minds are at a state of equipoise, the party with the burden of persuasion will lose because he has failed to carry his burden. See Ch. III, § 15. In a criminal trial, of course, the prosecutor has the burden of convincing the jury beyond a reasonable doubt.

30. The burden of producing evidence sometimes shifts to the opposing party. Under the orthodox rule, the burden of persuasion remains with the party to which the law initially assigned it. See Ch. III, § 15.

nesses to the stand, and the witness takes the oath or, in lieu thereof, makes an affirmation.[31]   Then, the plaintiff's counsel conducts the direct examination.   This interrogation consists of a series of question and answer exchanges: counsel simply presents questions to the witness that elicit from him an account of pertinent facts and occurrences.

How closely does counsel control and direct the testimony of his witness?   At one end of the scale is the possibility of minimal guidance: occasional questions which direct the witness's attention to pertinent incidents, but which allow considerable freedom of narration.   At the other extreme is the possibility of asking a number of narrow, highly directive, questions which call upon the witness to respond in a sentence or two.[32]   To some extent, whether counsel uses the technique of free narrative or that of specific question and answer depends upon his individual choice.   He will be influenced by the capabilities of his witness and the nature of the testimony expected.   If the witness is articulate and can be expected to make an orderly, favorable presentation, counsel might decide to exercise only minimal direction.   The trial judge, however, has considerable discretionary authority over the form in which testimony is elicited.[33]   Most judges and even more opposing attorneys prefer the question and answer technique.   Frequently it is more efficient.   It also facilitates anticipation by opposing counsel, making it easier to interpose an objection between the examining counsel's question and the expected, inadmissible answer. Consequently, the court often responds favorably to a request by opposing counsel that testimony be elicited by specific questions.

After the direct examiner completes the first phase of questioning, the opposing counsel may, as a matter of right,[34] conduct his cross-examination.   Of course, a lawyer is always entitled to waive cross-examination and, for reasons of trial strate-

---

31. An affirmation simply is a solemn declaration that the declarant will tell the truth. See Adv.Comm. Note to Fed.R.Evid. 603.

32. McCormick, § 5, at 7.

33. McCormick, § 5, at 8 nn. 4–6.

34. Alford v. United States, 282 U.S. 687, 691 (1931). See Aluminum Industries Inc. v. Egan, 61 Ohio App. 111, 116–17, 22 N.E.2d 459, 462–63 (1938); McCormick, § 19, at 43–46.

gy, it is usually sound practice to do so unless the direct testimony of the witness has been harmful. Further interrogation always presents the risk that the witness's answers may damage the cross-examiner's case. This risk should be avoided when the direct testimony has been innocuous, unless counsel finds it necessary to the proof of his claim or defense to elicit additional testimony from the witness. Even in these circumstances it may be necessary for the cross-examiner to call the witness later in the case, for in most jurisdictions the scope of inquiry on cross-examination can not exceed that of direct.[35]

Theoretically, a cross-examiner has the same leeway to elicit free narration as has the direct examiner. In practice, however, the cross-examiner usually tries to control closely the witness by asking precise, narrowly-drawn questions which call for specific answers, often a "yes" or "no." This high degree of direction responds to the hostility normally existing between a witness and his cross-examiner. If counsel were to ask broad, general questions, calling for a lengthy narrative response, the witness could use the opportunity to repeat and emphasize his direct testimony or to give additional testimony which could be unfavorable. Of course, if the witness is not hostile, the examiner may relax the usual tightly structured exchange.

Following cross-examination, the counsel who called the witness may conduct redirect examination. Although the scope of redirect examination is subject to the discretionary control of the trial judge, he must permit the examiner to ask questions regarding aspects of the witness's testimony that were first revealed during cross-examination.[36] Finally, there may be a fourth phase of interrogation: recross-examination. This last part of the examination process is likely to be at or near the point of diminishing returns. Accordingly, the trial judge may

---

35. See infra § 30.

36. See McCormick, § 32, at 64. New matters may arise on cross that are within the scope of inquiry of the direct examination. In cases where the cross-examiner raises new matters that exceed the proper scope of inquiry, his examination is subject to several procedural consequences. These consequences are discussed infra § 30. Note also that some jurisdictions do not limit the inquiry of cross-examination to that of direct.

exercise his discretion to disallow recross questions, although he should permit recross as to new points developed during redirect questioning.[37]

Just as interrogation of a witness may have four distinct phases (direct, cross, redirect and recross), so too may the trial of a case consist of four-part sequence. After the plaintiff's (or prosecutor's) case in chief, in which he presents the witnesses and real evidence necessary to permit his recovery, the defense presents its case. (Here, of course, the defense counsel calls witnesses for direct examination and plaintiff's counsel becomes the cross-examiner.) The next phase of trial is the plaintiff's case in rebuttal, following which comes the final phase: the defendant's case in rejoinder.

Observe, however, that all of the evidence might be presented during the first two trial stages, or even during plaintiff's case in chief. The defendant may elect to present no case in defense, choosing instead to rely upon his cross-examination to negate the trier's belief in the plaintiff's evidence. Furthermore, at the conclusion of plaintiff's case in chief the defendant may move for a directed verdict (or in a criminal case, an acquittal), arguing that he is entitled to a judgment as a matter of law because the plaintiff (or prosecutor) has failed to present sufficient evidence. To revert to an earlier discussion, the defendant is arguing that the plaintiff has not discharged his burden of production because he has failed to provide evidence sufficient to enable a reasonable trier to find the existence of an essential element of the plaintiff's case.[38]

§ 26. Examining the Witness: Leading, Misleading and Argumentative Questions

Much of the law of evidence, as we shall see, rests upon assumptions about human conduct. Subsequent chapters contain

---

37. For a further discussion of this rule, see State v. McSloy, 127 Mont. 265, 271–73, 261 P.2d 663, 665–67 (1953); McCormick, § 32, at 65 n. 57.

38. See Ch. III, § 15. In rare instances, court rules or decisions permit or require that one party interrupt the other's case to present evidence "out of order." See, e. g., State v. Lovett, 345 So. 2d 1139 (La.1977).

illustrations of evidentiary rules grounded upon suppositions about how a jury will evaluate certain types of evidence, and about the conditions under which a person is likely to speak truthfully.

The familiar rule that generally forbids the use of leading questions during direct examination rests upon two assumptions. The first, a factual assumption, is that a cooperative relationship exists between the direct examiner and his witness. Presumably, the witness will give testimony favorable to the examiner's client; further, it is likely that examining counsel and witness have met prior to trial and discussed or even rehearsed the latter's testimony. The second assumption, a psychological one, is that if the direct examiner phrases his questions in language that impliedly suggests the desired answer, the witness will conform to the suggestion and tailor his answer accordingly. The second assumption is grounded on the first: the friendly witness will respond to suggestive questions.[39]

Accordingly, as a general rule, the direct examiner is prohibited from asking leading questions—that is, he is usually forbidden to ask questions that suggest the desired answer. The judgment whether a question is leading is a contextual one, which takes account of such factors as phrasing and voice intonation. In a suit for breach of contract for the sale of goods the following would constitute a leading question: after establishing that the defendant had spoken with the plaintiff, counsel for the plaintiff asks the witness:

> "During this conversation, didn't the defendant declare that he would not deliver the merchandise?"

On the other hand, counsel could rephrase his question:

> "Will you state what, if anything, the defendant said, during this conversation, relating to the delivery of the merchandise?"

---

39. For an account of behavioral research that indicates that the wording of a question has a profound effect upon the respondent's answer, see Loftus & Zanni, Eyewitness Testimony: The Influence of the Wording of a Question, 5 Bull. of Psychonomic Society 86 (1975).

and thereby avoid the suggestive characteristic which makes the first question improper.

The leading questions doctrine embodies the view that the trier should hear the witness's testimony, not that implanted by partisan counsel. The objective of minimizing partisan influence is promoted by prohibiting leading questions during direct examination.[40] Three points, however, should be noted. First, practical considerations sometimes militate against entering an objection to a leading question. The damage incurred from the leading question may not justify the interruption or jury impatience occasioned by an objection.[41] Second, the trial judge is rarely reversed solely on the ground that he ruled erroneously on objections to leading questions. Third, there are situations outside the reach of the general prohibition, and in these leading questions are deemed proper.[42] Leading questions are permitted, for example, in eliciting preliminary information that is not in contention. Counsel can use leading questions to establish his witness's identity, address, and other incidental testimony. Leading questions are also proper, at least for a brief period, if the witness is forgetful. Counsel may attempt to stimulate recollection[43] by directing the witness's attention to the specific event in question. There is some risk that if the leading questions do not revive memory, the witness may nonetheless give an answer based upon the suggestion implied by the examiner's question. Whatever the theoretical extent of this risk, it is minimized by the practical controls, first, of the opponent's right to object that

---

40. This theory that leading questions may cause bias is supported by behavioral research. Note 38 supra; McCormick, § 6, at 8 n. 7. But see Cleary, Evidence as a Problem in Communicating, 5 Vand.L.Rev. 277, 287 (1952).

41. Experienced counsel generally objects sparingly, reserving his objection for situations in which he wishes to exclude evidence capable of significantly harming his case. A constant objector does not draw favor from the jury. Unless leading questions constitute a pattern or pertain to a significant point, it usually is advisable not to object.

42. Morgan at 51–52.

43. See infra §§ 27–28 for a discussion of what additional techniques are available when a witness has a failure of memory.

recollection has not been refreshed and, second, of further testing, during the cross-examination, of the witness's memory. Finally, leading questions are usually permitted in the interrogation of a very young witness. Again, some risk is encountered, especially since a youthful witness is presumably quite susceptible to suggestion. As a practical matter, however, leading questions may present the only effective method of eliciting this testimony. In all of these permissive instances, the trial judge has ample power to prevent abuse and on objection, or occasionally on his own initiative, he can restrict or terminate a leading inquiry.

The prohibition against leading questions is generally inapplicable during cross-examination. Here the assumption is that the cross-examiner and the witness are antagonistic, and that there has been no preparatory conference between them. It is further assumed that an uncooperative witness is not amenable to implied suggestion. In short, leading questions are proper during cross-examination because the risks assumed to be present in direct examination are thought to be absent in the supposedly hostile atmosphere of cross-examination.[44] Note that the use of leading questions aids the cross-examiner in controlling an adverse witness. His inquiries can be narrow and specific, designed to limit the range of response, and consciously framed to induce the witness to give the desired answer. Thus, the cross-examiner can question a hostile witness on the examiner's terms, thereby lessening the damaging effect that might otherwise accrue.

It should be apparent that the factual assumptions of cooperativeness (during direct examination) and hostility (during cross) which underlie the rule governing leading questions may be inapposite with regard to many witnesses. Some witnesses have no allegiance to either of the parties. Furthermore, tactics may force the direct examiner to call a hostile witness, or the cross-examiner may have the opportunity to interrogate a witness who is friendly. If, for a particular witness, the usual assumption is erroneous, the opposing counsel may request a

---

44. For further discussion of the reasons for the different treatment of direct and cross-examination, see Lempert & Saltzburg at 13–15.

change in the mode of examination. The trial judge has the power to permit or deny leading questions, depending upon the actual relationship between examiner and witness. Federal Rule of Evidence 611, which codifies the common-law practice, contains the following pertinent provisions:

> (a) Control by Court—The court shall exercise reasonable control over the mode and order of interrogating witnesses and presenting evidence so as to (1) make the interrogation and presentation effective for the ascertainment of the truth, (2) avoid needless consumption of time, and (3) protect the witnesses from harassment or undue embarrassment.

> . . . . .

> (c) Leading Questions—Leading questions should not be used on the direct examination of a witness except as may be necessary to develop his testimony. Ordinarily leading questions should be permitted on cross-examination. When a party calls a hostile witness, an adverse party, or a witness identified with an adverse party, interrogation may be by leading questions.[45]

Note that the rule makes special reference to calling an adverse party. In this situation, a hostile exchange can be predicted. Consequently, the general rule is that the sponsoring counsel can, from the outset, treat the adverse party as a hostile witness. In many states this rule is contained in a statute or rule of court which declares that a party opponent may be questioned under the rules that normally apply to cross-examination. For example, the Virginia Code provides:

> A party called to testify for another, having an adverse interest, may be examined by such other party according to the rules applicable to cross examination.[46]

---

45. See United States v. Schoupe, 548 F.2d 636 (6th Cir. 1977) for an illustration of excessive use of leading questions by a prosecutor interrogating an uncooperative witness whom he had called to the stand.

46. Va. Code Ann. § 8.01–401.A. (Repl.Vol.1977).

Although the general thrust of this and similar provisions is to allow leading questions, some jurisdictions, either by judicial interpretation or by the passage of a companion statute (or rule) also permit the party calling his adversary to the stand to impeach the latter,[47] that is, to present evidence which raises doubts about the witness's credibility.[48]

Closely allied with leading questions are so-called argumentative questions which are improper during either direct or cross-examination. As the term suggests, an argumentative question is one which is designed to induce the witness to affirm counsel's interpretation of the evidence.[49] The question "From your testimony that X pointed to the building that was on fire, we can assume, can't we, that the fire was visible?" would be argumentative[50] and on objection, should be struck or rephrased. Although argumentative questions are always improper, (since the jury, not counsel and the witness, is supposed to draw the inferences), judges sometimes permit cross-examiners to ask questions which, in the strict sense, fall into this category.

Misleading questions[51] are also inappropriate during either direct or cross-examination. The vice of these questions is that they assume as true a fact that either is not in evidence, or is in dispute. For example, the question "At any time during this assault, did anyone attempt to leave?" assumes the existence of

---

47. Va. Code Ann. § 8.01–403 (Repl. Vol.1977); McCormick, § 38, at 77. The Federal Rules of Evidence go further and permit the impeachment of *any* witness, by either party. Fed.R.Evid. 607. For a discussion of the relationship between impeachment and leading questions, see S. Saltzburg & K. Redden, Federal Rules of Evidence Manual 364 (2d ed. 1977).

48. See Ch. VIII, § 80. As noted elsewhere, the common law generally forbids a party from impeaching witnesses he calls to the stand. Id.

49. McCormick, § 7, at 11.

50. See Di Bona v. Philadelphia Transp. Co., 356 Pa. 204, 207, 51 A. 2d 768, 770 (1947). Judges and lawyers sometimes use the adjectives "misleading" and "argumentative" loosely, or even interchangeably.

51. For some illustrations, see Life & Cas. Ins. Co. v. Garrett, 250 Ala. 521, 523–24, 35 So.2d 109, 111 (1948); In re Yale's Estate, 164 Kan. 670, 675, 191 P.2d 906, 909 (1948); Reardon v. Boston Elev. R. Co., 311 Mass. 228, 231, 40 N.E.2d 865, 866–67 (1942).

the assault, yet the fact of the assault may be contested. Of course, if the witness in the foregoing example had just testified that there was an assault, the question would be relatively harmless. Sometimes, however, counsel uses the misleading question in an attempt to get a second witness to affirm the testimony of an earlier witness. For example, suppose one witness testifies as to the assault, and another witness gives testimony pertaining to persons leaving the scene of the alleged affray. The question to the second witness, "Did anyone leave during the course of the assault?" is misleading because an affirmative answer might mean (1) only that someone left the scene or (2) that there was an assault and someone left. The problem is whether the witness affirmed the premise of the question or simply its specific inquiry, and it is this ambiguity which makes the question misleading.[52]

§ 27. Examining the Witness: Refreshing Recollection

Leading questions, we have noted, are permitted in circumstances in which they serve as a catalyst to recollection. This form of interrogation is not, however, the only courtroom technique that can be used to stimulate memory. Sometimes it is possible to revive the memory of a forgetful witness by showing to him an object, usually a writing, or by allowing him to listen to a recording.[53] The association of the writing or recording with the forgotten event may induce recollection.[54] Frequently, the item used to aid the witness with a faltering memory is a writing prepared at some prior time by the witness himself. (Anything, however, may be used to revive the witness's present memory.) Under the majority and preferred view, the witness

---

52. McCormick, § 7, at 11. A question is also misleading when it assumes a fact for which there is no supporting evidence. A question in point: "Did you stop using narcotics before or after these headaches about which you complain?"

53. "Anything may in fact revive a memory: a song, a scent, a photograph, and [sic] allusion, even a

past statement known to be false." United States v. Rappy, 157 F.2d 964, 967 (2d Cir.), cert. denied, 329 U.S. 806 (1947); see also Steele v. Coxe, 225 N.C. 726, 36 S.E.2d 288 (1945).

54. See Annot., 125 A.L.R. 19 (1940), supplemented by Annot., 82 A.L.R. 2d 473 (1962), discussing the subject of refreshing recollection.

can refer to this writing, even though it describes the event about which he is to testify.[55] It is important to recognize, however, that the purpose for which the writing is used is limited: it serves *only to refresh* the witness's recollection and not as an independent source of evidence. If after examining the writing the witness states that he now has a present recollection of the event, he may continue his testimony. Even though he may occasionally consult the writing, it is his *testimony*, given from his restored memory, that constitutes the evidence received.

The procedure for refreshing present recollection often calls upon the trial judge to make a difficult judgment, particularly where the object used to refresh recollection is a writing which contains an account of the occurrence in question. He must determine if the witness's recollection has actually been refreshed or whether the witness merely is reciting the contents of the writing. An affirmation by the witness that his memory is restored is a persuasive, but not controlling, factor, especially if he continues to falter. It is apparent, of course, that if the judge determines that recollection has not been revived, he can no longer assume that the witness's testimony constitutes the primary evidence. The primary evidence is the writing itself. Whether this writing is admissible is a question addressed in the next section. It now suffices to reemphasize that any object can be presented to a witness for the limited purpose of reviving his memory. If this procedure is effective, the witness's testimony, not the writing, constitutes the evidence received by the court.

The theory that denies evidentiary status to the writing (or other object) used to refresh present recollection has a practical consequence: even though the examiner has the writing marked as an exhibit for purposes of identification, he is not entitled to admit it into evidence. This means, in practical effect, that he cannot submit the writing for jury examination; the trier must rely entirely upon the testimony of the witness.

---

55. United States v. Riccardi, 174 F.2d 883 (3d Cir.), cert. denied 337 U.S. 941 (1949) is a leading case. See Neff v. Neff, 96 Conn. 273, 278–79, 114 A. 126, 127–28 (1921). But see Morgan at 55–56.

At the end of his examination, the questioner relinquishes the writing to his opponent (often the cross-examiner) who may then use the item in conducting his examination. This affords the opponent an opportunity to test the extent to which the witness actually recalls the event in question: he can attempt to expose discrepancies between the witness's testimony and the writing, or otherwise try to demonstrate that memory is not revived or is inaccurate. Most jurisdictions also allow the opponent to introduce the writing into evidence for purposes of impeachment. These jurisdictions permit the jury to examine the document and assess the witness's testimony in light of the writing, even though the writing can be utilized only for the limited purpose of determining credibility.[56]

In most cases, of course, a direct examiner has consulted his witness prior to calling him to the stand. Thus, the refreshing of the witness's memory, if any such prompting is necessary, normally takes place outside the courtroom. When this occurs, the cross-examiner may not know whether or not his opponent has used a writing to stimulate the witness's memory. Sometimes, however, through investigation, discovery, or cross-examination, the opponent learns that a document has been used to refresh recollection. The question then arises whether counsel has a right to use this item during the conduct of his cross-examination. A convincing argument can be made that refreshing a witness's recollection before trial, when the process can not be observed by the trier, should give the cross-examiner the same right of access to the underlying writing as he has when the process of refreshing memory takes place in the courtroom. Some authorities, particularly in criminal trials, so hold.[57]

---

56. This is an example of limiting the use of evidence to a particular purpose. See Ch. 1, § 5; Ch. VI, §§ 50, 52. The subject of impeachment is covered in Ch. VIII.

57. See, e. g., State v. Mucci, 25 N.J. 423, 436–40, 136 A.2d 761, 766–70 (1957); State v. Bradshaw, 101 R. I. 233, 240–41, 221 A.2d 815, 818–19 (1966). The rule requiring production still is a minority view. In civil matters, documents that have been or might be used "to refresh" often can be reached through the discovery process. See Fed.R.Civ. P. 34. But see Fed.R.Civ.P. 26(b)(3).

Rule 612 of the Federal Rules of Evidence provides in part:

> Except as otherwise provided [by the Jencks Act, 18 U.S.C.A. § 3500] . . ., if a witness uses a writing to refresh his memory for the purpose of testifying, either—
>
> (1) while testifying, or
>
> (2) before testifying, if the court in its discretion determines it is necessary in the interests of justice,
>
> an adverse party is entitled to have the writing produced . . . to inspect it, to cross examine the witness thereon, and to introduce in evidence those portions which relate to the testimony of the witness.

Under these provisions, there is no absolute right to compel production of a writing used to refresh a witness's memory prior to his courtroom appearance. The rule reflects a judgment that in view of other means, notably discovery, available to parties [58] to gain access to pertinent materials in the adversary's hands, it suffices to leave to the judge's discretion the issue of whether the opponent is entitled to a writing used to aid memory prior to trial.

Rule 612 makes specific reference to the Jencks Act [59] which entitles an accused in a federal criminal proceeding to demand delivery of a written or recorded statement of a prosecution witness.[60] This right becomes effective only after the witness

---

58. See H.Rep.No.93–650, 93d Cong., 2d Sess. reprinted in 1974 U.S. Code Cong. & Admin. News 7086. Neither the federal rule nor the accompanying Advisory Committee Report makes clear whether a claim of privilege overrides the court's power under this rule to order one side to show the other a document. Probably, the privilege will prevail. S. Saltzburg & K. Redden, Federal Rules of Evidence

Manual 380 (2d. ed. 1977). See also United States v. Schoupe, 548 F.2d 636 (6th Cir. 1977).

59. 18 U.S.C.A. § 3500.

60. 18 U.S.C.A. § 3500. The Act applies only to "written statements made by said witness and signed or otherwise adopted or approved by him; [or] a stenographic, mechanical, electrical or other recording

has testified, and entitles the defense to such of the witness's statements as "relate to the subject matter" of his testimony.[61] The right of access provided by the Jencks Act is not dependent upon whether or not the prior statements were used to refresh recollection.

§ 28. Examining the Witness: Past Recollection Recorded

This subject is explained in detail elsewhere,[62] where it is treated as an exception to the hearsay rule. A brief exposition appears here because past recollection recorded (variously called recorded recollection or recorded past recollection) is governed by a rule which bears close kinship to the rule pertaining to refreshing present recollection. Nonetheless, these two rules should be sharply distinguished.

The rule pertaining to past recollection recorded is not applicable, at least under the orthodox approach, if the witness is able to testify from revived memory. However, if resort to the procedures described in the preceding section fails to restore memory, it may be possible to introduce into evidence a writing that describes the unrecalled event. It is necessary, however, to establish carefully a foundation comprised of the several requirements of admissibility. First, the witness must testify that the writing was made or verified by him soon after the event in question and at a time when memory was fresh. That is, even though the witness has no present recollection of the event, he must recognize the writing and be able to state that he remembers making it or verifying it soon after the event. Second, the witness must state that he believes the writing is accurate. These requirements are necessary to ensure the accuracy and reliability of the writing, aspects which are particularly important since the cross-examiner, faced with a witness who can not remember the event, may find it impossible to disprove the event by cross questions. Obviously, he can not directly interrogate

---

. . . which is a substantially verbatim recital of an oral statement made by said witness and recorded contemporaneously . . . ."

61. 18 U.S.C.A. § 3500(a)–(b).

62. See Ch. VII, Part D.

the witness about the occurrence, since the witness can not now recall it.

It is important to recognize that past recollection recorded, unlike present recollection refreshed, involves the use of the writing itself as evidence. It is introduced into evidence by the sponsoring counsel—assuming he is able to fulfill the requirements of a proper foundation.

§ 29. Examining the Witness: The Opinion Rule

In deciding the historical facts, the factfinder (often a jury) frequently must rely upon circumstantial evidence. When direct proof is unavailable, the trier finds the historical facts by a process of inference: from the evidence supporting one fact, the trier infers the existence of a related fact. Since the jury has the principal responsibility of deciding the facts through the inference-drawing process, it is generally deemed inappropriate for a lay witness to incorporate in his testimony his own inferences in the form of an "opinion" or "conclusion." This prohibition applies generally to any testimonial statement or description in which the lay witness's opinion is *unnecessary*—that is, the rule forbidding opinions is applicable in circumstances where the witness could, if requested, describe his observations in "factual" terms. If the witness can adequately reveal the facts, the jury is then in a position to draw the necessary inferences.

The rule against opinion stems in part from the apprehension that testimonial opinion might unduly influence the jury and, in larger part, from the conviction that the allocation of function between witness and jury makes lay opinion unnecessary. Perhaps there is some risk that the trier's factual determinations will be unduly influenced by a witness who, refusing to confine himself to an objective statement of what he has seen or heard, goes further and gives an interpretation or opinion. The fundamental and more persuasive rationale for excluding lay opinion, however, rests upon the assumption that if the jury is in a position to draw the inferences, opinion offered by a lay witness is superfluous.[63] Many courts now accept this rationale, and re-

---

63. VII Wigmore, § 1918, at 10.

cent cases display a tendency to justify the admission of a witness's opinion on the straightforward ground that, in the circumstances, its reception appears helpful to the trier.[64] This preferred ratiocination also explains the long-standing practice of courts to admit expert opinion (which is usually helpful) while prohibiting most, but not all, lay opinion.

The traditional formulation of the rule against opinion holds that a lay witness should recite the observed "facts," but should not offer his "opinion." The difficulty of administering this rule is that there is no precise method of classifying a testimonial statement as either fact or opinion. Almost every statement contains some degree of inference. As McCormick indicates, the difference between fact and opinion is one of degree.[65] When a witness describes a tree as "gnarled and decaying" he is, in the strict sense, giving an opinion, although, as we shall see, the courts would deem this statement one of fact. The same is true when a witness states that the voice he heard was that of *X*. Brief reflection about routine social and business conversation demonstrates that it is saturated with inferences. What, then, is the judicial dividing line between fact and opinion?

The more general and conclusory a statement, the more likely it will be classified an opinion. Conversely, the closer a statement comes to describing the separate components of an observation, the more likely it will be deemed a statement of fact.[66] The statement "*X* is drunk" is a statement of opinion [67] (although, perhaps, admissible anyway); the statement "*X* had poor muscular control, and the odor of alcohol on his breath" is a statement of fact, as that term is used by the courts. Obviously, these two statements are not diametrically opposed. The difference between them is found in the degree to which the

---

64. See, e. g., Reed v. Allen, 522 S. W.2d 339 (Tenn.App.1974); Foundation Reserve Ins. Co. v. Starnes, 479 S.W.2d 330 (Tex.Civ.App.1972).

65. McCormick, § 11, at 24–25.

66. Professor McCormick presents a particularly illuminating discussion of the fact-opinion distinction. Id. at 23–24.

67. This testimonial statement might significantly assist the trier and, hence, many modern courts would allow it. See infra note 70.

separate bases of a conclusion are individually identified and described. The opinion rule poses no barrier to any testimony that is deemed factual. However, the rule bans most, but not all, lay testimony that is cast in the form of an opinion.

A guiding principal of general application in common-law jurisdictions is one founded on practicality: lay opinion is usually inadmissible if it is reasonably practical and efficient for the witness to express the separate factual components underlying it. If it is feasible to break an opinion into its rudimentary factual parts, then, presumably, the trier will be in as favorable a position as the witness to draw inferences. The opinion, thus unnecessary, is inadmissible. Conversely, when it is impractical to place the trier in a position of equal competence to draw inferences, the witness may give his opinion.[68] Suppose, for instance, the witness testifies that *"X became angry when his appointment was cancelled"* or that *"Y looked fatigued and worried* when he reported to work." These statements are, under the usual judicial classification, opinions. Nonetheless, they are admissible opinions because of the impracticality of reducing them into their component parts. It will thus be observed that all statements of fact and some statements of opinion are admissible.

Although most generalizations in this area can be challenged by some of the many disparate court rulings,[69] it is possible to further characterize that class of statements regarded as permissible lay opinion. Where the observer-witness forms an impression immediately upon perceiving an event—that is, where he would naturally gain an impression or opinion without time for reflection and deductive reasoning—he can usually convey his perception to the trier in a conclusory statement. This situation normally occurs where perception is not sequential, but rather

---

68. Many illustrations are contained in Parker v. Hoefer, 118 Vt. 1, 100 A.2d 434 (1953). For a recent case allowing lay opinion concerning vehicle speed and intoxication, see Howard v. State, 346 So.2d 918 (Miss.1977).

69. See, e. g., Daniell v. State, 37 Ala.App. 559, 563–64, 73 So.2d 370, 373 (1954), which collects a sample of the many conflicting authorities. Maguire et al. at 304–10.

the witness perceives a thing or an event at once, as a unified whole. Thus, when a witness testifies that a car "passed at high speed," or that "*Y* looked youthful," an objection based upon the opinion rule should fail. The same may be said of the statement "*X* was drunk", although one could argue that it is feasible to dissect this statement into such components as impaired speech, telltale breath, poor physical coordination, and so forth. Often, however, observers do not isolate these separate manifestations; rather they perceive drunkenness as an integrated whole. Even where separate observations can be detailed, the witness's account may not adequately convey the total impression, and thus his opinion is still helpful. Accordingly, many recent decisions have approved lay opinion that the actor in question was intoxicated.[70]

A number of cases express the principle that lay opinion on the ultimate issue is improper. It appears, however, that this should be true only in certain circumstances. A witness's opinion should be rejected if it contains conclusions or expressions of opinion that are superfluous and unhelpful (e. g., testimony that a party was negligent).[71] The same is true where his opinion contains a legal component which has not been adequately explained, and consequently might be misunderstood by the witness or jurors.[72] An example of this latter circumstance is found in testimony that "*X* had the capacity to make a valid

---

70. E. g., Rivers v. Black, 259 Ala. 528, 531, 68 So.2d 2, 4 (1953); State v. Durrant, 55 Del. 510, 515–516, 188 A.2d 526, 529 (1963) (witness detailed separate observations, then gave opinion); F. Busch, Trial Procedure Materials 319 (1961). Courts also have been lenient in receiving statements of general physical condition. See, e. g., State v. Garver, 190 Or. 291, 314–318, 225 P.2d 771, 782–783 (1950). As to lay opinion about the subject's sanity, see VII Wigmore §§ 1933–38, indicating a general receptivity. Note that such an opinion may not be formed spontaneously, again demonstrating that no statement of the ambit of the opinion rule can provide more than broad guidance.

71. Allen v. Matson Navigation Co., 255 F.2d 273, 278 (9th Cir. 1958); Commonwealth v. Brady, — Mass. —, 351 N.E.2d 199 (1976); Mc-Cormick, § 12, at 26–27. For a recent federal case allowing opinion on the ultimate issue, see United States v. Smith, 550 F.2d 277 (5th Cir. 1977).

72. See Fed.R.Evid. 701, 704 and Adv.Comm.Notes.

will." [73] Standing alone, this is objectionable opinion. Most jurisdictions explicitly define testamentary capacity in a rather technical manner as including a capacity to know the nature and extent of one's property, to identify the objects of one's bounty, and to understand the nature and effect of a will. During the evidence-taking stage of trial, neither the witness nor the jury may be aware of these legal requirements; thus a witness's opinion concerning X's capacity may be subject to ambiguity and misunderstanding. However, in situations where an opinion involving a legal criterion would be helpful to the trier, there is recent authority supporting admissibility if the legal concept is adequately explained to the witness and the jury.[74]

At an early date, a distinguished English jurist remarked that an opinion does not constitute evidence.[75] This assertion, which may have referred only to situations where the witness had no personal knowledge of the event in question, can not be given a literal meaning in the light of modern developments. A lack of any personal knowledge about the subject of one's testimony is one thing; rendering testimony in a general or conclusory mode is quite another. We have already seen that certain opinions are freely admitted for jury consideration and that the true basis of the opinion rule is the lack of necessity for the witness's opinion.[76] An opinion which is correctly permitted over objection or even one which comes in without objection may be considered as evidence by the factfinder. The only time an opinion does not constitute evidence is when a judge, on motion or objection, rules that the opinion is improper and orders it stricken from the record or instructs the jury to disregard it.

The Federal Rules of Evidence [77] provide:

> If the witness is not testifying as an expert, his testimony in the form of opinions or inferences is limited to

---

73. McCormick, § 12, at 28–29.

74. Fed.R.Evid. 704 and Adv.Comm. Note. See McCormick, § 12, at 29.

75. The statement is traced to Lord Mansfield in VII Wigmore, § 1917, at 6. For a full and illuminating history of the opinion rule, see id. § 1917.

76. McCormick, § 11, at 25.

77. Fed.R.Evid. 701. For similar provisions, see West's Cal.Evid. Code § 800; N.J.Evid. § 56(1).

those opinions or inferences which are (a) rationally based on the perception of the witness and (b) helpful to a clear understanding of his testimony or the determination of a fact in issue.

This provision should eliminate most of the useless quibbling that has been associated with enforcement of the rule against opinion. The first condition of the Federal Rule simply ensures that the witness has perceived the subject or event about which he gives opinion testimony. This is a familiar requirement, which has been uniformly recognized.[78] The second condition is a modest, but useful innovation. It shifts the focus of admissibility from practical necessity, still the principal criterion of admissibility in many common-law jurisdictions, to helpfulness. Whether an opinion is, under the formulation of the Federal Rule, "helpful to a clear understanding of . . . [the witness's] testimony" does not necessarily depend upon such factors as the spontaneity of the opinion or the ease with which its component parts may be separately stated. These factors are relevant, but not determinative. Accordingly, an opinion such as one in which *A* testifies that *B* was present and "should have heard *A*'s warning" should be helpful, even though under the traditional approach it might be excluded.[79]

§ 30. Examining the Witness: The Scope of Cross-Examination

The majority of jurisdictions in this country subscribe to what is commonly called the American Rule (or Federal Rule). It limits cross-examination to subjects or topics that were covered by the direct examiner and to matters relating to the witness's credibility.[80] These limitations are intended to achieve an

---

78. See Adv.Comm. Note to Fed.R. Evid. 701. See, e. g., United States v. Smith, 550 F.2d 277 (5th Cir. 1977); United States v. Butcher, 557 F.2d 666 (9th Cir. 1977).

79. See United States v. Smith, 550 F.2d 277 (5th Cir. 1977). Compare Commonwealth v. Moore, 323 Mass. 70, 76, 80 N.E.2d 24, 27 (1948) with State v. Taylor, 57 S.C. 483, 485–

86, 35 S.E. 729, 730 (1900). See Annot., 10 A.L.R.3d 258 (1966).

80. See, e. g., Conkling v. Conkling, 185 N.W.2d 777, 783 (Iowa 1971); Dinner v. Thorp, 54 Wash.2d 90, 95, 338 P.2d 137, 140 (1959). But the rule is variously stated as limiting the cross-examiner to the "same points" or "subjects" or "connected facts." McCormick, § 21, at 47–48.

orderly evidentiary presentation, supposedly resulting in a fuller understanding by the jury; the presentation of one party's case is not interrupted by proof of other facts which the opponent wishes to establish.

An incidental effect of the application of the American Rule is that it allows the party who makes the opening presentation of evidence (plaintiff or prosecutor) to present a more convincing case in chief since, by controlling the scope of his direct examination, he thereby limits the range of adverse testimony that can be elicited during cross-examination. Consequently, the opening party can sometimes postpone evidence of some of the unfavorable aspects of his case until his adversary presents the case in defense. Even if the adversary then adduces this adverse evidence, the direct examiner may have gained a psychological advantage by initially establishing a strong case. More important, the opponent will sometimes decide to abandon the point which he could not pursue on cross: the tactical advantage that might be gained in an immediate probe by cross-examination may be lost when the witness has a period of time away from the stand to collect his thoughts and, perhaps, confer with friendly counsel.[81] In short, the point that would have been explored on cross-examination, were it not for the American Rule, may not be worth the trouble and risk of recalling an adverse witness.

Obviously, situations arise in which it is debatable whether the cross-examiner is probing the topics covered on direct or whether he is inquiring into new matters.[82] The mosaic of human

---

81. McCormick, § 23, at 50. There also is confusion as to whether a cross-examiner who recalls a witness may use leading questions. This issue should be resolved on the basis of the relationship between the witness and the examiner (i. e., whether the witness clearly is identified with one side or the other) and not by the automatic application of the general rule that the party calling a witness can not lead him. See generally IIIA Wigmore §§ 909–18 (Chadbourn).

82. It seems clear that the direct examiner should not be entitled to elicit only a fragment of a transaction or statement, thereby presenting a misleading or distorted account, and to confine the cross-examiner strictly to the scope of the testimony on direct. See McCormick, § 23, at 48.

events does not always permit sharp lines between descriptive testimony. The amorphous division between testimonial subjects often leads to debate between counsel and, unfortunately, is the source of a number of appeals. The trial judge should be granted broad discretion to determine when the cross-examiner has exceeded permissible bounds. The rule limiting the scope of cross-examination is intended as a regulation governing the order in which evidence is presented and, as such, it should be administered with considerable latitude and practical adaptability.

A minority of jurisdictions follow the English (or Massachusetts) Rule, which does not limit cross-examination. The cross-examiner can thus inquire into any relevant matter.[83] He can, for example, not only attempt (as under the American Rule) to get the witness to retract or qualify part of his direct testimony, but also to have the witness testify as to matters bypassed by the direct examiner, including matters which aid in establishing a counter-claim, cross-claim, or affirmative defense. Finally, the cross-examiner may, as under the American Rule, probe topics which go to the witness's credibility.[84] This English or "wide-open" rule is easy to administer and minimizes the need for recalling witnesses.

A few jurisdictions have chosen a middle course between the American Rule and the English Rule. Under their approach, the cross-examiner may elicit any testimony that directly contests his opponent's allegations. He may not elicit testimony that goes solely to establish his own affirmative defense, counter-claim, or cross-claim, or other aspect of his case that does not controvert the opponent's allegations. In general, this means that the cross-examiner may not elicit testimony designed to substantiate claims or to avoid liability by disclosing additional facts upon which he has the burden of persuasion.[85] Under this intermediate rule, as under the American Rule, it is necessary to

---

83. McCormick, § 21, at 47.

84. J. Maguire, Evidence, Common Sense and Common Law 46 (1947); McCormick, § 23, at 49.

85. VII Wigmore, § 1889, at 545–46. The rule operates to prohibit the plaintiff from premature examination as to those new matters that he should reserve for his case in rebuttal. McCormick, § 23, at 48.

make discriminations among various parts of a witness's testimony in order to forbid that which does not properly belong within the scope of cross-examination.

Note that in all jurisdictions the cross-examiner may ask questions directed to credibility or impeachment. This means that he may propound questions designed to impugn the witness's motive to be truthful or to demonstrate aspects of the witness's prior conduct which cast doubt upon his veracity.[86] For example, the examiner may inquire whether the witness holds a grudge against one of the parties, whether he has a financial stake in the outcome of the case, or whether he has been convicted of a crime that raises doubt about his credibility. Even though inquiry about these facts carries the cross-examiner beyond the scope of direct examination, it is everywhere permissible to elicit testimony pertinent to impeachment. Two reasons justify this practice: first, credibility is always implicitly in issue and, second, a central purpose of cross-examination is to weaken or negate the testimony given during direct examination.

Except for questions pertaining to impeachment, the American Rule, as we have seen, obliges the cross-examiner to stay within the subject-matter bounds set by the direct examiner. On occasion, however, the cross-examiner will exceed the permissible scope; the question then arises as to what consequences attend this violation.[87] The opposing counsel can, of course, successfully object to the excessive questions, thereby containing the interrogation within the proper bounds; or he can permit the cross-examiner to pursue these excessive inquiries. As to those matters which are beyond the scope of direct examination, the cross-examiner is said to have "made the witness his own." That is, as to these new subjects the witness is treated as if he had been called by the cross-examiner. Thus, the direct examiner may successfully object to the cross-examin-

---

86. See, e. g., United States v. Fontana, 231 F.2d 807, 809–12 (3d Cir. 1956); Williams v. Graff, 194 Md. 516, 522, 71 A.2d 450, 452 (1950).

Impeachment is discussed in Ch. VIII.

87. See McCormick, § 24, at 50.

er's use of leading questions in regard to any new subject matter. In many jurisdictions, the cross-examiner is also forbidden to impeach the witness,[88] at least as to the testimony that is beyond the boundaries set by the direct examiner.

The Federal Rules of Evidence provide:[89]

> Scope of cross-examination — Cross-examination should be limited to the subject matter of the direct examination and matters affecting the credibility of the witness. The court may, in the exercise of discretion, permit inquiry into additional matters as if on direct examination.

Although these provisions ensure that federal courts will continue to apply the American (or Federal) Rule, they also reaffirm, and perhaps enlarge, the trial judge's discretion to permit the cross-examiner to inquire about subject matter beyond the scope of direct. If this discretion is exercised and new topics are explored, the interrogation must proceed in the mode of direct examination which means, under normal circumstances, without the use of leading questions. However, if the witness is actually hostile or uncooperative and leading questions are therefore justified, the cross-examiner should be entitled to continue to lead the witness, even in connection with the new topics.[90] This is but another way of saying that whether leading questions are appropriate should not depend upon who called the witness, but rather upon the responsiveness or hostility of the witness.[91] Finally, exceeding the scope of direct examination under the quoted Federal Rule has no effect upon the cross-examiner's right to

---

88. The rule against impeaching one's own witness is considered (and criticized) in Ch. VIII, § 80.

89. Fed.R.Evid. 611(b). See United States v. Callahan, 551 F.2d 733 (6th Cir. 1977); United States v. Ellison, 557 F.2d 128 (7th Cir. 1977).

90. Fed.R.Evid. 611(c); S.Rep. No. 93–1277, 93d Cong., 2d Sess., re-

printed in 1974 U.S.Code Cong. & Admin.News 7072. See United States v. Littlewind, 551 F.2d 244 (8th Cir. 1977) (rape case; reluctant victim may be led).

91. VI Wigmore, § 1887, at 538. In jurisdictions which have wide-open cross-examination, the use of leading questions similarly should be regulated.

impeach, since another Federal Rule ensures that either party may attack the credibility of any witness.[92]

§ 31. Examining the Witness: The Interaction of the American Rule and Certain Rules of Privilege

A major difficulty with the American Rule is the application of the amorphous standard "same subject or topic." [93] As a measure of the permissible range of cross-examination, this standard necessarily generates disagreements at trial and on appeal concerning the boundaries of interrogation that must be observed by the cross-questioner. Indeed, a few appellate courts have made a dispositive point of the housekeeping rule governing scope of interrogation, and have reversed judgments because the trial judge permitted (or denied) cross-examination in accordance with the dictates of the American Rule.[94] The cases also suggest that courts have sometimes applied the American Rule, combined with a rule of privilege, in a manner that absolutely precludes the admission of evidence which, arguably, should have been admitted at some point in the trial.

As elsewhere noted,[95] rules of privilege grant to the privileged person (called the "holder") the right to withhold relevant, but privileged, testimony from the factfinder. For example, by either statute or judicial opinion, confidential communications between attorney and client and those between husband and wife have been given a privileged status. As privileged matter, these communications are protected from disclosure, absent a waiver. A few rules of privilege are not confined simply to certain portions of a witness's testimony, but include the broader right not to take the stand. An example of such a privilege is the constitutional grant of freedom from compelled self-incrimination. As

---

92. Fed.R.Evid. 607.

93. See supra notes 80–82 and accompanying text.

94. Compare Conley v. Mervis, 324 Pa. 577, 188 A. 350 (1936) with Finch v. Weiner, 109 Conn. 616, 145 A. 31 (1929).

It should be noted that it may be unfair for the cross-examiner to ask leading questions throughout a far-reaching examination, especially if the witness is not hostile. See supra notes 81, 91.

95. See Ch. IX, § 86.

applied to an accused in a criminal trial, this fifth amendment privilege confers upon him the right not to be called to testify. If, however, he elects to testify, there is one line of authority suggesting that he thereby completely waives the constitutional privilege of self-incrimination as to the offense charged; [96] under this view, he may be subjected to a full cross-examination, excluding only questions as to separate offenses for which he still has not been tried. In other words, he can not selectively invoke the fifth amendment as to relevant aspects of the offense charged. If this constitutional interpretation is correct, it follows that the government should be allowed to broaden the scope of cross-examination to the constitutional limits, free from the usual restrictions of the American Rule. In the alternative (if the judge applies the American and confines the scope of cross-examination), the government should be entitled to later recall the accused. Either of these procedures recognizes that the rule of evidence which limits the scope of cross-examination is a rule only of trial administration, designed to regulate the order of proof. It does not embody a major policy or principle underlying the factfinding process.

A difficulty arises because most cases,[97] either expressly or by implication, make the rule prescribing scope the determinative factor governing the extent to which the accused is deemed to have waived his privilege against self-incrimination. Thus, by offering only selective testimony on direct examination, the accused testifying in a jurisdiction that has the American Rule thereby limits his waiver and confines the prosecutor to the

---

96. Johnson v. United States, 318 U.S. 189, 195–96, (1943); VIII Wigmore, § 2276, at 465–66 (McNaughton). But see Brown v. United States, 356 U.S. 148, 154–56 (1958); Tucker v. United States, 5 F.2d 818, 822 (8th Cir. 1925). The extent of the accused's waiver is discussed in Ch. IX, § 92. An accused may testify in connection with a preliminary motion without effecting a waiver for trial purposes. Sim-

mons v. United States, 390 U.S. 377, 389–390 (1968); Fed.R.Evid. 104(d). But see Harris v. New York, 401 U.S. 222 (1971).

97. E. g., United States v. Pate, 357 F.2d 911, 915 (7th Cir. 1966); Ziegler v. United States, 174 F.2d 439, 446 (9th Cir.), cert. denied 338 U.S. 822 (1949). See Weinstein & Berger, ¶ 611[03], at 35–36 nn. 13, 14.

subject or topics covered during direct examination. Under the rationale of these cases, the prosecutor not only is prohibited from exceeding the scope of direct examination, but also is forbidden to later recall the witness, who has not waived his privilege against self-incrimination as to those matters outside his direct testimony. Thus, a lowly rule designed to produce trial efficiency takes on the far-reaching significance of prescribing the boundaries of a great constitutional principle. Aside from this anomaly, the use of the rule regulating cross-examination to determine the extent to which the privilege against self-incrimination is waived produces the incongruity of a narrow waiver in a jurisdiction adhering to the American Rule, but a broad waiver in a jurisdiction following the English Rule. It is not easy to explain why the defendant taking the stand in Arizona (which applies the English Rule) triggers a broad waiver of his constitutional rights, whereas the accused testifying in Pennsylvania (which applies the American Rule) does not.[98]

§ 32. The Components of Trial: Closing Argument and Judge's Charge

After the close of the evidence, the lawyers have an opportunity to address the trier and to state their respective arguments concerning the evidence and what it proves. The plaintiff's counsel (or, in a criminal case, the prosecutor) makes his closing argument first. The defendant's lawyer then delivers his closing argument and following this, the plaintiff's counsel gives his argument in reply. Observe that the party who has the burden of persuading the jury of the existence of the facts necessary for a recovery (or conviction) has the opportunity to make the final argumentative presentation.

Counsel have considerable latitude in setting the form and content of closing argument.[99] They may urge the factfinder to believe certain evidence and to draw reasonable inferences from

---

98. For two commentators' view of what criteria should govern the extent of the waiver, see Weinstein & Berger, ¶ 611[03], at 39–48.

99. For a helpful discussion of closing argument with an emphasis upon tactical considerations, see R. Keeton, Trial Tactics and Methods § 7.12 (2d ed. 1973).

it.[1] They may not, however, allude to evidence that was not offered or that was rejected, nor may they urge that evidence admitted only for a limited purpose be considered for another, improper purpose.[2]

In the federal system and in most states, the judge instructs the jury after, rather than before, the closing arguments of counsel.[3] In his charge, the judge always sets out the applicable law; he may also include instructions to guide the jury in the proper use or evaluation of the evidence.[4] As elsewhere noted,[5] some jurisdictions permit the judge to comment upon the evidence.

NOTES

1. *Stages of a Jury Trial.* The selection of a jury is, in the broad sense, part of the trial. In a jury case, the phases of a typical trial may be summarized as follows:

    (a) Jury Selection (Voir Dire)

    (b) Counsels' Opening Statements

---

1. Roberts v. State, 346 So.2d 473 (Ala.Crim.App.1977). Compare Hayes v. Coleman, 338 Mich. 371, 382, 61 N.W.2d 634, 640 (1953) with Harvey v. Aubrey, 53 Ariz. 210, 214–15, 87 P.2d 482, 483–84 (1939). For cases in which counsel exceeded permissible bounds, see United States v. Barker, 553 F.2d 1013, 1024–25 (6th Cir. 1977); Robinson v. Pennsylvania R.R., 214 F.2d 798, 800–03 (3d Cir. 1954).

2. See People v. Housholder, 74 Mich.App. 399, 253 N.W.2d 780 (1977); VI Wigmore, § 1807, at 261. See also I Wigmore, § 13, at 300–01. Counsel can make reference to matters that are judicially noticed. VI Wigmore, § 1807, at 266. For examples of potential abuses in closing argument, see Lempert & Saltzburg at 832–48.

3. Charging the jury before closing argument rather than afterwards makes it more convenient for counsel to argue about the jury's duties under the instructions as, for example, where counsel stresses the elements that must be found to constitute fraud or assumption of risk. However, the prevailing view, which reserves the judge's instruction until last, has the advantage of concluding the trial on an impartial note. Furthermore, counsel's preceding arguments are made with knowledge of what the instructions will be, since the lawyers and judge already have conferred in chambers over the latter's charge and he has made a final decision concerning what instructions he will give.

4. See Ch. I, § 5.

5. See note 2 following Ch. I.

(c) The Presentation of Evidence
Plaintiff's Case in Chief
Defendant's Case in Defense
Plaintiff's Case in Rebuttal
Defendant's Case in Rejoinder

(d) Counsels' Closing Arguments

(e) Judge's Charge

(f) Jury Deliberation and Verdict

2. *Order of Counsels' Argument.* The plaintiff or prosecutor, it will be recalled, gives his opening argument first, makes the first evidentiary presentation, and is entitled to make the last closing argument. Are there psychological (forensic) advantages in having the first and last "word"? Consider the following closing argument to the jury by defense counsel:

> The plaintiff's counsel, Mr. Agee, made the first opening statement, he presented his evidence first, he made the first closing argument and in a moment he will have yet another chance to address you. I was second in line to present my evidence, and this is my only opportunity to address you with a closing presentation. Perhaps it is fair that the plaintiff has the first and last word, because as His Honor will instruct you, the plaintiff has the burden of persuasion in this case. He must convince you that his alleged facts are the true facts and, if you don't believe that, you are sworn to return a verdict for my client, Mr. Woodson.

> And I would like to make one other point before I review the evidence with you. If you will bear with me during this one chance I have to speak, if you will closely observe the weaknesses in the plaintiff's case and the ways in which the evidence fails to support it, then, if Mr. Agee should confront you with some new argument, please ask yourself, Ladies and Gentlemen, what I might say to answer that argument if I were able to address you again.

> Turning now to the evidence, you will recall that the very first witness, Mrs. Kline, stated that she was uncertain whether the . . . .

3. *Past Recollection Recorded.* Under the orthodox approach, the rule allowing the introduction of a witness's prior writing as past recollection recorded is not applicable if the witness is able to testify from present (aided or unaided) recollection. Why should not a witness's prior written account of an event be admissible even if he can testify from memory, especially if the writing was not prepared for litigation?

4. *Opinion Rule.* A distinguished professor has commented on the opinion rule as follows:

> The rule of evidence that (normally) excludes from judicial proof laymen's opinions is designed to keep the witness' language at the neutral descriptive level and to exclude his erroneous or biased references; and the exceptions to the rule show recognition that the language of common nouns and adjectives is inadequate to communicate to a jury the data from which it can infer that, for instance, a voice heard by the witness was X's voice. Hence the witness is allowed to state directly that the voice he heard was X's voice.

E. Patterson, Jurisprudence, Men and Ideas of the Law, § 1.15, at 47 (1953).

5. *Scope of Cross-Examination.* Most jurisdictions applying the American Rule make it applicable to all witnesses, including parties who testify. In a few jurisdictions, when a civil party calls himself as a witness the opponent (cross-examiner) can exceed the scope of direct examination. McCormick, § 25, at 52. Is there any reason why the usual restriction should be lifted in this instance?

CHAPTER V

RELEVANCE: RECURRING PROBLEMS OF CIRCUMSTANTIAL PROOF

§ 33. Scope

The requirement of relevance, we have noted elsewhere,[1] is one of general application. Even when this fundamental requisite of admissibility is satisfied, however, a trial judge has general discretionary authority to exclude evidence if he determines that its probative value is outweighed by such practical policy considerations as prejudice, confusion of the issues, time consumption, or misleading the jury.[2] The application of this balancing process takes full account of the particular facts and circumstances of the case being tried; differences among cases, coupled with the broad discretionary authority vested in the trial judge, limit the precedential value of these ad hoc rulings.

The materials in this chapter focus upon recurring patterns of circumstantial proof. Certain issues of evidence have repeatedly arisen, and courts and legislatures have responded by pronouncing rules of exclusion (or admissibility) that are intended to yield uniform results in similar situations. The bases underlying these rules are varied, but the dominant influences are probative force, the practical considerations noted above, and various public policies discussed later in this chapter. To the extent these rules are formulated as specific, absolute directives (as opposed to broad principles subject to the trial judge's exceptions) they restrict or eliminate ad hoc discretionary rulings by the trial judge.[3] Thus, these rules add an element of uniformity to evidentiary law; they also produce predictable tensions when, as is often the case, the "similar" situations purportedly governed by one of the rules have in fact significant differences among them. This chapter examines many of these rules, their underlying bases, and their effect upon the trial process.

---

1. Ch. II, § 8.

2. Ch. II, § 13.

3. McCormick, § 185, at 440.

§ 34. Character Evidence: In General

As McCormick states, character evidence is a "conspicuous instance" in which specific rules have been developed in an effort to strike the proper balance between the probative value of evidence and the countervailing practical policy considerations.[4] The potential probative force of character evidence is not difficult to see. We know that historical or adjudicative facts often are established at trial by circumstantial proof. In many instances, issues of fact involve questions about someone's conduct. Because character evidence is often circumstantially probative of one's actions, it is usually relevant. There are a variety of situations in which character evidence could be important, but several examples will illustrate typical contexts:

(1) In an automobile accident case, the only issue may be whether either or both of the two parties were negligent. The plaintiff wants to introduce evidence that the defendant has been involved in numerous automobile accidents, many of which have resulted in his conviction for some act of wrongful driving. Or the plaintiff may offer a witness who has observed the defendant for many years and is willing to testify that the defendant is generally a careless driver.

(2) In a case for assault and battery, the defendant may claim that he acted in self-defense because the plaintiff was the first aggressor. To support this allegation, the defendant offers evidence that the plaintiff is a person of turbulence and violence.

(3) In a prosecution for larceny, the prosecutor may offer to show that the accused has a record of past convictions for shoplifting, embezzlement, and robbery.

In all of these examples one can reasonably argue that the evidence of the actor's character is probative of the specific conduct in question. The countervailing considerations, however, should also be apparent. Evidence of carelessness, turbulence, or past crimes may be given excessive weight by the jury or may cause it to judge the actor on his past rather than on his present conduct. Character evidence may also distract the jury

---

4. Id., § 186, at 442.

from the central elements of the case, and its introduction may considerably lengthen the trial.

Recognition of these potential countervailing dangers has produced strict limits on the admissibility of character evidence. These limits respond to three determinants: the purpose for which character is to be used, the form of character evidence offered, and the type of proceeding, civil or criminal. The primary factor is the ultimate purpose for which evidence of character is offered, that is, whether the character which is supported by the evidence is to be used directly or circumstantially. Note that in the three foregoing hypothetical illustrations, the proponent seeks to use character circumstantially: from the evidence offered the trier is, first, to infer the existence of the relevant aspects of character *and, then, to infer* that the subject acted consistently with that character. In contrast, the direct use of character occurs when character, or more specifically a character trait, is an essential element in the case. This direct use is freely allowed in all courts.[5] Circumstantial use of character, however, is disallowed in most jurisdictions in civil cases and, although everywhere allowed in criminal cases, its use in criminal trials is hedged with restrictive rules. The major restrictions limit the circumstances in which character evidence is admissible and also prescribe what form or type of evidence is admissible to show character.

Possible forms of character evidence include (1) specific instances of past conduct that are probative of the relevant character trait; (2) testimony by a witness who is familiar with the person in question and who can state his opinion whether the subject has a certain character trait; and (3) evidence of the subject's community reputation for possessing the character trait in question. All of these types of character evidence carry dangers of prejudice, confusion, misleading the jury and time-consumption; these practical counterweights must be weighed against the potential probative value of character evidence.

---

5. Character is an essential element in only a few types of civil suits; it is very rarely an essential ele- ment in a criminal proceeding. See McCormick, § 191, at 454.

Arguably, evidence of specific acts has the greatest potential to show character accurately, and evidence of community reputation has the least. However, the courts have emphasized judicial expedition (probably at the expense of probative force) and have shown a distinct preference for reputation evidence because its presentation requires comparatively little time. Only in recent years has opinion evidence gained favor, largely because the shift in residential patterns from small towns to urban centers has weakened the assumption that most persons have a community reputation.[6] Because evidence of specific instances possesses the greatest potential to consume time (as well as to arouse prejudice), its admission is limited to those cases in which character is a central element in the litigation, that is, cases in which character is used directly.[7] In these instances its greater probative force is a prevailing consideration; further, since character is a central issue, evidence that reveals character can not be said to distract the trier from the principal aspects of the case.

§ 35. Character Evidence: Character An Essential Element of a Claim, Charge or Defense

The substantive law sometimes makes character a dispositive issue at trial: the existence or nonexistence of a character trait is itself an issue that directly determines the outcome of the case. In these instances, it is not necessary to utilize character as the basis for inferences about particular conduct—that is, to use character circumstantially. Such a case is a libel or slander suit where character is defamed and the defense is truth.[8] The defendant, for example, states that the plaintiff is "corrupt and

---

6. Courts also have begun to admit evidence of a person's reputation in his employment community as well as his residential community. See supra § 38 at note 29; Ch. VIII, § 80.

7. Fed.R.Evid. 405(b) and Adv.Comm. Note. See United States v. Brown, 547 F.2d 438 (8th Cir. 1977).

8. See McCormick, § 186, at 443 n. 8; Maguire et al. 970–71 n. 3; Conner v. Dart Transp. Serv., 65 Cal. App.3d 320, 135 Cal.Rptr. 259 (1976).

dishonest"; in the resulting suit for defamation, the defendant bases his defense upon the truth of his statement. Plaintiff's character for dishonesty and corruption is directly in issue, and the inferential chain stops with the establishment of these traits: further inferences about particular conduct are not required. Likewise, where an employer is sued for negligently engaging an employee of uncontrollable temper or intemperance, the character of the employee is placed directly in issue.[9]

The distinguishing characteristics of these cases, or of any action in which character is said to be "directly in issue," is that character constitutes an essential "element of a charge, claim or defense." [10] In these cases, of course, there exists no question as to the relevance of character evidence. Because character is itself a dispositive issue in the case, evidence intended to establish (or refute) the character trait in issue is always received.[11] Furthermore, many jurisdictions admit any *form* of character evidence that has probative value including testimony of (1) specific past acts; (2) opinions held by qualified observers; and (3) reputation in the community.[12] This generous receptivity stands in marked contrast to the begrudging approach that has traditionally prevailed when character is used circumstantially. In the latter instance, which is described in more detail below, not only are there strict limitations as to when character may be shown, but there are additional restrictions upon the type of evidence that may be used to establish character.

---

9. See, e. g., Christy v. United States, 68 F.R.D. 375 (N.D.Tex. 1975); Winchester v. Padgett, 167 F.Supp. 444, 448 (N.D.Ga.1952); Guedon v. Rooney, 160 Or. 621, 87 P.2d 209 (1939). Cf. International Security Life Ins. Co. v. Melancon, 463 S.W.2d 762 (Tex.Civ.App.1971).

10. Adv.Comm.Note to Fed.R.Evid. 404. Fed.R.Evid. 405(b) uses this phrase in declaring that specific instances of conduct are admissible to prove character only when it is an essential element in the action.

For other cases, see McCormick, § 186, at 443 n. 8.

11. I Wigmore, § 71, at 495. See Adv.Comm.Note to Fed.R.Evid. 404.

12. See West's Ann.Cal.Evid.Code § 1100, Law Rev.Comm.Comment; Morgan at 200. Contra, Guedon v. Rooney, 160 Or. 621, 87 P.2d 209 (1939). McCormick asserts that the particular kind of character trait in issue determines which one(s) of these various types of evidence will be received. McCormick, § 187, at 443–44.

§ 36. Character Evidence: Character Used Circumstantially

The circumstantial use of character involves not only the establishment of the relevant character trait, but also the inference that the conduct in question was consistent with the actor's character. If, for example, the issue in a prosecution for criminal assault is who attacked first, the defendant or the victim, the defense may wish to offer evidence that the victim has an aggressive and violent character; the desired inference is that his actions were commensurate with his character and, hence, that he attacked first. Specifically, the inferential chain is this: from the evidence presented, the factfinder infers a particular character trait, from which it further infers relevant actions that are manifestations of this trait. Used circumstantially, character serves only the subsidiary function of helping the trier reach an ultimate proposition about conduct. The probative value of character evidence is thus attenuated and such convincing force as it does possess must be measured against the countervailing practical costs attending its introduction.[13]

It should be emphasized, however, that the probative value of character evidence can vary considerably from case to case. The degree of probative force associated with this evidence is affected by the strength and nature of the character trait (i. e., how dominant and specific it is), by the forcefulness of the evidence to establish that trait, and by the strength of the inference that the act in question is likely to result from the character trait. Some further examples, set out in subsequent sections, will illustrate these points.

§ 37. Character Evidence: Circumstantial Use of Character in Civil Cases

Arguably, one could have a character trait of carelessness or, more specifically, of carelessness in performing a certain activity such as driving. Should the trier of fact be permitted to infer, in accident litigation, that an automobile driver who had such a trait was at fault on the occasion in question?[14] The risk in

---

13. Adv.Comm.Note to Fed.R.Evid. 404.

14. For a thoughtful article that suggests a negative answer, at least where accident proneness is involved, see, James and Dickinson, Accident Proneness and Accident Law, 63 Harv.L.Rev. 769 (1950).

drawing this inference is that careless drivers often drive properly and, to state the obvious but inverse proposition, even generally careful drivers sometimes drive carelessly. Nonetheless, the evidence has a degree of probative force that seemingly satisfies the basic test of relevance: it increases somewhat the probability that the generally careless driver was at fault.[15]

Observe that the value of this evidence of a specific character trait (careless driving) appears to have more probative value than does evidence that would demonstrate a general carelessness in all activities. But even the inference from a frequent lack of driving care to a specific act or omission (e. g., speeding or failure to stop at an intersection) carries with it several probative difficulties. First, the actor's careless driving may not be manifested in the particular negligent conduct at issue in the suit: one's careless disregard of speed limits, for example, is not very revealing on the issue of whether he failed to signal that his car was turning. Secondly, as noted above, due care may have been exercised on the occasion in question despite a usual pattern of careless driving. These considerations weaken the case for admitting character evidence because they present uncertainty and heighten the apprehension that the trier might give undue weight to evidence of prior negligence.

Arguably, in another context the probative force of character evidence is stronger. Suppose the plaintiff has a propensity toward truculence and physical violence. Injured in an affray with the defendant, he brings suit for assault and battery. The defendant pleads self-defense and offers evidence of the plaintiff's violent character to support the inference that the latter was the initial aggressor. The test of relevance is clearly satisfied: evidence of the character trait makes it more probable than it would be without the evidence that the plaintiff was the aggressor.[16] Of course, a violent or aggressive person will sometimes exercise restraint, thereby acting inconsistently with his character trait. However, the inference from aggressive character to violence may be stronger than the inference from traits

---

15. See Ch. II, §§ 10–11.

16. See supra note 15 and text at note 4.

of carelessness to a specific careless act.   Physical aggression is purposeful activity;   carelessness is often the result of inattention. Similarly, one could argue, a trait of turbulence and violence is likely to be manifested in a physical encounter, whereas carelessness, even in driving, can be evinced in a variety of ways. The validity of these tentative assertions remains an open question.   The courts, however, have had to make both tentative assumptions and practical judgments about the admissibility of character evidence.

The civil cases dealing with character evidence reflect an inconsistent pattern.   The dominant view, embodied in the Federal Rules, is that character evidence offered to support the circumstantial use of character in civil cases is generally not worth its cost in time, distraction, prejudice, etc., and is, accordingly, rejected.[17]   Another view admits character evidence in limited cases, such as those involving fraudulent misconduct or assault and battery.   The distinguishing characteristic of these cases is that the alleged conduct usually involves moral turpitude or at least carries the stigma of strong societal disapprobation; [18] typically, punitive damages are available to the complaining party. The quasi-criminal nature of these civil suits has persuaded some courts to extend to the civil party against whom such misconduct is alleged a right which, as we shall see, is usually reserved for the accused in a criminal case.   The party charged with misconduct may introduce evidence that his character is favorable and thus inconsistent with the conduct alleged.[19]   Of course, the favorable character trait he seeks to establish must be inconsistent with the alleged activity or else its probative value would be marginal or nonexistent.   A character trait of honesty would be inconsistent with an allegation of deceitful misrepresentation, but a character trait for nonviolence would not.

---

17. Fed.R.Evid. 404(a). Note, however, that character evidence can be used circumstantially to impeach a witness. See Ch. VIII, § 81.

18. McCormick, § 192, at 459–60.

19. McCormick, § 192, at 459–60; I Wigmore, § 64, at 477–80. An early leading case supporting this minority view is Hess v. Marinari, 81 W.Va. 500, 94 S.E. 968 (1918).

The minority courts which allow character evidence in specific kinds of civil cases have had their greatest precedential influence in one particular type of case: assault and battery where the defendant claims self-defense. Here, many courts that generally disallow in civil cases character evidence when character has only a circumstantial use, permit the defendant to introduce not only evidence of his peaceful character, but also to introduce evidence of the victim's propensity for violence or aggression. The evidence is offered, of course, to support by inference the defendant's claim that the victim was the first aggressor.[19a] The victim-claimant may respond to the evidence by introducing evidence of the defendant's turbulent or aggressive character [20] (or, for that matter, by rebuttal evidence that the victim's character is nonviolent). The more general acceptance of character evidence in assault and battery,[21] but not in other civil contexts, is difficult to explain. Perhaps this receptivity is an implied acknowledgment that the probative relationship between a violent character and truculent conduct is stronger than the usual character-to-conduct nexus.[22]

§ 38.   Character Evidence: Circumstantial Use of Character in Criminal Cases

Because most criminal acts involve deliberate conduct, it is plausible that the trier would be especially aided by knowledge

---

19a. A related, but distinct, situation exists when the civil defendant offers evidence of the victim's reputation for violence and couples this evidence with evidence that the defendant was aware of the victim's reputation. Here, admissibility is widespread. McCormick, § 192, at 460–61. The theory is that the victim's reputation bears upon defendant's apprehension and, of course, the defendant's state of mind is a significant factor in determining whether he acted reasonably.

20. McCormick, § 192, at 461. Contra, Fed.R.Evid. 404(a)(1)(2) which uses the terms "accused" and "prosecution," making it clear that the circumstantial use of character evidence is restricted to criminal cases.

21. In Rich v. Cooper, 234 Or. 300, 380 P.2d 613 (1963) the Oregon Supreme Court refused to extend the circumstantial use of character evidence to civil cases other than assault and battery where the defendant claims self-defense. A police officer, sued by the plaintiff-arrestee for assault and battery, sought to introduce evidence of the plaintiff's violent character for the inference that the plaintiff was likely to resist arrest. The court held this evidence inadmissible.

22. See text § 37 at n. 16.

of the accused's character. If the accused is generally disposed towards criminal acts, this disposition increases the likelihood that he committed the act with which he is charged. Further, the probative link between character and conduct is strengthened in cases where a *specific* character trait directly relates to particular alleged conduct. For example, the character trait of dishonesty relates directly to a criminal act involving fraud, cheating, or deception. Again, however, the probative value of character evidence must be weighed against the policies of exclusion. At least two related risks of serious prejudice to the accused attend the use of character evidence. First, the trier might accord undue probative force to evidence of the accused's bad character, using it as the major determinant of guilt in the crime charged. Secondly, the trier might deemphasize the risk of an incorrect determination of the crime charged because evidence of the accused's unfavorable character provokes the belief that he should be confined or otherwise penalized. These dangers of prejudicial effect, when combined with the counterweights of time consumption, distraction, and confusion of the issues have caused the courts to unite in a general principle: the prosecution may not initially show the defendant's bad character trait(s) for the inference that he is more likely to have committed the crime charged.[23]

The accused, on the other hand, is entitled to use character evidence in presenting his defense. The gravity of a criminal conviction, involving the possible loss of life or liberty, has influenced all courts to give special dispensation to an accused: he is permitted to show character traits (e. g., honesty, peacefulness) inconsistent with the crime charged.[24] The dangers of prejudice to the accused do not exist with respect to evidence of a relevant trait of "good" character offered by the accused, although the

---

23. McCormick, § 190, at 447; Fed. R.Evid. 404 (a) (1).

24. McCormick, § 191, at 454; Fed. R.Evid. 404 (a) (1). But see United States v. Davis, 546 F.2d 583 (5th Cir. 1977) excluding good behavior evidence offered to negate willfulness in trial for prison escape; a difficulty with admitting this evidence is that it supports good character by specific acts. See supra § 34.

potential costs to the trial process of increased time consumption and distraction are present. The courts, however, consider paramount the accused's interest in protecting his freedom and hence they subordinate the countervailing practical considerations.

The principle that the accused may "place his character in issue," [25] as the cases often express it, does not answer the question of what kind of evidence is admissible for this purpose. In addressing this problem, it first should be recalled that the basic requirement of all evidence is that of relevance. In the present context, the principle of relevance demands a showing that the character trait portrayed by the defendant is inconsistent with the crime charged. We have noted that this requirement would not be satisfied, for example, where an accused charged with criminal fraud offered evidence that he was a nonviolent person. Assuming, however, relevance is satisfied, there are several types of character evidence which have probative value to establish the accused's desirable character traits. These are, as we have already observed: (1) previous acts relevant to the character trait in question; (2) opinion testimony given by one or more witnesses who know the accused and who testify as to his (relevant) good character; and (3) testimony of witnesses familiar with his (relevant) good reputation.

The traditional view, which emphasizes judicial expedition, still prevails in most jurisdictions and limits the accused to evidence of his community reputation.[26] His "character witnesses" are subjected to a comparatively brief period of interrogation during which they state their familiarity with his reputation.[27]

---

25. McCormick notes that this phrase is misleading because character is almost never one of the ultimate issues in a criminal case. McCormick, § 191, at 454.

26. McCormick, § 191, at 456.

27. "In America the usual method of proof of character . . . is by general reputation after foundation testimony has been given to show that the character witness knows the reputation of the person in question. Following the foundation proper questions are: Does the person have a general reputation as to the trait involved (designating it) in the community of (naming it) or in larger centers in the area in which he is well known (stating it)? Do you know that reputation? Is it good or bad?" Ladd & Carlson at 233.

Increasingly, however, courts have come to doubt the existence of a community reputation for many persons, especially those who reside in large metropolitan areas.[28] A partial escape from the restrictions of the orthodox rule is found in those jurisdictions that allow evidence of reputation within the employment community where the accused works.[29] A more direct approach, endorsed by the Federal Rules and a minority of jurisdictions, is to permit proof of character by receiving the opinion of persons who are sufficiently familiar with the accused to be able to testify concerning the trait in question.[30] The probative force of opinion evidence surpasses that of reputation evidence: the former is the product of direct observation and conclusion; the latter is merely the recital of an opinion or conclusion that is based on the more remote source of community hearsay.[31]

Proof by opinion evidence may, however, involve a greater expenditure of time than proof by reputation because the cross-examiner can (within reasonable limits set by the trial judge) probe the specific occurrences and observations that underlie the opinion.[32] Surely, however, this expenditure of time is a small

---

28. "Such a faith [in reputation evidence as a measure of character] is a survival of more simple times. It was justified in days when men lived in small communities. Perhaps it has some justification even now in rural districts. In the life of great cities, it has made evidence of character a farce." Cardozo, Nature of the Judicial Process 157 (1921).

29. United States v. Parker, 447 F. 2d 826, 830–31 (7th Cir. 1971); People v. Kronk, 326 Mich. 744, 40 N. W.2d 788 (1950); Hamilton v. State, 129 Fla. 219, 176 So. 89 (1937). See also Mass.Gen.Laws Ann., Ch. 233, § 21A (1959). McCormick states that evidence of reputation should be permitted when it is developed within "any considerable group with whom [the accused] . . . constantly associate[s] in his business, work, or other continued activity, and who might reasonably be thought to have a collective opinion about him." McCormick, § 191, at 456. Fed.R.Evid. 803(21) excepts from the hearsay rule "Reputation of a person's character among his associates or in the community."

30. Fed.R.Evid. 405(a); United States v. Morgan, 554 F.2d 31 (2d Cir. 1977); State v. Scalf, 254 Iowa 983, 119 N.W.2d 868 (1963); McCormick, § 191, at 455 n. 68. See VII Wigmore, § 1986.

31. Michelson v. United States, 335 U.S. 469, 477 (1948) (characterizing reputation evidence as opinion-based-on-hearsay).

32. As will be discussed in the next section, a prosecutor may probe a reputation witness's knowledge of

price for the increased probative force of personal opinion. Additional reasons supporting the admissibility of opinion by a knowledgeable witness are, first, the practical difficulty of finding a qualified "reputation witness" willing to testify and, second, the superiority of opinion in providing the trier with a basis for making an intelligent evaluation of the subject's character.

Note, however, that most courts do not permit the accused to establish his character by introducing evidence of specific instances of past conduct. Evidence of specific occurrences is potentially the most time consuming and distracting of the three possible means of showing character.[33] The consequence of admitting this evidence is that the principal focus of both direct and cross-examination of the character witness is upon selected past acts of the accused. These inquiries can raise collateral issues concerning the existence, number, or nature of past acts, thus exacting additional costs in time consumption, distraction, and possibly, confusion and surprise.

§ 39. Character Evidence: Presenting and Cross-Examining the Reputation Witness

The procedures that control the proof of character through the use of one or more reputation witnesses [34] promote trial expedition by sharply focusing the scope of the examination. A criminal trial provides a convenient illustration of proof by reputation, although the same principles apply in civil cases in which reputation evidence is admissible. Assume that the accused calls a character witness. The witness first states the association, such as residence within the accused's community, that enables him to be familiar with the accused's reputation for the relevant character trait.[35] The witness is then asked the nature of that

---

rumors and certain occurrences which should be generally known to the community. This inquiry, however, is limited to a yes or no answer by the witness, so ordinarily it should not consume as much time as the cross-examination of an opinion witness.

33. Fed.R.Evid. 405 and Adv.Comm. Note. See, e. g., United States v. Davis, 546 F.2d 583 (5th Cir. 1977).

34. See generally supra §§ 34–38.

35. Sample questions appropriate to establish the necessary foundation

reputation and, if he replies as expected, he will simply state, "It is good."

It should be apparent that this terse portrayal not only lacks color and impact, but it also eludes a discriminating assessment because the trier is without any guidance as to the kind or number of occasions which lie behind the asserted reputation. Furthermore, the trier does not know if the witness personally observed any of these occasions, a fact that might have influenced his answer. The process of cross-examination does, however, afford a somewhat ritualistic test of the accuracy of the witness's assertion about the accused's reputation. As a first step, the prosecutor may further examine the witness's opportunity to know the accused's reputation. For example, he may inquire how long the witness has been a member of the accused's community. Second, he may ask the witness about damaging rumors of which one familiar with the accused's reputation should presumably be aware.[36] A major thrust of these questions, which must be asked in a "have-you-heard" form [37] is to test the witness's familiarity with the accused's reputation. A further purpose of these inquiries is to ascertain the standard that the witness is applying in his assertion that the accused has a good reputation. Thus, the prosecutor might ask a question such as "Have you heard that the accused was convicted last year for receiving stolen property?" In the leading case, Michelson v. United States,[38] the question "Have you heard that the accused

---

for a character witness are set out in Ladd, Techniques and Theory of Character Testimony, 24 Iowa L. Rev. 498, 519–527 (1939).

36. See, e. g., Snead v. State, 243 Ala. 23, 8 So.2d 269 (1942) (character witness appearing in a prosecution for rape asked if he had heard of defendant ravishing other women on specified occasions).

37. When character evidence is restricted to reputation only, the inquiries are addressed in the "have you heard" format rather than "did you know" because the former

focuses on the witness's acquaintance with the general talk about the accused in the community, while the latter questions the witness's personal knowledge. Michelson v. United States, 335 U.S. 469, 482 (1948). The federal rules (which permit opinion evidence) avoid any problems over the form of cross-examination questions by stating "[o]n cross-examination, inquiry is allowable into relevant specific instances of conduct." Fed.R.Evid. 405 and Adv.Comm. Note.

38. 335 U.S. 469, 472–87 (1948).

was arrested for receiving stolen property?" was approved by the United States Supreme Court on the theory that an arrest (even when there is no subsequent conviction) affects one's reputation and, hence, inquiry into the witness's knowledge of the arrest is proper.

Note that if the character witness has not heard of an unfavorable event, his familiarity with the accused's character is brought into question; if he had heard of an unfavorable event, but nonetheless states that the accused enjoys a good reputation, his standard for determining that the reputation is favorable is brought into question. The event—or, more precisely, the rumor inquired about—must be one that would affect the reputation to which the witness has testified.[39] Thus, where the witness has testified that the accused has a good reputation for veracity, it would be improper to ask a have-you-heard question about an incident involving aggressive conduct.

The technique of cross-examination described above presents an ambitious or overzealous prosecutor with opportunities for abuse. For example, the prosecutor might ask about a rumor for which there is not a reasonable basis. The courts therefore require that the cross-examiner ask only questions that he can propound in good faith—that is, questions based upon a reasonable belief of the actual existence of the rumor inquired about. Many authorities add the qualification that this belief is reasonable only if based upon reliable information that confirms the *actual existence* of the event giving rise to the rumor.[40] The trial judge has the responsibility of ensuring that the prosecutor's questions are not spurious. Misconduct should trigger the imposition of sanctions upon the offending attorney, and should also give rise to a mistrial where the transgression is too prejudicial to ameliorate by a curative instruction.[41]

---

39. In *Michelson*, the Court rejected the "Illinois rule" which would restrict inquiry about arrests only to "very closely similar if not identical charges." Id. at 483.

40. McCormick, § 191, at 458.

41. Id. Such reversals, however, have been rare. Id. n. 78. See generally, Annot., 3 A.L.R.3d 965 (1965). For an example of appellate tolerance, see United States v. Morgan, 554 F.2d 31 (2d Cir. 1977).

During the prosecutor's case in rebuttal, he may present reputation witnesses to refute the accused's asserted good reputation
for the particular character trait in question. This opportunity,
of course, is conditioned upon the accused first placing his character in issue. Thus, if the accused has attempted to show that
he has a good reputation for honesty and obedience to law, the
prosecutor may try to show that he has a bad reputation for
these traits. Just as the accused's reputation witnesses are subject to cross-examination, so too are the government's reputation witnesses. Their qualifications may be probed and they
may be asked "have-you-heard" questions concerning an incident which is likely to be known in the community and which is
consistent with the character portrayed by the defense.

Considerations of the time consumption and distraction limit
the inquiry that may be conducted by have-you-heard questions:
the cross-examiner must settle for the answer of the witness. If
the prosecutor's question is "have you heard that the accused
was arrested for receiving stolen property?" and the witness answers "no," the prosecutor's only recourse is to repeat the question—and even this tactic may be blocked if the judge, in his
discretion, sustains the opponent's objection. The prosecutor
may not present extrinsic evidence to demonstrate to the jury
that the arrest occurred or, at least, rumors to that effect exist.
More importantly, neither the questioned witness nor the accused may attempt to erase the damaging inference of the question by proving the nonexistence of the arrest or any such rumors. Additional inquiry into this collateral subject is considered not to be worth the cost in judicial expedition and efficiency. This truncation in allowable proof underscores the importance of the cross-examiner's good faith.

Wigmore argues that the testing of an accused's reputation
witness by "have-you-heard" questions is an unjustified practice.[42] In his view the jury is unable to limit its concern to
the credibility of the reputation witness. Instead, it is likely to
use the rumor communicated by the question to infer that the

---

42. IIIA Wigmore, § 988, at 920–21
(Chadbourn).

rumor exists and that it is true. The jury may then infer that the accused is likely to be guilty of the acts for which he is now on trial. Obviously, this technique of testing a witness's qualifications does involve risks of prejudice.[43] However, without such questions the trier has little or no basis for evaluating the character witness's assertion that the accused has a good reputation for the relevant character trait. It is true, of course, that the prosecutor can weaken the effect of the accused's reputation witness by presenting government witnesses who will state that the accused has a bad reputation for the trait in question. As a practical matter, however, such witnesses may be difficult to produce, since many persons might be reluctant to proffer this testimony. Furthermore, even if the prosecutor can produce one or more contradictory witnesses who will assert that the accused has a bad reputation, it is difficult for the trier to evaluate the conflicting lines of reputation evidence unless the witnesses' knowledge and standards are tested. A similar need exists for adequately testing, usually by questions in a "did you know," format, character witnesses who give opinion testimony. Thus, courts which allow opinion testimony permit the cross-examiner to test the basis of the witness's opinion.

There are additional reasons why probing the basis of the testimony of a character witness does not, on balance, treat the accused unfairly. The accused alone determines whether to make an issue of his character. If he decides to offer character evidence, he has a comparatively free choice in the selection of persons who will act as his reputation (or opinion) witnesses. These advantages, it seems, justify the current practice of allowing the cross-examiner to probe specific rumors or events that bear upon the direct testimony of a character witness.

§ 40. Character Evidence Pertaining to a Victim or Other Non-Party

In some circumstances, the character of one who is not a party is circumstantially relevant to an issue involving conduct.

---

43. The prejudicial dangers are equally great with the "did you know" questions permissible in jurisdictions that allow opinion evidence to establish character.

Because the circumstantial use of character usually is disallowed in civil cases,[44] the issue of the admissibility of evidence of a non-party's character most frequently arises in a criminal setting. Usually the issue is whether either the accused or the prosecution can introduce evidence of the victim's character. A typical setting is a trial for murder in which an accused claims self-defense, alleging that the victim was the first aggressor. May the defendant introduce evidence that the victim was a person of violence and aggression? A similar issue arises in a prosecution for rape in which an accused claims the defense of consent and offers to support it with evidence of the victim's trait of unchastity or for sexual promiscuity.[45]

There is general recognition that the *accused* may introduce evidence of a victim's character when the defense asserted makes it relevant.[46] In many jurisdictions the manner of proof is limited to evidence of reputation.[47] Of course, when the accused presents testimony of the victim's character trait(s), the prosecutor may cross-examine the reputation or (where allowed) the opinion witness and may present reputation (or opinion) witnesses of his own.[48]

A difficult question arises when the accused does not offer one or more character witnesses to establish the victim's character, but through the pleadings and the evidence, the accused makes an issue of the victim's conduct and, by inference, of the latter's character. This indirect attack on character occurs most fre-

---

44. See supra § 37.

45. See Morgan at 181.

46. Fed.R.Evid. 404(a)(2); I Wigmore, §§ 62–63, at 464–72; McCormick, § 193, at 461 (discussing homicide cases where self-defense is asserted); Morgan, at 181 (noting that in rape cases where consent is the defense, the right to introduce evidence of the victim's character is extended to the prosecution); S. Saltzburg & K. Redden, Federal Rules of Evidence Manual 130 (2d ed. 1977) (observing that some states exhibit a tendency to exclude character evidence of the victim in rape cases).

47. See McCormick, § 193, at 461 (homicide cases); I Wigmore, § 62, at 467 (rape cases). Fed.R.Evid. 404(a)(2) and 405(a) permit reputation and opinion evidence to show a victim's character.

48. McCormick, § 193, at 461 (homicide cases); Morgan at 181 (rape cases).

quently in a trial for violent homicide when the accused pleads self-defense and offers evidence that the victim was the first aggressor. A number of courts and the Federal Rules hold that in prosecutions for homicide, a plea of self-defense coupled with evidence that the deceased was the first aggressor is sufficient to trigger the prosecutor's right to offer rebuttal evidence that the victim was a person of peaceful character.[49] This position recognizes that in cases of physical violence evidence of character has sufficient probative value to warrant admission; the special need for the evidence, occasioned by the unavailability of the victim, strengthens the case for admissibility. Furthermore, the risk of unfair prejudice to the accused is reduced in such instances because the evidence is directed to the victim's character, not to that of the defendant. In this circumstance, the trier is likely to use the evidence for its intended purpose: determining who was the first aggressor. Some risk does exist, however, that the character evidence may arouse sympathy for a praiseworthy victim and provoke in the trier vengeful feelings against the accused. This possible prejudice may be largely avoided by the trial judge strictly limiting character evidence to a showing of no more than the victim's nonviolent nature.

Many courts have rejected the arguments above, and have limited rebuttal evidence of a victim's peaceful nature to those cases in which the accused *directly attacks* the victim's character through the use of reputation (or opinion) witnesses.[50] McCormick notes that this approach not only avoids the danger of the sympathetic trier and praiseworthy victim, but that it also has an "attractive consonance" with the general principle that the criminal defendant has the exclusive privilege to put his own character in issue.[51]

When the accused makes an issue of the victim's character through a direct attack, there is a diversity of opinion as to whether he has thereby placed his own character in issue.

---

49. Fed.R.Evid. 404(a)(2); McCormick, § 193, at 462; Waltz, Criminal Evidence 55 (1975).

50. I Wigmore, § 63, at 471–72.

51. McCormick, § 193, at 461. For discussion of the accused's privilege as to making his own character an issue in a criminal case, see supra § 38.

Some courts emphasize that it is difficult for the trier to evaluate evidence bearing upon initial aggression when the character evidence is limited to the victim—only one of the two participants in the occurrence.[52]   While it is true that if the victim is a truculent person, he is more apt to have been the first aggressor than would a person of nonviolence, it is also true that if the accused is likewise aggressive, the character trait of the victim may be entitled to little or no probative weight.   Thus, the argument runs, in order to make a rational judgment based upon character, the trier needs to know the propensities of both defendant and victim: a direct attack by the accused upon the victim's character should permit counterbalancing evidence of the accused's character.[53]   It should be stressed, however, that even if this argument is accepted the accused does not open the door to a *general* attack upon his character; rather, he triggers the prosecutor's right to show that he has the same character trait as that which he imputes to the victim.

Another line of cases,[54] endorsed in the Federal Rules of Evidence,[55] holds that unless the accused first offers evidence of *his* character, the government is forbidden from doing so. These jurisdictions take a protective attitude toward the accused, emphasizing the fear of prejudice that, in part at least, underlies the accused's basic right to keep his character out of the proceeding.[56]   This right should not be forfeited, the argument goes, simply because the accused bases his defense on the character of another person.   Viewed from the standpoint of an accurate reconstruction of the facts, this latter position is difficult to defend; obviously, if the trier is made aware only of the victim's character, there is a greater chance that it may draw erroneous inferences.   On the other hand, if there is a risk of undue prejudice against the accused resulting from evidence of

---

52. E. g., State v. Robinson, 344 Mo. 1094, 130 S.W.2d 530 (1939); State v. Padula, 106 Conn. 454, 459, 138 A. 456, 458 (1927). See also Comment, 99 U.Pa.L.Rev. 105 (1950).

53. Supra note 52; I Wigmore, § 63, at 472.

54. E. g., Roberson v. State, 91 Okl. Cr. 217, 218 P.2d 414 (1950); Stearns v. State, 266 Ala. 295, 96 So.2d 306 (1957). *See* Comment, 99 U.Pa.L.Rev. 105 (1950).

55. Fed.R.Evid. 404(a)(1).

56. See supra § 38.

his violent character, it seems unfair to attach the price of prejudice to his decision to reveal the victim's truculent character.

§ 41. Reputation, Incidents, and Threats as Bearing Upon the Defendant's State of Mind

A criminal defendant who pleads self-defense raises the issue whether in light of all of the circumstances he acted reasonably in defending himself against the victim. Likewise, in a civil suit for assault and battery, a defendant who asserts self-defense poses the question of the reasonableness of his conduct. In either instance, the issue of whether the defendant's conduct was reasonable is normally one for jury resolution. The required determination involves an assessment of the defendant's actions in view of both the victim's conduct *and* the defendant's realistic apprehension of harm. This latter aspect of the determination requires an inquiry into the reasons why the defendant may have feared the victim. Hence, evidence of the victim's reputation, his threats against the accused, or instances of violent conduct, *if known to the defendant*,[57] is admissible on the issue of the defendant's state of mind. The purpose of the evidence is to demonstrate that the victim's reputation or activity made the defendant apprehensive or fearful, thus justifying his self-protective measures.[58] The evidentiary use just described requires, of course, a showing that the defendant had knowledge of the victim's reputation for violence, threats, or aggressive conduct. To this general requirement an exception should be noted: evidence of a *threat* directed at the defendant, but disclosed only to a third person, should also be admitted.[59] Admissibility in this latter instance, however, can not rest upon relevancy that is derived from the probable effect of the threat upon the defendant's state of mind. The basis upon which the evidence is received is

---

57. II Wigmore, § 247, at 54, 60.

58. McCormick, § 295, at 700. Sometimes the *accused's* reputation if known to the victim is relevant. See Carbo v. United States, 314 F. 2d 718, 740–41 (9th Cir. 1963) (extortion accomplished by using underworld figure whose reputation for violence was known to victims).

59. I Wigmore, § 110, at 546–47; McCormick, § 295, at 700–01.

that the threat makes it more likely that the victim was the aggressor.[60]

§ 42. Evidence of Habit

The line between character and habit is not always easy to discern, but the division can mark the difference between exclusion and admissibility. Character evidence, as we have seen, is usually rejected in civil cases, except in those instances where character forms an essential element of the claim or defense.[61] Even in criminal cases the circumstantial use of character is not generally favored, and character evidence is admitted only in carefully prescribed circumstances.[62] On the other hand, evidence of habit, used circumstantially to prove particular conduct, generally is admissible.[63] The jurisdictions differ, however, in their degree of receptivity. In some courts, evidence of habit is admissible only if there is no eyewitness to the conduct in question.[64]

Character may be thought of as a trait or disposition which can manifest itself in a variety of activities. Thus viewed, character is more general than habit; the latter is a particular activity, routine, or response that is frequently repeated over a protracted period of time. A person with a character trait for

---

60. For discussion of the admissibility of evidence of the victim's *character*, even when unknown to the defendant at the time of the incident in question, see supra § 40.

61. See supra §§ 34–35.

62. In most jurisdictions, the accused alone determines if his character or that of the victim will be used circumstantially. See supra §§ 38–40.

63. Morgan at 185.

64. McCormick, § 195, at 463. This view is difficult to defend because its premise is the superior reliability of eyewitness testimony—a proposition which is highly dubious. A very good summary of the weaknesses of testimonial proof, which collects many authorities, appears in Maguire et al. at 52. Even if testimonial proof were considered reliable, should evidence of habit be rejected? It seems that this added evidence still should be presented for the trier's evaluation. The case for habit evidence especially is strong when the eyewitness is one of the parties (or identified with one of the parties) and evidence of habit is offered by the adversary.

punctuality and orderliness may have a habit of picking up and sorting his mail each day at noon.

The probative value of habit is considered greater than that of character. When evidence of habit is introduced, the desired inference from habit to the conduct in question is grounded upon a series of specific, repetitious actions. The trier is asked to infer that on the occasion in question the actor conformed to habitual practice or procedure. When evidence of character is considered, the desired inference is grounded upon a trait, tendency, or disposition which may be displayed in somewhat varied circumstances. A general tendency to drive carefully could be displayed in a variety of driving activities.[65] Thus, evidence that a person generally exercises care in driving is usually classified as evidence of character and rejected. Conversely, evidence that each workday a person traversed a particular railroad track and always stopped before crossing is generally classified as habit.[66] The character-habit line becomes blurred when the evidence offered is that the actor always stopped at railroad crossings, but surely this is an area where the judge's discretion should be sustained.[67]

The business environment, which is characterized by standardized procedures and routines, offers many opportunities to develop evidence of habit. Frequently, courts refer to habit within a business organization as "custom," but this difference in label does not alter the requirement of a repeated response to a particular circumstance. Some courts have required that the admissibility of evidence of custom be dependent upon corroborating evidence that the custom was followed on the particular occasion in question.[68] This is an inadvisable limitation which loses sight of the rationale of evidence showing a habit or custom: the theory is that a pattern of continuous activity increases the

65. McCormick, § 195, at 462.

66. See, e. g., Missouri Pacific Ry. v. Moffatt, 60 Kan. 113, 55 P. 837 (1899). Cf., Glatt v. Feist, 156 N. W.2d 819 (N.D.1968). See McCormick, § 195, at 462.

67. See generally I Wigmore, § 97, at 530–32; McCormick, § 195, at 462–63.

68. Slough, Relevancy Unraveled, 5 Kan.L.Rev. 404, 444–450 (1956).

likelihood that the custom was followed on the particular occasion.

The modern approach to the admissibility of habit and custom is expressed in the following provision of the Federal Rules of Evidence:

> Evidence of the habit of a person or of the routine practice of an organization, whether corroborated or not and regardless of the presence of eyewitnesses, is relevant to prove that the conduct of the person or organization on a particular occasion was in conformity with the habit or routine practice.[69]

Note that the Federal Rule expressly rejects the eyewitness requirement [70] and leaves open the question of what kind of evidence is admissible to prove habit or custom.[71] The usual method of proof is by the testimony of a witness who has observed the habit or custom over a sufficient period to state that it is a routine, repeated practice. Sometimes, however, the proponent must resort to proof of a number of specific instances which, taken together, demonstrate the required regularity. This manner of proof is generally accepted, although dissimilarities between the instances or the apparent lack of a sufficient number to establish a routine may result in the judge's discretionary rejection.[72] The Federal Rule also rejects the requirement, imposed by some courts, that business custom be corroborated as a condition

---

69. Fed.R.Evid. 406. In a recent criminal case the trial judge was reversed for excluding evidence of business custom. United States v. Callahan, 551 F.2d 733 (6th Cir. 1977).

70. See supra n. 64 and accompanying text.

71. The House Committee on the Judiciary deleted a provision that would have authorized the proof of habit by opinion evidence and evidence of specific instances of conduct. This deletion was made to allow the courts to deal with this issue on a case-by-case basis. The Committee noted that it did not intend to sanction a general authorization for the use of opinion evidence to show habit. H.Rep. 93–650, 93d Cong., 2d Sess. reprinted in 1974 U.S. Code Cong. & Admin. News 7075, 7079. In any event, it would appear that an opinion whether a habit was followed on the occasion in question would not be appropriate unless there was evidence of repetitious conduct.

72. See McCormick, § 195, at 465.

precedent to its admission. Corroboration is viewed correctly as relating to the sufficiency of evidence rather than to its admissibility.[73]

§ 43. Other Criminal Acts: In General

Neither the prosecutor nor the civil plaintiff initially can use reputation or opinion evidence to show that the accused or defendant has a bad or criminal character consistent with the crime or conduct charged.[74] We already have observed that in most jurisdictions character evidence offered to support the circumstantial use of character is confined to criminal cases and its introduction is the exclusive right of the accused. The government may not elicit character evidence except in rebuttal.[75] From this, it follows that the government cannot prove one or more past criminal acts in an effort to support the inference that the accused has a bad or criminal disposition.[76] Permitting this line of proof would be inconsistent with the general principle that disallows character evidence when offered for circumstantial use against the accused. Furthermore, the use of evidence of specific acts to establish bad character runs afoul of the accepted rule disallowing this form of evidence to establish a character trait. In short, the forbidden line of proof invokes with full force the considerations of distraction, confusion of the issues, time consumption and, especially, prejudice.

A different issue is raised, however, when the prosecutor seeks to introduce evidence of other criminal acts, not to show the accused's character or his criminal propensity, but rather to

---

73. Adv.Comm.Note to Fed.R.Evid. 406.

74. In criminal trials, the accused has the exclusive privilege of initially using evidence to support the circumstantial use of his character. See supra § 38. In civil trials, a minority of courts permit a civil party charged with conduct of a quasi-criminal nature to introduce evidence supporting the circumstan-tial use of character. See supra § 37.

75. See supra, § 38.

76. This section, and the one following, refer to past criminal and immoral acts of an accused whether he was criminally convicted for the acts or not. The effect of an acquittal on the admissibility of the evidence is discussed, infra nn. 80–81 and accompanying text.

establish circumstantially an element of the crime charged.[77] When evidence of other crimes is so used, the factfinder is asked to engage in the following inferential reasoning: from a finding that the defendant has committed other criminal acts, the trier draws inferences about the accused's conduct or state of mind in connection with the offense for which he is now on trial. If, for example, the factfinder knows that a defendant now charged with embezzlement has committed criminal fraud on another occasion, it might disbelieve his defense of innocent mistake and conclude that he acted purposefully. To illustrate further: a showing that a defendant, who is being tried for the murder of a drug addict, previously killed another addict with a similar weapon and under the same distinctive circumstances may serve to identify him as the slayer. Here, evidence of another crime is circumstantially relevant to the accused's conduct.

In each of these hypotheticals, the evidence of other crimes reveals something more than the accused's defective character or general criminal disposition: it provides the basis for inferences concerning a specific element (either mental state or conduct) of the crime in question. In general, evidence of collateral crimes is admissible if its purpose is not to show criminal disposition, but rather to prove immediately or ultimately one or more elements of the crime charged. The first task of the proponent is to convince the judge that the probative force of the proffered other-crimes evidence is directed toward a specific proposition that is either an element of the offense charged (such as intent) or else, if the proposition is more remote (as, for example, motive), its establishment provides a basis for inferring the existence of an element of the crime charged. Even when such a proposition is properly identified, the probative force of the other-crimes evidence must, as in the case of all evidence, be shown to outweigh the practical reasons for exclusion:

---

77. Although generally confined to criminal trials, evidence of other crimes may be relevant and admis- sible in certain civil cases, such as in a suit for a fraudulent act. See infra § 47.

time consumption, confusion, distraction, surprise, and, particularly, prejudice.[78]

§ 44. Other Criminal Acts: Degree of Certainty With Which Collateral Crime Must be Shown

A preliminary issue sometimes arising in connection with an offer of other-crimes evidence is the question: by what degree of certainty must the commission of the collateral crime be shown? Arguably, before other-crimes evidence is admissible, the proponent should be required to show either that the accused was convicted of the collateral crime or that its existence is clear beyond a reasonable doubt. A rule imposing this standard of certainty ensures against the possibility of using evidence of a collateral crime of which the defendant was not in fact guilty. But a rule of such strictness is at odds with the basic principle that individual items of evidence need not meet a standard of proof intended to apply to the totality of evidence presented. Although the sum of all of the evidence presented in a criminal case must, in order to sustain a conviction, support belief beyond a reasonable doubt, the requirement that a reasonable-doubt standard be met for each item of evidence would make it virtually impossible to build an evidentiary record. Of course, no such general requirement exists; to the contrary, the basic test for the admission of evidence is satisfied if the evidence has a tendency to make the existence of a consequential fact more probable.[79] The telling impact of other-crimes evidence, however, coupled with its high potential for inducing prejudice, justifies some special safeguards. Accordingly, most authorities hold that the defendant's commission of the collateral crime must be shown by "substantial" evidence or, in some jurisdictions, by evidence that is "clear and convincing." [80]

---

78. Adv.Comm.Note to Fed.R.Evid. 404. Surprise is a practical reason for exclusion recognized in many states, but not included in Fed.R. Evid. 403 which specifies the counterweights to admissibility. See Ch. II, § 13.

79. Ch. II, § 10.

80. See, e. g., United States v. Brown, 548 F.2d 1194 (5th Cir. 1977); United States v. Beechum, 555 F.2d 487 (5th Cir. 1977); People v. Albertson, 23 Cal.2d 550, 145

A special difficulty arises if the accused has been tried and acquitted for the commission of the collateral crime. In a technical sense, an acquittal means only that the jury (or, possibly, the judge) decided that the evidence was insufficient to convince it beyond a reasonable doubt of the existence of each essential element of the collateral offense. This finding does not preclude a subsequent determination of criminal conduct by a lesser standard, such as one calling for substantial evidence; nor does it preclude reconsideration of one particular aspect or element of a collateral offense. Observe the possibility that evidence in the collateral trial may have been very strong regarding conduct, but comparatively weak as to a mental element (such as intent) of the collateral offense. In the present trial for a different offense, the prosecutor may seek only to introduce evidence of the accused's conduct connected with the (alleged) collateral offense. In short, the use of evidence of the other crime in the present trial should not be precluded by the *terms of the result* in the unsuccessful collateral prosecution, nor should use necessarily be foreclosed on grounds of untrustworthiness.

Notwithstanding the foregoing conclusion, there is a countervailing consideration: admission of evidence pertinent to a collateral crime for which the defendant has been acquitted does, in practical terms, cause him to defend against the same charge a second time. Even though different consequences may accompany the subsequent use of other-crimes evidence, the accused is required to again challenge and rebut evidence pertaining to an offense for which he has already won an acquittal. The force of this consideration, raising policy concerns that are related to those underlying the prohibition against double jeopardy, has caused a minority of courts to hold that other-crimes evidence cannot be used where the trial of the collateral crime resulted in an acquittal.[81]

P.2d 7 (1944); State v. Billstrom, 276 Minn. 174, 149 N.W.2d 281 (1967); State v. Hyde, 234 Mo. 200, 136 S.W. 316 (1911). Other cases are cited by McCormick, § 190, at 452 nn. 51–52. A few cases require that the collateral crime be established beyond a reasonable doubt.

See, e. g., Ernster v. State, 165 Tex.Cr.R. 422, 308 S.W.2d 33 (1957).

81. See, e. g., State v. Little, 87 Ariz. 295, 350 P.2d 756 (1960); Annot., 86 A.L.R.2d 1132, 1146–47 (1962).

Although this minority approach has immediate appeal, reflection suggests that it is unsound, at least when it operates as an absolute rule. Suppose, for example, an accused bookkeeper, prosecuted for the offense of embezzling funds from his employer, asserts the defense of innocent mistake, and, after a trial, is acquitted. Subsequently, he becomes employed by another firm, and thereafter bookkeeping discrepancies of a similar type are discovered. If the accused is again prosecuted for embezzlement and again he asserts that the bookkeeping irregularities resulted from an innocent mistake, should the prosecutor be foreclosed from presenting evidence of the earlier incident? At the least, it appears unwise to reject out-of-hand the evidence of the other crime on the sole ground that the earlier prosecution resulted in an acquittal.[82] This is especially true where the losses sustained by the two employers reveal a similar pattern. The earlier trial put the accused on notice of the potential criminal nature of his activity making it less likely that the subsequent discrepancies were the product of a benign state of mind. A similar unsound result would occur in these circumstances: an accused is prosecuted for the arsenic poisoning of A, a child in her care. The evidence shows that the arsenic was administered in small doses over a period of time and that the accused was the beneficiary of a life insurance policy on A's life. Nonetheless, the accused is acquitted. Subsequently, the accused is arrested and charged with poisoning, by similar means, B, another insured child in her custody; this trial too results in an acquittal. If later, child C is found poisoned under similar circumstances, should evidence of the prior crimes be excluded in the resulting prosecution of the same accused? At some point in successive prosecutions, the *cumulative* prior circumstances become so highly probative,[83] that

---

82. Some commentators note that cases such as those described in the text are rare, and they argue that other crimes evidence should not be admissible after an acquittal unless later developments suggest the verdict was incorrect. Lempert & Saltzburg at 214–15.

83. For cases suggesting this kind of problem, see United States v. Woods, 484 F.2d 127 (4th Cir. 1973), cert. denied 415 U.S. 979 (1974); Tucker v. State, 82 Nev. 127, 412 P.2d 970 (1966); People v. Peete, 28 Cal.2d 306, 169 P.2d 924 (1946); Lyles v. State, 215 Ga. 229, 109 S.E.2d 785 (1959); McCormick, § 190, at 450 n. 42.

evidence of the other instances should be admitted. Finally, it should be kept in mind that when evidence of a collateral crime is relevant in the trial for the present offense, the prosecutor must present his own evidence of those relevant aspects of the other crime—he can not simply rely upon a description of what witnesses in the collateral trial said.[84] This evidence may differ in probative quality from that presented in a prior prosecution for the other offense. Sometimes, the evidence in the present proceeding will be stronger. In instances when the evidence concerning the collateral crime is significantly more convincing than that which was presented in the collateral trial, there is a reduced risk of using untrustworthy evidence (pertaining to a collateral crime) to convict the accused in the present trial.[85]

These various considerations suggest that it is undesirable to bar absolutely evidence concerning a collateral offense because of an earlier acquittal. What is desirable, it will later be suggested, is a flexible policy that avoids an absolute rule, but recognizes the unfairness and general undesirability of causing an accused to respond twice to the same charge.

§ 45.   Other Criminal Acts: Application of the Governing Principle

The rule which forbids other-crimes evidence to establish criminal propensity, but admits this evidence to establish a specific consequential (material) proposition may be stated in either of two ways.[86] A positive or "inclusive" formulation of the rule is that relevant evidence of other criminal activity is admissible unless its *sole* probative value is to show a criminal propensity or disposition. A negative or "exclusive" statement of the rule holds that evidence of other criminal activity is inadmissible

---

84. It may be however, that the prosecutor can, in certain instances, introduce portions of the transcript from the collateral trial. See Ch. VII, Part G, §§ 73–74.

85. Of course, this does not lessen the policy objection of having the accused respond twice to the government's assertions concerning the collateral offense.

86. See Stone, The Rule of Exclusion of Similar Fact Evidence: America, 51 Harv.L.Rev. 988, 989 (1938).

unless the evidence has probative value to establish one or more *enumerated* propositions, such as knowledge, identity, absence of accident or mistake, intent, or motive.[87] A characteristic of the exclusive form of the rule is that it specifies these admissible purposes, not simply as an illustration, but rather as a complete list of the approved propositions to which other-crimes evidence may be directed. Under this formulation, evidence not fitting within an established category is rejected.[88]

A possible difficulty with the limited or exclusive formulation is that it lacks the breadth and flexibility to take account of the varied factual patterns in which evidence of other crimes may have probative force for a purpose other than simply showing criminal disposition. That is, the proffered evidence of other crimes may have a legitimate probative use, yet the proposition to which it is directed may not be listed among the enumerated permissible categories.[89] A system confined to limited, specified exceptions also has been criticized on the ground that judges sometimes unwittingly admit evidence offered as relevant to one of the enumerated exceptions without a careful assessment of its probative value.[90] As will be emphasized shortly, the critical inquiry in considering evidence under either statement of the rule governing other-crimes evidence is a careful assessment of the purpose, probative worth, and possible prejudice of the evidence. Thus, the inclusive statement of the rule, which may encourage more careful analysis and does permit flexibility, is to be preferred. In most cases, however, either formulation of the rule produces the same evidentiary result.[91]

---

87. See State v. Johnson, 183 N.W. 2d 194 (Iowa 1971). For additional possibilities, see McCormick, § 190, at 448–51.

88. See State v. Lyle, 125 S.C. 406, 118 S.E. 803 (1923) discussed in Stone, supra note 86, at 1006.

89. Note, Other Crimes Evidence At Trial: Of Balancing and Other Matters, 70 Yale L.J. 763, 767–69 (1961).

90. See Stone, supra note 86, at 1005–07 where this and other criticisms of the second formulation of the rule are forcefully detailed.

91. Weinstein and Berger state that the actual "decisions are not appreciably affected by the form of the rule." Weinstein & Berger, ¶ 404[08], at 42.

Whenever a proponent offers evidence of a collateral crime, it is important that both counsel and judge identify clearly the consequential fact to which the evidence is directed. A criminal offense consists of proscribed conduct accompanied by a specified state of mind. It would appear, therefore, that the outer boundaries of the relevance of other-crimes evidence is established by inquiring if evidence of another crime provides a basis from which the trier can draw inferences about either the accused's conduct or state of mind in connection with the crime charged. Although the consequential facts to which the evidence might be addressed can vary widely, certain factual categories, such as those described below, are repeatedly cited by the courts; the frequency with which these arise justifies their careful consideration.

Federal Rule of Evidence 404(b) which forbids the use of evidence of other crimes to "show that [the accused] acted in conformity therewith," nonetheless provides that this evidence "may . . . be admissible for other purposes . . . ."[92] By way of illustration, the Rule lists purposes such as "proof of motive, opportunity, intent, preparation, plan, knowledge, identity, or absence of mistake or accident."[93] From the language of the Rule and its legislative history, it is clear that the federal drafters created an open system in which a trial judge neither mechanically excludes nor routinely accepts other-crimes evidence: rather, he determines admissibility on the basis of such factors as probative value, potential prejudice and the availability of alternative forms of evidence.[94] The elaborative material below contains a sampling of the circumstances in which consequential propositions normally can be established by the introduction of other-crimes evidence.[95]

---

92. Fed.R.Evid. 404(b).

93. Id.

94. Id.; Adv.Comm. Note to Fed.R. Evid. 404(b); 2 Weinstein & Berger, ¶ 404[08], at 40–42.

95. For further examples, see Annot., 93 A.L.R.2d 1097 (1964)

(other-crimes evidence in drug prosecution); Annot., 78 A.L.R.2d 1359 (1961) (fraud prosecutions); Annot., 34 A.L.R.2d 777 (1954) (forgery prosecutions); Annot., 20 A. L.R.2d 1012 (1951) (bribery prosecutions).

(1) In the prosecution of *D* for the murder of *V*, evidence that *V* had threatened to expose *D*'s participation in a land fraud scheme would be relevant to show *motive*, i. e., the reason why *D* might have committed the criminal offense charged.[96] Existence of a motive usually supports an inference about conduct, but motive might also have probative value in establishing a mental state such as intent (purpose).[97]

(2) In the trial of *D* for a criminal assault upon *V*, *D* asserts that he was in another city on the day in question. Evidence that on the same day *D* attempted to rob a liquor store in the city where the offense against *V* occurred would be relevant to show that *D* had the *opportunity* to commit the assault.[98]

(3) In the prosecution of *D* for the theft of a rented automobile, he asserts that he intended to return the car. Evidence of the theft of other rented cars would be relevant to establish *D*'s *intent*.[99] The term "intent"

---

96. United States v. Cyphers, 553 F. 2d 1064 (7th Cir. 1977) (defendant's purchase of $1000 worth of heroin after robbery relevant to show motive for the crime); Dillon v. United States, 391 F.2d 433, 435–36 (10th Cir.), cert. denied 393 U.S. 825, 889 (1968) (accused's participation in abortion scheme supplied motive for present crime of bribery); Fuller v. State, 269 Ala. 312, 334–37, 113 So.2d 153, 172–76 (1959), cert. denied 361 U.S. 936 (1960) (accused's receipt of illegal gambling payoffs supplied motive to murder nominee for public office who pledged to eradicate gambling and other illegalities in that county); McCormick, § 190, at 450–51.

97. See McCormick, § 190, at 450–51.

98. See United States v. Stover, 565 F.2d 1010 (8th Cir. 1977); People v. Tranowski, 20 Ill.2d 11, 169 N.E.2d 347 (1960). A similar result should obtain in a case in which D is prosecuted for the theft of jewelry from a retail shop, and evidence is introduced to show that he broke into and entered the building in which various retail shops, including the shop in question, were located. In Snead v. State, 243 Ala. 23, 8 So.2d 269 (1942) evidence of prior assaults was introduced to rebut defendant's claim that his physical incapacity prevented him from committing the assault in question.

99. See United States v. Dudley, 562 F.2d 965 (5th Cir. 1977); United States v. Welborn, 322 F.2d 910 (4th Cir. 1963). See also United States v. Rocha, 553 F.2d 615 (9th Cir. 1977) (previous arrest for possession of marijuana admitted to show intent to distribute); Mar-is, generally speaking, synonymous with "purpose." Thus, since the crime of theft is usually defined so as to require a taking of goods with the purpose of depriving the owner (either permanently or for a substantial period of time), evidence of other thefts bears upon the mental element of intent.

(4) In the trial of D for exploding a bomb in a public building, evidence that a week before the bombing he stole explosive materials would be relevant to show his *preparation* for the crime charged.[1] Preparatory activity increases the likelihood that the act in question was accomplished. Preparation may also reveal the state of mind of the actor, e. g., by showing deliberation or purposefulness.

(5) In the prosecution of D for arson of building A, evidence that D had wrongfully burned building B would be relevant, if coupled with other evidence to show that D had a *plan* (scheme or design) to destroy these buildings in order to collect insurance proceeds.[2]

---

childon v. United States, 519 F.2d 337, 346–47 (8th Cir. 1975) (other drugs in defendant's possession relevant to show intent to distribute drug in question); United States v. Brettholz, 485 F.2d 483, 488 (2d Cir. 1973), cert. denied, 415 U.S. 976 (1974) (prior transactions with cocaine make it more likely that defendants intended to sell cocaine rather than purchase marijuana); State v. Wyman, 270 A.2d 460 (Me. 1972) (evidence that accused almost drove automobile into B and C while shouting "Do you want to be Number 2?" is relevant to show that accused intentionally ran into the first victim, A); State v. Darling, 197 Kan. 471, 475–81, 419 P. 2d 836, 840–42 (1966) (that defendant intended to cause an abortion by use of certain therapy is shown by evidence that on other occasions he used the same medical procedures to produce abortion); People v. Shea, 147 N.Y. 78, 98–101, 41 N. E. 505, 511–12 (1894) (evidence of election fraud in connection with which accused armed himself and went to polls is relevant to show purposeful killing as opposed to a homicide that resulted from sudden passion).

1. King v. State, 230 Ga. 581, 582, 198 S.E.2d 305, 306 (1973); II Wigmore, § 238, at 33–34 n. 1.

2. State v. McClard, 81 Or. 510, 160 P. 130 (1916) (evidence of similar fire that destroyed other insured property). See United States v. Krohn, 560 F.2d 293 (7th Cir. 1977) (scheme to use forged checks) Leonard v. United States, 324 F.2d

If the crime charged is shown to be part of a plan, inferences can be drawn concerning conduct or, perhaps, state of mind. In its pristine form, this exception entails the evidentiary use of acts separate from the crime charged in order to infer the existence of a plan or scheme.[3] An inference is then drawn that the act charged is part of the larger scheme.[4] From this conclusion, further inferences can be made about the actor's conduct or intent (or other mental state) in connection with the offense charged. However, courts have occasionally admitted evidence of similar criminal acts under the rubric of plan, scheme, or design, in circumstances that render it doubtful whether a general or comprehensive plan existed.[5]

(6) In the trial of *D* for receiving stolen property from *A*, evidence that on other occasions and under similar circumstances *A* had supplied *D* with goods known by *D* to have been stolen is relevant to show that *D* had *knowledge* that the goods in question were

---

911 (9th Cir. 1963) (scheme to forge and pass treasury checks); McWhorter v. Commonwealth, 191 Va. 857, 870–71, 63 S.E.2d 20, 26–27 (1951) (plan to persuade workers to quit their jobs; evidence of insults to worker admitted); II Wigmore, § 304, at 202–3.

3. See State v. Marquez, 222 Kan. 441, 447–448, 565 P.2d 245, 251 (1977); II Wigmore, § 304, at 202–04. But the plan may be conceived during or shortly after the commission of the collateral crime, as where *D* robs *A* and in so doing learns the location of *B* who possesses certain funds. *D* then seeks out and robs *B*. State v. Toshishige Yoshimo, 45 Haw. 206, 364 P.2d 638 (1961).

4. See, e. g., United States v. Little, 562 F.2d 578 (8th Cir. 1977). For a case in which the government failed to provide sufficient evidence of a comprehensive scheme, see State v. Little, 87 Ariz. 295, 303–04, 350 P.2d 756, 761 (1960) (effect of prior acquittal also considered by court).

5. See, e. g., Perry v. People, 116 Colo. 440, 181 P.2d 439 (1947); Griffin v. State, 124 So.2d 38 (Fla. Ct.App.1960); Payne, Jr.: The Law Whose Life is Not Logic: Evidence of Other Crimes in Criminal Cases, 3 U.Rich.L.Rev. 62, 79–80 (1968). However, even though collateral acts may not be sufficiently integrated with the act charged to constitute an overall plan, the collateral acts nonetheless may be admissible for another purpose such as motive, intent, etc.

stolen.[6] The element of knowledge is closely related to and frequently overlaps that of intent (or purpose) since both require awareness. From an evidentiary standpoint, the difference between intent and knowledge is not critical because evidence offered to show knowledge also has probative value to show intent (or purpose). Similarly, because intent includes knowledge, evidence offered to establish intent would also have probative force on the element of knowledge. The substantive criminal law, however, will often distinguish between intent and knowledge.[7] For some crimes, knowledge, unaccompanied by any intent or purpose concerning the actor's conduct, satisfies the culpability requirement for mental state. Other crimes are defined so that intent is a prerequisite to culpability as, for example, in the case of retaining possession of lost property with the intention of depriving the owner.[8]

(7) In the prosecution of *D* for passing a forged check for $75 purportedly made payable to *D* by *A* Company, evidence that *D* passed similar false checks from *A* Company under like circumstances (e. g., buying a small item and receiving a substantial sum in change) is relevant to *identify* *D* as the actor in the offense charged.[9] Evidence of other crimes is admissible to

---

6. Peters v. United States, 376 F.2d 839 (5th Cir. 1967) (other transactions with counterfeit bills relevant to show accused knew that bills in question were counterfeit); United States v. Allen, 303 F.2d 915 (6th Cir. 1962); People v. Rife, 382 Ill. 588, 598–99, 48 N.E.2d 367, 373 (1943) (possession and concealment of similar items that were stolen); II Wigmore, §§ 324, 326, at 227–32. But see Bullard v. United States, 395 F.2d 658 (5th Cir. 1968) (willingness to defraud insurance company through car theft not probative of knowledge that another car was stolen).

7. See Model Penal Code § 2.02, Comment (Proposed Official Draft). See also II Wigmore, § 300, at 192–93.

8. See Model Penal Code § 223.5.

9. State v. Bock, 229 Minn. 449, 39 N.W.2d 887 (1949); see Durns v. United States, 562 F.2d 542 (8th Cir. 1977) (prior attempted kidnapping using same modus operandi);

prove identity when conduct is in question (that is, when the accused denies that he participated in a criminal event, and when the modus operandi of the collateral crime(s) and the crime charged are sufficiently distinctive to be substantially probative of identity. A mere showing that D has committed other crimes in the same class as the offense charged is insufficiently probative of identity to justify admission. However, even where the principal and collateral crimes are somewhat dissimilar, it may be possible to introduce evidence that a distinctive feature or instrumentality linking the defendant to the collateral crime(s) is also involved in the crime charged. For example, it may be possible to show that a certain weapon was used in perpetrating both crimes or that an instrumentality acquired during the collateral crime (e. g., a check-writing machine) was used in the commission of the crime charged (passing forged checks).[10]

(8) In the trial of D, a bookkeeper, for embezzling the funds of A Company, evidence that D embezzled

United States v. Maestas, 546 F.2d 1177 (5th Cir. 1977) (similar use of forged checks); State v. King, 111 Kan. 140, 206 P. 883 (1922) (other buried bodies, along with accused's possession of decedent's personal effects, relevant to identify D as murderer of A, whose buried body also was discovered on D's premises and whose personal effects were in D's possession); Whiteman v. State, 119 Ohio St. 285, 164 N.E. 51 (1928) (similar offenses characterized by using uniforms to impersonate officers). But see United States v. Myers, 550 F.2d 1036 (5th Cir. 1977) (insufficient similarity between bank robbery charged and subsequent bank robbery); Drew v. United States, 331 F.2d 85, 92–94 (D.C.Cir. 1964) (two ice cream stores held up by black

with sun glasses; insufficient similarity especially since one of the offenses did not involve threat with gun).

10. United States v. Barrett, 539 F. 2d 244 (1st Cir. 1976) (extraordinary expertise in avoidance of burglar alarm activation); United States v. McMillian, 535 F.2d 1035 (8th Cir. 1976) (same gun used in principal and collateral crime); State v. Latta, 246 Or. 218, 425 P. 2d 186 (1967) (burglary trial; evidence admitted to show tool in defendant's possession was burglary tool); People v. McMonigle, 29 Cal.2d 730, 177 P.2d 745 (1947) (stolen naval T-shirt worn during commission of subsequent crime).

the funds of *B* Company by making false entries is relevant to negate a defense that the erroneous entries in *A*'s records were the result of innocent *mistake*.[11] A similar theory of admissibility would permit evidence that *D*, who defends a murder charge on the ground of *accidental* shooting, fired at the decedent on another occasion.[12]

Note that each of the foregoing examples is directed either to the defendant's conduct or to his mental state. It is true that sometimes the evidence is ostensibly directed to a more remote proposition, such as plan, opportunity, or motive, that is not an element in the crime charged; however, from such an intermediate proposition, further inferences about conduct or mental state can be drawn. Of course, there are other consequential propositions, not included in the illustrations above, which ultimately bear upon conduct or state of mind and which usually can be shown by evidence of collateral crimes.[13] For example, the destruction of evidence or attempted flight, when apparently undertaken to avoid conviction or apprehension, can give rise to an inference of guilt.[14] Courts also admit evidence of a crime

11. Crider v. Commonwealth, 206 Va. 574, 145 S.E.2d 222 (1965). See also United States v. Fairchild, 526 F.2d 185 (7th Cir. 1975), cert. denied 425 U.S. 942 (1976) (possession of counterfeit bills probative of intent and ability); United States v. Kaplan, 416 F.2d 103 (2d Cir. 1969) (possession of check issued without consideration relevant to present charge against bank teller of falsifying entry); II Wigmore, § 329, at 233–34 (where the author treats the basis of admissibility, at least in most cases, as intent).

12. Cf. State v. Cunningham, 173 Or. 25, 41–43, 144 P.2d 303, 310 (1943); II Wigmore, § 302, at 196 (where author treats the basis of admissibility as intent).

13. See, e. g., United States v. Woods, 484 F.2d 127 (4th Cir. 1973), cert. denied 415 U.S. 979 (1974) (prior episodes of cyanosis of children in defendant's care probative that criminal activity was cause of the asphyxiation of victim child); United States v. Montalvo, 271 F.2d 922, 927 (2d Cir. 1959), cert. denied 361 U.S. 961 (1960) (possession of penknife caked with heroin shows accused about to join illegal enterprise); McCormick, § 190, at 448–51.

14. McCormick, § 190, at 451; United States v. Howard, 228 F.Supp. 939, 942–43 (D.Neb.1964) (in narcotics prosecution, evidence admitted that accused had murdered principal witness against him); Mattox v. State, 243 Miss. 402, 413–16, 137

not charged when its commission is so closely related in time or circumstance to the principal crime that revelation of the collateral crime is necessary to a complete understanding of the principal offense.[15] It will be observed that the various illustrative purposes justifying other-crimes evidence overlap, so that evidence of collateral crimes often falls within more than one category.

§ 46. Other Criminal Acts: Balancing the Competing Considerations that Govern Admissibility

Commentators have generally been critical of the judicial treatment of other-crimes evidence;[16] much of this critical comment has been directed toward decisions which admit this evidence under the various labels without a careful analysis. Certainly there are examples of evidential admission which can not be reasonably justified under any theory.[17] Often, however, the courts simply have seized upon a wrong label to justify an otherwise proper ruling of admissibility.[18] This latter mistake, al-

---

So.2d 920, 922–24 (1962) (attempt to arrange murder of witness). Maguire et al. cites these and other cases at 898–99.

15. Carter v. United States, 549 F.2d 77 (8th Cir. 1977); United States v. Roberts, 548 F.2d 665 (6th Cir. 1977); Howard v. State, 346 So.2d 918 (Miss.1977); State v. Villavicencio, 95 Ariz. 199, 388 P.2d 245 (1964); Weinstein & Berger, ¶ 404[08], at 404–45.

16. E. g., Payne, Jr., The Law Whose Life is Not Logic: Evidence of Other Crimes in Criminal Cases, 3 U.Rich.L.Rev. 62, 68–69, 85–87 (1968); Slough & Knightly, Other Vices, Other Crimes, 41 Iowa L. Rev. 325, 349–50 (1956).

17. E. g., Nunez v. United States, 370 F.2d 538 (5th Cir. 1967) (per

curiam) (discussed in Weinstein & Berger, ¶ 404[09], at 59); Commonwealth v. Kline, 361 Pa. 434, 65 A. 2d 348 (1949). But see Commonwealth v. Boulden, 179 Pa.Super. 328, 345–47, 116 A.2d 867, 875–76 (1955) (refusal to extend *Kline* decision). For a recent case where the basis of admissibility is left in doubt, see United States v. Davis, 551 F.2d 233 (8th Cir. 1977).

18. See, e. g., Carter v. United States, 549 F.2d 77 (8th Cir. 1977) ("res gestae"); Canty v. State, 244 Ala. 108, 11 So.2d 844, cert. denied 319 U.S. 746 (1943) ("res gestae"). In Williams v. State, 110 So.2d 654 (Fla.1959), a rape case, the court cites plan and identity as justifying evidence of a similar occurrence; yet the accused's defense was consent. Yet the collateral crime did have probative force to

though regrettable because it muddles judicial analysis and adds to a body of divergent and confusing precedents, is harmless error for the case at hand.

Neither the commentators, nor the courts, have been completely successful in articulating an ideal formula for determining when evidence of collateral crimes should be admitted. All authorities agree that any rule governing the admission of other-crimes evidence must require a probative value greater than simply a showing of bad disposition or criminal proclivity. There is general agreement, also, that the judge should exclude any evidence, the probative value of which is outweighed by the danger of prejudice (or some other adverse practical consequence).[19] But these are general propositions, abstractly stated. Disagreement erupts in their application to specific facts. Because of the great potential for prejudicial consequences inherent in other-crimes evidence, a judge often encounters difficult problems of analysis and balancing. His determination can involve a number of variables, and it is important that he identify these and assess each with care.

If there has been a trial on the collateral crime and an acquittal resulted, this fact should be considered an important, though not necessarily determinative, element in the balancing process.[20] As noted earlier, if evidence of the other offense is used to show that the accused was on notice of the potential criminal nature of his conduct (and hence an innocent state of mind with regard to the present crime is unlikely), the fact of acquittal should not usually dictate exclusion.[21] Also, prior acquittals involving offenses with characteristics similar to those in the

---

negate the likelihood of consensual conduct.

19. Fed.R.Evid. 403; Adv.Comm. Note to Fed.R.Evid. 404(b); Weinstein & Berger, ¶ 404[10], at 66; McCormick, § 190, at 453: "[S]ome of the wiser opinions (especially recent ones) recognize that the problem is not merely one of pigeonholing, but one of balancing. . . ." See United States v.

Hearst, 563 F.2d 1331 (9th Cir., 1977).

20. See People v. Griffin, 66 Cal.2d 459, 426 P.2d 507 (1967); Weinstein & Berger, ¶ 404[09], at 46–48; Annot., 86 A.L.R.2d 1132 (1962).

21. State v. Darling, 197 Kan. 471, 478–81, 419 P.2d 836, 842–44 (1966). See supra § 44.

present crime may be admissible if the cumulative probative impact of the several offenses, considered together, justifies the costs of prejudice, distraction, or time consumption that may be involved in receiving evidence of the collateral offenses.[22] Other situations will arise in which admissibility is justifed, despite an earlier acquittal.

Of course, other-crimes evidence must meet the basic requirements of relevance. In making the relevance determination, it is always important to identify precisely the proposition to which such evidence is directed and to evaluate carefully its probative force. Other important factors include: (1) whether the accused contests the proposition for which the evidence is offered; and (2) whether other evidence, with less potential for prejudice, appears sufficient to establish the proposition.[23] It is sometimes easier to assess these variables after much of the evidence is in, the strength of the government's case against the accused is known, and the issues have been clarified. The judge should not hesitate to exercise his full control over the order of proof and, in appropriate cases, to postpone his decision regarding other-crimes evidence until the end of the government's case in chief, or even until after the accused has presented his evidence in defense.[24]

The opinion in United States v. Byrd,[25] authored by Judge Friendly, is illustrative of the kind of assessment and careful balancing that is necessary when considering the admissibility of collateral-crimes evidence. This case involved the prosecution

---

22. See supra § 44. Cf. People v. Fox, 126 Cal.App.2d 560, 569, 272 P.2d 832, 838 (1954) (evidence that accused gave same explanation for a previously dismissed charge as he gave in connection with present crime is admissible).

23. McCormick, § 190, at 452–53.

24. Weinstein & Berger, ¶ 404[10], at 70; McCormick, § 190, at 452. In United States v. Juarez, 561 F. 2d 65 (7th Cir. 1977), the court refused to find error in the trial judge's admission, during the government's case-in-chief, of evidence of a prior sale of heroin. Finding the evidence relevant to intent, the Court of Appeals ruled that since the accused could have contested intent, the prosecutor was not obligated to postpone the other-crimes evidence.

25. 352 F.2d 570 (2d Cir. 1965).

and conviction of an IRS employee for receipt of illegal fees in connection with his auditing of returns. The trial judge gave an erroneous instruction which, on appeal, resulted in a reversal. However, in the course of the appellate disposition, the court considered certain evidentiary points that were expected to arise again on retrial:

> One of these points concerns the admission by the trial court of evidence of Byrd's activities [receipt of payment] in connection with the auditing of the Sandberg tax return. The Government offered it as a part of its main case for the purpose of showing criminal intent. A vigorous objection was made by the defense but the court admitted it. The admissibility of this kind of evidence is "a matter in which the trial judge should be allowed a wide range of discretion." United States v. Feldman, 136 F.2d 394, 399 (2d Cir. [1943]). The exercise of discretion must be addressed to a balancing of the probative value of the proffered evidence, on the one hand, against its prejudicial character on the other. The probative value is measured by the extent to which the evidence of prior criminal activities, . . . closely related in time, and subject matter, tends to establish that the accused committed the criminal act charged in the indictment knowingly or with criminal intent or tends to negative the claim that the acts were committed innocently or through mistake or misunderstanding.
>
> It is generally recognized that there can be no complete assurance that the jury even under the best of instructions will strictly confine the use of this kind of evidence to the issue of knowledge and intent and wholly put out of their minds the implication that the accused, having committed the prior similar criminal act, probably committed the one with which he is actually charged. The court in its colloquy with defense counsel conceded that prejudice of this sort would result to Byrd in letting in the evidence.

From the quality of proof standpoint for proving knowledge and intent, its probative value was largely cumulative. The evidence came from the mouth of the same witness, Kaufman, who testified to the occurrences in the first two counts. If the jury believed his testimony as to those counts, the relating of the Sandberg incident added little, if anything, to a revelation of Byrd's state of mind. If they had disbelieved Kaufman's testimony about the first two counts, it is not very likely they would have believed his story about the Sandberg tax audit.

Another factor to be considered is whether the Government was faced with a real necessity which required it to offer the evidence in its main case. The defense had not, either in its claims or the statement of facts which it would seek to prove, "sharpened" the issue of intent by asserting that the act charged was done innocently or by accident or mistake. McCormick, Evidence, § 157 at 331 (1954). . . . Nor did the Government suffer from a lack of evidence of intent. Kaufman's testimony relating to the first two counts furnished ample evidence of knowledge and intent, of the same kind and quality as that shown by his testimony concerning the Sandberg tax return. There was therefore no pressing necessity that evidence of that prior occasion be offered on the Government's main case. . . . It is, of course, conceivable that in some cases proof of the offenses charged would contain little or nothing from which an inference of guilty intent could be drawn. In such a case a trial judge would, in the exercise of his discretion, be justified in admitting as part of the Government's case, proof of a prior similar offense to show knowledge or intent. For the present purpose of this discussion it is enough to point out that the scope of discretion does not include every offer of a prior similar offense which may contribute something to a showing of intent in the Government's main case. Where the prejudice is substantial and the probative value, through the nature of the evidence or the lack of any real necessity for it, is slight, its admission at that stage may be held to be an abuse of discretion. Under such circumstances the better practice would be to sustain the objection to the offer on the Government's main case without prejudice to its re-offer in rebuttal, if then warranted.[26]

A discriminating analysis of this kind fosters a sound result by clarifying the significant considerations in a given case. Of course, one should not expect the precedents to provide precise guidance. Invariable differences from case to case in such factors as the degree of certainty that the other offense was committed and the probable costs of admissibility in terms of prejudice and efficient trial administration may have a decisive influence upon admissibility.[27] For example, the introduction of other-crimes evidence might surprise the accused, putting his defense counsel at a disadvantage in presenting rebuttal evidence. This consideration should either lead to a continuance or count heavily against admission.[28] Furthermore, various judges view the admission of other-crimes evidence differently because of their differing assessments of its probative force in a particular case or their varying appraisals of the practical policy considerations underlying its general exclusion. Judicial disagreement is illustrated by those cases in which evidence of a collateral crime is relevant to a necessary element of the crime charged—for example, the element of intent—but that element is not directly contested by the accused, who asserts only that he did not engage in the conduct charged. In this situation, some courts

---

26. Id. at 574–75.

27. See, e. g., United States v. Johnson, 382 F.2d 280 (2d Cir. 1967) (per curiam) where the court distinguishes United States v. Byrd, 352 F.2d 570 (2d Cir. 1965). Both cases are cited (and part of the opinion in *Byrd* is quoted) in Maguire et al., at 907–08.

28. The Federal Rules prefer a continuance to avoid unfair surprise.

Adv.Comm.Note to Fed.R.Evid. 403. In a few jurisdictions there is a rule that notice, in certain circumstances, is a prerequisite to admissibility. See, e. g., State v. Spreigl, 272 Minn. 488, 139 N.W.2d 167 (1965) (charge of indecent liberties with a minor). Usually, however, a lack of notice is but a factor to be considered.

have permitted the use of other-crimes evidence to show intent,[29] while others have held that this evidence should be excluded because conduct and not intent is the element specifically contested by the defense.[30] Although the latter resolution generally is preferable, an invariable rule dictating exclusion probably is unwise. Certain proscribed conduct (such as robbery) itself may be highly suggestive of the requisite mental state, but other criminal activity (such as passing a counterfeit bill) is not so cogently probative of the actor's state of mind. Thus, even if the principal controversy at trial is the accused's conduct, the prosecutor sometimes may need to present evidence bearing upon intent to establish this element beyond a reasonable doubt. Furthermore, the collateral criminal activity may have some probative value for a specific purpose other than intent, yet if used solely for this other purpose, the propriety of admissibility may be questionable. If the evidence also bears upon intent, this additional value may strike the balance in favor of admissibility. If the accused wishes to protect himself against the proffered evidence, he can enter a stipulation on the issue of intent. The judge then will instruct a jury that intent is not an issue and that they are to return a verdict of guilty, if the other element(s) of the offense are found beyond a reasonable doubt.[31]

The courts have been especially receptive to other-crimes evidence in the prosecution of sex crimes.[32] The usual justification for a liberal policy of admission is the assumed propensity of sex offenders to repeat their illegal sexual activity, although this assumption is open to doubt.[33] Courts usually admit evidence of

---

29. See, e. g., United States v. Conley, 523 F.2d 650 (8th Cir. 1975), cert. denied 424 U.S. 920 (1976).

30. See, e. g., United States v. Byrd, 352 F.2d 570 (2d Cir. 1965); People v. Kelley, 57 Cal.Rptr. 363, 424 P.2d 947 (1967). In United States v. Coades, 549 F.2d 1303 (9th Cir. 1977) the court disapproved of evidence of another crime introduced to show intent when the defense was clearly based upon a denial

that the accused committed the act in question.

31. See Ch. I, § 5.

32. Annot., 77 A.L.R.2d 841, 846–49 (1961).

33. See Gregg, Other Acts of Sexual Misbehavior and Perversion as Evidence in Prosecutions for Sexual Offenses, 6 Ariz.L.Rev. 212, 231–35 (1965). A difficulty with the judicial assumption about the recidi-

collateral (prior and subsequent) sexual activity between the accused and the victim on the ground that it shows a propensity to practice an illegal sex act with a certain person.[34] This rule of admissibility is a special exception to the general prohibition against the use of other-crimes evidence to show criminal propensity. The distinction said to justify the exception is that between using other-crimes evidence to show a propensity for a certain crime with different victims and using it to show a propensity for particular criminal activity with a specific person.[35] The underlying assumption is that there is considerable likelihood that illegal sexual acts with the same person will be repeated. The assumption is probably valid, at least when applied to consensual sex crimes; its application to sex crimes of force, however, is questionable.[36]

Some courts have failed to apply the limitations of this special exception and, citing such reasons as intent, design, or propensity, have admitted evidence of sexual acts with third persons.[37] Usually, but not always,[38] this extended exception is applied in prosecutions for behavior considered uncommon or perverted, such as sexual acts practiced upon children.[39] Thus, in some prosecutions, evidence of other instances of generally similar conduct is admissible as bearing upon the accused's propensity

---

vism of sex offenders is that all such offenders are viewed as repeaters; there is evidence suggesting that the rate of recidivism as to most classes of sex offenses is low. Id. at 233.

34. See McCormick, § 190, at 449 n. 38.

35. Lempert & Saltzburg at 220–221.

36. Id. at 221.

37. Bracey v. United States, 142 F. 2d 85, 88 (D.C.Cir. 1944) (dictum); Lamar v. State, 245 Ind. 104, 195 N.E.2d 98 (1964).

38. State v. Finley, 85 Ariz. 327, 338 P.2d 790 (1959) (rape of another woman under somewhat similar circumstances, five days before). Rhine v. State, 336 P.2d 913, 920–23 (Okla.Crim.App.1958) (evidence that accused doctor drugged other patients and then had intercourse). In each of these cases, the court justified admission on the basis of a plan or scheme. Query whether there was a broad plan embracing all of the sexual acts?

39. See, e. g., State v. Spreigl, 272 Minn. 488, 139 N.W.2d 167 (1965) (sexual offense against young stepdaughter); State v. Schlak, 253 Iowa 113, 111 N.W.2d 289 (1961) (lewd act upon child); McCormick, § 190, at 449–50.

to commit a certain kind of sexual offense. This broadened receptivity also departs from the rule prohibiting evidence of other similar offenses to show only a proclivity to commit the crime charged.[40] The principle of extended admissibility in prosecutions for sex offenses has met resistance from some commentators who assert that, at least in cases allowing acts with third persons to be shown, the general prohibition against other-crimes evidence has been abandoned without adequate justification.[41]

§ 47. Similar Incidents in Civil Cases

Most jurisdictions reject the circumstantial use of character evidence in civil cases. Hence, evidence that a party acted negligently on prior occasions will not be received to show circumstantially that he was negligent at the time of the principal event. Reception of this evidence would not only violate the general rule forbidding the circumstantial use of character, but it would also contravene the rule that even where character can be shown, it may not be shown by evidence of specific instances. Of course, evidence indicating a habit—a long-term, consistent response to a particular situation—will be received for the inference that the consistent practice was followed on the occasion in question. Finally, as we saw in the preceding sections, in criminal trials the law raises a general prohibition against evidence of other crimes, but marks out exceptions when the evidence shows more than a criminal disposition. We now turn to some selected problems in the civil area which bear a close kinship to those discussed above.

---

40. The general prohibition normally excludes evidence of other crimes to show propensity even in instances where the collateral crimes involve the same offense as the crime charged. See People v. Lapin, 138 Cal.App.2d 251, 291 P.2d 575 (1956); People v. Kelley, 66 Cal.2d 232, 243–44, 424 P.2d 947, 957 (1967) (dictum); Morgan at 191–92.

41. For a thoughtful article on the subject of other-crimes evidence in sex cases, see Gregg, Other Acts of Sexual Misbehavior and Perversion as Evidence in Prosecutions for Sexual Offenses, 6 Ariz.L.Rev. 212 (1965). See also State v. McFarlin, 110 Ariz. 225, 517 P.2d 87 (1973) (limiting evidence of sexual acts with third persons, offered to show propensity or disposition to those cases involving abnormal sexual behavior).

Suppose that A sues B, a service station owner, alleging that B's attendant was negligent in placing a metal pipe over a walkway leading to a display rack. The plaintiff offers evidence that another person, X, tripped over the same pipe. B, on the other hand, offers evidence that in recent months many people have used the same walkway without an incident. The receipt of evidence of these collateral events may assist the trier in determining whether the walkway was hazardous and thus in resolving the issue of B's negligence (or A's contributory negligence). The probative force of these proffered items depends largely upon the coincidence of conditions that surround the earlier events and the event in question. Variables such as lighting, the condition of the walkway, and the attentiveness of X and the other pedestrians affect the strength of the inferences about the condition of the walkway at the time of A's fall. These factors may be difficult to prove, and the introduction of the evidence pertaining to the variables may be time-consuming. Similarity is particularly hard to demonstrate when one wishes to compare the conditions surrounding an event (A's fall) and one or more "non-events" (safe passage by the pedestrians who did not fall).

In most cases, these combined considerations persuade courts to reject evidence of similar incidents offered for the ultimate purpose of demonstrating negligence or a lack thereof.[42] The cost in terms of time, distraction and, possibly, prejudice is usually assessed as the prevailing factor. Although there are general statements in many cases that purport to forbid evidence of collateral accidents, differences from case to case in probative force and in the practical burdens that accompany admission have caused most appellate courts to repose in the trial judge a discretion to receive this type of evidence.

It is important to observe that, even when received, evidence of other accidents alone does not establish that the defendant was negligent. It may, however, establish that the surrounding conditions were dangerous or, if the other accidents were known to the defendant, that the defendant had notice that a possibly

---

42. Robitaille v. Netoco Community Theatres, 305 Mass. 265, 25 N.E.2d 749, 128 A.L.R. 592 (1940); Diamond Rubber Co. v. Harryman, 41 Colo. 415, 92 P. 922 (1907); Annot., 70 A.L.R.2d 167 (1960).

dangerous condition existed. When the evidence is offered to establish a hazardous condition, the desired inferences are (1) that the dangerous condition caused the other accident(s); (2) that the dangerous condition then existing also existed at the time of the plaintiff's injury; and (3) that this condition caused the plaintiff's injury. The ultimate question in a negligence suit, however, is whether the defendant acted unreasonably; proof of a dangerous condition alone is not usually dispositive of this question. Of course, this proof can be an important link in the process of establishing negligence, and its utility is seldom overlooked by claimants.

A careful proponent, seeking to persuade a trial or appellate court that "other-accident" evidence is admissible, should be prepared to state exactly why the evidence is relevant and why the probative force of evidence is sufficient to justify an exception to the usual prohibition. Note that not only is similarity of condition between the other accidents and the litigated event a critical point, but the number of other accidents can also be highly significant. It may be unreasonable to infer from a single prior accident that the condition alleged was in fact the cause. But two or more prior accidents at the same location, under substantially similar conditions, buttress the inference that the faulty condition existed and was the causal factor.

The importance of repetition and similarity varies depending on the proposition to which the evidence of collateral events is directed. Where prior accidents are used to show that the defendant was on notice that a possibly dangerous condition existed, even one accident known to the defendant has considerable probative force. Furthermore, where notice is the object of the proof, it is unnecessary to show that the other accident occurred under precisely the same condition as that involving the plaintiff; [43] it suffices that a dangerous condition, allegedly the cause of the present injury, was known or should have been known to the defendant because it was associated with a prior accident. This analysis again underscores the importance of carefully assessing and clearly stating probative value.

---

43. McCormick, § 200, at 475.

Considerable difficulty is encountered when a defendant wishes to show a lack of previous accidents for the inference that a dangerous condition did not exist. Although situations obviously vary, it generally holds true that evidence of an absence of other accidents is not so persuasive in demonstrating a safe condition as is evidence of prior accidents in demonstrating an unsafe condition. This is particularly true where the condition in question is subject to change. Someone, after all, must be the first to be harmed by an evolving hazardous condition. There are circumstances, however, notably those involving fixed or stable conditions and safe use or passage by a considerable number of persons, where probative force justifies admission. McCormick, with some judicial support, argues that the trial judge should be vested with discretion to admit evidence of a lack of prior accidents.[44] Furthermore, such evidence should be admissible to rebut the inference of a hazardous condition in cases where the judge has admitted evidence of prior accidents.

Other situations exist in which the probative value of a similar incident is high. In one case, for example, a plaintiff alleged that her skin was damaged by the defendant-manufacturer's cosmetic. One of the defenses was that any skin damage resulted from a source or cause other than the defendant's product. The plaintiff offered to show that X and Y, both users of defendant's preparation, sustained skin damage similar to that which she suffered. The court correctly admitted the evidence for the purpose of showing what had caused the skin condition.[45] A like result is usually appropriate where the sale price of property similar to the property in question is offered as relevant to value.[46]

Although more commonly encountered in criminal trials, other-crimes evidence—which discloses a similar event—has a paral-

---

44. McCormick, § 200, at 476–77.

45. Carter v. Yardley & Co., 319 Mass. 92, 64 N.E.2d 693 (1946); Annot., 42 A.L.R.3d 780 (1972). Cf. Hopkins v. Baker, 553 F.2d 1339 (D.C.Cir. 1977) (other persons use of railroad yard relevant on issue whether plaintiff's presence was foreseeable).

46. See McCormick, § 199, at 471–73 where a good discussion is accompanied by ample citations to authorities.

lel role in the context of certain civil trials,[47] notably those involving a claim based upon deceitful conduct. For example, when a
plaintiff seeks redress for an act of fraud or misrepresentation,
there are possibilities for introducing other, substantially identical acts to show a plan or scheme of which the present act is a
part; such evidence then can be used to prove conduct or identity
on the occasion in question.[48] Other fraudulent acts (bearing at
least some similarity to the act in question) may also have substantial probative force to prove mental state, such as knowledge
or intent.[49]

§ 48. Public Policy Considerations in Circumstantial Proof: Subsequent Remedial Action and Offers to Compromise or Plead Guilty

Public or social policy considerations frequently mold rules of
evidentiary exculsion as, for example, in instances where evidence of a privileged communication is rejected. A rule of evidence thought to promote socially desirable ends is that which excludes evidence of subsequent (post-accident) repairs or remedial measures in negligence cases. For example, in a suit for liability arising out of a defective walkway, evidence that the defendant repaired the condition after the accident is not admissible to show a prior defective condition. The same exclusionary
principle applies when the defendant institutes new safety regu-
lations or practices following an accident or injury. In both of
these instances the proponent of the evidence is attempting to
raise the inference that remedial steps were taken because the
actor thought the prior condition was hazardous or harmful;
therefore (the further inference goes), a dangerous or harmful
condition in fact existed.

An issue of relevance is, of course, raised by this inferential
chain. An after-the-incident precautionary measure may reflect
merely the exercise of extraordinary caution to avoid any possibility of future injuries, and may not indicate the actor's belief

---

47. For a broader discussion of other-crimes evidence, see supra §§ 43–
46.

48. McCormick, § 197, at 468–69.

49. Id., § 197, at 468.

that the condition in question was really hazardous. This hypothesis is sometimes cited as a reason for excluding post-injury measures.[50] It appears, however, that in many instances evidence of post-injury remedial steps increases the likelihood that the actor thought the prior condition or practice was unsafe. Thus, the traditional justification for refusing to admit evidence of repairs or other precautionary measures is that if this evidence could be used to establish a dangerous condition or practice, the person potentially liable would be reluctant to take corrective action. Since the law of evidence should foster the desirable policy objective of encouraging remedial action, it should reject evidence of post-injury protective measures offered for adverse use against the party charged with fault. Whether this rule of exclusion actually affects one's willingness to undertake remedial steps is problematic and the assumption that it does has been seriously questioned.[51] Arguably, even if the evidence of remedial measures were admissible, the actor would still make the necessary repairs or take other corrective action. Failure to do so poses for him the risk that another person would injure himself; furthermore, the case of the second claimant would be strengthened by the fact that the defendant had notice of a possibly dangerous condition by reason of the first accident. Doubts about the efficacy of the exclusionary rule have caused several courts to abandon it in strict liability cases.[52]

---

50. As the Advisory Committee to the Federal Rules noted "[A remedial measure] is not in fact an admission, since the conduct is equally consistent with injury by mere accident or through contributory negligence." Adv.Comm. Note to Fed.R.Evid. 407. The Committee notes, nonetheless, that it still is possible to infer fault. Id.

51. See Schwartz, The Exclusionary Rule on Subsequent Repairs—A Rule in Need of Repair, 7 The Forum 1 (1971). Professor Schwartz provides a careful analysis and notes, among other things, that in many cases the evidentiary rule is unknown to the potential defendant and thus could not influence his conduct. Id. at 6. He also observes that the motive to repair and avoid future accidents is strong and would prevail even if evidence of subsequent repairs were admissible. For a case that can be read as supporting this thesis, see Chart v. General Motors Corp., 80 Wis.2d 91, 258 N.W.2d 680 (1977).

52. Robbins v. Farmers Union Grain Terminal Ass'n, 552 F.2d 788 (8th Cir. 1977); Ault v. International Harvester Co., 13 Cal.3d 113, 117 Cal.Rptr. 812, 528 P.2d 1148 (1974).

The vast majority of courts, however, have at least purported to adhere to the rule in negligence suits.[53]

The distinction between cases of strict liability and those founded on negligence is probably justified for practical reasons. In negligence cases, liability attaches if the defendant acted unreasonably in view of the facts known (or which should have been known) to him before the incident in question. An after-incident remedial measure is usually taken on the basis of the additional facts revealed by the accident or injury. There is a risk that the trier, particularly a jury, might not keep this important distinction clearly in mind and might too easily infer prior knowledge from the subsequent remedial acts, which were generated by the knowledge learned from the incident itself.

Federal Rule 407 is in accord with most common-law decisions. It provides:

> When, after an event, measures are taken which if taken previously, would have made the event less likely to occur, evidence of the subsequent measures is not admissible to prove negligence or culpable conduct in connection with the event. This rule does not require the exclusion of evidence of subsequent measures when offered for another purpose, such as proving ownership, control, or feasibility of precautionary measures, if controverted, or impeachment.

A recent federal case has interpreted the phrase "negligence or culpable conduct" as not embracing strict liability.[54] The second sentence in this rule qualifies further the general rule of exclusion by adopting certain exceptions that were developed by the com-

---

53. Maine is an exception. Field, The Maine Rules of Evidence: What They Are and How They Got That Way, 27 Maine L.Rev. 203, 217–19 (1975); Note, The Repair Rule: Maine Rule of Evidence 407(a) and the Admissibility of Subsequent Remedial Measures in Proving Negligence, 27 Maine L. Rev. 225 (1975).

54. Robbins v. Farmers Union Grain Terminal Ass'n, 552 F.2d 788 (8th Cir. 1977) (exclusionary rule does not apply in products liability case). See also Farnar v. Paccar, Inc., 562 F.2d 518 (8th Cir. 1977).

mon law.[55] If a dispute arises over the ownership or control of property involved in an accident,[56] or if a defendant claims at trial that the condition in question cannot feasibly be corrected or made safer,[57] then remedial measures from which the trier can infer ownership, control, or feasibility may be entered in rebuttal. Occasionally, it may be necessary to reveal the fact of a repair or remedial step to impeach a witness by showing that he has acted or spoken inconsistently with his testimony at trial.[58] In these instances the evidence is not offered for the purpose of showing an unsafe condition, and its probative force may be considerably greater when directed to one of these propositions not governed by the rule of exclusion. Observe that the Federal Rule does not purport to exhaust the propositions to which evidence of subsequent measures might be relevant. It is important, however, that the judge ensure that an actual dispute exists concerning ownership, feasibility, etc. before he admits evidence of a remedial measure; otherwise there would be nothing left of the rule of exclusion.

Another example of an evidentiary rule designed to encourage socially useful conduct is that which excludes offers of compromise. Under this exclusionary principle, if there is an actual dispute between parties, evidence that one of the parties offered to settle or compromise the claim against him is inadmissible for the inference that he thought himself liable or that he had a weak case.[59] Sometimes such an offer has very little probative value: it may not be an implied admission of probable liability, but simply an attempt to avoid the expense and trouble of litigation. However, in some instances, as where a defendant offers a large settlement sum constituting a high percentage of the

---

55. Adv.Comm. Note to Fed.R.Evid. 407; II Wigmore, § 283; Annot., 64 A.L.R.2d 1296 (1959).

56. See, e. g., Boeing Airplane Co. v. Brown, 291 F.2d 310 (9th Cir. 1961).

57. See, e. g., Powers v. J. B. Michael & Co., 329 F.2d 674 (6th Cir. 1964).

58. See, e. g., Dollar v. Long Mfg., 561 F.2d 613 (5th Cir. 1977) (defendant's design engineer who testified product in question was safe impeached by letter he wrote to dealers warning of hazards).

59. See, e. g., Fed.R.Evid. 408 and Adv.Comm. Note; People v. Gill, 247 Mich. 479, 226 N.W. 214 (1929).

amount claimed by the plaintiff, an inference is justified that the offering party believes himself liable. Nonetheless, all jurisdictions exclude evidence of the offer, usually on the grounds that compromise should be encouraged. The decisions vary, however, as to the admissibility of statements made during the course of compromise negotiations. A statement made by either party in hypothetical terms—usually prefaced by such phrases as "without prejudice" or "assuming, but not admitting"—is protected. But factual statements not so couched or conditioned are usually admissible even if made during discussions about settlement possibilities.[60] The applicable Federal Rule reflects a more protective attitude and broadens inadmissibility to include evidence of "conduct or statements made in compromise negotiations . . . ." [61] This formulation avoids the difficult distinction between hypothetical and factual statements. However, under the Federal Rule, as under the common-law decisions, evidence of compromise or statements made in connection therewith are admissible if relevant for other purposes such as showing bias or rebutting a contention of undue delay.[62]

More jurisdictions also exclude evidence that one of the parties furnished or offered to furnish money in payment of medical or hospital expenses.[63] This "good Samaritan" rule is intended to encourage aid and assistance by preventing a disadvantage from accruing to a benefactor who provides economic benefits to an individual whose illness or incapacity might have been caused by the former's conduct. Likewise, in order to foster guilty pleas, evidence that an accused made an offer to plead guilty to the crime now charged or to a lesser charge is inadmissible.[64] Evidence that the accused pleaded guilty but later withdrew the plea is also usually excluded.[65]

---

60. State v. Stevens, 248 Minn. 309, 80 N.W.2d 22 (1956).

61. Fed.R.Evid. 408 and Adv.Comm. Note. See, e. g., Big O Tire Dealers, Inc. v. Goodyear Tire & Rubber Co., 561 F.2d 1365 (10th Cir., 1977).

62. Fed.R.Evid. 408.

63. The common-law rule is embodied in Fed.R.Evid. 409.

64. McCormick, § 274, at 665; Fed. R.Evid. 410. See United States v. Herman, 544 F.2d 791 (5th Cir. 1977).

65. Fed.R.Evid. 410; People v. Spitaleri, 9 N.Y.2d 168, 212 N.Y.S.2d

NOTES

1. *Evidence of Reputation.* As the text indicates in § 34, reputation evidence has been the preferred manner of proof in those instances when character may be shown for circumstantial use. When character is an essential part of a charge, claim, or defense, many courts admit any of the kinds of evidence that have a bearing on character: reputation, opinion or specific acts. Other courts prefer the more probative evidence of specific acts.

Note, however, that sometimes evidence of reputation is admissible on the issue of the appropriate amount of damages in a suit based upon defamation. Normally, the measure of proper damage in such a suit is the harm done to the plaintiff's reputation. If that reputation was bad even before the defendant's remark, the additional harm caused by the defamatory statement may be very small. Thus, the defendant may show that prior to his statement the plaintiff already had a bad reputation for the unfavorable character suggested by the defamatory remark. Morgan at 183.

2. *Evidence of an Accused's Prior Bad Conduct.* Note the possibilities, already explored, of an evidential showing that an accused has engaged in other criminal conduct: (1) "Have-you-heard" questions put to the reputation witness who, on direct, has asserted that the defendant has a good reputation (inconsistent with the crime charged); (2) Other-crimes evidence relevant to some proposition other than criminal propensity. In addition to these possibilities, a third avenue opens if the accused testifies. He is then subject to impeachment by evidence of criminal activity that bears on credibility. See Chapter VIII, § 81.

3. *Other-Crimes Evidence and Entrapment.* If an accused defends a charge on the ground of entrapment, evidence of other crimes similar to the one charged generally is admissible to show that he was predisposed to commit the offense. See Hampton v. United States, 425 U.S. 484 (1976); United States v. Russell, 411 U.S. 423 (1973). But see Hansford v. United States, 303 F.2d 219 (D.C.Cir. 1962), holding that it was reversible error to admit an officer's testimony that he had earlier observed the accused sell narcotics to addicts. Although the accused claimed that the officer had entrapped him—a claim that would normally permit evidence of other similar crimes—the officer's testimony of the earlier incident was not corroborated by other witnesses or by an official report and had not led to an arrest or indictment.

53, 173 N.E.2d 35 (1961). Cases yielding various results are collect- ed in Annot., 86 A.L.R.2d 326, 332–39 (1962).

4. *Other-Crimes Evidence Offered by the Accused.* Other-crimes evidence occasionally is offered by the accused to negate guilt as, for example, where criminal acts of the victim support a factual hypothesis that negates or lessens the defendant's guilt. In People v. Matlock, 51 Cal.2d 682, 336 P.2d 505 (1959), where the accused testified that he did not intend to strangle the victim but rather was helping him with a scheme to defraud an insurance company by choking him until unconsciousness set in, it was held error to exclude evidence that victim had been convicted of fraud. See also United States v. Kelley, 545 F.2d 619 (8th Cir. 1976) (construing Fed.R.Evid. 404(b) as applicable only to "other crimes" of the *accused*; those of victim not admissible.)

5. *Guilty Pleas.* Although an offer to plead guilty, like an offer to compromise, is excluded when offered to show a sense of guilt, a guilty plea that is made and received by the court is conclusive in the criminal case in which made and may be admitted in a civil case based upon the same conduct. Suppose, for example, *D* pleads guilty to the offense of reckless driving. This plea is a substitute for trial and has a conclusive effect. In a later civil suit grounded on the same alleged driving, some courts admit evidence of the guilty plea against *D* on the theory that it constitutes a party admission. See Chapter VII, n. 2 following § 58.

CHAPTER VI

THE HEARSAY RULE: ITS NATURE AND RATIONALE

§ 49. General Principle and Rationale

The general understanding among lay persons that hearsay evidence involves someone saying what he has heard elsewhere is partially accurate. Hearsay does involve a serial repetition: one person, the witness, repeats what an individual, whom we shall call the declarant, previously has said outside the courtroom.[1] But to constitute hearsay, the repeated statement must be offered for the purpose of proving that what the declarant said is true—just as if the declarant were on the witness stand, giving testimony which the proponent wants the trier to believe. Assume, for example, the declarant stated to a witness that the heating system in a particular warehouse was inoperative during the winter months; evidence of this statement is offered by the witness who overheard it to prove the system was not operating during this period. The proffered statement is hearsay. Unless an exception to the hearsay rule applies,[2] the opposing party can enter an objection and the judge will exclude the witness's testimony disclosing what the declarant said.

The basis for this hearsay objection is that the opponent is unable to confront and cross-examine the "real" witness—the declarant—and to expose weaknesses in his statement. It bears repeating, however, that a repetition is classified as hearsay only if the proponent of the evidence seeks to have the trier believe that the declarant's out-of-court statement is true, that is,

---

1. Under the prevailing view, a prior out-of-court statement by a witness now on the stand also is treated as hearsay. See infra § 52. In these circumstances, of course, the witness and the out-of-court declarant are the same person. In initially understanding the hearsay rule, the reader may be helped by assuming that the witness and the declarant are different persons.

2. The exceptions are considered in Ch. VII.

only if the proponent seeks to have the factfinder rely on the declarant's credibility.[3] It will be seen, momentarily, that it is only in instances in which a declarant's statement is "offered for its truth," as the cases say, that cross-examination of the declarant is necessary to protect the opponent. This proposition may be understood by recalling that the general purpose of cross-examination is to expose mistake or deception and thereby weaken or destroy the trier's belief in the truth of assertions made during direct examination. Thus, an adverse interrogation of the declarant is unnecessary when his statement is not offered for the truth of its assertion.

The following example illustrates further the nature of hearsay and the need for cross-examination: in a prosecution for the sale of illegal weapons, witness W testifies that declarant B stated that he (B) observed the accused selling a machine gun. If the proponent offers W's testimony to show that the accused made the sale, the trier is asked to believe B's account of the facts—to rely upon his credibility. The cross-examiner, unable to confront and interrogate the absent B, will find it difficult to expose weaknesses in B's statement. Cross-examination of the declarant, were he present, might reveal that he was deliberately lying or that, even though he was not consciously making a false assertion, his statement was inaccurate because of poor observation, faulty memory, or what might be called a "mistranscription" resulting from the declarant's unintended omission of a word or his ambiguous use of language. In sum, if B were on the stand the cross-examiner could probe not only whether B was willing to tell the truth, but also whether he had the ability to perceive the event clearly and to remember it adequately; the examiner could also ascertain whether B is using language that renders an unambiguous account of what occurred. The cross-examiner's interrogation of the witness, W, however, can only test whether W is accurately *repeating* what was said by the declarant B. It can not test the accuracy of B's statement.

---

3. The term "credibility" as here used includes both wilful and innocent (unknowing) misstatements. It may be thought of as synonymous with "accuracy."

Since we often shall refer to the potential defects in a declarant's statement—the so-called "hearsay dangers"—they are explicated below:

(a) *Defects in perception* refers to disabilities that arise from a failure or inability to observe or hear accurately.

(b) *Defects in memory* refers to inaccurate or incomplete recollection.

(c) *Defects in sincerity or veracity* refers to testimonial faults that arise from a reluctance to tell the complete truth, or from a conscious effort to distort or falsify.

(d) *Defects in transmission* refers to mistransmissions that arise because the declarant's statement is ambiguous (as, for example, when he uses a word or phrase that has a special or unusual meaning within a particular group or segment of society) or the declarant's statement is incomplete (as when he inadvertently leaves the word "not" out of a sentence). This potential defect is usually not considered by the courts as posing a significant risk.[4]

The assumption underlying the hearsay rule is that cross-examination reveals these infirmities; accordingly, the lack of opportunity for adequate cross-examination is the fundamental reason for excluding hearsay evidence. Although other reasons

---

4. Although it is true that defects in transcription can be exposed by cross-examination, this particular hearsay danger has received little attention in the reported cases. Possibly, this comparative inattention is a reflection that this hazard is not frequently encountered or, perhaps, not frequently recognized. It should be noted, however, that mistranscription by ambiguity often is a difficulty where the hearsay declarant communicates not by words, but rather by conduct. See infra § 51. However, mistranscription in this latter context is principally a problem of probative value, that is, the question is whether the actor's conduct is probative of the proposition for which it is offered. When the declarant communicates with words, but uses a special or "slang" meaning, other witnesses can sometimes help establish the particular denotation or connotation.

for rejecting hearsay have been advanced (for example, that the declarant did not speak under oath and his demeanor could not be observed by the factfinder), there now is a consensus that it is the untested nature of hearsay evidence that justifies its exclusion. This rationale, of course, is consistent with a major tenet of the adversary system: cross-examination is essential for ensuring accuracy and discovering truth.[5] Despite this consistency, however, the syllogistic application of the hearsay rule without exception would stultify judicial trials and impede accurate factfinding. Hence, as the next chapter demonstrates, there are numerous exceptions to the rule.

§ 50. Application of the General Principle

We have seen that the hearsay stigma attaches when, and only when, the proponent offers the declarant's assertion for a purpose which requires that the trier accept as true the facts it embodies. If the proponent's probative purpose can be achieved without the factfinder's reliance upon the truth of the declarant's statement, the hearsay rule is inapplicable.

There are several situations in which a serial repetition serves a recognized evidentiary purpose without requiring that the factfinder rely upon the declarant's credibility. One circumstance is where the proponent offers the declarant's statement because of its *legal significance independent of its truth*, or otherwise stated, independent of the declarant's subjective intent. For example, when the issue is whether B accepted A's offer for certain painting services, a witness W may testify that he overheard B say to A: "I accept your offer to paint my porch." Under the objective view of contract formation, the statement by B resulted in the formation of the agreement—assuming a reasonable offeror would have construed B's statement as an acceptance. The proponent only need establish that the operative words which formed the contract were spoken, not that these words were, in any sense, true. It is of no consequence that the cross-examiner is deprived of an opportunity to test the defects in B's perception, memory, sincerity or transcription. What

---

5.   V Wigmore, § 1367, at 32.

matters is that *B* spoke the words of acceptance, not (for example) that he may have been insincere because he secretly intended to reject *A*'s offer. Note there is no proper hearsay objection as to whether *B* spoke the words of acceptance, because *W*, who asserts he overheard *B*, is in court and available for cross-examination. The cross-examiner can interrogate *W* concerning what *B* said—that is, he can probe fully the issue of what (if any) words were spoken. Hence, *W*, who was, so to speak, the *auditor of B*'s statement can be cross-examined regarding what *B* said. *B*, the declarant, need not be examined because his statement is not offered for its truth.

The foregoing discussion reveals that there are two inquiries regarding the use of a declarant's out-of-court statement. The first question is whether there is admissible evidence that the declaration was made. If the statement is oral, it usually is necessary to call as a witness the auditor, who can give testimony concerning what the declarant said. If the statement is in writing, it usually is required that the writing be produced and identified as having been authored by the declarant. The proponent of the evidence must be able to prove the statement was made without violating any rule of evidence, *including the hearsay rule*. Assuming there is admissible evidence that the statement was made, the second inquiry is whether the declarant's statement is offered for its truth. In the illustration involving the formation of an oral contract, there was proper (admissible) evidence that the declarant-offeree spoke the words of acceptance. And since his declaration was not offered for its truth, it falls outside the exclusionary reach of the hearsay rule.

Consider Mr. Justice Holmes's classic example of the man who falsely shouts fire in a crowded theater.[6] Suppose that in the accused's prosecution for the resulting offense of disturbing the peace, a witness offers to testify that he heard the defendant shout "fire," and the defense objects on the grounds of hearsay. Because the statement is offered only to show that the declarant spoke the warning (and not to show that there was a fire in the

---

6. See S. Saltzburg & K. Redden,
   Federal Rules of Evidence Manual
   469–70 (2d ed. 1977).

theater), the objection fails. Note that the witness called to testify was an auditor-witness, in that he claims to have actually overheard the defendant shout the warning. What if the witness testified that another person, *B*, told him that the defendant shouted fire but the witness himself had not heard the shout? The proffered testimony would be hearsay. The prosecution would be introducing the witness's testimony for a purpose (viz, to show that the defendant shouted the warning) requiring the trier to accept the *truth of B's statement*. The defect in this latter instance is that the proponent offers hearsay evidence that the statement ("fire") was uttered: instead of calling an auditor, he calls a witness who did not hear the defendant's shout, and hence who can testify only that the auditor *B* stated that the defendant shouted "fire." The cross-examiner is denied the opportunity to test the *auditor's* assertion that the defendant gave the warning.

To summarize: in the last two illustrations, the statements of contractual acceptance and warning *do not themselves* constitute hearsay. If there is admissible, nonhearsay evidence that the declarant spoke the words, admission of the statements is proper. The reason these statements are not offered for their truth is because the law prescribes a legal effect to their mere utterance. This legal effect (the *formation* of a contract or the *utterance* of a prohibited warning) becomes operative without regard to the credibility of the declarant. This rationale of independent legal significance also applies to the utterance of a libel or slander, and to words that make a transfer a gift—assuming the substantive law provides that the gift is effected if delivery is accompanied by *words* of donation. Both defamatory words (e. g., "You are a thief") and the donative declaration (e. g., "Take this watch as a gift") are offered for their independent legal effect, without regard to the credibility of the declarant.

In a frequently cited case [7] involving a suit for conversion of plaintiff's corn by the defendant bank, it was necessary for the plaintiff to show that the corn in question belonged to him rath-

7. Hanson v. Johnson, 161 Minn. 229, 201 N.W. 322 (1924), the opinion in which is presented in pertinent part in Louisell et al. at 112.

er than to his tenant. The litigants agreed that one portion of the harvested corn belonged to plaintiff and the other portion belonged to the tenant; the issue was what corn belonged to whom. The plaintiff testified that prior to the alleged conversion by the bank, the tenant had pointed to certain cribs and stated for the first time that the corn in these belonged to the plaintiff. Was this hearsay? Under the controlling substantive law, the court correctly ruled that it was not. This holding was sound, despite the fact that the plaintiff was offering the statement to show that he owned the corn in question. Until the tenant's statement, the fungible crop had not been divided, and under the substantive law the tenant's statement resulted in endowing the plaintiff with sole ownership of the designated portion of the corn. The mere utterance of the statement had the independent legal effect of vesting ownership; it was unnecessary to rely upon the credibility of the tenant-declarant, since ownership was conferred regardless of his subjective intent. The result would have been contrary had the corn earlier been divided. In that event, a subsequent statement by the tenant which identified certain corn as belonging to the plaintiff would have been hearsay, because the trier then would be asked to accept as true the declarant's factual assertion that the designated portion of the corn already belonged to the plaintiff.

Another instance in which a statement is not offered for its truth is when the purpose of offering the statement is to *show its probable effect upon another person*. Suppose, for example, a patron sues a grocery store for injuries sustained from slipping on the contents of a broken ketchup bottle.[8] The defendant store calls to the stand a checkout clerk (the auditor) who will testify that he heard the manager cry out to the patron: "Lady, please don't step on the bottle of ketchup." The evidence is consequential (material) because the patron's conduct, which may involve contributory negligence, should be evaluated in light of the warning. The purpose for which the evidence is offered is satisfied if the trier decides that words of warning were spoken. It is unnecessary to use the declarant's statement for proof that

---

8. The example is based on Safeway Stores, Inc. v. Combs, 273 F.2d 295 (5th Cir. 1960); see Louisell et al. at 111; Maguire et al. at 503.

there was a bottle of ketchup on the floor. Without reliance upon the truth of the declarant's statement, the trier can evaluate the plaintiff's conduct in light of whether she was reasonably warned of the hazardous condition. The question is what effect the warning had or should have had upon her, a question that can be addressed without accepting the clerk's declaration for its truth. Indeed if the plaintiff maintains that she thought the manager was joking, she may so testify. Since it is the reasonableness of the *plaintiff's* conduct that is the issue on which the evidence is offered, it is immaterial whether or not the *declarant* actually thought there was a broken bottle of ketchup on the floor.

A similar rationale explains a British case involving a prosecution for the forbidden possession of ammunition in a battle zone.[9] In support of his defense of duress—grounded on the claim that he had been captured by enemy terrorists and forced to arm himself—the accused offered evidence of his captors' orders and threats. The statements of the captors were not hearsay because they were not offered for their truth. They were not offered, for example, to prove that the terrorists actually would have killed the accused had he not taken up arms. Rather, the statements were offered because their mere utterance was significant in proving duress. Evidence that the threats were made enables the trier to assess the probable effect of the statements upon the accused, permitting them to judge his conduct accordingly.[10]

In such cases as the foregoing, the fact that the statement was made is itself consequential because the utterance gives notice of

---

9. Subramaniam v. Public Prosecutor, 100 Solicitor's Journal 566 (Judicial Comm., Privy Council 1956) reprinted in pertinent part in Louisell et al. at 110.

10. In United States v. Kutas, 542 F.2d 527 (9th Cir. 1976) the Court of Appeals approved the admission of declarant's statement made in accused's presence on the nonhearsay ground that the statement reasonably could apprise the accused that the person he was harboring was an escaped prisoner. The fact that the person was an escapee was shown by other evidence, thus the declarant's statement could be used for the limited probative purpose of increasing the likelihood that the accused knew the person he was harboring was a fugitive.

a hazard or threatening circumstance which reasonably might affect the hearer's conduct. If the trier believes that the statement was made and that the actor heard it, it will weigh this evidence in deciding whether his actions were reasonable or justified. Compare the related but distinct case in which the substantive law makes it consequential that a declarant had an awareness or knowledge of a certain event or circumstance, and he makes a statement disclosing that knowledge. Here again the hearsay rule can be avoided. If, for example, it is consequential that the declarant knew that his brakes were defective, testimony that he stated that his brakes were bad would be admitted if the evidence were limited to showing that he had knowledge.[11] A similar rationale would admit evidence that a declarant stated that his company's manufacturing process was poisoning nearby aquatic life. These statements would be hearsay if offered to show defective brakes or that the declarant's firm was contaminating the water. However, if the evidence is *limited to the issue of the declarant's knowledge*, which under the substantive law (we have assumed) is a determinant of liability, there is no hearsay violation. Note that the proponent would have to supply additional evidence if he sought to prove that the brakes in fact were defective or that discharged pollutants in fact were killing fish.[12] But the words spoken demonstrate a knowledge or awareness, making it unnecessary to rely upon the declarant's credibility when awareness is the proposition at which the evidence is directed. Even though the statement of knowledge is couched in terms of the fact to be proved ("*I know* my brakes are bad") the statement "can still rest on the nonhearsay ground that (bad brakes having been otherwise shown) . . . [the declarant's] remark tends to show that if the brakes were bad he was aware of it."[13]

In an earlier chapter, we observed that evidence may have probative force pointing toward two or more consequential propositions.[14] It should now be apparent that there are instances when evidence offered for one probative purpose runs

---

11. See McCormick, § 249, at 591–92.   13. Id. § 249, at 592.

12. McCormick, § 249, at 592.   14. Ch. II, § 11.

afoul of the hearsay rule, but the same evidence offered for another purpose avoids a hearsay violation. Suppose, for example, golfer *A* sues country club *B* for injuries that resulted when *B* negligently provided *A* with a defective cart. It would be material that prior to *A*'s accident, *B* had knowledge that the cart was defective. Evidence is offered that golfer *C* (the declarant) had said to *B*'s agent in charge of the golf course, "Don't lease the red cart today, the brakes are bad." If this evidence is offered through an auditor-witness for the purpose of proving that the cart had defective brakes, a hearsay objection would be proper: the declarant made the statement out of court and the proponent offers it for the truth of the assertion that the brakes were defective. This use of the evidence requires that the trier rely upon the credibility of the declarant-golfer, yet his out-of-court assertion can not be tested by cross-examination. It is possible, however, to introduce this evidence to prove the defendant's agent had notice or knowledge of the defect [15] and thus acted carelessly in leasing the cart. Directed to the proposition of notice or awareness, evidence of the declarant's statement is not hearsay because its use does not require the trier to rely upon the statement. Of course, other evidence would have to be introduced to show that the brakes in fact were faulty, because the declarant's statement can not be used to establish this proposition.

The point to be emphasized is that a proponent, by carefully identifying the limited purpose for which evidence is offered, often can avoid application of the hearsay rule. When evidence is admitted for a limited, nonhearsay purpose, the opponent upon request is entitled to an instruction that the evidence is to be considered only for its admissible purpose. In the illustration, the judge would instruct the jury to consider the golfer's statement only with respect to the question of notice, not for the purpose of deciding whether the brakes were defective.[16]

---

15. See supra notes 9–10. Cf., Vinyard v. Vinyard Funeral Home, Inc., 435 S.W.2d 392, 396 (Mo.App. 1968).

16. It is doubtful, however, that even a conscientious jury can be entirely obedient to such an instruction. Tactical considerations thus might dictate that the opponent forego this request. It is difficult for the jury to abide by the instruction, and the instruction

We now have encountered three general classes of statements that fall outside the hearsay rule. In the first, the act of speaking certain words has an *independent legal effect* quite aside from the truth or falsity of the assertion. The acceptance of a contract is a classic example; the same rationale classifies as nonhearsay a statement made by a depositor to his bank, directing that his deposit be held in trust for his daughter—assuming that under the substantive law the very utterance of the words creates a trust.[17] In the second class of cases, the words spoken are offered for their probable *effect upon the listener*, for example, the statement made by the declarant to A that A should be careful of the broken bottle in the aisle.[18] A similar rationale supports the admission of a threat to kill made by declarant against the accused if the purpose of the evidence is to show that the accused was reasonable in taking steps to defend himself when he encountered the declarant. A third class of nonhearsay statements consists of those assertions by a declarant which exhibit his *knowledge of a fact or condition* in a case where this knowledge is material to the outcome. For example, a declarant states that his vehicle has defective brakes and this statement is offered to show his knowledge or awareness. A similar rationale might admit a statement by the declarant that he was forbidden by court order from visiting his child: this statement exhibits an awareness of that provision of the order, and would not be hearsay if offered in a contempt proceeding for the limited purpose of showing that the declarant knew of the restriction.

A fourth class of cases, regarding certain assertions of one's *state of mind*, falls on the borderline between hearsay and nonhearsay. Assume A transfers possession of a ring to B with the words "I want you to take this, as a gift." Suppose that the substantive law does not make the mere speaking of the words the determinant of whether the transfer was a gift, but rather it requires that the transfer be accompanied by a subjective dona-

serves to remind the trier of evidence which is unfavorable to the opponent.

17. Lempert & Saltzburg at 343.

18. Safeway Stores, Inc. v. Combs, 273 F.2d 295 (5th Cir. 1960). See also Player v. Thompson, 259 S.C. 600, 193 S.E.2d 531 (1972); Lempert & Saltzburg at 343.

tive intent. Is *A*'s statement hearsay because offered for the truth of its assertion? A similar issue is posed when the question is whether *A* selected the State of New York as his domicile, and the proponent offers a witness who will testify that *A* said "I want to live in New York permanently." Likewise, a hearsay question is raised if a suit for alienation of affections involves the issue whether *A*, the wife, loves *B*, the husband, and evidence is proffered that *A* said to *B* "I don't love you anymore." In each of these situations the principal hearsay danger is insincerity, although there also exists the possibility of mistranscription. Dangers resulting from defects in memory and observation are not present.

Neither the cases nor the commentators are harmonious in classifying, as hearsay or not, declarations of state of mind offered for the purpose of establishing the motive, intent, feeling or other mental state of the declarant. The differences, however, largely are conceptual because such statements, even if classified as hearsay, usually are admissible under a hearsay exception.[19] It is consistent with the generally approved definition of hearsay to consider as hearsay any declaration that directly asserts the declarant's state of mind if the declaration is offered for a purpose that requires the trier to accept as true the state of mind asserted. This resolution of the issues posed by the cases above includes within the hearsay category all of the illustrative declarations. This approach also classifies as hearsay a declarant's statement "New York is my favorite state" if offered to support the proposition that the declarant had changed his domicile to New York. The trier is asked to *believe* the statement and then to *infer* that the declarant intended to make New York his permanent home; [20] the first step involves accepting the truth of the statement.

---

19.   See Ch. VII, § 64.

20.   Some authorities suggest the declarant's statement is not hearsay because it has a circumstantial value in that the declarant is unlikely to speak in affectionate terms about a place or person unless he likes the subject of his remark. McCormick, § 249, at 590–91. Under this rationale the mere utterance of statements of praise, kindness, affection or disaffection, for example, have a probative value quite aside from the literal truth of the statement: the use of

None of the examples thus far discussed involves a written declaration, but it should be clear that assertive documentary evidence can be hearsay. If a declarant's writing is offered for the truth of the assertion it contains, the hearsay rule is applicable: the cross-examiner cannot test the reliability of the written assertion—unless, of course, the author testifies, in which case the writing may be superfluous.[21] As with verbal declarations, however, a writing may serve a nonhearsay purpose and, if properly offered, it escapes objection. Suppose, for example, A sues B for the fraudulent sale of a rare book. The complaint alleges that B, in connection with the sale, fraudulently stated that the volume bore the signature of Thomas Jefferson. Could B introduce into evidence a written warranty from his supplier (the declarant), authenticating Jefferson's signature as genuine? If B offers the warranty to support the proposition that the signature is genuine, the written evidence (an out-of-court assertion by the supplier) is hearsay. But if B offers the evidence only to show that he had no intent to deceive A (thus attempting to negate the element of deceit), there is no violation of the hearsay rule. Offering the statement contained in the warranty for the limited purpose of showing its probable effect upon B's mind enables the trier to consider the book supplier's assertion without relying upon his credibility.

§ 51. Conduct as Hearsay

Physical gestures such as those used in sign language, in pointing out a person or object, or in affirmatively nodding in response to a question, often are used as a substitute for words. When the declarant intends to make an assertion by physical manifestations and the proponent enters evidence of the declarant's actions for the truth of the assertion manifested, the

---

the words gives rise to an inference of an underlying state of mind consistent with the statement, even though the statement may not be literally true. The statements "I hate New York" and "I love New York" suggest on circumstantial grounds some measure, respective-

ly, of affection and disaffection— that is the utterance of the words reveals something about the declarant's state of mind.

21. But see Ch. VII, § 66; Ch. XIII, § 116.

hearsay rule applies. Thus, when *A*, asked to identify his assailant, points to *B*, his assertion would be hearsay if testimony from one who saw the gesture later is offered at *B*'s trial for the purpose of proving that *B* was the assailant.

A related but distinct situation is posed where the declarant does not intend to make an assertion, but his actions imply or suggest circumstantially his belief in a certain fact. A traveler who purchases a bus ticket and thereafter waits at a certain street corner may not intend to assert that a bus passes the corner, but his conduct implies this belief. If the traveler's conduct (standing at the corner with a bus ticket) is viewed simply as a substitute for words, equivalent in all respects to the statement "The bus passes this corner," then, like pointing or nodding, his conduct is hearsay if offered to show the passage of the bus. The argument, of course, is that since the declarant's out-of-court statement of the fact to be proved (the bus route) would be hearsay, so too should be his implied assertion of the same fact. This contention can be raised in many factual contexts. A sea captain inspects a vessel and then sets sail with his family aboard it. May a witness, offered by a party who seeks to show that the vessel was seaworthy, testify to the captain's actions? Again, the argument against admission rests on the ground that the captain's conduct belongs to the same prohibited hearsay class as his statement "This ship is seaworthy." A similar question is posed by evidence that a doctor performed an operation of a kind that usually is administered for a certain spinal disability. May a proponent seeking to establish this disability introduce evidence of the operation? [22]

A famous English case [23] considers in detail the issue of implied assertions. There, the proponents of a will sought to introduce letters to the testator from *X*, *Y*, and *Z* because the tone and content of the letters impliedly manifested the writers' belief that the recipient was sane and competent. So far as the letters disclosed, the writers (declarants) intended only to com-

---

22. See Maguire et al. at 521.

23. Wright v. Doe d. Tatham, 7 Adloph. & E. 313, 386, 112 Eng.Rep.

488 (Exch.Ch.1837) and 5 Cl. & F. 670, 739, 47 Rev.Rep. 136 (H.L. 1838).

municate various business and social matters, but the letters were *not offered to prove anything expressly said therein*: they were offered for the *implied assertion* that the writers believed their addressee to be competent. In other words, the writers' use of normal, unguarded language, coupled with the fact that they entrusted to the testator the discharge of certain business and social affairs, implied that they thought he was sane—just as the sea captain impliedly thought his vessel was a seaworthy craft.

Before attempting to resolve the hearsay status of what usually is called nonassertive conduct, it should be observed that in certain circumstances, silence or inaction also can be interpreted as an implied assertion of the existence or nonexistence of a certain fact. Suppose, for example, persons other than the plaintiff are exposed to an alleged condition which the plaintiff claims caused his injury, yet no one else complained or spoke about this condition. Can the trier draw an inference that the condition did not exist? This issue is sometimes posed when a plaintiff sues a restauranteur on the ground that the latter served unwholesome food. The hearsay question is whether the defendant can introduce evidence that no other customers complained.[24] In addition to the hearsay difficulty posed by this case, there is a problem of relevance. The probative force of evidence of "noncomplaints" depends, first, upon whether the other patrons consumed the same food as did the plaintiff and, second, whether they would have complained to the restauranteur had they become ill.

All of the foregoing examples, including those in which there is affirmative action, have in common the fact the declarant did not intend to make an assertion by his conduct. It is apparent that these nonassertive actions are different from those, such as a gesture, in which conduct *intended as an assertion* is offered to prove the assertion. Where nonassertive conduct is involved, the hearsay danger of insincerity is reduced or elimi-

---

24. See Landfield v. Albiani Lunch Co., 268 Mass. 528, 168 N.E. 160 (1929); Silver v. New York Cent. R.R., 329 Mass. 14, 105 N.E.2d 923 (1952) (issue: whether railroad passenger car became cold; evidence offered: other passengers did not complain).

nated because the actor does not intend to make the assertion
implied by his actions. The following illustration underscores
this distinction: A question arises as to whether a particular
day was warm or chilly. A witness, who on the day in question
was in a building, testifies that he observed from his window
that persons standing at a bus stop turned up their collars and
placed their hands in their pockets.[25] One can distinguish these
persons from the usual hearsay declarant because, in all likelihood, they did not intend to be making an assertion. They did
not say to the witness "The day is cold," nor did they affirmatively nod their heads when asked if it is chilly. Consequently,
it is unlikely that they were being deceptive or insincere. It
should be added that in this particular instance there are no
dangers from defects in the declarant's perception and memory
because the actors were responding immediately to perceived cli-
matic conditions.[26]

The absence of the hearsay risk of insincerity in situations involving nonassertive actions has caused most commentators to
place nonassertive conduct outside the hearsay ban. So viewed,
this conduct is simply circumstantial evidence of the proposition
it supports. Only recently, however, has this nonhearsay rationale expressly been adopted by courts and rulemakers. Probably
the weight of judicial authority, when one includes the older cases, supports a hearsay classification for nonassertive conduct.[27]
But as Professor Falknor notes:

> In any of these situations [of nonassertive conduct]
> the hearsay objection is likely to be overlooked. This
> is especially so when the evidence concerns "none-ver-

---

25. See Falknor, The "Hear-Say"
Rule as a "See-Do" Rule: Evidence of Conduct, 33 Rocky Mountain L.Rev. 133 (1960).

26. As to the danger of mistranscription, see supra note 4.

Some conduct, of course, would raise
dangers of defects in memory and
perception as, for example, where
letter-writers X, Y, and Z treat
their addressee as if he were competent, yet their contact with him
may have been limited (perception)
and in the remote past (memory).
See text supra at note 4. Note
that limited and remote contact
also affects probative force.

27. McCormick, § 250, at 599.

bal" conduct because the hearsay rule is almost always, in the abstract, phrased in terms of "statements" or "utterances" and the possible application of the rule to "conduct" may not be immediately apparent. And the same is true, although perhaps to a lesser degree, when the evidence is of "verbal" conduct [of the sort involved in the English case of the letters] relevant only circumstantially. Cases are legion consequently where the hearsay objection, with strong supporting authority, might have been raised but was not.[28]

Thus, in a prosecution of the defendant for keeping a house for the purpose of taking bets, an appellate court approved, with little discussion, the admission of evidence that while police officers were apprehending the defendant they answered his telephone and discovered that the callers were placing bets.[29] A concurring justice, however, argued that evidence of the calls, when offered to establish that the defendant used his house for taking bets, violated the hearsay rule. Under his view, the act of placing a bet was the equivalent of the assertion "This house is used for betting."

The trend [30] toward removing nonassertive conduct from the hearsay prohibition is endorsed in the Federal Rules of Evidence.[31] The rulemakers rejected a characterization of nonassertive conduct as hearsay on the ground that if the actor does not intend to make an assertion, there is little or no risk of insincerity. There are, of course, instances of apparently nonassertive conduct in which there is a risk of one or more hearsay dangers. The letter writers in the English case may have believed their addressee was subject to periods of insanity, but not wishing to offend him expressed themselves in a manner that falsely implied confidence in his abilities; the ticketed passenger awaiting the bus at the corner may have forgotten the bus

---

28. Falknor, The "Hear-Say" Rule as a "See-Do" Rule: Evidence of Conduct, 33 Rocky Mountain Law Review 133, 135 (1961).

29. People v. Barnhart, 66 Cal.App. 2d 714, 153 P.2d 214 (1944).

30. McCormick, § 250, at 598–99.

31. Fed.R.Evid. 801(a)(2) and Adv. Comm. Note.

route; the sea captain may not have had time to make a complete inspection, or may not have been inspecting the vessel at all, but rather was engaged in a search for a missing object.[32] In most of these instances, however, the possible infirmities should reduce the weight accorded the evidence, rather than dictate exclusion.[33] The minimal risk of insincerity associated with apparently nonassertive conduct supports a general rule of admissibility, subject to the judge's exclusion in cases where one or more dangers pose a substantial risk of jury misuse.[34] The approach of the Federal Rules probably will be widely adopted, thus reposing an issue that has fascinated academics, but been of little practical consequence.

§ 52. Prior Statements of a Witness

At common law, the hearsay rule encompassed any statement entered for its truth *other than one made from the witness stand in the present proceeding.* This broad definition places within the hearsay ban even a prior out-of-court statement made by a witness who testifies at trial. The reason for including a witness's own prior statement within the rule is not immediately apparent; if the declarant testifies at trial, each party can examine him regarding both his present testimony and his earlier out-of-court statement. Since the basis of the hearsay rule is the opponent's lack of opportunity to cross-examine the declarant, it would seem that the rule is inapplicable when the declarant is a present witness. Why, then, should a witness's prior, extra-judicial statement be classified hearsay?

Several preliminary points should be made. Although a majority of courts still take the view that a witness's prior statement is hearsay, evidence of the prior statement—even in these courts—often is admissible. Frequently, the earlier statement of a witness is inconsistent with his present testimony. In this circumstance, evidence of the prior statement is admissible for

---

32. See Lempert & Saltzburg at 350.

33. McCormick, § 250, at 599.

34. Under the modern approach, the judge must determine as an initial matter that the conduct is nonassertive—that is, that the actor did not intend to communicate the proposition for which his conduct is offered. See Ch. X, § 97.

impeachment. The immediate effect of revealing to the trier a prior contradictory statement is to discredit or impeach the witness's present testimony: one who gives inconsistent accounts of the same events should not readily be believed. All courts recognize the propriety of admitting evidence of prior inconsistent statements for this limited purpose of discrediting the witness. Difficulty arises, however, if the proponent in order to prove his case requires that the trier use the prior inconsistency as substantive evidence—that is, as evidence of the truth of the facts asserted in the out-of-court statement.

The following cases illustrate this difficulty: *A* sues *B* on a fidelity bond written to indemnify *A*, an employer, for losses occasioned by the defalcation of his employees.[35] At trial, the employee who allegedly misappropriated the goods takes the stand and denies any wrongdoing. The plaintiff then impeaches him by introducing a prior inconsistent statement in which the witness admitted the defalcations. All courts allow evidence of this prior inconsistency for purposes of impeachment. But can the trier also use the employee's statement as evidence that he misappropriated the goods? Stated in hearsay terms, the question is whether the earlier statement can be offered for the truth of the assertion that the employee-declarant converted the plaintiff's goods. Under the orthodox approach, the prior statement is hearsay if used to prove the misappropriation, since for this purpose it is an out-of-court statement offered for its truth.[36]

This traditional limitation upon the use of a prior statement becomes more than an academic formality in a case in which the proponent requires the substantive use of the impeaching evidence to prove an essential element in his case (that is, to satisfy his burden of production with regard to an element of his charge, claim, or defense upon which he has the burden of persuasion[37]). Assume, for example, in a prosecution for the illegal in-

---

35. See Letendre v. Hartford Accident & Indemnity Co., 21 N.Y.2d 518, 289 N.Y.S.2d 183, 236 N.E.2d 467 (1968).

36. Of course, if the statement constitutes an exception to the hearsay rule, see Chapter VII, it is admissible for its truth. However, this does not alter its characterization as hearsay.

37. See Ch. III, § 15.

terstate transportation of a female for purposes of prostitution, the government must prove as one element of the offense that the transported victim engaged in prostitution.[38] When called to the stand, the victim denies that she engaged in illegal sexual activity. As we have seen, she may be impeached by prior written or oral declarations to the contrary. But unless the prosecutor has other evidence that the witness engaged in prostitution, he will be unable to obtain a conviction because the witness-declarant's prior statements can not be used for the truth of their assertion that she engaged in prostitution. Such substantive use would violate the hearsay rule. Without additional evidence, the prosecutor would fail to meet his burden of production on the element of prostitution, and the judge would direct an acquittal. Similarly, in a wrongful death action against B, the plaintiff must prove that B and not C was the operator of a negligently driven vehicle.[39] Suppose plaintiff calls the only witness to the accident, who adversely testifies that C, not B, was the driver. The plaintiff then introduces evidence that the witness made an earlier written statement that B was the operator. If this prior statement cannot be used substantively, the plaintiff loses the case because there is no evidence to support the trier's finding that B was the driver.

Where there is other, sufficient evidence of the essential fact asserted in the prior inconsistent statement, the proponent suffers little or no practical disadvantage from the restriction that limits the earlier statement to the single purpose of impeachment. Although it is true that the opponent is entitled to an instruction directing the jury that the prior inconsistency is to be used solely to cast doubt on the witness's trial testimony, this restriction probably has little impact upon the jury's deliberations. Furthermore, it is impossible to ascertain whether the jury was obedient to the instruction. If the jury finds for the proponent and there is evidence aside from the earlier inconsistent statement to support the verdict, the resulting judgment will stand.

It is important to recognize that a prior inconsistent statement *can be used as substantive evidence* (that is, entered for its

38. See United States v. Biener, 52 F.Supp. 54 (E.D.Pa.1943).

39. See Ruhala v. Roby, 379 Mich. 102, 150 N.W.2d 146 (1967).

truth) *if it falls within one of the exceptions* to the hearsay rule.[40] This escape from the usual limitation that confines the trier's use of a prior inconsistent statement to the issue of credibility, however, does not alter the orthodox analysis that the statement is hearsay when used for substantive purposes: despite its hearsay character, it may be used for its truth because it fits within a hearsay exception.

What are the justifications for the traditional rule that prior inconsistent statements are hearsay? Various reasons have been advanced in support of the orthodox view. The principal ones are, first, that it is undesirable, especially in a criminal prosecution, to permit one to prove an element of his case by extra-judicial statements; and, second, that the examiner seeking to negate the effect of a prior inconsistent statement suffers a practical disadvantage that does not attend his attempts to nullify or weaken present testimony.[41]

The objection to permitting proof of one's case by extra-judicial statements is rooted in the belief that the most reliable statements are those made from the witness stand. Courtroom testimony is attended by all of the conditioning devices of a judicial inquiry, including the oath, the opportunity for the factfinder to observe demeanor, and the officialism of the proceedings. Of course, if this supportive rationale were extended to its logical end, the result would be to deny admission to all hearsay statements, even in the many instances where the statement falls within a hearsay exception. A related basis for the objection is the apprehension that permitting the substantive use of prior inconsistencies would encourage fabricated testimony. False evidence of prior inconsistent statements, it is feared, would be introduced in order to prove the essential elements of the proponent's case. It is doubtful, however, that the risk of fabricated testimony is graver in this instance than it is in many

---

40. Selected exceptions are discussed in Ch. VII.

41. See Rept., New Jersey Supreme Court Committee on Evidence (1963), where at pp. 132–135 arguments against liberalizing the traditional approach are set out. See also Maguire et al. at 549. For a judicial defense of the traditional view, see Ruhala v. Roby, 379 Mich. 102, 150 N.W.2d 146 (1967).

others, especially since the speaker is present in the courtroom to deny (or affirm) the inconsistency. The modification of a technical rule in order to permit the substantive use of prior inconsistent statements (which already are admissible to impeach) hardly seems the kind of reform that would increase significantly the incidence of perjury.

A more convincing defense of the traditional rule is the practical argument that effective interrogation relating to earlier inconsistent statements is difficult or impossible. To appreciate fully the basis of this contention, it is important to remember that the counsel who introduces evidence of the witness's prior inconsistent statement is trying to *neutralize* the witness's present assertions from the stand. Usually, it is the cross-examiner who introduces the prior contradictory statement, but occasionally the direct examiner, displeased or surprised by the testimony of his witness, offers evidence of a prior inconsistency.[42] The next examination is conducted by the opponent, who wants the trier to believe the witness's present testimony and disbelieve the prior inconsistent statement. That is, assuming that when confronted with the prior inconsistent statement the witness denies making it or else denies that the prior statement represents the truth, the counsel next examining the witness strives to support the witness's present testimony, while negating the impact of the evidence of the earlier inconsistency.

The obstacles faced by this subsequent examiner depend largely upon the witness's explanation of the evidence that he has made a prior contradictory statement. If he denies making the prior inconsistency or at least asserts that he has no memory of it, the subsequent examiner is hampered somewhat in eliciting an explanation of why the *unacknowledged* prior statement is inaccurate; the interrogator usually will have to settle for having the witness reassert that his preceding testimony, based upon present recollection of the event, is accurate. But the subsequent examiner faces a situation of even greater practical difficulty in the comparatively rare instance when the witness nei-

---

42. As to impeaching one's own witness, see McCormick, § 38, at 75–78; Ch. VIII, § 80.

ther acknowledges the prior inconsistency, nor remembers the event allegedly described in his prior statement (which event, if it existed, would be at odds with his present testimony). Here the interrogator neither can elicit testimony about the event, nor can he show why the prior inconsistency is inaccurate. In this circumstance, it is very difficult, if not impossible, for the subsequent examiner to interrogate the witness so as to demonstrate why the prior account should be rejected by the factfinder.

Contrast the situation in which the witness acknowledges he made the prior inconsistent statement, but denies its accuracy because he now purports to recall correctly the incident described in the statement. Here the subsequent examiner is not substantially handicapped. He can attempt to demonstrate why the facts he seeks to establish are shown reliably by the present testimony and why they should not be negated by the prior contradiction. As one source puts it:

> The declarant is in court and may be examined and cross-examined in regard to his statements and their subject matters. . . . The trier of fact has the declarant before it and can observe his demeanor and the nature of his testimony as he denies or tries to explain away the inconsistency. Hence, it is in as good a position to determine the truth or falsity of the prior statement as it is to determine the truth or falsity of the inconsistent testimony given in court.[43]

Although the subsequent examiner of a witness who has been challenged with a prior inconsistency will not attempt to generally discredit the witness (since he seeks to support the witness's in-court testimony), this hardly is a reason to disallow the substantive use of the prior inconsistent statement. The fact that the witness may be interrogated by both attorneys concerning the subject matter of his testimony, the conditions surrounding his prior inconsistent statement, and the reasons for the appar-

---

43. Calif.Law Rev.Comm. Comment on § 1235, Calif.Evid.Code (1965).

ent contradiction, surely avoids or minimizes the hearsay dangers.[44]

The question remains whether the practical disadvantage sometimes suffered by the subsequent examiner, when coupled with a preference for evidence given from the witness stand, provides a convincing basis for the traditional rule denying the substantive use of prior inconsistent statements.[45] This question is not easily resolved; any arguments for the orthodox approach must be weighed against several factors that support the substantive use of prior inconsistencies.[46] As noted, apprehensions about the abuse and frailty of extra-judicial statements have not prevented the courts and legislators from fashioning more than twenty-five exceptions to the hearsay rule. These permit substantive use of out-of-court statements in many instances in which the declarant does not even appear as a witness. It is also significant that compared with testimony from the stand, the prior statement was made closer in time to the event in question when, presumably, memory was fresher. And in many cases the prior statement was made before the possibly distorting influences of litigation, which include the witness's identification with one party, the psychological urge to make one's testimony consistent and believable, and the bias that may arise when an attorney prepares or "coaches" the witness.[47] These considerations have convinced a minority of jurisdictions to permit the substantive use of a witness's prior inconsistent state-

---

44. Cf. California v. Green, 399 U.S. 149, 160 (1970) indicating that in such circumstances it also is clear that the confrontation clause is satisfied. See Ch. VII, Part J.

45. For a defense of the orthodox view, see Beaver & Biggs, Attending Witness's Prior Declarations as Evidence, 3 Ind.L.Forum 309 (1970).

46. Note that the arguments supporting the orthodox view against admitting prior inconsistent statements for their substantive worth

apply equally against letting in party admissions for their substantive value. The recent trend is to remove party admissions from the category of hearsay instead of treating them, as has been the practice, as an exception to the hearsay rule. See Ch. VII, §§ 54, 58; Fed.R.Evid. 801(d).

47. For a careful and comprehensive analysis of the rule denying substantive effect to prior statements, see Lempert & Saltzburg at 478–89; McCormick § 251.

ment, even in instances when the prior statement does not fit within a recognized hearsay exception.[48]

When a prior inconsistent statement qualifies as an exception to the hearsay rule, it may be used, even under the orthodox rule, both as impeaching evidence and as substantive proof.[49] For example, where a party-witness has made an earlier contradictory statement,[50] that statement is a party admission which, because of an exception to the hearsay rule, may be received as substantive evidence.[51] Another escape from the hearsay rule is provided when the witness not only admits the prior inconsistency, but also recants part or all of his present testimony by stating that the assertion in the earlier statement is accurate. Here the cases hold the witness has adopted or merged his prior statement into his present testimony and hence his assertions, in effect, are contemporaneous statements from the stand.[52]

It remains to be considered whether a prior *consistent* statement should be classified as hearsay. The orthodox statement of hearsay, embracing as it does any statement offered for its truth which is made other than from the witness stand in the present proceeding, includes prior consistent statements. However, there is a significant difference between prior consistent and prior inconsistent statements. Where a prior statement is consistent with the trial testimony, the subsequent examiner has every opportunity for a full, forceful, and antagonistic interrogation. He may seek to impugn the general credibility of the witness, for the subsequent examiner is not trying to preserve one of the witness's accounts of an event while negating the other (as he must where a prior inconsistency exists). Thus, despite older precedents to the contrary, there is little logic to support

---

48. See Blakey, Substantive Use of Prior Inconsistent Statements Under the Federal Rules of Evidence, 64 Ky.L.J. 3, 35 n. 112 (1975).

49. Exceptions to the hearsay rule are discussed in Ch. VII.

50. Ch. VII, Part A.

51. McCormick, § 262, at 629–30. See United States v. Champion Int'l Corp., 557 F.2d 1270 (9th Cir. 1977).

52. This analysis is discussed in Ruhala v. Roby, 379 Mich. 102, 150 N.W.2d 146 (1967).

the application of the hearsay rule to prior consistent statements.[53]

This does not mean, however, that prior consistencies should be admitted freely. Evidence of these statements may constitute cumulative, superfluous proof; unlimited admission would encourage litigants and witnesses to strengthen their trial testimony by laying a groundwork of duplicative stories. Such a self-serving practice wisely is condemned by a generally recognized rule which prohibits bolstering a witness's testimony.[54] There are, however, occasions when a "fresh complaint" or prompt disclosure to a third party has special probative worth to show an event has occurred.[55] Indeed, silence by the victim of a crime might be viewed as inconsistent with the happening of the alleged occurrence. In many cases, especially those in which a criminal offense allegedly has occurred, there is often a special need for evidence of prompt disclosure because there are no eyewitnesses other than the perpetrator and the victim. Crimes such as rape or bribery, for example, are apt to be known only to the wrongdoer and the victim. Disclosure to a third person soon after an unusual occurrence is a natural and predictable response and, recognizing this, the courts have usually admitted evidence of a prior complaint or disclosure. Observe that by limiting the evidence to complaints which occur reasonably soon after the alleged event, the courts restrict the possibility of abuse.[56] Since the evidence is entered to confirm the happening

---

53. See McCormick, § 251, at 604. It also would seem that the prior consistency has been adopted by the witness and thus merges with his present testimony. See text supra at note 52.

54. See, e. g., United States v. Leggett, 312 F.2d 566, 572 (4th Cir. 1962); Graham v. Danko, 204 Va. 135, 129 S.E.2d 825 (1963).

55. United States v. Iaconetti, 540 F.2d 574 (2nd Cir. 1976). In theory, and under the practice in most jurisdictions, the evidence offered to strengthen the factual proposition that misconduct has occurred need only consist of testimony that the complaint was made; there is no need to recite to the trier the details of the disclosure or even the identity of the alleged wrongdoer. See IV Wigmore §§ 1135–36 (Chadbourn). But when prior consistent statements come in to rehabilitate a witness, details may be given. Id. §§ 1137–38.

56. Although most cases impose the requirement that the complaint be

of the event, many courts permit only evidence that there was a complaint about the act in question, but do not permit evidence of any details that were disclosed by the complaint.[57]

Prior consistent statements also have a special value in cases where a cross-examiner charges or implies that a witness's testimony is a recent fabrication developed for trial or that a witness has been corrupted or improperly influenced to distort or falsify his courtroom testimony. A prior consistency which predates the corrupting motive, event, or influence helps to rebut the express or implied accusation that the witness's testimony is tainted.[58] In these situations of "rehabilitating" the witness after an accusation of contrived testimony, the older cases admit the evidence of prior consistent statements only for the purpose of affecting credibility. Wisely, recent authority favors the use of this rebuttal or rehabilitative evidence for any purpose for which it is probative, including the truth of the assertion.[59] This accords with both sound theory and the practicalities of jury trial. Surely it is too much to ask a jury to accept a statement from the stand for its truth while using a prior consistent statement only as evidence of credibility.

Obedience to the traditional hearsay formula also precludes admission of prior out-of-court identifications of an individual. A pre-trial assertion, for example, that identifies the accused as the person who committed the act charged normally is offered for its truth and thus is hearsay. Yet in many instances an identification made closer in time to the encounter with the per-

---

made promptly, this condition is relaxed where there is a satisfactory explanation for the period of delay. People v. Mason, 301 Ill. 370, 379, 133 N.E. 767, 770–71 (1921). For a case admitting a "fresh complaint" in a bribery prosecution, see Commonwealth v. Friedman, 193 Pa.Super. 640, 165 A.2d 678 (1960).

57. See People v. Damen, 28 Ill.2d 464, 193 N.E.2d 25 (1963); IV Wigmore § 1136 (Chadbourn). But see Ch. VIII, Part B.

58. See United States v. Scholle, 553 F.2d 1109 (8th Cir. 1977); Sweazey v. Valley Transp., Inc., 6 Wash.2d 324, 107 P.2d 567 (1940); IV Wigmore, § 1128, at 268 (Chadbourn). See also Ch. VIII, § 85. But see United States v. Weil, 561 F.2d 1109 (4th Cir. 1977) (no proof bolstering statement made *prior* to promise of leniency).

59. See Fed.R.Evid. 801(d)(1); McCormick, § 251, at 604.

son whose identity is sought may be more reliable than a subsequent courtroom identification. This particularly is true where the earlier identification took place in circumstances that were not unfairly suggestive and the later courtroom identification occurred after a significant lapse of time in a courtroom setting which (because of the arrangement of counsels' tables and other indications of identity) makes it comparatively easy to identify the accused. This potentially greater reliability has prompted a growing number of courts to admit prior identifications as substantive evidence.[60] Most of these courts require that the identifying party be present and available for cross-examination.[61] Admission of a prior identification by one not present for cross-examination raises all the hearsay dangers, while not affording any opportunity for the cross-examiner to offset them.[62]

§ 53. The Hearsay Rule and the Federal Rules of Evidence

Under Federal Rule 801, hearsay is an oral or written "statement, other than one made by the declarant while testifying at the [present] trial or hearing, offered in evidence to prove the truth of the matter asserted."[63] A hearsay "statement" includes nonverbal conduct, *but only if the declarant intends* to make an assertion by his physical action, as, for example, when he points a finger to make an identification or nods his head in answer to a question.[64] Nonassertive conduct which, as we have seen, is conduct not intended by the actor as an assertion, is not within the federal definition of hearsay.[65]

---

60. See Fed.R.Evid. 801(d)(1)(c); S. Saltzburg & K. Redden, Federal Rules of Evidence Manual 459 (2d ed. 1977); McCormick, § 251, at 603.

61. See Annot., 71 A.L.R.2d 449, 456 (1960).

62. If a witness who testifies is unable to identify the accused in the courtroom, yet did make an earlier identification, the cross-examiner still can explore the circumstances of the prior identification and in-

quire as to the degree of certainty the witness had at the time of the earlier identification.

63. Fed.R.Evid. 801(c).

64. Fed.R.Evid. 801(a)(2). In United States v. Harris, 546 F.2d 234 (8th Cir. 1976), a declarant's laughter, when asked if he was really hurt, was treated as a "statement" subject to hearsay analysis.

65. Fed.R.Evid. 801(a), (c); Adv. Comm. Note to Fed.R.Evid. 801(a).

Subsection (d) of Rule 801 contains further refinements to the basic hearsay definition. Statements made by a party or by his representative (or those adopted by a party) are not classified as hearsay when offered against that party.[66] Traditionally, such statements, attributed to a party either by reason of his own utterance or on principles of adoption or agency, have been considered party admissions; as such, they have been admitted under the party admissions *exception* to the hearsay rule. Exceptions to the hearsay rule generally are limited to those out-of-court statements attended by circumstances that increase their trustworthiness. Guarantees of trustworthiness are not always associated with party admissions, since the test of their admissibility generally is only that a party or his representative (as defined in the cases or rules) made or adopted the extrajudicial statement which his opponent offers against the party at trial. For example, there is no requirement that the party's statement be against his interest at the time it was made, although in most instances the statement will have been disserving when made. Thus a disserving quality—which underlies an important exception to the hearsay rule and is associated with several others—may bolster the trustworthiness of most, but not necessarily, all party admissions.[67] The possible absence from party admissions of an element of trustworthiness persuaded the federal drafters to define such admissions as nonhearsay, rather than include them, as most courts have among the exceptions to the hearsay rule.[68]

In general, admissibility is the result under either classification, although the underlying rationale sometimes may be signif-

---

In United States ex rel. Carter Equip. Co. v. H. P. Morgan, Inc., 544 F.2d 1271 (5th Cir. 1977), the initialing of invoices was viewed as non-verbal assertive conduct within the Rule 801 definition of statement.

66. Fed.R.Evid. 801(d)(2). See, e. g., United States v. Porter, 544 F.2d 936 (8th Cir. 1976).

67. One exception to the hearsay rule, declarations against interest, is grounded on the assumption that a declarant is not likely to make a disserving statement unless it is true. See Ch. VII, Part I.

68. Adv.Comm. Note to Fed.R.Evid. 801(d)(2).

icant in defining the outer limits of admissibility.[69] Both the traditional and federal approaches cause a party to confront and explain his prior statements or those made by his representative.[70] And whatever the theoretical justification for party admissions, their admissibility is consistent with the Anglo-American adversarial system, which long has allowed a party considerable freedom in prescribing the course of litigation while enforcing the adverse consequences that flow from an adversary's mistaken strategy or tactics. The Federal rulemakers and many commentators assert that it is this consistency with the adversarial trial itself which justifies admissibility.[71] Other commentators propose that the principle of party responsibility [72] based upon personal or moral notions underlies the long-standing practice of admitting evidence of a party admission. Note that whether evidence of a party admission is presented is entirely in the hands of the adversary; a party can not introduce his own admission.

Finally, Rule 801 excludes certain prior statements of a declarant-witness from the definition of hearsay. Unwilling to re-

---

69. "[T]he degree to which the [party] admissions doctrine should be extended to statements other than those of a party himself rests on an assessment of the proper basis for admissibility." Weinstein & Berger, ¶ 801(d)(2)[01], at 111. The treatment of party admissions as nonhearsay has also led to drafting imperfections and ambiguities. For example, in the first sentence of Federal Rule 806, the drafters refer to hearsay statements and to non-hearsay party admissions, but in the second sentence they refer only to hearsay statements. The resulting difficulty is discussed in S. Saltzburg & K. Redden, Federal Rules of Evidence Manual 633 (2d ed. 1977).

70. See Kingsley v. Baker/Beech-Nut Corp., 546 F.2d 1136 (5th Cir.

1977); United States v. Porter, 544 F.2d 936 (8th Cir. 1976); United States v. Ojala, 544 F.2d 940 (8th Cir. 1976) (party's failure to protest a damaging remark made by his counsel in his presence made the remark an "adoptive admission" and therefore it was held to be nonhearsay).

71. Adv.Comm. Note to Fed.R.Evid. 801; Morgan at 241; Strahorn, A Reconsideration of the Hearsay Rule and Admissions, 85 U.Pa.L. Rev. 484, 564 (1937).

72. Lempert & Saltzburg at 366. These commentators assert that the probable basis for the rule is the accepted notions of morality that require an individual to be responsible for his own action.

move the hearsay ban entirely in circumstances where the out-of-court declarant also is a trial witness, the drafters compromised by passing a provision that classifies a witness's prior statements as nonhearsay in limited, specific situations. If a prior *inconsistent* statement "was given under oath subject to the penalty of perjury at a trial, hearing, or other proceeding, or in a deposition," [73] the statement constitutes substantive evidence. This provision limits the substantive use of a prior inconsistent statement to those situations where, as a practical matter, there usually will be convincing proof (often by a transcript or sworn deposition) that the statement was made. Hence, it is unlikely that an examiner wishing to negate the impact of the previous inconsistency will face a witness who denies the existence of the prior statement.[74] The Federal Rule also recognizes, as it should, that the prior inconsistent statement made under oath and under conditions where a perjury charge could result increases the likelihood that the statement is reliable. The Federal approach also encourages litigants who anticipate the need to offer a witness's prior statement for substantive purposes to take his deposition or, where possible, to call him to testify in a grand jury proceeding or preliminary hearing.

The treatment of prior *consistent* statements under Rule 801 largely is congruent with the common-law development. The Rule follows the common-law practice of admitting prior consistent statements of a witness when "offered to rebut an express or implied charge against him of recent fabrication or improper influence or motive . . . ." [75] Unlike the common law, however, the Rule allows the proponent to use such consistent statements not only to rehabilitate (accredit) the witness, but also as substantive evidence. As elsewhere noted,[76] permitting the sub-

---

73. Fed.R.Evid. 801(d)(1). United States v. Scholle, 553 F.2d 1109 (8th Cir. 1977); United States v. Jordano, 521 F.2d 695 (2d Cir. 1975). For a discussion of "other proceedings," see United States v. Castro-Ayon, 537 F.2d 1055 (9th Cir. 1976).

74. See supra § 52; Ch. VIII, § 83.

75. Fed.R.Evid. 801(d)(1)(B). See United States v. Navarro-Varelas, 541 F.2d 1331 (9th Cir. 1976); United States v. Iaconetti, 406 F. Supp. 554 (E.D.N.Y.1976).

76. See supra § 52 at note 53.

stantive use of prior consistent statements accords with sound theory and practice. The Federal Rule also endorses a recent common-law trend by admitting prior identifications for their substantive use, provided the identifying witness is on the stand and subject to cross-examination.[77] No express provision is made for the admission of a "fresh complaint"—at least not under Federal Rule 801. But in some circumstances, such a complaint will fit within an exception.[78]

Care must be taken to observe that Federal Rule 801(d)(1), which covers various kinds of prior statements by a witness (inconsistent statements, consistent statements and prior identifications), contains quite different criteria controlling when these statements fall outside the hearsay rule. The characterization of a prior inconsistent statement as nonhearsay depends upon whether the earlier statement was under oath and subject to the penalty of perjury, whereas the characterization of a prior consistent statement as nonhearsay is conditional upon whether it is used to rebut a charge of improper influence or recent fabrication. A prior identification is considered outside the hearsay rule if no more is shown than that the testifying witness, now subject to cross-examination, made an earlier identification of the person in question "after perceiving him." [79]

NOTES

1. *Nonassertive Conduct.* Consider a divorce suit brought by husband against wife on grounds of wife's adultery with X. The wife denies having sexual relations with X, and wants to testify that after she and X were discovered together in wife's bedroom, the wife immediately insisted that a physician be called to examine her and to verify that she had not recently had intercourse. Assuming the physician could not be contacted, is the testimony of the wife's request hearsay? See Corke v. Corke and Cooke, 1 All.E.R. 224 (1958), which holds that the wife's statements are inadmissible hearsay. Even if the wife intended to imply that she had not had relations,

---

77. Fed.R.Evid. 801(d)(1)(C); see supra § 52 at note 60.

78. In particular, note the possibility that the complaint may consti-

tute an excited utterance. Ch. VII, Part B, § 61.

79. Fed.R.Evid. 801(d)(1)(C).

isn't the jury in a position to decide how much, if any, probative value should be attributed to the wife's demands for an examination?

2. *Prior Statements.* How do you explain the fact that Fed.R. Evid. 801(d) classifies as nonhearsay only those prior inconsistent statements made under oath, while the same rule prescribes a nonhearsay classification for prior consistent statements offered to rebut a charge of recent fabrication even though the prior consistent statement was *not* attended by an oath?

3. *Recognizing Hearsay.* Professor Laurence Tribe has made a significant contribution to an understanding of the hearsay rule and the exceptions which attend it. Tribe, Triangulating Hearsay, 87 Harv.L.Rev. 957 (1974). The diagram which follows draws upon his work, as does a portion of the following explanatory discussion.

Suppose it is necessary for a party to show that the door of a storage building was left unlocked prior to a theft occurring on the evening of January 15. A witness testifies that a worker (declarant) at the building told the witness that the door in question "was not secured at the end of the workday on January 15." If this evidence is offered for the proposition that the door was not locked, all four hearsay dangers are present:

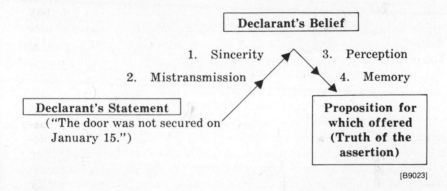

[B9023]

The trier must conclude that the declarant actually *believed* (sincerity) that the door was *unlocked* (note also the possible mistransmission resulting from use of the word "secured"). Next the trier must conclude that the declarant's belief was correct—that he had a chance to *observe* the door (perception) and that he correctly *recalls* that it was unlocked on January 15 (memory). This line of reasoning, which proceeds from the declarant's statement to his belief and then to the accuracy of that belief, involves reliance upon the declarant's credibility. The hearsay prohibition clearly is applicable.

Suppose, however, the question is not simply whether the door was unlocked, but also whether the owner of the storage building took reasonable steps to keep its contents secure. A witness testifies that at the end of the workday on January 15th he overheard the declarant report to the owner that the door in question was not secured. Offered for the purpose of showing that the owner was made aware of a condition of insecurity, the evidence is not hearsay:

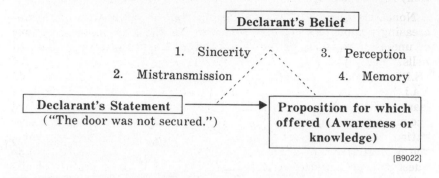

[B9022]

In using the evidence of declarant's statement, it is unnecessary for the trier to rely upon the declarant's credibility, and therefore the hearsay dangers are avoided. Other evidence must be introduced as the basis for a finding that the door was unlocked. Of course, the owner can explain why it was reasonable to take no action following the declarant's statement to him. He may say, for example, that he thought the declarant was mistaken in his assertion. However, it is still unnecessary for the trier to rely upon the declarant's credibility: the question is what the owner thought or should have thought in light of all surrounding circumstances, including the declarant's statement.

The case of Thomas v. State, 14 P.2d 953 (Crim.Ct.App.Okl.1932) involved a prosecution for forgery accomplished by passing a check bearing the signature of one "B. F. Smith." The prosecution wished to show that, contrary to the accused's contention, B. F. Smith was a fictitious person and thus the check in question actually was forged with this name by the accused. A deputy sheriff testified that he had inquired of persons in the area whether they knew of B. F. Smith and had received negative answers. Did the deputy's testimony violate the hearsay rule? The court held it did not. Is this decision sound?

4. *Polls or Opinion Surveys and the Hearsay Rule.* The applicability of the hearsay rule to opinion polls varies with the particular survey. Some surveys do not involve a hearsay response from the person

polled. For example a poll to determine how many people *express* an opinion on the subject of world disarmament does not involve a hearsay response: it is sufficient for purposes of the survey that the respondent does or does not express an opinion. If the survey seeks to determine how many people favor disarmament, it is necessary to believe the respondent's statement that he does or does not favor disarmanent, thus raising the hearsay danger of insincerity. A poll not directed at opinion, but rather at determining what the respondent may have done in the past (e. g. whether he voted in a particular election) raises the additional hearsay danger of a defect in memory.

Nonetheless, even when the hearsay rule is applicable, courts increasingly admit the evidence under one of the traditional exceptions or under an exception of recent origin that is specifically addressed to polls. See Zippo Mfg. Co. v. Rogers Imports, Inc., 216 F.Supp. 670 (S.D.N.Y.1963); Note, Opinion Polls and the Law of Evidence, 62 Va.L.Rev. 1101 (1976). A well-designed poll produces results that, at least within limits, are reliable. However, it is important to afford the cross-examiner an adequate opportunity to test the design and execution of the poll. Such factors as the selection of a sampling area, the determination of a random selection within it, the design of the questions, the experience of the poll-takers, and the execution of the interviews can be important.

CHAPTER VII

THE HEARSAY RULE: SELECTED EXCEPTIONS

PART A. PARTY ADMISSIONS

§ 54. In General

Although the Federal Rules treat admissions by a party as nonhearsay,[1] the common law considers such statements hearsay but admits them under the party admissions exception to the hearsay rule. The federal departure in classification traces the rationale for admitting party admissions offered by an opponent more to the spirit of the adversary system than to the considerations of trustworthiness which more commonly characterize the various hearsay exceptions;[2] as elsewhere noted,[3] however, neither the federal innovation nor the common-law view supplies a unifying theme that adequately explains the admissibility of party admissions.

Despite the federal approach, the classification here accorded party admissions is the traditional one: the extra-judicial statements of a party are hearsay when offered for their truth, yet are received into evidence as an exception. This treatment comports with most of the existing cases without sacrificing innovation, for the range of admissibility under the federal and common-law classifications is substantially similar (at least between the federal judiciary and those states which have followed the recent trend toward broadening the party admissions exception). The Federal Rule governing party admissions receives special attention in a section below, where differences between it and the traditional common-law approach are noted.

A party admission is a hearsay "statement" comprised of words or conduct, made or adopted by a party (or made or

---

1. Fed.R.Evid. 801(d)(2).

2. Adv.Comm.Note to Fed.R.Evid. 801(d)(2). See Ch. VI, § 53, at note 66.

3. Ch. VI, § 53.

adopted by his representative, agent or "privy"), which is offered against the admitting party by his opponent. As a tactical matter, an adversary will present evidence of a party admission when the admission is inconsistent with the "admitting" party's contentions at trial.

It is important to recognize that an extra-judicial party admission is not conclusive. After evidence of a party admission has been introduced, the admitting party may try to negate the evidence, either by denying the statement (if appropriate) or by rebutting the inferences which the proponent seeks to draw from it.[4] Suppose, for example, A offers against opposing party B the latter's extra-judicial admission of driving at an excessive rate of speed prior to an automobile accident. B may deny that he made the statement, admit making it but explain he was only joking, or seek to lessen the impact by testifying that speed was not the cause of the collision. A party admission, in other words, has only such evidential value as the trier accords it, and the adversaries are free to argue about probative weight. This inconclusive feature distinguishes evidentiary party admissions from the parties' formal admissions which usually are made in the pleadings, through a discovery rule, or by a stipulation. These formal admissions remove the fact conceded from further contest.[5]

---

4. As discussed in Ch. VI, § 49, the basis for the hearsay rule is the inability of the opposing party to cross-examine the declarant. Notice that when a party, as opposed to his representative, has made an admission, a hearsay objection lodged against evidence of the admission is really an assertion that the objector-party did not have an opportunity to examine himself when the statement was made. While the awkward posture of the objector serves as a rationale to justify admissibility when the objecting party is also the declarant, this rationale arguably does not extend to admissions made by representatives or by those in privity. See infra § 57.

5. See, e. g., Fed.R.Civ.P. 36 which facilitates the admission of facts. Some courts hold that testimony by a party from the witness stand, as distinguished from extra-judicial statements, has a conclusive effect. This rule applies when he testifies concerning a matter within his personal knowledge and his testimonial statement contradicts his asserted claim or defense. See, e. g., Holland v. Holland, 217 Va. 874, 234 S.E.2d 65 (1977); Bell v. Harmon, 284 S.W.2d 812 (Ky.App.1955).

Two issues frequently are raised by offers of evidence intended as party admissions. First, are the actions or words of the admitting party sufficiently unambiguous to be probative? Second, to what extent should the admitting party be held responsible for statements or actions of affiliated persons such as his agents or privies? The first issue is a familiar one of relevance. The second issue involves a policy judgment concerning the ambit of party responsibility. We shall return to this question shortly.

§ 55. Party Admission: An Illustration

The most common party admission is an oral or written statement by a party which, in the context of litigation, is determined by his adversary to be disadvantageous to the admitting party and hence is offered in evidence against him. In an Iowa automobile accident case,[6] the defendant introduced as a party admission the plaintiff's signed statement that the defendant (in whose car plaintiff was a passenger) was not intoxicated and had driven carefully. The inconclusive nature of party admissions is demonstrated by the fact that the plaintiff testified in rebuttal that he had signed the statement (which had been drafted by defendant's insurance agent) without reading it and while in the hospital under the influence of pain-killing drugs.

The foregoing case illustrates another point about party admissions: frequently admissions by an adversary party are inconsistent both with the admitting party's contentions at trial, as advanced through the pleadings or other witnesses, and with his trial testimony.[7] In this situation, the introduction of the earlier, extra-judicial statement serves both a substantive purpose and an impeaching or discrediting function. Hence, even though a party admission can be introduced against a party whether or not he takes the stand, it has enhanced probative value if it is inconsistent with the party's trial testimony and can be used to impeach him. This additional value may induce the proponent of a party admission to withhold its presentation until his adversary testifies.

---

6. Olson v. Hodges, 236 Iowa 612, 19 N.W.2d 676 (1945).

7. See, e. g., Peterson v. Richards, 73 Utah 59, 272 P. 229 (1928).

§ 56.　Party Admission by Conduct

Nonverbal action, such as flight from the scene of the crime [8] or changing one's appearance or name,[9] also can constitute a party admission, provided, of course, these actions have probative value. Such conduct usually is offered to demonstrate a sense of guilt or wrongful conduct. If a party conducts himself inconsistently with his trial contentions, his contradictory conduct may be introduced against him under the exception for party admissions. An alternative analysis finding increased acceptance characterizes conduct not intended as a substitute for words as nonassertive and thus outside the definition of hearsay.[10] Obviously, where this latter analysis prevails, it is unnecessary to invoke the present exception. Thus, evidence of the accused's flight from the scene of the charged offense might be received as nonhearsay, circumstantial evidence.

A failure to take action or to speak out sometimes may have probative value to confirm the existence of a certain fact or condition. This occurs most frequently when a party, confronted with a statement or accusation, fails to deny or protest its accuracy. A failure to correct or deny such a statement constitutes an implied admission, assuming it reasonably can be expected that a person in the party's position would protest the statement were it untrue. An implied admission occurred, for example, in a federal case [11] in which the evidence showed that the defendant in a tax evasion prosecution had removed bundles of money from a safe and stated to interested beneficiaries that each bundle contained $500. One of those present said to him "No; $5000", and the defendant remained silent. The court held that the defendant's failure to deny the accuracy of the onlooker's statement was an implied admission of the higher amount.

A trial judge should exercise a high degree of care in admitting evidence of admissions implied because of silence. It first is essential that he determine the statement was heard and understood by the admitting party and that the latter had an op-

---

8. State v. Townsend, 201 Kan. 122, 439 P.2d 70 (1968).

9. McCormick, § 271, at 655.

10. See Ch. VI, § 51.

11. United States v. Alker, 255 F.2d 851 (3d Cir. 1958).

portunity to reply. Second, the judge should be alert to constitutional difficulties. It would violate one's constitutional right against self-incrimination to admit evidence that he failed to respond to a statement or allegation if he were properly exercising his fifth amendment right to remain silent.[12] An accused in a criminal proceeding must be warned, when governmental officials deprive him of his "freedom of action in any significant way," [13] that he has the constitutional right to remain silent, and this right may not be infringed. Finally, the judge should recognize that some statements or accusations, especially those which might be exaggerated or inflammatory, reasonably may not warrant a reply. Consequently, he should condition admissibility upon his determination that a reasonable person in the position of the nonanswering party would have replied had such person thought the statement inaccurate.[14]

§ 57. Vicarious or Representative Admissions

A principal issue associated with party admissions is the range of admissibility—the extent to which a party may be held responsible (in the evidentiary sense) for statements made by someone else. The strongest case for a representative or vicarious admission is found where the principal-party expressly has authorized an agent to speak for him on a particular subject or expressly has adopted another's prior statement. If, for example, an injured person commissioned his doctor or lawyer to speak for him at a hearing before an insurance claims adjuster, his representative's statements would constitute authorized party admissions and, as such, would be admissible against the authorizing party. Similarly, if an independent doctor or lawyer

---

12. Adv.Comm.Note to Fed.R.Evid. 801. See Miranda v. Arizona, 384 U.S. 436, 468 n. 37 (1966).

13. Miranda v. Arizona, 384 U.S. 436, 444 (1966); see McCormick, § 161, at 353–58.

14. State v. Guffey, 261 N.C. 322, 134 S.E.2d 619 (1964); see Arpan v. United States, 260 F.2d 649, 655 (8th Cir. 1958); Heller, Admissions by Acquiescence, 15 U.Miami L. Rev. 161, 163–64 (1960). Suppose the subject matter of the unanswered statement is not within the knowledge of a party against whom the evidence is offered. Lack of knowledge would, in most circumstances at least, make it reasonable not to reply. McCormick, § 270, at 652–53.

spoke at the hearing, and subsequently a party expressly assented to the former's statements, these would be admissible as adoptive party admissions.

A change in the facts requires a somewhat different analysis, grounded upon the principles discussed in the preceding section. Suppose a physician writes a letter to his patient setting out the former's diagnosis and prognosis. If the patient then appends the letter to his claim for insurance reimbursement and forwards it to the insurer, it might be inferred that he acquiesced in the physician's findings. In these circumstances, a court probably would find that the patient impliedly had adopted the physician's statement; hence the doctor's letter would be admissible against the patient as a party admission.[15] Of course, if in forwarding the letter the patient protested the doctor's findings, there would be no implied adoption. This, however, does not preclude the proponent from showing that the patient had *authorized* the physician to speak for him; such a showing would provide an alternative basis for admitting the physician's statements.

An adoptive admission, then, may be any statement expressly or impliedly accepted by the admitting party. If the judge finds that a party has adopted another's statement, the opponent may enter it as a party admission. As to other statements by third persons (not involving adoption), admissibility traditionally has been restricted to previously authorized statements. Until recently, the courts have drawn a sharp distinction between an agent's conduct, for which his principal may be vicariously liable, and an agent's statements, which can not be imputed to the principal absent conferral of authority to speak. The fact that an agent speaks while engaged in *activity* that is clearly within the scope of his delegated duties does not mean that he *speaks for* his principal, even if he speaks about such activity. Authority to speak is a matter for separate determination.[16] Conse-

---

15. See Wade v. Lane, 189 F.Supp. 661 (D.D.C.), aff'd 290 F.2d 387 (1961). In the circumstance, affirmative action implies adoption; in the analogous situation discussed supra at note 11, inaction in the form of silence resulted in adoption.

16. See Restatement of Agency, Second, § 286.

quently, difficulty is encountered with statements made by agents not employed to speak for the principal,[17] but rather engaged primarily to perform physical acts such as making repairs, ushering, driving a truck, and so forth.[18] In these cases, many courts, especially in their early decisions, take the narrow view that the authority to speak either is nonexistent or does not extend to statements of fault or misdeeds that could result in the principal's liability.[19] A truck driver, the reasoning goes, is engaged to drive the principal's truck, not to speak for him; hence a statement by the driver that he was speeding is not a party admission of his employer-principal,[20] and can not be admitted against the employer under a party admissions theory.

Fortunately, this restrictive view, which often results in excluding reliable, probative evidence, is losing favor. There is a clear trend toward admitting the agent's statement as the employer's party admission if the statement concerns a "matter within the scope of . . . [the] agency or employment, made during the existence of the [agency or employment] relationship." [21] The requirement that the employment or agency relationship exist at the time of the representative's statement protects the principal against disserving statements of former, perhaps disgruntled, employees.

Even in those jurisdictions that abide by the orthodox approach and take a narrow view of the employee's authority to

---

17. As the drafters of the federal rules noted, "[s]ince few principals employ agents for the purpose of making damaging statements, the usual result was the exclusion of the statement." Adv.Comm.Note to Fed.R.Evid. 801(d)(2).

18. E. g., Semprini v. Boston & M. R.R., 87 N.H. 279, 179 A. 349 (1935); Rudzinski v. Warner Theatres, Inc., 16 Wis.2d 241, 114 N. W.2d 466 (1962). Are paid informants "agents" of the police with authority to speak? See United States v. Pena, 527 F.2d 1356 (5th Cir.), cert. denied 426 U.S. 949 (1976),

where the issue is raised but not resolved.

19. IV Wigmore, § 1078, at 166 (Chadbourn). A review of cases applying the traditional view may be found in Nobero Co. v. Ferro Trucking, Inc., 107 N.J.Super. 394, 258 A.2d 713 (1969).

20. McCormick, § 267, at 640–41.

21. Fed.R.Evid. 801(d)(2); see Nobero v. Ferro Trucking, Inc., 107 N. J.Super. 394, 258 A.2d 713 (1969); McCormick, § 267, at 641.

speak, careful evidentiary planning often results in the admission of his statement. To begin with, various exceptions to the hearsay rule, such as those for spontaneous declarations and declarations against interest, may apply with the result that an employee's statement is freely admissible against any party, including the principal. The rationale of admissibility is the satisfaction of the conditions of reliability prescribed by the applicable hearsay exception and not the rationale of adversarial responsibility which underlies party admissions. Furthermore, if the employee or agent is made a party, his prior statement often will constitute *his own party admission*, even if it is not that of his principal. As always, the test of relevance must be satisfied, which in this context means that the prior statement must have probative value to establish the agent's liability. If the relevance test is satisfied and the agent is joined as a party defendant in the suit against the principal, the agent's statement is admissible against the agent himself, although, as we shall see, there are restrictions upon how this use affects the employer's liability.

Note that a statement by an agent might support one or more of the following propositions: (1) the agency relationship or scope of employment ("I was making a delivery."); (2) the agent's fault ("I forgot to give a signal."); (3) the principal's fault ("My employer told me to ignore the overloaded cargo and make the delivery by noon."). As to the first of these uses, the traditional requirement is that the fact of agency must be proved by evidence independent of the statement offered as a party admission [22]—to hold otherwise would amount to assuming

---

22. IV Wigmore, § 1078, at 176 (Chadbourn). See infra note 1 at the end of Part A. Even the approach of the Federal Rules appears to require independent evidence that the employment or agency relationship existed at the time of the agent's statement. Further, if an issue arises under Federal Rule 801(d)(2) whether the agent's statement concerns "a matter within the scope of his agency or employment," the proponent should be required to produce independent evidence of the scope of the agency. Note, however, that the *judge* makes the necessary findings with regard to the existence of the employment relationship and what matters fall within it. See Ch. X, § 97. In making these determinations, he is "not bound by the rules of evidence except those with respect to privileges." Fed.R.Evid. 104(a).

the agency existed and then validating that assumption by using the agent's statements as a party admission against the principal. If there first is produced evidence of an agency relationship that includes "speaking authority," the agent's declaration then becomes admissible against the principal. With respect to the second use, regarding the agent's fault, the evidence—as we just observed—constitutes the agent's party admission and is clearly admissible to establish his liability. Note, however, that under principles of vicarious liability and respondeat superior, the superior is liable if the employee's conduct is actionable, regardless of any wrongful conduct on the part of the superior. Hence, the trier's use of the employee's declaration, ostensibly only to find the employee's wrongful conduct, nonetheless may affect the employer's liability. This indirect or derivative use of the evidence to impose liability on the employer [23] results from the substantive law; the evidentiary use is against only the employee. Unfortunately, some courts have not made this distinction and have resisted even this derivative use by requiring "that the agent's liability be established by evidence also admissible against the principal." [24]

Finally, when the agent's statement speaks to the principal's fault, courts traditionally have required that the statement be made within the scope of the employee's employment *and* that there be preliminary evidence that the employee had the requisite authority to speak.[25] As noted above, however, the trend is toward admitting an agent's or employee's statement if it concerns a matter within the scope of his duties. Such a statement may inculpate either the agent or the superior or, for that matter, both of them.

---

23. A good analysis is found in Madron v. Thomson, 245 Or. 513, 419 P.2d 611, clarified 423 P.2d 496 (1966).

24. E. Cleary & J. Strong, Evidence, Cases, Materials, Problems 632 (2d ed. 1975). See Annot., 27 A.L.R.3d 966 (1969); Note, 11 Hous.L.Rev. 481, 484 (1974).

25. See, e. g., Madron v. Thomson, 245 Or. 513, 518–20, 419 P.2d 611, 614–15 (1966). For a federal case decided prior to the effective date of the Federal Rules of Evidence, see Northern Oil Co. v. Socony Mobil Oil Co., 347 F.2d 81 (2d Cir. 1965).

An interesting aspect of the judicial development of vicarious or representative party admissions is the growth of coexisting doctrines illustrative of contrasting extremes between exclusion, on the one hand, and admissibility, on the other. A hinderance to the full exposure of relevant evidence is the doctrine—still viable in some jurisdictions—that renders inadmissible statements which the principal has authorized to be made *only* between agents or from an agent to himself. Under this restrictive doctrine, such statements are not party admissions of the principal for the reason that he conferred no authority to speak to third persons, but rather he gave only limited authority to speak to one or more designated persons (i. e., the principal or another agent). This limited authority is exceeded in instances where the agent speaks to a person not within these classes.[26]

Although the precise extent of an agent's real or apparent authority constitutes an appropriate line of demarcation for some purposes (such as the power to contractually bind the principal), this fine distinction serves no useful purpose when applied to evidentiary matters. The law of evidence is concerned with such interests as trustworthiness and adversarial fairness. An employee's statement, made to his superior or to a co-employee may be highly trustworthy, especially if it concerns a matter within the scope of the employee's duties. It is not usually in the employee's interest to make false statements adverse to his principal. Furthermore, the employer often has access to any available evidence that casts doubt upon the accuracy of his employee's statement. In short, the trier of fact should be allowed to weigh the employee's statement in light of all of the circumstances developed at trial. These considerations have caused a

---

26. Application of this rule often results in the exclusion of accident reports, internal reviews, investigations, etc., prepared at the principal's request. Unless the court finds the principal conferred upon the agent(s) preparing the report the authority to speak to persons outside the business organization, admissibility against the principal under a party admissions theory is precluded. See Dilley v. Chesapeake & Ohio Ry., 327 F.2d 249 (6th Cir. 1964). Note, however, that the *Dilley* case would now be governed by Fed.R.Evid. 801(d)(2) (D) which supports admission.

growing number of courts to abandon the technical restriction placed upon intra-business communications.[27]

A second, contrasting doctrine also has judicial support. Although the exclusion of intra-organizational communications should be deemed unduly confining, the admission of statements made by a party's "privy" probably is an unwarranted extension of the admissions exception. To understand this aspect of party admissions, it first is necessary to consider what is meant by the relationship of "privity." Although imprecise, the term (in the present context, at least) denotes a relationship between a party and another, derived by means of a consensual undertaking (usually a transfer) that purports to confer something of value. A relationship of privity is said to exist where one transfers to a party a right, title, or interest in some tangible or intangible asset; in many jurisdictions a relationship of privity also exists where a party and another jointly hold certain proprietary interests. Buyers and sellers stand in a relationship of privity, as do deceased persons and those who take their property through will or intestacy.[28] Many courts also apply the privity label to joint owners, joint tenants, and joint obligees.[29]

In its most important application, the doctrine of party admissions by a privy holds that statements by a predecessor in interest [30] which concern the property (or right) transferred *and*

---

27. See, e. g., Johnson v. Grand Trunk Western R. Co., 58 Mich. App. 708, 719, 228 N.W.2d 795, 800 (1975).

28. McCormick, § 268, at 647–48.

29. Id., at 647; IV Wigmore, § 1077 (Chadbourn). "Privity" perhaps is a confusing label to use in connection with the party admission of a joint holder, since it is not immediately apparent why a joint holder should be treated like a predecessor in interest—which aptly describes the other privity situations. But note that the party admissions

doctrine is applicable only to joint ownership as distinguished from ownership in common. Morgan at 251–52. Apparently the theory is that "identity of substantive interests should determine the scope of admissible evidence." Id. at 252. In a joint tenancy, the interest of the deceased tenant passes to the surviving tenant; in a tenancy in common, the interest of the deceased tenant passes to his heirs or devisees. Thus each joint tenant is a potential transferee or a transferor.

30. In the case of joint owners the privy is not a predecessor, but one

which are made while the predecessor-declarant purportedly owned the property [31] are admissible against the successor in interest. Thus, if *A* sold a painting to *B*, an earlier statement by *A* that the painting had a flaw that had been retouched would be admissible in litigation between *B* and *C* concerning the condition of the painting. That is, *C* could introduce *A*'s statement as *B*'s party admission, assuming *A* made the statement while he still owned the painting.

This result is supported by the dubious rationale that one taking property (or at least colorable title to it) [32] assumes the burdens of the evidentiary admissions that are traceable to his predecessor. This is not a satisfying ground for the admissibility of hearsay evidence. The major concern here is trustworthiness. It is true that *A*'s prior position to know about the condition of the painting favors admissibility. But the application of the present exception denies to *B* the chance to cross-examine *A* concerning the latter's assertion.[33] The major hearsay dangers of insincerity, inaccurate perception, and faulty memory all are present. *A*'s relationship to *B* is an arm's length transaction; it carries no authority, express or implied, entitling *A* to speak for *B*. A weak analogy supporting admission is found in the increasingly accepted rule admitting an agent's statement concerning a matter within the scope of his employment if made during the employment relationship. The privity rule requires that the statement be made during the period of ownership and it admits only statements about the right, title, or interest transferred. The single arm's length transaction giving rise to privity is a

---

who holds the property contemporaneously. See supra note 29.

31. Colorable title would suffice. As Morgan notes at 280, the requirement that the predecessor make the statement " 'while owning the interest' [later transferred to a party] does not denote or connote actual or legal ownership of any interest. It means simply, while the declarant had whatever interest, if any, the party in the action is claiming to have derived from him, so that the party has the same legal position with reference to the property that the declarant had at the time of the declaration."

32. See supra note 31.

33. For a careful criticism of the privity rationale of party admissions, see Morgan, Admissions, 12 Wash.L.Rev. 181, 203 (1937).

tenuous link, however, compared with the more substantial relationships that characterize other representative or vicarious party admissions. Further, the likelihood that the declarant's declaration concerns a subject about which he is knowledgeable does not lessen the danger of insincerity. One might urge that the exception for a predecessor's statement is supported by the fact that such a statement usually is against the financial or proprietary interest of the predecessor-declarant,[34] but this argument assumes too much: any statement, whether self-serving or disserving, made by the predecessor concerning his interest or title in the thing later transferred comes within the exception.[35] Furthermore, there is another exception to the hearsay rule that specifies when declarations against interest are admissible.[36] It is thus difficult to justify the admission of a predecessor's statements, at least on the grounds that normally support exceptions to the hearsay rule. Beneath the surface of many of the cases, however, practical considerations such as the unavailability of the declarant, his known familiarity with the property in question, and, often, the fact that his statement was disserving when made, operate to subordinate sound theory to pragmatic considerations and account for the considerable recognition of the rule extending party admissions to statements of a privy.

A discussion of party admissions would be incomplete without mention of the admissibility of the statements made by a coconspirator. A conspiracy is analogous to a business partnership in the sense that its participants act in concert to achieve a desired end.[37] Thus, the courts have viewed a party as having authorized all acts and declarations of a coconspirator made during and in the furtherance of the conspiracy.[38] The line between declarations which further the conspiracy and those which do not is shadowy. As Professor McCormick notes, the criterion often applied in practice is whether the statement was made

---

34. See McCormick, § 268, at 649 for a summary of the arguments for and against the privity exception.

35. Morgan at 279–80

36. See infra Part I.

37. McCormick, § 267, at 645.

38. Morgan at 249; United States v. Diez, 515 F.2d 892 (5th Cir. 1975), cert. denied 423 U.S. 1052 (1976).

during the continuance of the conspiracy,[39] although cases can be found which reject statements on the ground that the declarations did not further the conspiracy.[40] A more common basis for exclusion is that the conspiracy had terminated before the statements were made. Yet here, too, there is room for a difference of opinion, and acts of concealment sometimes are considered within the conspiracy.[41]

The exception for coconspirators' statements applies in both civil and criminal cases. It is unnecessary that the pleadings or indictment charge a conspiracy, and the declarant-coconspirator need not be a party to the proceeding in which his statement is introduced against a conspiring party. However, the proponent of the statement must make a preliminary evidentiary showing sufficient for the judge to find that the conspiracy existed, that the declarant and the party were members of it, and that the declarant made the statement in question in its furtherance.[42] The evidence used to establish the existence of the conspiracy and its membership must be in addition to and independent of the declaration which the proponent offers as being within the coconspirator's admissions rule. Some difficult problems involving the proper roles of judge and jury arise in cases involving admissions

---

39. McCormick, § 267, at 645.

40. E.g., State v. Podor, 154 Iowa 686, 135 N.W. 421 (1912).

41. McCormick, § 267, at 646.

42. There is disagreement among the courts concerning the proper role of the judge in assessing the evidence of a conspiracy. Under one view, the judge need only determine that the evidence supporting the proponent's claim that a conspiracy existed is sufficient to constitute a "prima facie" showing —that is, the evidence is sufficient for a reasonable jury to find that there was a conspiracy, that the declarant and the party against whom the declaration is offered were coconspirators, and that the statement in question was made in furtherance of the conspiracy. Carbo v. United States, 314 F.2d 718 (9th Cir. 1963). Under a second view, the judge himself must determine that there was a conspiracy and so forth; in making this determination, he assesses the credibility of the evidence offered. United States v. Petrozziello, 548 F.2d 20 (1977). A very good discussion of these and other approaches is contained in Saltzburg & Redden, Federal Rules of Evidence Manual, 462–69 (2d ed. 1977). The role of the judge in connection with a coconspirator's admission is discussed further in Ch. X, § 98.

by a coconspirator, especially in criminal cases in which conspiracy is charged as a substantive offense. These problems are treated elsewhere.[43]

§ 58. Party Admissions Under the Federal Rules

As noted previously, the Federal Rules of Evidence remove party admissions from the classification of hearsay. In their nonhearsay form, admissions against a party opponent are governed by Rule 801(d)(2).[44] A party's own statement may be offered against him whether he made it in his individual or representative capacity. Authorized statements made by a party's agent and offered against the party also are admissible; it is immaterial that the authorized statement was made to another agent or to the principal.[45] Significantly, the rule also includes as a party admission a statement by an "agent or servant concerning a matter within the scope of his agency or employment," if the statement is made while the employment or agency relationship still exists. As noted, this provision is part of a modern trend toward eliminating the restrictive traditional approach that rejects evidence on the ground that the employee or agent was not authorized to speak for his principal. Arguably, the broader test adopted in the Rules is consistent with a party's adversarial responsibility: since he has engaged the agent to act on his behalf and he has some control over the agent's duties, it is fair that the statements of the agent related to his employment be admissible against the party-principal. Also, there is

---

43. Ch. X, § 98; supra note 42.

44. The pertinent provisions exclude from the definition of hearsay:

(2) Admission by party-opponent. —The statement is offered against a party and is (A) his own statement, in either his individual or a representative capacity or (B) a statement of which he has manifested his adoption or belief in its truth, or (C) a statement by a person authorized by him to make a statement concerning the subject, or (D) a statement by his agent or servant concerning a matter within the scope of his agency or employment, made during the existence of the relationship, or (E) a statement by a coconspirator of a party during the course and in furtherance of the conspiracy.

45. Adv.Comm. Note to Fed.R.Evid. 801(d)(2). See United States v. Pena, 527 F.2d 1356 (5th Cir.), cert. denied 426 U.S. 949 (1976).

reason to think that an agent's statement made under the conditions prescribed by the Rule are reliable: the agent usually is well informed about matters related to his employment, and those of his statements which are introduced against his employer normally are against the interest of the agent, the employer, or both. It is not likely that the employee would make false inculpatory declarations or statements jeopardizing his continued employment.[46]

Rule 801(d) makes no provision for admitting the declarations of one in a relationship of privity to a party, a step which may trigger the demise of this aspect of party admissions. It is possible, however, that some declarations by a privy could be received under the "catchall" exceptions, 803(24) and 804(5),[46a] designed to admit evidence deemd trustworthy, but which does not fit any of the specific exceptions. Furthermore, a privy's statement, if disserving when made, will qualify as a declaration against interest under Federal Rule 804(b)(3) if the declarant is unavailable as a witness.[47]

NOTES

1.   Where the admission of a statement against a party depends upon the conferral of authority or upon a particular relationship (such as one of employment, agency, or conspiracy) between the declarant and the party, that authority or relationship must be established by evidence independent of the declaration itself. Thus, even though the declaration may allude to the relationship, etc. that, if established, can give the declaration an admissible status, the relationship first must be shown to exist by evidence independent of the admission. Under the preferable practice, the judge determines if the relationship exists. See Ch. X, §§ 97-98.

2.   Sometimes a single transaction or event which involves an infraction of the criminal law also gives rise to one or more suits for civil damages. A traffic accident, for example, may involve both a misdemeanor (or felony) and a tortious activity. If the public offense is tried first and a guilty plea is entered, many jurisdictions allow evidence of the plea to be introduced in the civil action based upon the same event. See Smith v. Southern Nat. Ins. Co., 134 So.2d 337 (Ct.

---

46.   McCormick, § 267, at 641; Lempert & Saltzburg at 373.

46a.   See infra Part J at notes 94-95.

47.   See infra Part I.

App.La.1961). This evidence does not, however, have a conclusive effect in the civil action. It should be noted that some jurisdictions deny admission to evidence of pleas of guilty in traffic offenses when later offered in a civil suit, but admit evidence of other guilty pleas. Although the status of a plea of nolo contendere has been debated, Federal Rule of Evidence 410 states that neither a plea of nolo contendere nor a withdrawn guilty plea is admissible in any other civil or criminal action. See Ch. V, § 48.

A different situation exists if an accused pleads not guilty but nonetheless is convicted. May his conviction be introduced in a civil trial based upon the same transaction? It is clear that there has been no party admission. There is growing authority, however, that the doctrine of collateral estoppel makes the first judgment conclusive as to those facts actually and necessarily decided. See Cardillo v. Zyla, 486 F.2d 473 (1st Cir. 1973). Compare Eastern Renovating Corp. v. Roman Catholic Bishop of Springfield, 554 F.2d 4 (1st Cir. 1977).

Another view admits evidence of the criminal conviction in the civil trial, but permits the jury to accord to the evidence such weight as they desire. Finally, many courts, perhaps still a majority, exclude evidence of the criminal conviction. A factor which may be determinative is whether the party is in a defensive posture in the second proceeding or whether he is, as the courts say, "seeking to profit from his criminal acts." An example of the latter is where an individual is convicted of arson, but nonetheless brings suit against the insurer of the burned structure. Courts tend to admit evidence of the earlier conviction.

3. A basic principle of evidence is that personal knowledge of the witness or declarant is essential to admissibility. The speaker must have seen, heard, or otherwise perceived the event about which he speaks. But if the admissibility of a party admission is grounded on the adversary system, it is unnecessary that the party have personal knowledge of the event or condition about which he speaks. The cases so hold. Janus v. Akstin, 91 N.H. 373, 20 A.2d 552 (1941); see also Adv.Comm. Note to Fed.R.Evid. 801. Should this exemption from the usual requirement of personal knowledge apply when a party's agent, employee or privy makes the declaration in question? Since one basis of admitting another's declaration as an admission of a party is that the declarant probably knows the subject about which he speaks, it should be required that the representative have personal knowledge.

PART B. SPONTANEOUS DECLARATIONS

(PRESENT SENSE IMPRESSIONS AND
EXCITED UTTERANCES)

§ 59. In General

The term "spontaneous declaration" as used here includes two related but distinct hearsay exceptions for statements made under circumstances minimizing the dangers of insincerity and inaccurate memory. The first of these exceptions is made for a statement of "present sense impression." Such a statement draws its trustworthiness from the fact that it is made contemporaneously with, or immediately after, the event that it describes. The requirement of substantial contemporaneity minimizes the dangers of deliberate misrepresentation (since there is little time during which to conceive a false assertion) and of a faded memory. The second exception is made for a spontaneous declaration usually called an "excited utterance." This statement is made under a sense of excitement, shock, or stress and at a point in time fairly close to the event it describes. Here, it is the state of nervous excitement or shock that is thought to still the speaker's ability to practice deception. Requiring the statement to be made soon after the event in question helps ensure against defects in memory.

Both the statement of present sense impression and the excited utterance must pertain to the event that caused the immediate or excited response. A statement about an unrelated matter indicates that the speaker's attention is not confined to the immediately preceding event, thus increasing the possibility of conscious deception. An unrelated event also may be farther in time from the declaration, and the greater the time lapse, the more significant the possibility of a memory flaw. The admissibility of both types of spontaneous statements is conditioned upon a preliminary determination by the judge that the various requirements of the applicable exception have been met.

§ 60.   Present Sense Impression

This exception is of comparatively recent origin. The leading case supporting it is Houston Oxygen Co. v. Davis,[48] decided by the Texas Supreme Court in 1942. Some courts have not recognized the exception as such, but nonetheless have admitted statements bearing the characteristics of a present sense impression.[49] Increasing recognition can be expected now that the Federal Rules provide a hearsay exception for it:

> *Present sense impression*—A statement describing or explaining an event or condition made while the declarant was perceiving the event or condition or immediately thereafter.[50]

Although judicial disagreement may develop concerning how soon after the event (or condition) the statement must be made, the central idea is that the statement follows so closely the perception of the event that deliberate falsification and memory defects are unlikely. In most instances, the person who heard the declarant's statement about the event also will have been in a position to observe the circumstances described. This opportunity for confirmation further reduces the chance of a purposeful misstatement. The rule, however, does not, require that the hearer be in a position to observe the event or condition. Nonetheless, the courts are likely to take this factor into account, especially when there is an issue concerning the lapse of time between the event or condition and the statement describing it.

The qualifying language "describing or explaining" restricts admissibility to a statement which details the perceived event. A statement which may have been evoked by the event but which does not describe or explain what happened does not come

---

48. 139 Tex. 1, 161 S.W.2d 474 (1942). See also Morgan at 298–300.

49. McCormick, § 298, at 710. The exception usually applied to justify admission is that for res gestae, the most amorphous of the exceptions. See infra note 3 following Part B.

50. Fed.R.Evid. 803(1). See, e. g., MCA Inc. v. Wilson, 425 F.Supp. 443 (S.D.N.Y.1976) (after hearing a song, declarant remarked that it sounded like "Bugle Boy"—a song to which *P* held the copyright).

within the exception.[51] Two aspects of the present exception which may be contrasted with the exception for an excited utterance are (1) the extent to which contemporaneity is required, and (2) the extent to which the statement must directly describe the event or condition to which it pertains.

§ 61. Excited Utterances

Unlike the exception for present sense impressions, the exception for an excited utterance requires that the declarant speak while under the stressful influence of a startling event or condition. The necessary state of excitement may embrace the consequent shock of emotional distress.[52] The rationale supporting admission is that the emotional stress suspends the process of reflective thought necessary for conscious fabrication, and that the recentness of the event minimizes the danger of faulty memory. Section 803(2) of the Federal Rules adopts the exception as it has been developed by the common law in most jurisdictions:

> *Excited Utterance*—A statement relating to a startling event or condition made while the declarant was under the stress of excitement caused by the event or condition.

There are several distinctions and refinements to be made with regard both to the Rule and the common-law tradition which underlies it. The time lapse between the event and the declaration obviously is an important factor. A state of excitement, of course, can linger for a period of time after the causal event has occurred, but the longer the interval between event and declaration, the greater the chance of exclusion.[53] Observe, however, that the required immediacy for present sense impres-

---

51. Weinstein & Berger, ¶ 803(1)[01], at 77–78.

52. Wright v. Swann, 261 Or. 440, 493 P.2d 148 (1972); People v. Damen, 28 Ill. 2d 464, 193 N.E.2d 25 (1963); Keefe v. State, 50 Ariz. 293, 297–98, 72 P.2d 425, 427 (1937); McCormick, § 297, at 704–06.

53. Staiger v. Gaarder, 258 N.W.2d 641 (N.D.1977); Tait v. Western World Ins. Co., 220 So.2d 226 (La. App.1969); Marshall v. Thomason, 241 S.C. 84, 127 S.E.2d 177 (1962). But see State v. Stafford, 237 Iowa 780, 23 N.W.2d 832 (1946).

sions does not necessarily accompany an excited utterance: if a declarant makes the statement as he regains his faculties after a period of unconsciousness or extreme shock, the passage of several or more hours between the exciting event and the statement usually is not fatal to admissibility.[54]

Consider also the directness with which the utterance must relate to the startling event. A present sense impression must describe or explain an event or condition, but the excited utterance need only relate to the startling event. This difference in scope is illustrated by the leading case Murphy Auto Parts Co. v. Ball,[55] a suit against a defendant-employer in which the action of an allegedly negligent employee accidentally had injured the plaintiff. An issue in the case was whether the employee was engaged in his employer's business at the time of the accident. In a post-accident remark, the employee stated that he had been on an errand for his employer. The trial judge admitted this statement, and the Court of Appeals for the District of Columbia approved the admission, holding that the statement qualified as an excited utterance. The test, said the court, is whether there is an exciting event which prompts the declaration and if it is so prompted, it need not be confined only to a description of the event.

The *Murphy* case is interesting for still a second point. Under the traditional view, the declaration in question would have qualified as a party admission if an agency relationship were shown to exist by evidence outside the employee's declaration *and,* under the old strict view, *if* the agent had authority to speak. The proponent of the evidence in *Murphy* had failed to prove these elements, so that the statement in question could not come in as a vicarious party admission. Yet it did qualify for admission as an excited utterance. The point, made earlier in this text[56] but illustrated in *Murphy* is that imaginative think-

---

54. Allen v. McLain, 75 S.D. 520, 530, 69 N.W.2d 390, 396 (1955); State v. Stafford, 237 Iowa 780, 23 N.W.2d 832 (1946); Davis Transport, Inc. v. Bolstad, 295 S.W.2d 941 (Tex.Civ.App.1956). But see Staiger v. Gaarder, 258 N.W.2d 641 (N.D.1977).

55. 249 F.2d 508 (D.C.Cir. 1957), cert. denied 355 U.S. 932 (1958).

56. See supra § 57.

ing about possible alternate avenues of admission may yield positive results.

The proponent of an excited utterance may be faced with the question whether he must provide independent evidence (aside from the excited declaration itself) of the startling occurrence. Although there is some disagreement, the weight of authority appears to accept the declaration as proof that the exciting event has occurred.[57] The Federal Rule, which is silent on this point, probably will be interpreted so as to permit the declaration to serve as evidence that the event took place.[58]

NOTES

1. Arguments about the reliability of an excited utterance usually center upon the proposition that while one who is startled may not falsify, the chances of impaired perception are increased when he is excited. See Hutchins & Slesinger, Some Observations on the Law of Evidence—Spontaneous Exclamations, 28 Colum.L.Rev. 432 (1928). In short, as the risk of one hearsay danger goes down, the risk of another is increased. However, this infirmity need not result in exclusion, but rather could be considered in weighing the evidence. Apparently, no jurisdiction has rejected the excited utterance exception.

2. It is the responsibility of the trial judge to determine if the exception for excited utterances is applicable. In People v. Poland, 22 Ill.2d 175, 181, 174 N.E.2d 804, 807 (1961) the court stated the necessary factors consisted of "(1) an occurrence sufficiently startling to produce a spontaneous and unreflecting statement; (2) absence of time to fabricate; and (3) the statement must relate to the circumstances of the occurrence." The fact that the declaration was in the form of an opinion or conclusion or that it was made in answer to a question should not preclude admissibility. The rule against opinion

---

57. E. g., State v. Hutchison, 222 Or. 533, 353 P.2d 1047 (1960); Armour v. Industrial Comm., 78 Colo. 569, 243 P. 546 (1926). See Slough, Res Gestae, 2 Kan.L.Rev. 41 (1953).

58. See Traveler's Ins. Co. v. Mosley, 75 U.S. (8 Wall) 397, 19 L.Ed. 437 (1869). Weinstein & Berger, ¶ 803(2)[01], at 82–83 discuss the *Mosley* case and Rule 803(2). They point out that Fed.R.Evid. 104(a) lends support to the assumption that the declaration may be received as evidence of the happening of the event. That rule frees the judge from the rules of evidence (except with regard to privileges) in making preliminary determinations about the admissibility of evidence. This suggests that the hearsay declaration could be used to establish the event.

is designed to apply to testimony from the stand, where there is an opportunity to rephrase a question or answer. That an excited utterance was given in response to a question should not itself defeat admissibility; this fact, however, may be relevant in the judge's determination whether the declaration was made under the influence of excitement or stress. See McCormick, § 297, at 706, 708.

3. The phrase "res gestae" still appears in judicial opinions despite widespread condemnation. A declaration is said to be admissible despite the hearsay rule if it constitutes a part of "the thing done." Often, the term is used to justify the admission of a statement having independent legal significance. But, as we saw in the preceding chapter, such a statement is not hearsay and thus need not be entered under an exception. Unfortunately, the res gestae label is sometimes indiscriminately applied to hearsay declarations that fit within the exceptions for statements of excited utterance, present sense impression, physical condition, or state of mind. See infra Part C. The imprecision of the term, coupled with careless usage by the courts, has been a source of perplexity for students and lawyers. See generally VI Wigmore §§ 1757, 1766–70.

PART C. PHYSICAL OR MENTAL CONDITION

§ 62. In General

The hearsay exceptions for statements about the declarant's physical or mental condition are well established. Their recognition in part is based upon the realization that one's primary means of learning about another's bodily condition or state of mind often is through his statements. These exceptions also are defined so as to ensure trustworthiness. Reliability is achieved by the general requirement (subject to several qualifications) that the excepted statement must describe a currently existing physical or mental condition—that is, the declaration must refer to a condition that exists at the time of the statement and not to some past condition. This requirement of contemporaneity reduces somewhat the chance of reflective fabrication; it also eliminates the risk of faulty memory. Note that faulty perception is usually not a problem. Arguably, out-of-court statements of presently existing physical or mental condition are as reliable as subsequent courtroom testimony.

Federal Rule 803(3), which is based upon the common law, provides a hearsay exception for:

> Then existing mental, emotional, or physical condition—A statement of the declarant's then existing state of mind, emotion, sensation, or physical condition (such as intent, plan, motive, design, mental feeling, pain and bodily health), but not including a statement of memory or belief to prove the fact remembered or believed unless it relates to the execution, revocation, identification, or terms of a declarant's will.

The sections which follow explicate these provisions. Note, however, that the Federal Rule adopts the general requirement which limits the excepted declaration to a "then existing" condition, but suspends this requirement in cases involving a will. As we shall see, the courts have considered a declarant's statement relating to his will as falling within a special category and have been willing to broaden the present exception to include a statement about past events or conditions.

§ 63. Present Physical Condition

Physical condition is a familiar courtroom issue. The existence of an injury to a party (or in some cases to a non-party) may be an element of a cause of action. And the extent of injury usually affects the damage award. Although many physical ailments and conditions can be ascertained by the trier's visual inspection or by a physician's testimony giving the results of a medical examination, it generally is helpful and sometimes essential to consider an individual's own statement of his physical condition. This is especially true with regard to such subjective internal symptoms as pain, headaches, nausea, and so forth.

The present exception admits relevant hearsay declarations in which the declarant, either by exclamation or narration, indicates his then existing bodily condition.[59] Thus, a declarant's out-of-court statements that he was having difficulty hearing and

---

59. Casualty Ins. Co. v. Salinas, 160 Tex. 445, 333 S.W.2d 109 (1960); Frangos v. Edmunds, 179 Or. 577, 173 P.2d 596 (1946); Kickham v. Carter, 335 S.W.2d 83 (Mo.1960).

that he was experiencing headaches would be admissible under the present exception.[60] There is no danger of a defect in memory and only a minimal danger of erroneous perception. Although insincerity is a risk, the jury readily can appreciate the possibility of a self-serving motive. Furthermore, the judge has the authority to reject evidence of a statement of physical condition in instances where there appears to be a high risk of fabrication.[61]

The extra-judicial statement of bodily condition may be recounted by any witness who overheard it. There is no requirement (at least in the majority of jurisdictions) that the person overhearing the statement be a medical specialist.[62] However, in a growing number of jurisdictions it is significant whether the statement was made to a physician who is being consulted for purposes of treatment. In this setting, many jurisdictions, including the federal judiciary,[63] now expand the exception for physical condition to include statements of *past* physical condition.[64] This relaxation of the usual requirement that the declaration describe a condition existing at the time of the statement rests on the rationale that effective treatment normally depends upon an accurate statement of condition; thus the patient has an incentive to be truthful. Statements of past physical condition, of course, raise the possibility of a defect in memory.

The common-law cases reflect a marked reluctance to admit declarations of condition made to a physician consulted not for treatment, but rather solely for the doctor's preparation of his expert testimony. In this setting, the rationale justifying the expanded exception for statements of past condition does not apply. Furthermore, many cases reject even statements of *present* condition when made to the medical expert not engaged

---

60. Frangos v. Edmunds, 179 Or. 577, 173 P.2d 596 (1946).

61. McCormick, § 291, at 690.

62. VI Wigmore, § 1718, at 63 (Chadbourn); McCormick, § 291, at 689.

63. See Fed.R.Evid. 803(4) set out in the text infra at note 66.

64. Meaney v. United States, 112 F. 2d 538 (2d Cir. 1940); Peterson v. Richfield Plaza, Inc., 252 Minn. 215, 89 N.W.2d 712 (1958).

in treatment or in diagnosis undertaken for purposes of treatment.[65]

Federal Rule 803(4) creates the following hearsay exception:

> Statements for purposes of medical diagnosis or treatment—Statements made for purposes of medical diagnosis or treatment and describing medical history, or past or present symptoms, pain, or sensations, or the inception or general character of the cause or external source thereof insofar as reasonably pertinent to diagnosis or treatment.

The Federal Rule is explicit in its provision that statements of past symptoms are admissible when made "for purposes of medical diagnosis or treatment. . . ." By not specifying that the statement be made directly to a physician, the Rule allows admission of remarks made to other medical attendants.[66] Note that the wording of the Rule is broad enough to admit statements made to a physician consulted for the purpose of enabling him to testify even if no treatment is contemplated. The Advisory Committee's Note explains that many common-law decisions allowed the nontreating physician to state to the trier the patient's account of his past symptomatology when such testimony helped to explain the basis of the expert's diagnosis and prognosis. In theory, these statements were to be not considered for their truth, but rather for their bearing upon the physician-expert's opinions. The Committee thought the jury could not be obedient to this distinction and that, on balance, the declarations should come in and be accepted for their truth if the trier so wished to treat them.[67]

NOTE

Sometimes statements to a doctor include references to the cause of the accident, e. g., "I was struck on the right hip by a bicyclist." If the

---

65. See McCormick, § 293, at 692.

66. The drafters noted that under Rule 803(4) "[s]tatements to hospital attendants, ambulance drivers and *even members of the family* might be included." Adv.Comm. Note to Fed.R.Evid. 803(4) (emphasis added).

67. Adv.Comm. Note to Fed.R.Evid. 803(4).

statement of the immediate cause of the accident is pertinent to treatment and if one safely can presume that the patient knew this, the patient's statement to a treating physician (or other medical personnel associated with treatment) arguably encompasses even that portion of the statement which details the external cause of the injury. Thus viewed, the entire statement including reference to the external cause is admissible. Some courts have so held, but the greater number have refused to receive statements of external cause. See McCormick, § 292, at 691. The Federal Rule, 803(4), quoted in the text above does provide for the admission into evidence of a statement describing "the inception or general character of the cause or external source . . .." Even this provision, which adopts the position of the most liberal cases, would not justify the admission of statements of fault, e. g., "I was injured by X, who drove his bicycle through a stop sign." Adv.Comm. Note to Fed.R.Evid. 803(4).

§ 64. Present State of Mind: In General

Professor McCormick reminds us of the frequency with which the "substantive law . . . makes legal rights and liabilities hinge upon the existence of a state of mind in a person involved in the transaction at issue." [68] The law inquires into one's mental state in both criminal and civil litigation. A crime normally is defined so as to require a particular mens rea or state of mind; the measure of civil damages sometimes depends upon the mental suffering of the victim or the malicious intent of the defendant. The cases are replete with other instances where mental state is in issue: the question of where one is domiciled is answered in part by ascertaining his intention; the issue of whether a will was validly executed (or whether it was revoked) may turn upon intent; the question whether one fraudulently conveyed his assets is in part answered by his intentions. In these and other situations, the substantive law is drawn so that the existence or nonexistence of a particular state of mind itself is a pivotal element in the case.[69] In other words, mental state is often the ultimate proposition to which the evidence (whether direct or circumstantial) is addressed.

---

68. McCormick, § 294, at 694.

69. Extortion cases provide frequent examples. See United States v.

Adcock, 558 F.2d 397 (8th Cir. 1977); United States v. Taglione, 546 F.2d 194 (5th Cir. 1977).

Observe, however, that state of mind, once established, also can serve as circumstantial evidence of behavior. In this situation, state of mind is not the ultimate proposition to be proven, but serves as an intermediate basis for further inferences about conduct. Suppose, for example, there is an issue in a case as to whether an individual has left the United States. If it can be established (by direct or circumstantial evidence) that he intended to leave, this intention (state of mind) can be used as a basis for the further inference that he departed.[70]

The central problem of the following section is the scope and application of the exception to the hearsay rule that allows into evidence a declarant's statements of his mental condition when these statements are offered for the truth of their assertion. It should be observed, however, that some statements bearing upon mental attitudes, condition, or intent, which appear to involve the present exception may be seen upon closer inspection not to invoke it. Close examination may show that the statement in question is not hearsay and thus requires no exception. If, for example, a declarant-testator refers to his son-in-law, X, as a "crooked politician" and evidence of this statement is offerred in a case where the issue is whether the testator intended to include X as a beneficiary under his will, the present exception need not be invoked. The proffered utterance is not offered for its truth (that is, to show that X is a dishonest politician), but only as circumstantial evidence of the declarant's dislike of his son-in-law. In contrast, if the testator's statement had been "I hate X and intend to exclude him from any share in my estate," evidence of this declaration should fall within the present exception. The trier is asked to believe that the declarant entertained the hatred and intention to foreclose X. In cases involving statements of mental condition, the first question to be asked is whether the intended use of the evidence requires that the trier accept as true the declaration of mental state.[71]

---

70. Note that even direct evidence of the actor's state of mind (e. g., his declaration "I intend to leave") is circumstantial evidence that he left. See Ch. 2 § 9.

71. Consider in the setting of a child-custody case, a statement by the child that her stepfather "killed my brother and he'll kill my mommie too." This declaration is not

What elements of trustworthiness qualify a statement of mental condition for an exception to the hearsay rule? Because the declarant expresses an existing (as distinguished from a past) state of mind, there is no danger of faulty perception or memory. The contemporaneous nature of the statement also reduces somewhat the possibility of insincerity, at least where the statement is made with apparent spontaneity.[72] Hence, in many instances, a declarant's hearsay statement describing an existing emotional or mental state carries as high a degree of reliability as does his subsequent testimonial statement describing retrospectively the mental condition.

§ 65. State of Mind to Prove Conduct: Use and Limitations

Selected illustrations from cases in which the substantive law makes mental state an ultimate (as opposed to an intermediate) issue have been set out in the preceding section. We have also seen that state of mind can be used as part of an inferential chain which, ultimately, is directed toward conduct.[73] For example, a declarant's intention to undertake a certain act increases somewhat the probabilities that he pursued his intention and

hearsay if offered only to show circumstantially that the declarant regarded the stepfather with fear and anxiety. Betts v. Betts, 3 Wash.App. 53, 473 P.2d 403 (1970). On the other hand, the statement that "I hate my stepfather and don't want to live with him," if offered to show the child's wishes concerning her custodian probably would be viewed as hearsay, but within the present exception. Some authorities, however, would hold that the statement had a circumstantial use to show the child's lack of affection and preferences for another guardian. The reasoning is that the use of the words, even if not accepted as true, show a lack of affinity and a probable preference for someone else as a guardian. See Ch. VI, § 50, the text preceding and following n. 19.

72. If the statement appears to be a contrivance, the judge should exercise his discretion and exclude it. See Fed.R.Evid. 403. For an interesting case that calls for an analysis of the hearsay/nonhearsay distinction as well as careful consideration of the risk of insincerity, see State v. Baldwin, 47 N.J. 379, 221 A.2d 199 (1966).

73. Deane Buick Co. v. Kendall, 160 Colo. 265, 417 P.2d 11 (1966) (declarant's statement that he intended to return to work admitted on the issue of whether he was going to work when he sustained a fatal accident).

accomplished the contemplated act. But where the evidence of an actor's state of mind consists of his own declarations, the factfinder's use of this evidence necessitates a reliance upon the truth of the declarant's statement, and the present hearsay exception must be invoked.

In the leading case of Mutual Life Ins. Co. v. Hillmon,[74] the central issue was whether a body discovered at Crooked Creek, Kansas was that of Hillmon, the insured, or that of Walters, a companion. Part of the evidence offered by the defendant insurance company consisted of letters written by Walters to his family and fiancee in which he declared his intention to leave Wichita and journey with Hillmon to the vicinity of Crooked Creek. The United States Supreme Court held Walters's written statements admissible under the state of mind exception, since they showed his present intention to travel with Hillmon to Crooked Creek.[75] This intention was relevant because it increased somewhat the probabilities that Walters embarked upon his intended journey and reached his destination, thereby increasing the likelihood that the body was his.

Despite this straightforward analysis there is a latent question of relevance (and, as we shall see, an additional hearsay difficulty) in the *Hillmon* case that was not satisfactorily addressed by the court. Walters's communications indicated that he was going to accompany Hillmon to their common destination. Walters's journey to Crooked Creek appeared to have depended upon the cooperation of another (Hillmon); this contingency operates to reduce the probative force of the evidence, for if Hillmon decided not to undertake the journey, Walters probably would not have embarked for Crooked Creek.[76] However, so long as Wal-

---

74. 145 U.S. 285 (1892).

75. For a detailed account of this case and its ramifications, see Maguire, The Hillmon Case—Thirty-three Years After, 38 Harv.L.Rev. 709 (1925).

76. Under the circumstances of *Hillmon*, the probability that Walters would not have gone to Crooked Creek alone or with a person other than Hillmon is increased by the fact that Walters was to be employed by Hillmon when the latter found a site satisfactory for a sheep ranch. See Mutual Life Ins. Co. v. Hillmon, 145 U.S. 285, 288 (1892).

ters's declarations were offered to show his probable future conduct and not that of Hillmon, this contingency should affect only the weight to be given to the evidence, not its admissibility.[77]

A more difficult question arises from the inferences that can be derived from the contingency that Walters was travelling with Hillmon. Suppose the question in the case were whether Hillmon had journeyed to Crooked Creek and, suppose further, that Walters's declarations were offered not to show his conduct, but to show that of Hillmon. To admit the portion of the declaration that Walters intended to accompany Hillmon allows the inference that Hillmon intended to accompany Walters and that, in fact, he did so.[78] This chain of proof permits a statement, admitted because of the exception for Walters's present state of mind, to show Hillmon's state of mind from which Hillmon's conduct is inferred.[79]

The rationale behind the state of mind exception does not support such an extension: the declarant's express or implied statement of the intent and conduct *of another person* possesses all the dangers of hearsay and none of the assurances associated with the present hearsay exceptions.[80] Despite this "theoretical awkwardness," [81] the language of the Supreme Court in the *Hillmon* case is broad enough to admit that portion of Walters's declaration alluding to Hillmon which carries the associated inference that Walters went with Hillmon.[82] It is to be stressed, how-

---

77. See United States v. Pheaster, 544 F.2d 353, 376 & n. 14 (9th Cir. 1976) (noting that contingencies always are present that could frustrate a person's asserted intentions).

78. See discussion in United States v. Pheaster, 544 F.2d 353, 377 (9th Cir. 1976).

79. Note that the state of mind exception would allow Walters or any other competent witness to testify that *Hillmon stated* his present intention to make a certain

trip. This would enlarge the probabilities that Hillmon undertook the journey.

80. Lempert & Saltzburg at 414.

81. United States v. Pheaster, 544 F.2d 353, 377 (9th Cir. 1976).

82. Mutual Life Ins. Co. v. Hillmon, 145 U.S. 285, 294–296 (1892): "Evidence that . . . [Walters] had the intention of leaving Wichita with Hillmon would tend . . . to show that he went from Wichita to Crooked Creek with Hillmon."

ever, that the issue in the *Hillmon* case was Walters whereabouts; it was not argued that Hillmon was elsewhere than in the Crooked Creek area. Nonetheless, most courts have followed the apparent lead of the Supreme Court on this question of how much of a declaration is admissible and have permitted a declarant's statement of his present intention to undertake a course of action requiring the cooperation of another to serve as evidence that the *contemplated act was accomplished.*[83] The opponent of the evidence is entitled to a limiting instruction that directs the jury to consider the declarant's statement as evidence only of his conduct and not as evidence of the conduct of the other possible participant.[84]

This practice of limiting the use of the state-of-mind declaration may be of little efficacy where the real interest of the trier is not in the declarant's future conduct, but in that of the co-participant. In People v. Alcalde,[85] the exception for present state of mind was applied by the Supreme Court of California (over the strong dissent of Justice Traynor) in a most interesting set of circumstances. The prosecution was for murder, the accused was one Frank, and the victim was his girlfriend Bernice. In an effort to show that Bernice was with Frank on the evening of her murder, the state offered her statements to a witness that she was "going out [to dinner] with Frank tonight." A limiting instruction that the hearsay declaration could be used only as evidence of Bernice's intention was given, but it is argu-

---

Id. at 295. The court states: "The letters in question were competent . . . as evidence that, shortly before the time when other evidence tended to show that he went away, he had the intention of going, and of going with Hillmon, which made it more probable both that he did go and that he went with Hillmon . . . ." Id. at 295–96.

83. Lempert & Saltzburg at 414:
Most courts follow the Supreme Court . . . and allow a state-

ment of an intention to engage in some action with another to support the inference that this action was done with the other and, since the two are not separable, to support the inference that the other did the action with the declarant.

84. McCormick, § 295, at 699. But see supra note 83.

85. 24 Cal.2d 177, 148 P.2d 627 (1944).

able that the evidence should have been rejected. Neither Bernice's whereabouts at the time of her death, nor her identity, was a point of dispute at trial. What was in dispute was whether Frank was with her. Hence, the evidence was of little probative worth for its limited purpose of showing that the declarant went out to dinner, but was highly probative (or so the trier may have thought) to show that Frank was the declarant's companion. Note also, that in the *Hillmon* case, where Walters declared his intention to travel to Crooked Creek with Hillmon, Walters's intention to go to Crooked Creek might have been fulfilled even if Hillmon had decided not to make the journey.[86] But in *Alcalde*, the girlfriend could not "go out *with Frank*" unless the latter consented to participate in this social engagement. The primary value of the evidence was not to show that she went out, but that Frank was her escort.

Despite the foregoing analysis, the result in *Alcalde* may be defensible. There was evidence in the record that Bernice dressed for dinner and that she left her apartment. One witness testified that she thought she saw Bernice leave in a car with a male. Would she have gone out with an escort other than Frank or, assuming the witness was mistaken, would she have gone out alone? Of course, these possibilities exist. It is significant, however, that she asserted an intention to pursue a course of conduct (go out to dinner) with a particular person (Frank) and there was evidence that the conduct was undertaken. In these circumstances, where there is evidence of a declarant's intention and evidence that she undertook the predicted course of conduct, the probability that the other individual participated is increased. The declarant's intention to go out with Frank is fulfilled only if he is her escort and evidence showing that she went out (or further evidence showing that she went out with a male) serves to confirm the realization of her intention.[87] Like-

---

86. In Walters's letters, he expressed a keen interest in seeing the part of the country to which he intended to travel. See Mutual Life Ins. Co. v. Hillmon, 145 U.S. 285, 288–89 (1892). But see, supra note 76.

87. A careful analysis of People v. Alcalde, supra note 85, appears in Lempert & Saltzburg at 414–15.

wise, were there independent evidence that the other alleged participant took steps to implement the contemplated joint activity (such as dressing to go out, and, thereafter driving in the direction of his purported companion's apartment), the dangers associated with the declarant's statement of intention would be lessened.

Under this suggested approach, the admissibility of a declarant's statement that he will undertake a course of conduct with X, when offered as evidence tending to show that the conduct was accomplished depends upon (1) independent evidence that the declarant or X undertook the activity and (2) the likelihood that the declarant would not have undertaken it unless X participated (i. e., the degree of cooperation required of X). Hearsay dangers still exist: for example the declarant may have a defective memory concerning the prior arrangement with X, or the declarant may be lying. But in the circumstances of a particular case, corroborating evidence may lessen the dangers enough to justify the admission of a declaration of the kind encountered in *Alcalde*, even in the face of a very real danger that the trier will use the declaration as evidence of X's conduct.

In a recent federal prosecution for a kidnapping conspiracy, the United States Court of Appeals for the 9th Circuit approved the trial judge's admission of the victim's statement that he intended to meet Angelo, the accused, in a nearby parking lot, obtain some marijuana, and then return.[88] Although there was no independent evidence that Angelo had travelled to the purported meeting place, there was undisputed evidence that the victim had left his companions with the avowed purpose of going to the

---

88. United States v. Pheaster, 544 F.2d 353, 374–80 (9th Cir. 1976). The trial preceded the effective date of the Federal Rules of Evidence and both the trial and appellate courts applied Rule 26 of the Federal Rules of Criminal Procedure (The "admissibility of evidence" shall be governed by "the principles of common law as they may be interpreted by the courts of the United States in the light of reason and experience."). However, the Court of Appeals notes that under one interpretation of Federal Rule of Evidence 803(3), its decision would be the same even if the case had been tried after the effective date of the Rules. Id. at 379–80. See infra note 89 and accompanying text.

parking lot to rendezvous with the accused. The victim was not thereafter heard from.

The admission into evidence of the victim's declaration of intention, including the name of the accused, makes it highly probable that the jury used the statement as evidence that Angelo was the individual whom the victim encountered after leaving his companions. The act of meeting Angelo required his cooperation, since the meeting place was a parking lot to which Angelo presumably would have to travel. All hearsay dangers are present. Against these persuasive reasons for rejection, it is necessary to weigh the corroborating evidence that the victim took the initial steps to accomplish the joint action. Undoubtedly, there was a pressing need for the evidence, but that need was to connect Angelo with the offense and not to show that the victim was to meet some unidentified person in the parking lot. Thus, the real utility of the evidence falls outside of its permissible limited use (to show only the victim's action). If admissibility is to be justified on the basis of the need to connect Angelo with the kidnapping, the limiting charge instructing the jury to consider the victim's declaration only with regard to the victim's conduct not only belies the real purpose of the evidence, but also asks of the jury a discrimination at odds with common sense.

We see, then, that one line that may mark the boundaries of the present exception lies between a declarant's statements of present intention regarding his future conduct and his statements asserting the future conduct of another. This distinction is consistent with the language of Federal Rule 803(3). It is noteworthy that the House Judiciary Committee which reviewed this rule commented that it "intended that the Rule be construed to limit the doctrine of . . . Hillmon . . ., so as to render statements of intent by a declarant admissible only to prove his future conduct, not the future conduct of another person." [89]

---

89. H.R.Rep.No.93–650, 93d Cong., 2d Sess. 13–14, reprinted in 1974 U.S.Code Cong. & Admin.News 7075, 7087. In United States v. Pheaster, the court notes that this quoted sentence reflects a cutback in the prevailing common law. It also notes that this restrictive interpretation apparently is contrary to the Advisory Committee's intent to incorporate the *Hillmon* doctrine in full. 544 F.2d 353, 379–80 (1976).

It remains to be seen whether the courts will take seriously the Committee's intention by denying admissibility or whether they will give it only the perfunctory attention of a limiting instruction.

Another major restriction on the use of the state-of-mind exception may be considered in connection with the leading case Shepard v. United States.[90] In *Shepard*, the United States Supreme Court again turned [91] its attention to declarations of mental state offered as circumstantial proof of conduct. Dr. Shepard was prosecuted for taking the life of his wife. The indictment charged that death had been effected by means of poison. There was evidence that shortly before dying, Mrs. Shepard summoned her nurse and asked to examine the contents of a whiskey bottle. Stating that this was the liquor she had taken just before collapsing, she inquired whether there was enough remaining in the bottle to permit a test for the presence of poison. She then remarked that the taste and smell were unusual and stated "Dr. Shepard has poisoned me."

The government at first had Mrs. Shepard's statements admitted under the hearsay exception for dying declarations;[92] however, on appeal it was held that the prosecutor failed to show that all of the necessary elements of this exception were present.[93] There remained, however, other appellate issues: could admissibility be sustained, as the government urged, on the grounds either that Mrs. Shepard's declarations were not hearsay or that they fell within the state-of-mind exception? There was testimony in the record that Mrs. Shepard had remarked at various times that she had no further will to live and that she had stated that she might take her own life. Since these statements showed a depressed state of mind (a mental condition consistent with the defense theory of suicide), the gov-

---

90. 290 U.S. 96 (1933).

91. Mutual Life Ins. Co. v. Hillmon, discussed supra at note 74, was decided in 1892. The *Shepard* case was decided four decades later.

92. See infra Part H.

93. There was a failure to demonstrate that the declarant had a sense of impending death. See Shepard v. United States, 290 U.S. 96, 99–100 (1933); infra, Part H, § 76.

ernment argued that Mrs. Shepard's declarations that her husband had poisoned her should come in as rebuttal evidence, because they were inconsistent with a suicidal intent. So used, the argument ran, no hearsay problem was involved because the declarations were not entered for their truth, but only as circumstantial evidence bearing on the will to live. Furthermore, the government apparently urged, if hearsay were involved, the exception for mental state was applicable.

The Court, in an opinion by Justice Cardozo, found the evidence objectionable on two grounds. First, since the declarations in question clearly were treated by the trial judge as coming within the hearsay exception for dying declarations, it was prejudicial to the defendant if subsequently, on appeal, admissibility was placed upon a different ground: had this different ground been identified at trial, the accused could have objected to it and if successful would have been entitled to a limiting instruction cautioning the jury that the declarations only could be considered for the limited purpose for which they were offered. Second, the court expressly disapproved the admission of Mrs. Shepard's statements as indicative of her state of mind. The declarations, said the court, showed little about the victim's will to live; rather, they were forceful, accusatory statements about an act committed by another, and the jury necessarily would have to regard them as such. Citing the *Hillmon* case, Justice Cardozo remarked:

> Declarations of intention, casting light upon the future, have been sharply distinguished from declarations of memory, pointing backwards to the past. There would be an end, or nearly that, to the rule against hearsay if the distinction were ignored.
>
> The testimony now questioned faced backward and not forward. This at least it did in its most obvious implications. What is even more important, it spoke to a past act, and more than that, to an act by some one not the speaker.[94]

---

94. Shepard v. United States, 290
U.S. 96, 105–06 (1933).

This passage summarizes the major limitations upon the use of the state-of-mind exception. Generally, the exception does not include statements of memory or belief about past actions or events,[95] nor does it usually include declarations offered to prove the actions of a person other than the declarant. Note also Justice Cardozo's concern that the hearsay rule would be weakened seriously should "backward looking" declarations be viewed as within the exception for state of mind. A declarant's statement of past conduct ("I was in Chicago last January 15th".), involves the hearsay risk of a defective memory, a danger not involved with declarations of intended conduct ("I intend to go to Chicago in January".). It also would appear—although no data exist —that the problem of doubtful veracity (sincerity) might be more severe where past conduct is concerned. Arguably, statements about past conduct made in the light of subsequent events might, on the whole, carry a greater risk of insincerity than statements of mere intention.

Suppose the state-of-mind exception were broadened generally to include statements not only of the declarant's past conduct but also of "external" events, including the observed actions of others. *Every* relevant declaration about a past event then would be admissible under the theory that the declaration evinced a belief or memory about the event, and that this belief or memory constituted, in the broadest sense, a state of mind. It is apparent that statements of such "remembered" past events usually would present all the hearsay risks: faulty perception, defects in memory, insincerity, and mistransmission.[96] Thus, by the circuitous approach of enlarging the state-of-mind exception, the hearsay rule would be emasculated.

There is one area where the exception for mental state has been broadened so as to include at least statements of the *declar-*

---

95. Occasionally a declaration looking toward future conduct is coupled with a related past event of recent origin ("*X* just called and demanded money and I intend to deliver it this afternoon."). There is authority for admitting the statement in its entirety. United States v. Annunziato, 293 F.2d 373 (2d Cir. 1961). But see United States v. Mandel, 437 F.Supp. 262 (D.Md.1977).

96. See Ch. VI, § 49.

ant's own past conduct. Moved, perhaps, by a sense of special need, the courts increasingly have been receptive to declarations of a deceased person concerning his estate or will.[97] The Federal Rules of Evidence acknowledge this trend and Rule 803(3) permits the admission of "a statement of memory or belief to prove the fact remembered or believed [if the statement] relates to the execution, revocation, identification, or terms of declarant's will." [98] It is likely, of course, that the declarant-testator knew the most about his will (that is, whether it had been executed, modified, or revoked). Often this knowledge, coupled with the unavailability of the declarant, creates a special need for evidence of his declarations. These considerations combine to persuade a majority of courts to admit even "backward looking" declarations in these limited circumstances. Nonetheless, the hearsay risks all are present. Perhaps the innovation for wills points toward a broader recognition that in circumstances characterized by need and substantial probative value, the hearsay rule should yield. It should not be overlooked that the hearsay risks relating to perception, memory, sincerity and mistransmission are pertinent in deciding questions of evidentiary weight. Hence, the presence of dangers that account for the hearsay rule need not always result in exclusion, but can be considered in the trier's evaluative process.

NOTES

1. The general limitation which restricts the exception for mental condition to statements of existing state of mind does not, of course, prohibit the trier from reasonably inferring that the declared state of mind existed on another occasion. Suppose that on August 15 the declarant states that he is depressed. If the issue were whether the declarant committed suicide on August 20th, the proponent of the declaration would urge the trier to infer that the state of mind persisted (or that it returned) on August 20th. The only issue to be resolved by the trial judge in making his evidentiary ruling would be one of relevance.

---

97. McCormick, § 296, at 702.

98. The drafters observed that this exception rested "on practical grounds of necessity and expediency rather than logic." Adv.Comm.Note to Fed.R.Evid. 803(3).

2. There is now some case support for the application of the mental state exception to statements of recently perceived events when these statements are coupled with a declaration that looks toward the future. A case in point is United States v. Annunziato, 293 F.2d 373 (2d Cir.), cert. denied 368 U.S. 919 (1961), where the admitted declaration alluded to a recent phone call from X and an intention to respond to it by sending to X some money. See McCormick, § 296, at 704; supra note 95.

3. Suppose in the course of litigation the sanity of the declarant develops as an issue. Evidence is offered that the declarant frequently states that he is Chairman Mao Tse-tung. Under one view, this declaration is not hearsay because the proponent is not offering it for its truth; under another analysis, the statement is hearsay because it is the equivalent of the declaration "I think that I am Chairman Mao Tse-tung." Even under the latter approach, the statement is admissible because it constitutes a declaration of presently existing mental state. Of course, the trier may consider the danger of insincerity in assessing the weight to be accorded this evidence.

PART D.   RECORDED RECOLLECTION

§ 66. In General

The present exception, past recorded recollection, should be considered in conjunction with the principles that govern refreshing a witness's present recollection. These principles, which are treated in more detail elsewhere,[99] may be summarized as follows: when a witness evinces an inability to remember, interrogating counsel may attempt to revive the witness's memory by producing a writing (or some other item) intended to induce recollection. If the interrogator succeeds in restoring the witness's memory so that the latter can testify from present recollection, the only evidence received by the court is the witness's testimony, not the writing. The writing serves the limited purpose of aiding memory; consequently, the counsel who used the writing for this narrow purpose has no right to introduce it into evidence. Under these circumstances, which are usually designated "present recollection refreshed," there is no hearsay difficulty because no "off-the-stand" assertion is offered for its truth. The witness testifies from present (revived) mem-

---

99. Ch. IV, § 27.

ory just as if he had not experienced a temporary inability to recall the event in question.

A different situation is encountered when the witness's memory cannot be revived satisfactorily and an earlier writing, authored or previously verified by the witness, if offered *in lieu of* his present testimony. If the proponent introduces the writing for a purpose which requires the trier to accept the truth of the assertions it contains, the writing is hearsay: the cross-examiner neither can cross-examine the writing, nor can he interrogate the witness about the details of the events described in it, since the witness is unable to recall these. Under these circumstances, admissibility must rest upon the use of some exception to the hearsay rule.[1] If the witness can provide a foundation which attests to the accuracy of the writing by reason of its timely and accurate preparation, the present exception for recorded recollection will suffice.

§ 67. Recorded Recollection: Rationale and Application

Although a forgetful witness may be unable to recall the occurrence or condition described in an earlier writing, he may be able to testify that he authored the writing (or at least verified its accuracy) when the event was fresh in his memory. If he also can affirm that the writing is accurate—either because he recalls making an accurate recordation or because it was his habitual practice to make correct notes—then the present exception applies.[2] The requirements or recorded recollection reduce the hearsay risks of insincerity and faulty memory.[3] Since the wit-

---

1. United States v. Edwards, 539 F. 2d 689 (9th Cir. 1976); see Maguire and Quick, Testimony: Memory and Memoranda, 3 How.L.J. 1, 9 (1957).

2. Walker v. Larson, 284 Minn. 99, 169 N.W.2d 737 (1969); State v. Bradley, 361 Mo. 267, 275, 234 S. W.2d 556, 560 (1950) (dictum); Annot. 82 A.L.R.2d 473, 525–31. Often, a notary, stenographer, or bookkeeper can testify to a habit

of making correct entries. For a case which considers at length the requirements of a proper foundation, see Hodas v. Davis, 203 A.D. 297, 196 N.Y.S. 801 (1922). The *Hodas* decision is criticized in Walker v. Larson, supra, 169 N.W. 2d at 742–43.

3. The risk of mistranscription also is reduced, since the witness probably can correctly interpret his earlier language.

ness must testify in the presence of the trier (and subject to cross-examination) that the writing is accurate, there is some assurance of sincerity.[3a] The further requirement that he affirm that the writing was made at a time when he had a strong recollection of the event or condition in question minimizes the danger of a defective memory.

Federal Rule 803(5) describes the exception for recorded past recollection:

> Recorded Recollection—A memorandum of record concerning a matter about which a witness once had knowledge but now has insufficient recollection to enable him to testify fully and accurately, shown to have been made or adopted by the witness when the matter was fresh in his memory and to reflect that knowledge correctly. If admitted, the memorandum or record may be read into evidence but may not itself be received as an exhibit unless offered by an adverse party.

This statement of the exception generally is in accord with the case law.[4] Usually, the witness will have written the memorandum or record that is offered as recorded recollection, but 803(5) expressly takes account of the case in which the witness was not the author. It is enough that the witness adopted the writing which, in this context, means that he examined the writing and affirmed its correctness at a time when memory was fresh.

Note that applicability of the exception hinges upon a finding that the witness "now has insufficient recollection to enable him to testify fully and accurately . . . ." There still is disagreement among state jurisdictions as to whether impaired memory is essential to the applicability of the present exception and, if so,

---

3a. The danger of insincerity is further reduced when the writing was made prior to the existence of any motive to falsify.

4. See United States v. Kelly, 349 F.2d 720 (2d Cir. 1965); Jordon v. People, 151 Colo. 133, 376 P.2d 699 (1962); Annot. 82 A.L.R.2d 473 (1962). For a recent case construing Fed.R.Evid. 803(5) and upholding its validity against a Sixth Amendment claim of a denial of the right to confront an adverse witness, see United States v. Marshall, 532 F.2d 1279 (9th Cir. 1976).

whether there must be a complete inability to remember the pertinent event before the prior writing may be introduced. A minority of courts take the view that because the memorandum was prepared soon after the event which it describes, it is more reliable than subsequent courtroom testimony. Hence, it is admissible (if the other requisites of the exception are met) without regard to the present ability of the witness to remember the event.[5] Most courts, however, require a substantial or total loss of memory before the exception for recorded recollection is available.[6] In these courts there is concern that dispensing with the requirement of impaired memory would lead to the increased use of statements prepared for litigation and often drafted or influenced by interested parties, claims adjusters, or attorneys.[7] The requirement embodied in the Federal Rule (inability to "testify fully and accurately") strikes a sensible balance and is apt to emerge as the dominant formulation.

The last sentence of the Federal Rule prohibits the proponent from treating the recorded recollection as an exhibit. The practical effect of this prohibition is to prevent the jury from examining the writing and from carrying it to the jury room, unless, of course, the adverse party enters the writing as an exhibit. The position expressed in the rules has some case support, although the authorities are divided.[8] The rationale for prohibiting jury inspection, and thus treating the memorandum differently from other items of documentary evidence, apparently lies in the notion that the memorandum is a substitute for present testimony; consequently, the reasoning goes, the jury should have no greater exposure to the evidence than it has to other testimonial proof. This approach avoids the risk, if indeed there is one, that extensive jury use and inspection of the writing will result in exaggerating its probative force.

---

5. E. g., State v. Sutton, 253 Or. 24, 450 P.2d 748 (1969).

6. E. g., Noumoff v. Rotkvich, 88 Ill.App.2d 116, 232 N.E.2d 107 (1967).

7. McCormick, § 302, at 715.

8. Compare State v. Folkes, 174 Or. 568, 150 P.2d 17 (1944) cert. denied 323 U.S. 779 with Curtis v. Bradley, 65 Conn. 99, 31 A. 591 (1894).

NOTE

An interesting problem of proof by means of recorded recollection arises when an observer reports facts to another, who records them. It then becomes important that the proponent produce both participants—the first to affirm that his oral transmission, rendered when his memory was fresh, correctly portrayed the facts observed, and the second to affirm that he faithfully recorded the verbal statements. See United States v. Booz, 451 F.2d 719 (3d Cir. 1971); Primeaux v. Kinney, 256 So.2d 140 (La.App.1971).

PART E.   RECORDS OF BUSINESS AND RELATED ENTERPRISES

§ 68. In General

Every jurisdiction has created a hearsay exception permitting admission of the records of business concerns and related enterprises such as hospitals, educational institutions, and governmental departments.[9] The principal characteristic of an entity which constitutes a "business" is its engagement in regular, systematic activity.   The overwhelming majority of jurisdictions provide for the so-called "business entry" exception by either statute or rule of court, although a few states have fashioned this exception through the common-law decisional process.[10]

---

9. As to departments and agencies of the federal government, see infra Part F.

10. For example, the State of Virginia has no statute or rule of court that sets out the exception. Nonetheless, there is a judicially created exception. See Neeley v. Johnson, 215 Va. 565, 211 S.E.2d 100 (1975).

The rule first developed at common law was called the "shopbook rule." It may be traced to the English practice of allowing a merchant to prove an account receivable upon which he brought suit. The shopbook rule was necessitated, both in England and America, by the rule of incompetence that disqualifed parties from testifying. Ch. IV, § 22. Admission of the merchant's books of account supplied the proof necessary to establish the debt claimed. Even though the merchant did not, technically at least, testify, he had to comply with elaborate procedures, such as taking a special ("suppletory") oath and opening his books to judicial inspection, designed to ensure the validity of his claim. For a concise, careful description of the common law and statutory development of the business entry exception, see Lempert & Saltzburg at 423–26.

Underlying the exception for business records is the recognition that business entities rely heavily upon regularly-kept records and, consequently, that there is an organizational motivation to be thorough and accurate. While it may be true, as we shall see shortly, that some business entries carry a significant risk that the entrant has departed from objectivity and cast the entry in self-serving terms, most entries are attended by circumstances that encourage accuracy. The general practice of reliable and prompt record-keeping reduces the hearsay dangers and justifies the admission of business records for the truth of the assertions within them. The exception for business records also is a practical necessity in the modern business environment because a "business transaction" often involves several or more participants, each of whom has personal knowledge of only a portion of the transaction. Thus, the central records of a department store chain may show that certain goods were shipped from warehouse inventory, received by a branch store, stocked, and then sold. Yet the shipping clerk can testify only that he placed the goods on a delivery truck, the driver only that he delivered certain packages to the branch store, the stock clerk only that the goods were shelved, and the sales clerk only that all of the goods were sold. Likewise, different individuals may participate in installing a telephone, repairing it, assigning the number, billing the user, and so forth. It would be highly burdensome to call as witnesses all participants in these segmented transactions. An attractive alternative is to present the composite business record, supported or sponsored by a custodian or other qualified person who can state (1) that the proffered record systematically was made in the course of regularly conducted business activity, and (2) that the information entered came from an individual with personal knowledge.

§ 69. Records of Business and Related Enterprises: Illustrations and Refinements

Federal Rule 803(6) is illustrative of the statutory (or rule-of-court) provisions that govern the admissibility of business entries and related records. Under this Rule, an exception is made for—

> Records of regularly conducted activity—A memorandum, report, record, or data compilations, in any

form, of acts, events, conditions, opinions, or diagnoses, made at or near the time by, or from information transmitted by, a person with knowledge, if kept in the course of a regularly conducted business activity, and if it was the regular practice of that business activity to make the memorandum, report, record, or data compilation, all as shown by the testimony of the custodian or other qualified witness, unless the source of information or the method or circumstances of preparation indicate lack of trustworthiness. The term "business" as used in this paragraph includes business, institution, association, profession, occupation, and calling of every kind, whether or not conducted for profit.

The Rule and its various counterparts in state jurisdictions contemplate that the person(s) who provides the basic information for the entry will have personal knowledge of the act or event that is recorded. There is no requirement, however, that this person be called to testify;[11] it suffices that the custodian or other qualified witness states that it is the business practice to base the entry upon data supplied by one with personal knowledge.[12] It is essential under the Federal Rule and its state counterparts that the report was made in the regular course of business, that it was the regular practice to make the kind of entry in question, and that the entry was made "at or near the time" of the condition or event described in the entry.

Although the language of the Rule is somewhat ambiguous, it almost certainly will be construed to require that both the informer (who supplies the information from personal knowledge) and the entrant-recorder (who makes the written entry) act in the regular course of business.[13] That is, the informer must be

---

11. United States v. Page, 544 F.2d 982 (8th Cir. 1976).

12. Weinstein & Berger, ¶ 803(6)[02], at 150. See United States v. Wigerman, 549 F.2d 1192 (8th Cir. 1977) (business records used to show interstate movement); United States v. Carranco, 551 F.2d 1197 (10th Cir. 1977) (business manager provides necessary foundation and establishes that it is regular practice of company to make changes and additions on freight bill).

13. See United States v. Yates, 553 F.2d 518 (6th Cir. 1977). But see

making the basic communication (either verbal or written) in the course of his regular business duties, and the entrant must be recording the information as a consequence of his regular business duty. On some occasions, of course, the informer and entrant will be the same person, as where an office manager routinely observes which of his employees are on duty and records their presence. Frequently, however, the informer may be different from the entrant, as where the doctor states that the patient has a broken wrist and the nurse records this information in the appropriate medical files.

A problem arises where either the informer or the entrant is not acting under a business duty. In the leading case of Johnson v. Lutz [14] several bystanders reported to a policeman certain observed facts about a traffic accident. The policeman recorded these statements in his police report, which later was offered into evidence for the purpose of proving the truth of the recorded facts. The Court of Appeals of New York ruled against admitting the report. Its holding was based principally on the view that the state statute governing business entries never was intended to support the admissibility of statements volunteered by observers not acting in the course of business. This construction of the statute is consistent with the rationale of the business entries exception, for it draws upon the reliability which presumably attends the dutiful conduct of those engaged in business. It can be argued that the entrant's business-motivated *recording* of information gratuitously supplied by an informer should satisfy the statute in cases where persons within the business organization would rely on the information. The courts, however, generally have adhered to the *Johnson* requirement and insisted upon the additional reliability present when all participants in the making of the record are acting under a

---

United States v. Rent-R-Books, Inc., 538 F.2d 519 (2d Cir. 1976). For a brief but persuasive discussion that a business duty is required of both participants, see S. Saltzburg & K. Redden, Federal Rules of Evidence Manual 593 (2d ed. 1977) where the authors review

Griffin, The Big Civil Case and the Federal Rules of Evidence, 49 Temp.L.Q. 898 (1976).

14. 253 N.Y. 124, 170 N.E. 517 (1930). For a criticism of this decision, see V. Wigmore, § 1530a, n. 1.

business duty.[15] This judicial requirement confirms that the court—not the business community—remains the primary arbiter of admissibility.

It should be noted that in those instances in which only one participant in the recordation is acting under a business duty, admissibility still can be gained if the statement of the non-business participant qualifies under another hearsay exception.[16] For example, where the communication of the non-business declarant qualifies as a spontaneous declaration or a party admission, the applicable exception *can be linked* with the business entry exception to render the statement admissible. Suppose, for example, a bystander excitedly reported to a policeman certain facts about a startling event and the latter (acting under a business duty) recorded the bystander's statement. The linking principle would be operative: the business-entry exception is used (in lieu of the testimony of the entrant-policeman) to prove the statement was made; the excited-utterance exception is invoked to permit the trier to accept the bystander's statement for its truth. Of course, where one policeman—the informer—reports to another policeman—the entrant—there is no need to rely upon the principle of linking, since the exception

---

15. See, e. g., United States v. Plum, 558 F.2d 568 (10th Cir. 1977); Standard Oil Co. of California v. Moore, 251 F.2d 188 (2d Cir. 1957), cert. denied 356 U.S. 975 (1958); Yates v. Bair Transport, Inc., 249 F.Supp. 681 (S.D.N.Y.1965); Annot., 69 A.L.R.2d 1148 (1972); McCormick, § 310, at 726. The essential element is that the participants in the business record act under a business duty. The involvement of separate business entries in the creation, use, or storage of a particular record does not defeat admissibility. See United States v. Pfeiffer, 539 F.2d 668 (8th Cir. 1976).

16. Kelly v. Wasserman, 5 N.Y.2d 425, 185 N.Y.S.2d 538, 158 N.E.2d 241 (1959) (business entry coupled with party admission); see United States v. Smith, 521 F.2d 957 (D.C. Cir. 1975) (business entry may be used to show statement was made by one not under business duty; since statement not offered for its truth, but only to show inconsistency, no linking hearsay exception necessary). In United States v. Vacca, 431 F.Supp. 807 (E.D.Pa. 1977) the court overlooked the double hearsay problem arising when the informer is not acting under a business duty. See the comments of Professor John Schmertz in 2 Federal Rules of Evidence News 77–65 (Aug. 1977).

for business entries is applicable both to the declaration and its recordation.[17]

Several restrictive interpretations of business-entry provisions call for cautious evidentiary planning. In Palmer v. Hoffman [18] the ·United States Supreme Court held inadmissible an accident report prepared and offered at trial by a defendant railroad because the entries were made primarily for purposes of litigation and not for the systematic conduct of the railroad business. In the deceptively simple analysis of Justice Douglas, the record was not made " 'in the regular course' of business [railroading] within the meaning of the [then controlling federal] Act." [19] This approach could render inadmissible a variety of documents prepared in the regular course of activity, but in light of possible litigation.

The *Palmer* holding had not been given a broad construction,[20] perhaps because of a realization that accident reports and other documents that may pertain to a potentially litigated event are prepared for a variety of reasons, including assessing present and projected financial losses, determining cause, undertaking the least costly remedial measures, and so forth. However, in circumstances presenting a strong self-serving motivation, the *Palmer* principle will apply and the proffered business record will be rejected.[21] Federal Rule 803(6) expressly provides for this result by directing that the exception for business entries

---

17. For a discussion of the admissibility of police reports under Fed. R.Evid. 803 and its statutory predecessor, see Annot., 31 A.L.R. Fed. 457 (1976).

18. 318 U.S. 109 (1943).

19. Palmer v. Hoffman, 318 U.S. 109, 111 (1943).

20. See Pekelis v. Transcontinental & W. Air Inc., 187 F.2d 122 (2d Cir.), cert. denied 341 U.S. 951 (1951) and cases therein cited.

21. In Yates v. Bair Transport, Inc., 249 F.Supp. 681 (S.D.N.Y.1965) the court rejected medical reports prepared for purposes of litigation by doctors of the plaintiff's choice, but admitted physician's reports prepared at the request of the defendant. All of the reports were proffered by the plaintiff. See also Korte v. New York, N.H. & H.R. Co., 191 F.2d 86 (2d Cir. 1951). See Hartzog v. United States, 217 F.2d 706 (4th Cir. 1954) (prosecution for tax evasion; error to admit deputy collector's worksheets prepared for case).

does not apply where "the source of information or the method or circumstances of preparation indicate lack of trustworthiness." However, this provision should be invoked sparingly because the trier usually can identify the temptation to be self-serving and discount the weight of the evidence accordingly.

There are two other problems attending this exception. Some courts still engage in the restrictive practice of rejecting medical diagnoses found by the judge to be conjecturable.[22] (Just how the judge, presumably trained in law but not in medicine, is supposed to determine which diagnoses fall into this speculative category is a question not easily answered.) Other courts, expressing a similar concern about trustworthiness, purport to exclude from the present exception diagnostic "opinions," [23] thus confining the admissible evidence to medical findings that can be confirmed objectively either by sight or standard testing procedures. These rather arbitrary blockages of medical evidence apparently are cast aside in Federal Rule 803(6), which provides for the admission into evidence of "opinions, or diagnoses." [24] Of course, as noted above the Rule does expressly provide for the exclusion of any business record which, because of the source of its contents or the circumstances of its preparation, is deemed untrustworthy.

A second difficulty with the present exception is encountered when a medical record contains assertions as to the immediate cause of the patient's injury or assertions about fault. Although the cause of the injury (that is, whether it came from a fall, a collision, etc.) usually is pertinent to a medical determination regarding proper treatment, statements about fault ("*D* was speeding and hit patient") generally are viewed as outside the entrant's business duty to record.[25] Even when the recorded

---

22. Loper v. Andrews, 404 S.W.2d 300 (Tex.Civ.App.1966).

23. See, e. g., Thomas v. Fred Weber Contractor, Inc., 498 S.W.2d 811 (Mo.Ct.App.1973); Jackson v. Cherokee Drug Co., 434 S.W.2d 257 (Mo.Ct.App.1968).

24. See Myers v. Genis, 235 Pa.Super. 531, 344 A.2d 691 (1975) (citing Fed.R.Evid. 803(6)).

25. Lindstrom v. Yellow Taxi Co., 298 Minn. 224, 214 N.W.2d 672 (1974); Kelly v. Sheehan, 158 Conn. 281, 259 A.2d 605 (1969). See Maguire et al. at 669-78.

statement concerns only the immediate cause of the patient's condition, it usually is necessary to link the business entry with another hearsay exception in order to gain admissibility. Typically, the statement explaining the cause comes from the patient or some other person not under a business duty to speak. Consequently, even though the entrant may be under a business duty to record matters pertaining to immediate cause (and hence to treatment) it still is required that another exception be invoked to cover the patient's or other non-business speaker's statement.[26] Special consideration should be given to the possibility of linking the business entry exception with that for party admissions, spontaneous declarations, or statements of physical condition made to a treating physician. When the linking principle applies, the medical record shows that the statement in question was made; the other applicable exception permits the statement to be used for its truth.

NOTES

1. If a regularly-kept entry is admissible to show certain facts or events, the absence of an entry (that normally would be made if an event occurred) may have probative force to show that the event did not occur. To illustrate, if P company routinely records shipments of goods that are prepaid, the absence of an entry pertaining to certain goods indicates that there was no prepayment. Federal Rule 803(7) which permits an absence of entry to be shown is aligned with the weight of authority. Is the absence of an entry hearsay?

2. Federal Rule 803(8) provides for the admission of records compiled by public offices or agencies. There is authority that government records and reports are governed exclusively by this provision and are not within 803(6). See, e. g., Complaint of American Export Lines, Inc., 73 F.R.D. 454, 459 (S.D.N.Y.1977); United States v. American Cyanamid Co., 427 F.Supp. 859, 867 (S.D.N.Y.1977). In United States v. Oates, 560 F.2d 45 (2d Cir. 1977) the court analyzed the relationship between 803(6) and 803(8) and concluded that a report of a United States Customs chemist fell within Rule 803(8) and under its applicable provisions could not be introduced against an accused, since

---

26. Felice v. Long Island Railroad Co., 426 F.2d 192, cert. denied 400 U.S. 820 (1970).

that Rule does not except from the hearsay rule records prepared by law enforcement personnel when offered against an accused.

3. The introduction of computer business records generally requires a more comprehensive foundation than that necessary for conventional records, since it usually is necessary to provide evidence of the procedure utilized in gathering, storing, and retrieving information. See United States v. Scholle, 553 F.2d 1109 (8th Cir. 1977).

PART F. PUBLIC RECORDS

§ 70. In General

Most frequently created by statute or rule of court, the hearsay exception for public records rests upon the assumption that persons discharging the public's business accurately will maintain public records because of substantial reliance by users.[27] The force of public duty and the presence of routine, systematic practices combine to make the analogy to the exception for business records compelling. The shared characteristics of these exceptions account for the abbreviated treatment here given to the public records exception. Note, for example, the common problem of whether the informer and entrant were responding to an obligation that, either expressly or impliedly, arose from official duties. As a general rule, if only the entrant (or only the informer) has such a public duty another hearsay exception, applicable to the statement of the declarant who is not under a duty, must be linked to that for public records to admit the record for the truth of its assertion.[28]

The use of the public records exception, however, often involves a hearsay problem not found with the business records exception because the former usually does not require that the public custodian (or other appropriate official) appear as a witness. The exception is applicable if the entry or statement in question merely is part of a public record (as defined by statute,

---

27. Another practical reason asserted for the exception is "the unlikelihood that [a public official] will remember details independently of the record." Adv.Comm.Note to Fed.R.Evid. 803(8).

28. See, however, infra § 71 and especially the comment on investigative reports.

rule of court, or judicial opinion) *in the custody* of a public official. The frequency with which public records are used as evidence makes it impractical to require that the public custodian or his surrogate appear in court to verify that the record is genuine and is held in proper custody. Practical difficulties are also posed if the original record is removed from the public repository each time it is presented in court. Thus, most statutes provide that when the appropriate public custodian attests by official written certification or by seal that the original is a public record in his custody and that the proffered duplicate is a "true copy," the duplicate will be accepted for its truth on the basis of the custodian's hearsay statement that it is within the present exception.[29] There thus is no need that he appear in court.

§ 71. Public Records: Application of the Exception

Because the judicial and statutory treatment of this exception varies among the jurisdictions, generalizations must be viewed with particular caution. The usual prerequisite for admissibility is a showing that the proffered document or written assertion was made by a public official or employee acting within his official duties. A few jurisdictions require that the record have been open to public inspection.[30] Some statutes specifically designate as admissible certain certificates or documents;[31] others, more general in application, are framed in terms of records, statements, or reports of public officers or agencies.[32] Typically, the public records exception, either by general provision or by a multiplicity of specific ones, includes rather generous provisions for the receipt in evidence of assertions or data from first-hand knowledge of persons acting under a public duty. It also usually is recognized that data and facts sent to a public agency by a "semi-public" source such as a physician or clergyman come

---

29. This statement of genuineness serves to authenticate the document. See Ch. XIII, §§ 113–15.

30. Morgan at 280.

31. See, e. g., Va.Code Ann. § 58–48.3 (1974 Repl.Vol.) (tax returns filed with State Tax Commissioner).

32. See, e. g., West's Ann.Cal.Code, Ev. § 1280 (1966).

within the exception—at least where there is a statutory or professional duty to report.[33]

There is growing recognition that factual findings of official investigations should fall within the exception, despite the awareness that much of the factual information may come from persons with no public or business duty.[34]   Admission here is justified, if at all, by the probability that the officials conducting the investigation (who themselves are under a public duty) will be careful and discriminating in selecting the factual data upon which to rely in reaching their findings and conclusions.

The Federal Rules of Evidence contain a number of provisions governing the admissibility of public documents.[35]   Principal among these is Rule 803(8) which provides a hearsay exception for:

> Public records and reports—Records, reports, statements, or data compilations, in any form, of public offices or agencies, setting forth (A) the activities of the office or agency, or (B) matters observed pursuant to duty imposed by law as to which matters there was a duty to report, excluding, however, in criminal cases matters observed by police officers and other law enforcement personnel, or (C) in civil actions and proceedings and against the Government in criminal cases, factual findings resulting from an investigation made pursuant to authority granted by law, unless the sources of information or other circumstances indicate lack of trustworthiness.

The Rule confers general admissibility upon investigative findings, but not when offered against an accused.   This protective provision may be required by the accused's constitutional right

---

33.   McCormick, § 316, at 736.

34.   See e. g., Givens v. Lederle, 556 F.2d 1341 (5th Cir. 1977) and Hodge v. Seiler, 558 F.2d 284 (5th Cir. 1977), both construing Fed.R.

Evid. 803(8)(c) ; Smith v. Universal Services, Inc., 454 F.2d 154 (5th Cir. 1972) ; McCormick § 317.

35.   Fed.R.Evid. 803(8), (9), (10), (11), (12), (14).

to confront witnesses against him.[36] The Rule also excludes, in criminal cases, records of matters personally observed by police officers. This restrictive provision rests upon the assumption that the relationship between the police and an accused will be antagonistic;[37] thus, hostility could diminish the objectivity and accuracy of official entries.

NOTE

Much litigation and judicial discussion have surrounded the question of the scope of the duty and authority of an officer who, in an official or professional capacity, reports vital statistics to a public agency. Where statutes provide that a death certificate can be received as proof of the facts therein stated, see, e. g., Va.Code Ann. § 32–353.- 27(b) (1973), most courts have held either that the official duty does not extend to entries about the cause of death (e. g., "suicide," "food poisoning") or that the "facts" referred to in the statute are only those facts of which the entrant had a first-hand knowledge, not those derived from third persons not under a public duty. See Edwards v. Jackson, 210 Va. 450, 171 S.E.2d 854 (1970). Thus, a death certificate may be admissible only to prove the fact of death (perhaps including date or time of death), not to show causation. Query whether such an interpretation would preclude admission where a medically observable cause of death (such as a crushed larynx) which may raise an adverse inference (in the example, strangulation) is listed on the certificate by an entrant with a duty to report but no first-hand knowledge. Cf. Fed.R.Evid. 403, 803(9).

---

§ 72. Transitional Note: The Hearsay Exceptions and Declarant's Unavailability

The applicability of the hearsay exceptions discussed so far is not conditioned upon whether or not the declarant is unavailable as a witness. All of the foregoing exceptions (along with others omitted from the preceding discussions) are grouped under Federal Rule of Evidence 803. These exceptions are similar to

---

36. U.S.Const. amend. VI. See infra Part J.

37. S.Rep.No.93–1277, 93d Cong., 2nd Sess. reprinted in 1974 U.S. Code Cong. & Admin.News 7051.

For a case in which an *accused* introduces a police record under Fed.R.Evid. 803(6), see United States v. Smith, 521 F.2d 957 (D.C. Cir. 1975).

those developed by the states through the process of judicial decision or statutory enactment. But the incorporation of these exceptions under a single federal rule emphasizes their salient common feature: the availability (or unavailability) of the declarant is immaterial to their application. This shared feature is founded upon the determination that the admissible declarations described in Federal Rule 803 have guarantees of trustworthiness that make them the substantial equivalent of testimony from the stand; this conclusion renders unimportant the question whether the hearsay declarant could be called upon to testify in person about the subject matter of his out-of-court statement. Since the hearsay statement is on an equivalent footing with live testimony, it comes into evidence either in addition to, or in lieu of, the testimony of the declarant.

We now encounter additional exceptions, grouped under Federal Rule 804,[38] in which the declarant's unavailability to testify conditions admissibility. Before these exceptions are applicable, the proponent must demonstrate to the judge that he can not reasonably secure the declarant's testimony. Rule 804 exceptions, which generally are consistent with the common law, may be thought of as "second class" exceptions. The hearsay within these exceptions is not equal in quality to the "class one" exceptions of Rule 803 [39] (or, of course, to live testimony), but the statements are thought sufficiently reliable to be considered by the trier if the declarant is unavailable as a witness.

It is not always easy to predict the circumstances under which a declarant will be considered unavailable. This especially is true under the common law, where the requirement of unavailability usually was defined separately for each of the exceptions conditioned upon it.[40] The clear cases are those in which ab-

---

38. There are four specific exceptions and one "catch all" or residual exception contained in Rule 804(b). Three of the specific exceptions are discussed in the materials immediately following. One of the specific exceptions is briefly considered infra Part J, note 88. The residual exception is considered in the text, infra Part J, at note 95.

39. This generalization, perhaps, is inaccurate when applied to former testimony. See infra, Part G, § 74.

40. Adv.Comm. Note to Fed.R.Evid. 804. A good discussion of the unavailability requirement is found in McCormick § 253.

sence from the jurisdiction, death, or some other incapacity (such as serious illness) renders it impossible to present the declarant as a witness. Federal Rule 804(a), which draws upon substantial common-law support, announces other conditions, such as the successful claim of a privilege or a persistent refusal to testify,[41] that satisfy the requirement of unavailability.[42] Under the Federal Rule, an inability to remember the event to which the witness is asked to testify also renders the witness unavailable.[43] Common-law decisions, in contrast, are not uniform on the question whether a lack of memory suffices.[44]

---

41. See United States v. Carlson, 547 F.2d 1346 (8th Cir. 1976) (co-conspirator who was granted use immunity refused to testify for fear of reprisals and was thereafter incarcerated for contempt; held unavailable).

42. *(a) Definition of unavailability* —"Unavailability as a witness" includes situations in which the declarant—

(1) is exempted by ruling of the court on the ground of privilege from testifying concerning the subject matter of his statement; or

(2) persists in refusing to testify concerning the subject matter of his statement despite an order of the court to do so; or

(3) testifies to a lack of memory of the subject matter of his statement; or

(4) is unable to be present or to testify at the hearing because of death or then existing physical or mental illness or infirmity; or

(5) is absent from the hearing and the proponent of his statement has been unable to procure his attendance (or in the case of a hearsay exception under subdivision (b)(2), (3), or (4), his attendance or testimony) by process or other reasonable means.

A declarant is not unavailable as a witness if his exemption, refusal, claim of lack of memory, inability, or absence is due to the procurement or wrongdoing of the proponent of his statement for the purpose of preventing the witness from attending or testifying.

Note that the proponent seeking to use the exceptions for (1) statements under belief of impending death ("dying declaration") or (2) statement against interest or (3) statement of family history ("pedigree") must show not only his inability to produce the witness by "process or other reasonable means" but also his reasonable inability to obtain the declarant's deposition. Fed.R.Evid. 804(a)(5).

43. See United States v. Davis, 551 F.2d 233 (8th Cir. 1977).

44. McCormick, § 253, at 611.

PART G.   FORMER TESTIMONY

§ 73.   In General

This exception, invoked in various contexts, is applicable where the proponent in the present trial seeks to utilize testimony given in an earlier hearing or proceeding. The hearsay dangers are minimized by the prior opportunity to test or develop the testimony. In one familiar setting, a witness is called by one side—for example, by the plaintiff—and, after direct examination, is made available for cross-questions. Subsequently, the case is appealed and, for reasons unrelated to the testimony of the witness, a new trial is ordered. If the witness cannot be produced to testify at the new trial, the original proponent (the plaintiff) now may offer to prove, usually by means of a transcript, the witness's testimony from the first trial. In theory, and occasionally also in practice, the *opponent* of the witness in the first trial (the defendant, in the present example) may introduce the prior testimony against the earlier proponent.

In the foregoing illustration, the parties to both proceedings (the original and the new trial) are the same. Each had the opportunity to interrogate the witness at the earlier trial. Suppose, however, that the first suit was brought by one plaintiff and the second was initiated by another. This difference in plaintiffs would occur, for example, where the first suit resulted from a claim by an infant for injuries occasioned by the negligence of a defendant railroad, and the second suit resulted from a claim by a parent for loss of the child's services. If the witness who testified against the railroad in the first trial is unavailable at the second trial, may his testimony be used by either party? If the defendant railroad seeks to use all or part of the former testimony against the second plaintiff, a difficulty is encountered: the second plaintiff was not a party to the first suit and had no opportunity to interrogate the witness and to develop his testimony. This lack of opportunity has caused most courts to exclude the former testimony when offered against one not a party or not in privity with a party to the first suit.

However, there remains the possibility that the second plaintiff could introduce the former testimony against the defendant railroad which was a party to the earlier suit and thus was afforded the opportunity to test the prior testimony. Nonetheless, the early cases denied admissibility. The reasoning was this: since the railroad can not use the former testimony against the second plaintiff, fairness dictates that the plaintiff not be permitted to use the prior testimony against the railroad. This logic underlies the so-called doctrine of mutuality which requires that there must be at least the possibility of mutual use of the former testimony before one party can introduce it. Modern scholarship and recent cases [45] reject the doctrine, taking the view that in a factfinding proceeding the concern only should be whether it is fair to offer the testimony against a party who also was a party to the prior trial.[46] Under this recent approach, fairness is not assessed on the basis of whether either party could offer the prior testimony. The question of fairness turns upon whether the party against whom the evidence of prior testimony is offered had an earlier opportunity to develop or test the former testimony.

§ 74. Former Testimony: Application of the Exception

When evidence of prior testimony is offered against an opponent who was a party to the earlier proceeding, it may not be apparent why the hearsay rule should apply at all. Since the rule barring hearsay rests upon the opponent's lack of opportunity to cross-examine, it seemingly is inapplicable where a full opportunity has been afforded. Arguably, then, there often is no reason to classify prior testimony as an *exception* to the hearsay rule; the proper approach is to view the prior testimony as nonhearsay—at least in instances where the opponent already has had adequate opportunity to conduct an adverse examination.

---

45. McCormick, § 256, at 618–19.

46. See infra § 74 and Note 1 at the end of Part G, suggesting that the pertinent inquiry is whether a party to the prior suit conducted an interrogation with the same motive and interest as that of the present party. Under such a view, it is not essential that there be any identity of parties; the test is identity of interest.

The traditional approach, however, which now has the endorsement of the Federal Rules of Evidence,[47] is to treat previous testimony as hearsay and then, under appropriate circumstances, to invoke the present exception. This treatment is consistent with the orthodox definition of hearsay, which brings within the rule any statement offered for its truth which was made at a time and place other than from the stand in the *present proceeding*. A plausible justification for treating prior testimony as hearsay is that its evidentiary use denies to the trier in the second trial the opportunity to assess the witness's demeanor. It should be noted, however, that the trustworthiness of prior testimony arguably is higher than the other "class two" exceptions, which (as we have seen) give a preference to live testimony by conditioning admissibility upon the unavailability of the hearsay declarant. Indeed, trustworthiness may be equal to or even greater than most of the exceptions contained in class one, thus qualifying the generalization made earlier in this text that class two exceptions are less trustworthy than their class one counterparts.[48]

Although many states have passed statutes governing the admission of former testimony, this exception took root and grew to maturity in the common-law tradition.[49] There are variations from state to state in statutory language and in case-developed law, but the formulation contained in Federal Rule of Evidence 804(b)(1) has substantial statutory and judicial support. If the declarant is unavailable, the court may receive in evidence:

> Former testimony—Testimony given [by one who was] . . . a witness at another hearing of the same or a different proceeding, or in a deposition taken in compliance with law in the course of the same or another proceeding, if the party against whom the testimony is now offered, or, in a civil action or proceeding, a predecessor in interest, had an opportunity and

---

47. See Fed.R.Evid. 804(b)(1).

48. See supra § 72 at n. 38.

49. McCormick, § 254, at 615.

similar motive to develop the testimony by direct, cross, or redirect examination.

The exception requires a showing of unavailability, coupled with a showing that the party against whom the evidence now is offered had a fair opportunity and a probable motive to test or develop the testimony at the earlier proceeding.[50] The requirement is satisfied that there was an *opportunity* to examine the witness at the prior proceeding; it is not essential that there was an actual interrogation, so an earlier waiver of cross-examination does not render the exception inapplicable.[51] Although the Federal Rule does not expressly state that the prior testimony must have been given under oath or affirmation, such a setting no doubt is contemplated.[52]

In civil cases, it is sufficient that the *predecessor in interest* to the present party had an opportunity and a similar motive to examine the now-unavailable witness. Although the phrase "predecessor in interest" (which the courts frequently use interchangeably with the phrase "persons in privity") [53] has an exasperating inexactness about it, the expression generally refers to the predecessor from whom the present party received the right, title, or interest that is at issue in the current litigation. For example, a decedent is a predecessor in interest to ("in privity with") both his personal representative and those, such as heirs and legatees, who take from him; so, too, is a grantor of proper-

---

50. Note that the Rule does not limit the use of former testimony only to the party *against* whom (or against whose predecessor) the earlier testimony was offered. The drafters reasoned that, for the purpose of the application of the present exception, direct and redirect examination of one's own witness is the equivalent of cross-examination of the opponent's witness. Adv.Comm.Note to Fed.R.Evid. 804 (b). See Falknor, Former Testimony and the Uniform Rules: A Comment, 38 N.Y.U.L.Rev. 651 (1963).

51. McCormick, § 255, at 616. In a recent Virginia case, however, the court apparently makes actual prior cross-examination a condition of the present exception. See Fisher v. Commonwealth, 217 Va. 808, 232 S.E.2d 798 (1977).

52. See Weinstein & Berger, ¶ 804(b)(1)[02], at 51–52.

53. For a discussion of the term privity as it is used in connection with the exception for party admissions, see supra § 57, text at nn. 28–36.

ty a predecessor to his grantee. Joint owners, joint obligors and joint obligees often have been considered within a relationship of privity.[54] It is not clear, however, that a joint interest satisfies the Federal Rule, since, strictly speaking, a joint holder is not a *predecessor*. The fundamental requirement of Rule 804(b)(1) is that the proponent of prior testimony show that the successor against whom the evidence is offered is attempting to protect or advance substantially the same interest as his privy-predecessor. If this requirement is satisfied, the term "predecessor" should be construed accordingly.[55] A functional approach is more desirable than one which emphasizes the arcane aspects of privity.

The link of property or interest succession infrequently applies in a criminal context. In cases where it arguably applies —as, for example, where two business partners are tried separately for the receipt and sale of stolen property—the confrontation clause of the Constitution casts doubt upon using prior testimony against the last party tried.[56] The constitutional doubt is avoided under the Federal Rule by limiting the privy-predecessor concept to civil actions.

It should be observed that the Federal Rule, in common with most states, limits the exception for prior testimony to circumstances in which the present opponent shares with the earlier examiner (whether himself or a predecessor) a "similar motive to develop the [prior] testimony by direct, cross, or redirect examination."[57] Similarity of motive is determined by ascertaining the interests and objectives of the party in the first proceedings and, where interrogation actually has taken place, by examining the prior interrogation. If the motive of the previous examiner is substantially different from that of the present party against whom the prior testimony now is offered, the prior

54. Morgan at 251–52.

55. See Re Master Key Antitrust Litigation, 72 F.R.D. 108 (D.Conn. 1976) (federal government is predecessor in interest to private antitrust plaintiff).

56. See Weinstein & Berger, ¶ 804(b)(1)[05]. For further discussion of the confrontation clause, see infra Part J.

57. Fed.R.Evid. 804(b)(1); McCormick, § 256, at 620. See supra note 55.

interrogation should not be an adequate substitute for present questioning.

It sometimes is said that the issues in the first and second trials must be identical, but this overstates the requirement. When the judge in the second proceeding is trying to determine similarity of motive, he should determine only whether the issues to which the now unavailable declarant *directed his proffered testimony* are the same, or substantially the same, in both trials.[58] These are the issues that are determinative; congruence of other issues in the two cases is unnecessary. Circumstances, however, might dictate that the judge weigh the relative importance of the witness-declarant's testimony in both trials, at least where the role of the testimony in the first trial was so minor as to raise questions about the motive of the earlier party to develop or test it.

An illustration of the considerations that attend the application of the former testimony exception can be found by recourse to an earlier example. Suppose an injured child sues a railroad for installing a mechanically defective signal; subsequently the child's parent sues for loss of the child's services, alleging negligent maintenance of the signal. Testimony by a witness in the first trial (in which the infant was the plaintiff) that the signal was not working at the time of the accident would be material to both cases. In the second proceeding, where—we shall assume—the witness is unavailable, the testimony would be offered against the same party (the railroad) which defended the first suit, thus satisfying the condition of party similarity. If the judge concluded that the motive of the railroad in the first trial was similar to its motive in the second trial, the exception for former testimony would apply. Application of the exception should not be denied on the ground of a difference in the ultimate issue between the two trials; rather, the inquiry should be whether as to those issues to which the witness's testimony was responsive the railroad had a common motive.

---

58. McCormick, § 257, at 620.

NOTES

1. A minority of jurisdictions do not require that the party to the first proceeding be either the same party who later opposes the former testimony or a predecessor in interest. Rather, these jurisdictions require only that the prior testimony was first developed or tested by *a* party who had the opportunity to examine the witness-declarant and who had an interest and motive *similar* to the opponent-party in the second trial. Thus, in some circumstances, former testimony is receivable against one who was neither a party to the first trial, nor a successor in interest. See Cal.Evid. Code § 1292; Travelers Fire Ins. Co. v. Wright, 322 P.2d 417 (Okla.1958). Nonetheless, the broader rule is intended to ensure that the prior examination adequately protects the present party. Is this a more desirable approach than that of making admissibility depend upon an analysis of whether the party to the first proceeding was a predecessor in interest?

2. Use of an official transcript is the most convenient and reliable method of proving that the testimonial statements from the first trial or proceeding were made by the witness-declarant. The official (public) records exception to the hearsay rule usually enables the proponent to introduce the transcript as proof of the testimonial statements in question. However, the proponent can use other methods of proof. For example, one who heard the former testimony can take the stand in the present trial and state what the testimony was, i. e., recite what he heard the declarant say. If the witness had made notes, these might come into evidence as recorded recollection, or might be used to refresh recollection. See Weinstein & Berger, ¶ 804(b)(1) [01] at 50. Observe that proving that the prior testimonial statements were made involves a hearsay problem when the evidence proffered is an official transcript or a writing which is a recordation of past recollection. An exception (for public records or recorded recollection) allows the transcript or writing to serve as evidence that the prior statements were made. Of course, the second hearsay problem—that involving the use of the statements for their truth—normally is resolved by reference to the present exception for former testimony. But suppose the prior testimony consists in part of statements by the (now unavailable) witness reciting what someone else (a declarant) said. To use the declarant's words for their truth, the proponent must invoke an appropriate exception if one can be found. Cf. United States v. Davis, 551 F.2d 233 (8th Cir. 1977) (prior testimony recites statement of D; D's statement constitutes a party admission).

3. Assume that the testimony at the first trial would have been excluded had appropriate objection been made. At the second proceeding an opponent for the first time raises the proper objection. Is the

objection waived? Most courts would answer that if the witness were present and testifying in the second trial, a proper objection would be entertained and sustained; therefore, the opponent can object when the witness's statements from the first proceeding are offered as former testimony. Note, however, that when the objection that could have been made attacks only the form of the testimony (e. g., incomplete foundation, violation of the opinion rule, etc.) and not its relevance or competence (e. g., violation of the hearsay rule), it will not defeat admissibility in the second trial. McCormick, § 259, at 623.

PART H. DYING DECLARATIONS

§ 75. In General

The exception for dying declarations has a curious history, revealing judicially-imposed restrictions that range from debatable to senseless.[59] For our purposes, it suffices to say that during the Nineteenth Century, courts increasingly admitted *in criminal homicide prosecutions* the victim's dying statement identifying his slayer or revealing the cause of his pending death. Only in cases of homicide, the reasoning went, was there a special need because the alleged murderer has silenced the witness-victim.

Application of this arbitrary rule results in excluding dying declarations in all civil cases and in all criminal prosecutions except those for homicide.[60] This limitation gives little weight to the supposed reliability of any "deathbed statements"[61]—a reliability derived from the belief that one thinking himself about to die will be motivated to speak truthfully.[62] If this belief is

---

59. A cogent account appears in McCormick §§ 281–85.

60. See Carver v. Howard, 280 S.W. 2d 708 (Ky.1955) (dying declaration not admissible in civil action for wrongful death and personal injury); Hansel v. Commonwealth, 260 Ky. 148, 84 S.W.2d 68 (1935) (dying declaration not admissible in prosecution for rape, even though victim died in resulting childbirth).

61. Adv.Comm. Note to Fed.R.Evid. 804(b)(2) (recognizing the "powerful

psychological pressures" present at death).

62. "Dying declarations in homicide cases have from ancient times been admitted in evidence either (1) because of solemnity—the solemnity of the occasion and the fear of punishment in the hereafter if one tells a lie just before death, or (2) because of necessity—since the victim of the homicide cannot testify its admission is necessary to protect the public against homicidal suspect, it should not support the admission of dying declarations in homicide cases, where the consequences of a conviction are quite serious. Indeed, one can argue that these declarations should be excluded in criminal cases, but admitted in civil cases where the results of erroneous factfinding are less severe.

In homicide cases, courts generally sanction the exception for dying declarations, but have been unwilling to accept statements that do not pertain to the injury or death of the victim-declarant; they have restricted admissibility to those statements which describe the circumstances (including identity) surrounding the slaying. The basis for this restriction is the lack of immediacy of any other subject matter. Statements about other topics carry a greater risk of insincerity or faulty memory. Curiously, there also is authority that the dying declaration must have been uttered by the victim whose murder is the subject of the trial where the declaration is offered. Strictly applied in a case where the defendant contemporaneously kills two persons, the limitation results in excluding a statement of the declarant-victim in the trial for the murder of the other victim.[63] Such a limitation can not be justified on the ground that a special need is lacking. It also is difficult to see how the assumed element of trustworthiness is weakened in these circumstances.

Thus, while the rhetoric of courts affirms that statements made in anticipation of death are likely to be accurate,[64] admissibility often has been restricted in ways that cannot be reconciled with the premise of trustworthiness. Furthermore, as Professor Morgan has noted, the judicial rulings on admissibility cannot be reconciled with a rationale of special need, for even where there are eyewitnesses to the homicide, a dying declara-

---

criminals and prevent a miscarriage of justice. . . . In our judgment, both grounds justify the admissibility of dying declarations . . . ." Commonwealth v. Brown, 388 Pa. 613, 616–17, 131 A.2d 367, 369 (1957) (footnotes omitted).

63. A few courts have so held. See Westberry v. State, 175 Ga. 115,

164 S.E. 905 (1932) (soundly criticized in V Wigmore, § 1433, at 281); Commonwealth v. Stallone, 281 Pa. 41, 126 A. 56 (1924).

64. E. g., Commonwealth v. Brown, 388 Pa. 613, 616–17, 131 A.2d 367, 369 (1957). But see Kidd v. State, 258 So.2d 423, 429–30 (Miss.1972) (concurring opinion).

tion is admissible if the conditions of the exception are satisfied.[65]

§ 76. Dying Declarations: Application of the Exception

Despite the apparent inconsistencies noted in the preceding section, the central feature of dying declarations—and the condition that is essential to admissibility—is that the statement be made at a time when the declarant has a settled expectation of death. All hope of recovery must have been abandoned; equivocal statements ("I may die") are insufficient to satisfy the exception. The judge must find from all of the attending circumstances, including statements by the declarant, that the declarant felt a sense of impending death.[66] Of course, in jurisdictions still adhering to the traditional approach, admissibility is conditioned further upon a showing that death actually ensued and that the prosecution is for the resulting homicide. If the prosecution is for some lesser offense—such as abortion or rape—the declaration is inadmissible even though death in fact ensued.[67]

An increasing number of jurisdictions have taken steps to expand the exception, usually by sanctioning admissibility in criminal prosecutions other than homicide or in civil actions (such as wrongful death) where there necessarily is an inquiry as to cause of death.[68] The Federal Rules of Evidence contain the following provision: [69]

> Statement under belief of impending death—In a prosecution for homicide or in a civil action or proceeding, a statement made by a declarant while believing that his death is imminent, concerning the cause or circumstances of what he believed to be his impending death.

65. Morgan, at 268.

66. Shepard v. United States, 290 U.S. 96 (1933); Wilson v. State, 86 Nev. 320, 468 P.2d 346 (1970).

67. Winfrey v. State, 174 Ark. 729, 296 S.W. 82 (1927); supra note 60; Morgan at 268.

68. McCormick, § 287, at 685; Morgan at 268.

69. Fed.R.Evid. 804(b)(2).

Note that this formulation extends to any civil case, subject, of course, to the requirements of relevance. However, on the criminal side of the docket the exception is limited to prosecutions for homicide. This restriction apparently rests upon the old "necessity" theme.[70] The exception operates only where there is a belief that death is imminent, but there is no requirement that the declarant actually die. (Of course, death will have occurred in homicide cases.) Note the general limitation that the statement must refer to the cause or circumstances attending the supposed impending death.[71] Finally, the application of this exception hinges upon the unavailability of the declarant; however, the absence of the declarant need not be caused by his death: any of the reasons set out in Federal Rule 804(a) will suffice.

NOTES

1. Dying declarations most frequently are offered by the prosecution in an effort to convict the accused of the murder of the declarant. But the exception is equally available to the defense. See State v. Proctor, 269 S.W.2d 624 (Mo.1954); State v. Puett, 210 N.C. 633, 188 S.E. 75 (1936).

2. The argument has been made, usually without success, that a lack of religious conviction or belief should defeat admissibility because there is no fear of divine punishment. Courts generally have been satisfied that there is a psychological stimulus to be truthful when facing the uncertainties of death, even though the declarant has no fear of divine or supernatural sanction. Under this view, irreverence may be shown for the purpose of affecting the weight to be accorded the declaration, but not to defeat its admissibility. Maguire et al. at 645–46; Annot. 16 A.L.R. 411 (1922).

3. As with other evidence (except party admissions, supra note 3 following Part A, and statements of family history, infra Part J, note 2), there is a requirement that the proponent of a dying declaration show that circumstances support the conclusion that the declarant had first-hand knowledge. However, if this requirement is met, the better-reasoned cases do not reject the declaration simply because it is phras-

---

70. Adv.Comm. Note to Fed.R.Evid. 804(b)(2).

71. The drafters of the Rule believed the influence of the impend-

ing death was not sufficient to ensure the trustworthiness of statements dealing with other matters. Id.

ed in terms that appear to violate the opinion rule. This position is sound, for it recognizes that the opinion rule should be confined in application to courtroom testimony that can be rephrased so as to eliminate unnecessary inferences or conclusions. Morgan at 267. See also Ch. IV, § 29.

4. Does the exception for dying declarations implicate the confrontation clause of the Sixth Amendment, particularly where the victim is the only accusing "witness"? See infra Part J., n. 1 and accompanying text.

PART I.   DECLARATIONS AGAINST INTEREST

§ 77.   In General

Statements or declarations against interest should be distinguished from party admissions: declarations against interest must be adverse to the interest of declarant *at the time* of the utterance and the declarant must be unavailable. Unlike party admissions, which may be offered only against the admitting party, declarations against interest may be offered by any party. Party admissions, as we have seen,[72] do not have to be against interest when made and are not conditioned upon a showing of unavailability.

Because the use of declarations against interest is conditioned upon a showing of unavailability, the exception has its most frequent application where the declarant is not a party. When the declarant is a party, the hearsay exception more often applied is that for party admissions. Although a party can not introduce his own statement as a party admission, he can in theory (and does occasionally in practice) put into evidence his declaration against interest. This seldom happens, however, because of the dual requirements that the proffered statement be disserving when made and that the declarant be unavailable. From a tactical standpoint there usually is no incentive for the declarant-party to offer the statement because it is apt·to be inconsistent with his posture at trial. Further, from a practical standpoint, the party-declarant usually is available with the result that an essential condition of the exception for declarations against interest is

---

72.   See supra §§ 54, 72.

not met. Hence, it may be generalized that declarations against interest are disserving statements, made by an unavailable, non-party declarant.[73]

The assumption that underlies the present hearsay exception is that a declarant is unlikely to make a disserving statement unless it is true. Common observation probably supports this proposition, putting aside special psychological conditions characterized by self-denegration. In this regard, it is interesting that until recent years statements coming within the declarations-against-interest exception were limited to those that were directly against the declarant's pecuniary or proprietary interest.[74] Thus, assertions coming within the exception have tended to have a business or financial flavor in that they deal with matters of ownership or money. Statements against penal interest usually were rejected, although the law here is undergoing a change. Statements against one's social interest, often discussed by the commentators and considered in scattered cases, even today have gained acceptance in only a few jurisdictions.

§ 78. Declarations Against Interest: Application of the Exception

If the unavailable declarant has made a statement admitting that he owes money or acknowledging that he does not own property (or that his ownership is limited, impaired or encumbered), he usually has satisfied the condition that his statement be against pecuniary or proprietary interest. Conversely, if the declarant has made a statement or a written entry indicating that he is owed $2,000 by X, the assertion normally is self-serving and outside the present exception. But a subsequent statement or entry showing that $2,000 has been received from X is an acknowledgment that the debt is no longer owing; thus, this last entry (the statement of receipt) has a disserving quality.[75] Al-

---

73. For a comprehensive and incisive treatment of this exception, see Morgan, Declarations Against Interest, 5 Vand.L.Rev. 451 (1952); see also the influential article, Jefferson, Declarations Against Interest: An Exception to the Hearsay Rule, 58 Harv.L.Rev. 1 (1944).

74. McCormick, § 277, at 671.

75. Knapp v. St. Louis Trust Co., 199 Mo. 640, 98 S.W. 70 (1906) (admitting not only that portion of a physician's entry regarding payment, but also that portion showing date of treatment and condition treated).

though it is arguable that the trustworthiness of a statement of
receipt of monies owed is suspect because the declarant may not
realize that his assertion is against his interest, such a general
contention probably should not defeat admissibility. Analytically, the courts correctly conclude that the statement of money received impairs or defeats a claim that a collectable debt still is
outstanding.[76]

   The question whether a statement is against interest must be
answered in context, taking into account the circumstances attending the declaration.[77] A statement that a debt is owed normally is against the declarant's interest, but it would not be in
circumstances where it is to the declarant's advantage to establish the debt. For example, it might be advantageous to the declarant to establish a debt in order to show that a transfer of his
real property was not absolute but was made only to secure an
outstanding debt.[78] In the usual case, the court will assess the
nature of the statement (as disserving or not) by inquiring
whether, under all of the known circumstances, a reasonable

---

76. A different problem is presented
when an agent acknowledges receipt of money on behalf of his
principal. Here the against-interest requirement arguably is satisfied because the agent indirectly is
acknowledging his obligation to re-
mit the sum received to his principal. A false entry might result in
his liability to the principal for the
amount recorded. See Jefferson,
Declarations Against Interest: An
Exception to the Hearsay Rule, 58
Harv.L.Rev. 1, 12 (1944).

77. "A fact . . . stated may or
may not be against interest according to the *circumstances*. For example, a statement that one is *not*
a partner in a certain firm states
a fact which favors one's interest
if the firm is insolvent (and a defi-
cit is therefore to be made up), but
disfavors one's interest if the firm

is solvent (and profits are thus
shared); while a statement that
one *is* a partner in the firm states
a fact for or against interest in
just the reverse situations." V
Wigmore, § 1463, at 269. For a recent federal case analyzing the
"against requirement," see United
States v. Gonzalez, 559 F.2d 1271
(5th Cir. 1977).

78. Barrera v. Gonzalez, 341 S.W.2d
703 (Tex.Civ.App.1960). Similarly,
an entry of partial payment received, which arguably is against interest (because it is a recognition that
part of the debt is no longer owed),
made after the running of the statute of limitations may favor the declarant's interest if the effect of
the payment is to revive the obligation. See Small v. Rose, 97 Me.
286, 54 A. 726 (1903).

man would consider the statement against his interest. The trial judge, however, will consider any evidence regarding the mental attitude of the particular declarant, and he will exclude the proffered hearsay declaration if he finds that this particular declarant did not consider the statement adverse to his interest.[79] This result is consistent with the rationale underlying the exception, that is, it would be inconsistent with the psychological basis of the exception for the judge to admit a declaration even though he was unable to satisfy himself that the *particular* declarant thought the statement disserving.

Courts have been faced with continuing pressure to expand the kinds of interests that will qualify under the exception. One argument finding increasing acceptance is that a statement sufficiently disserving should be admissible even though it may not be *directly* or *immediately* adverse to a proprietary or pecuniary interest: in other words, a contingent adverse interest should suffice. The major step in accepting this argument came when American courts began to hold that a statement indicating fault or other actionable conduct qualified as being against pecuniary interest. Probably a majority of courts now endorse the view that a statement which, if true, would render a declarant liable for damages in an action for tort is sufficiently adverse to pecuniary interest to justify admission.[80] Similar reasoning should uphold the admissibility of any declaration that, if true, would result in civil liability, such as a declarant's assertion that he was the father of an illegitimate child.[81] This statement, of

---

79. The cases do not make this point clearly; however, most courts appear willing to consider evidence about the mental state of the particular declarant in question. See, e. g., Demasi v. Whitney Trust & Sav. Bank, 176 So. 703 (La.Ct.App.1937), where the court refers to the declarant as ignorant and not realizing the consequences of her statement. See also 4 Weinstein & Berger, ¶ 804(b)(3)[02], at 84–85.

80. Home Ins. Co. v. Allied Telephone Co., 246 Ark. 1095, 442 S.W. 2d 211 (1969); Neely v. Kansas City Pub. Serv. Co., 241 Mo.App. 1244, 252 S.W.2d 88 (1952); Duncan v. Smith, 393 S.W.2d 798 (Tex. 1965). But see Morgan at 259, citing cases that illustrate a "sharp conflict in the decisions."

81. In Ferguson v. Smazer, 151 Conn. 226, 196 A.2d 432 (1963), the court acknowledged that such a

course, raises the possibility of judicially imposed support payments. A further extension, recognized in a growing number of jurisdictions, permits declarations against *penal* interest to come within the present exception. Thus, if the declarant makes a statement acknowledging conduct that would subject him to a criminal penalty, the statement is admissible. Some of the jurisdictions that admit this kind of disserving statement limit admissibility to *civil* trials where the criminal conduct described also constitutes a tort.[82] Thus, some courts bring declarations contingently against penal interest within the more familiar rule that recognizes the admissibility of statements acknowledging tortious conduct. Other jurisdictions have taken a direct approach. They frankly recognize that statements against penal interest, which implicate both monetary loss and more severe penalties such as incarceration, potentially are the most disserving of all adverse statements.[83] These courts hold that declarations that could lead to criminal liability fall within the present exception, and admit these statements in both civil or criminal trials.[84]

In the minority of jurisdictions that generally extend the exception to penal interests, there nonetheless is apprehension about fabricated evidence, especially in a criminal trial. This judicial skepticism most often occurs when an accused, attempting to raise a reasonable doubt, offers a hearsay declaration, inculpating an unavailable declarant, to prove that the declarant, not the accused, committed the crime. Often these minority jurisdictions adopt a special requirement intended to reduce the chance of false or untrustworthy evidence: they condition admissibility of a declaration against penal interest offered by the accused in a criminal trial upon the existence of corroborative

---

declaration was against pecuniary interest, but then rejected the statement on several grounds that should have affected weight, not admissibility.

82. McCormick, § 278, at 673–74. Cf. State v. Gorden, 356 Mo. 1010, 204 S.W.2d 713 (1947) (statement held inadmissible).

83. See, e. g., Hines v. Commonwealth, 136 Va. 728, 117 S.E. 843 (1923).

84. See, People v. Brown, 26 N.Y.2d 88, 308 N.Y.S.2d 825, 257 N.E.2d 16 (1970). But see State v. Gordon, supra note 11. See also N.J.Evid. Rule 63(10).

evidence increasing the likelihood that the absent declarant committed the crime in question.[85]　Such corroborative evidence, for example, might indicate the declarant's motive, establish his presence at the scene of the crime, or show other circumstances tending to confirm the trustworthiness of the declaration.

Federal Rule of Evidence 804(b)(3) adopts the holdings of recent decisions:

> Statement against interest—A statement which was at the time of its making so far contrary to the declarant's pecuniary or proprietary interest, or so far tended to subject him to civil or criminal liability, or to render invalid a claim by him against another, that a reasonable man in his position would not have made the statement unless he believed it to be true.　A statement tending to expose the declarant to criminal liability and offered to exculpate the accused is not admissible unless corroborating circumstances clearly indicate the trustworthiness of the statement.

The Federal Rule uses a reasonable man standard for determining whether a statement is disserving, but this standard should not prohibit an inquiry by the judge as to whether the *particular* declarant in question viewed the statement as against his interest.　In the vast majority of cases, no issue arises whether circumstances peculiar to a particular declarant should render self-serving or neutral a statement that a reasonable man would find adverse.　But where the opponent produces evidence to show that the declarant in question did not view the proffered statement as one against interest, the judge should exercise the power conferred by Federal Rule 403 to exclude the statement on the ground that its probative value is outweighed by the risk that it will mislead the jury.

Rule 804(b)(3) also takes a cautious approach to the introduction of a statement against penal interest offered to exculpate the accused in a criminal case.　Admissibility of the against-penal-interest declaration is made dependent upon a

---

85.　See, e. g., N.M.Stat.Ann. 20–4–804; Maine R.Evid. 804(b)(3).

showing of "corroborating circumstances [that] clearly indicate the trustworthiness of the statement." [86] Thus, in a criminal case, the accused seeking to show that another person committed the crime in question must couple his offer of the other person's inculpatory hearsay statement with a showing of corroborating evidence.

NOTES

1. Should a statement that exposes the declarant to hatred, ridicule, or disgrace come within the against-interest exception to the hearsay rule? Such statements against one's social interest have received more attention from the commentators than acceptance by the courts. Earlier drafts of the Federal Rules of Evidence contained a provision that included disserving social statements among those that qualified as "against interest." But Congress found such declarations "lacking sufficient guarantees of reliability" and deleted the provision. H.R.Rep.No. 650, 93rd Cong. 2d Sess. 16 (1973). For cases discussing declarations against social interests see United States v. Dovico, 261 F.Supp. 862 (S.D.N.Y.1966), aff'd, 380 F.2d 325 (2d Cir.), cert. denied 389 U.S. 944 (1967); State v. Sanders, 27 Utah 2d 354, 357–59, 496 P.2d 270, 272–73 (1972). For statutes providing that such declarations are admissible, see Nev.Rev.Stat. § 51.345; Kan. Code Civ. Proc. § 60–460(j).

2. Courts still struggle with the admissibility of statements that in part are disserving and in part are self-serving or neutral. Severance of the declaration by admitting *only* the disserving portions is one possibility, although in some contexts such a procedure may distort impact and meaning. Another possibility is for the trial judge to evaluate the statement as a whole to try to determine whether the disserving aspects preponderate. The cases are not harmonious. See McCormick, § 279, at 677–78; Weinstein & Berger, ¶ 804(b)(3) [02], at 87–88. Where portions of the statement(s) that are not adverse are more or less neutral, the case for admission of the entire statement is strong. Where the balance is close and severance is not a practical alternative, much deference should be given to the trial judge's discretion. One noted commentator makes the suggestion that the judge should explain to the jury the rationale of the hearsay exception for against-interest statements so as to enable them to evaluate more accurately combined statements that are not entirely disserving. See Weinstein & Berger, ¶ 804(b)(3)[02], at 89.

---

86. Compare United States v. Atkins, 558 F.2d 133 (3rd Cir. 1977) (corroboration sufficient) with United States v. Guillette, 547 F.2d 743 (2d Cir. 1976) (insufficient).

3.   In certain circumstances, rejection of a declaration against penal interest, when coupled with other restrictive rulings, is a violation of due process.   The leading case is Chambers v. Mississippi, 410 U.S. 284 (1973), the peculiar facts of which arguably confine the holding to comparatively few situations.   Chambers, the accused, moved to call as an adverse witness, *X*, an *available* declarant who had confessed to the crime of murder with which Chambers was charged.   The trial judge denied this motion, but did allow Chambers to elicit from *X* during direct examination testimony that the latter had given a written confession admitting guilt for the crime in question; on cross, the prosecutor showed that *X* had repudiated the confession and, further, secured testimony from *X* that he was not at the scene of the crime when the fatal shot was fired.   Because the court refused to permit Chambers' lawyer to treat *X* as an adverse witness, counsel was denied the opportunity to conduct a hostile examination designed to weaken or destroy *X*'s claim of alibi and to attack the credibility of *X*'s repudiation of his written confession.   Blocked from this line of proof, Chambers sought to present certain witnesses to whom *X* orally had admitted his (*X*'s) perpetration of the killing in question.   The trial judge ruled the evidence inadmissible on hearsay grounds.

In reversing the conviction on the basis that the sum of the judge's rulings denied Chambers due process of law, the United States Supreme Court discussed declarations against penal interest.   It found that the corroborating circumstances made *X*'s verbal declarations against penal interest trustworthy.   These circumstances included testimony that *X* was at the scene, that he had a gun of the type used in the killing, that he had admitted his guilt soon after the murder and on more than one occasion, and that his declarations unequivocally were against his interest.   The court also found it significant that *X* was in the courtroom and subject to examination under oath.   Note, however, the usual requirement, applied in both federal and state cases and adopted in Fed.R.Evid. 804(b)(3), that the declarant be unavailable before the exception for declarations against interest is applicable.

PART J.   HEARSAY AND EXCEPTIONS:
PAST AND FUTURE

No aspect of Anglo-American evidentiary law has drawn more attention and commentary than the hearsay rule and its various exceptions.   As with other controversial subjects, the hearsay rule has its ardent defenders and critics.[87] The basic rule and its exceptions—some of which are omitted [88] from this brief text

---

87. See, e. g., Taylor, The Case for Secondary Evidence, 81 Cas. & Com. 46 (Jan.-Feb. 1976); 2 Jones on Evidence, §§ 8:1–8:3 (6th ed. 1972) (collecting authorities pro and con); Maguire, The Hearsay System: Around and Through the Thicket, 14 Vand.L.Rev. 741 (1961).

88. The Federal Rules of Evidence contain twenty-nine exceptions to the hearsay rule, not including party admissions which the Federal Rules treat as nonhearsay. The exception for learned treatises appearing as 803(18) is briefly consid: ered in connection with expert testimony. Ch. XII, § 106. Particular attention is called to another Rule 803 provision, the exception for ancient documents. Rule 803(16) excepts from the hearsay exclusionary rule:

Statements in ancient documents —Statements in a document in existence twenty years or more the authenticity of which is established.

Necessity plays a dominant role in this exception because the declarant who makes assertions in a document aged twenty or more years likely is unavailable or without sufficient memory to testify. Note, however, that the unavailability of the declarant is immaterial to the application of the exception. To the extent this exception rests on trustworthiness, such reliability probably is found in the fact that the statement far antedates the present controversy; if there was a motive to misrepresent, it is unlikely that the source of the motive is the controversy in which the aged document is offered. Further-

more, additional reliability is gained if the accuracy of the document —assuming its existence was continuously known—has not been challenged for twenty or more years. Presumably, if the case were otherwise and the document were suspect, the judge could exclude it. See Fed.R.Evid. 403.

Many, but not all, common-law jurisdictions recognize the exception for statements contained in ancient documents. At common law the document must be thirty or more years old. Some jurisdictions limit the exception to dispositive statements or recitals in documents that are likely to be drafted carefully. The hearsay exception for ancient documents should be distinguished from the ancient document rule pertaining to the authentication of writings. See Ch. XIII, § 114.

One use of the ancient documents exception is to prove family relationships where an issue of kinship arises. But all jurisdictions recognize in some form the "pedigree exception," which can be used in establishing family relationships such as births, marriages, divorces, degree of kinship, etc. The common-law doctrine was hedged with restrictions: where the issue concerns X (for example, his birth, death, etc.) or the relationship of X to Y, the proponent must show that the declarant was related by blood to X (in the first example) or to X or Y (in the second example). It also sufficed that the declarant was married to X (first example) or to X or Y (second example), but relationships of affinity more distant than that of the spouse

—can be criticized as resting upon untested premises and assumptions. Arguably, the hearsay rule operates to block valuable evidence, whereas many of the exceptions admit evidence that is suspect.[89] The validity of the critical hypothesis can not

---

of the subject of the declaration would not suffice under the orthodox common-law view. Morgan at 301–02. Some courts even required that where the statement concerned X and Y, the proponent must show the declarant's relationship *to both*. Id. at 304. Thus although Z, a declarant married to Y, in *most* jurisdictions could make a statement about Y and X that would fall within the exception, it was clear that members of Z's family (unrelated to X or Y by consanguinity) could not give admissible declarations about the relationship of X and Y. Recent decisions, however, extend the exception to include persons, such as a physician or minister, so situated as to know the facts even though the kinship is missing. Id. at 302.

The common law insisted that the declaration be made prior to the present controversy or, at least, before the controversy was known to the declarant. As developed under the common law, the reliability of this exception depends upon (1) the usual knowledge (even though not firsthand) of family members about their own family and (2) absence of a motive to falsify. The assumption is that a family-member declarant is likely to speak truthfully about relationships within his own family; for one thing, his statements often are subject to verification through other family members. The common law also required that the declarant be unavailable, thus heightening the need for the

hearsay evidence falling within the exception.

The Federal Rules expand the pedigree exception under the title "statement of personal and family history." Rule 804(b)(4) provides that when the declarant is unavailable, there shall be an exception for:

(A) A statement concerning the declarant's own birth, adoption, marriage, divorce, legitimacy, relationship by blood, adoption, or marriage, ancestry or other similar fact of personal or family history, even though the declarant had no means of acquiring personal knowledge of the matter stated; or (B) a statement concerning the foregoing matters, and death also, of another person, if the declarant was related to the other by blood, adoption, or marriage or was so intimately associated with the other's family as to be likely to have accurate information concerning the matter declared.

This provision discards by omission the common-law requirement that the declaration predate the controversy, extends the exceptions to include declarants closely associated with the family in question, and requires only a relationship between the declarant and one of the persons spoken of in the declaration.

89. Note, Erosion of the Hearsay Rule, 3 U. of Richmond L.Rev. 89, 103 (1968).

be tested here, but the rule and its exceptions deserve some further exploration.

The basic exclusionary rule, rejecting all extrajudicial statements offered for their truth and not within a recognized exception, accepts the proposition that cross-examination can expose evidential infirmities such as inaccurate perception, poor memory, insincerity, and mistransmission. Although it is difficult to imagine an adversarial system in which no value is placed upon the efficacy of cross-examination, no one yet has empirically demonstrated that adversarial cross-questioning usually lays bare these infirmities. What repeatedly is shown by common experience, however, is that cross-examination often causes a witness to express uncertainty, give additional information, or, sometimes, modify or repudiate his direct testimony. Thus, even without a convincing demonstration that cross-examination is beyond any doubt "the greatest legal engine ever invented for the discovery of truth," [90] a showing that it often causes a witness to change his testimony, either in emphasis or context, is enough to justify cross-questioning as a central feature of the adversary system. This suggests that attempts to abandon or nullify the rule against hearsay evidence are unlikely to be unsuccessful so long as the basic tenets of the adversary proceeding are retained. Because the adversarial posture demands the opportunity for cross-examination, the hearsay rule—which protects that right by rejecting "untested" evidence not within an exception—is not easily forsaken.

As to the exceptions, these are the product of an evolutionary process that began two centuries ago.[91] The result of pragmatic accommodation, they lack the symmetry and consistency of a comprehensive design or preconceived plan. The behavioral assumptions underlying the exceptions more readily are traced to the judges' view of human nature than to the controlled inquiry of behavioral scientists. Research has confirmed the validity of some of these assumptions, while casting doubt upon others.[92]

---

90. V Wigmore, § 1367, at 129.

91. V Wigmore, § 1426, at 208.

92. See, e. g., Stewart, Perception, Memory, and Hearsay: A Criticism of Present Law and the Proposed

The recognition or retention of an exception, however, should not depend entirely upon the law's accuracy in pronouncing conditions in which a declarant is likely to be truthful. The ultimate question is whether accurate factfinding is advanced by acceptance of the hearsay evidence in question. A reasoned answer to this depends not only upon the probable degree of reliability of the evidence, but also upon the tribunal's need for the evidence and the extent to which the trier can be alerted to its possible infirmities. Testimonial infirmities, such as defects in memory or sincerity, that underlie the hearsay rule also may be valuable in assessing the probative force of hearsay evidence. The justification for an exception need not rest upon a showing of high reliability; it is sufficient that the exception generally operates to admit evidence that has a sufficient degree of truthworthiness to promote accuracy in the factfinding process. Tested by this standard, the present exceptions are more defensible.

A suggestion that there is a degree of permanence to the present hearsay system, consisting of a basic exclusionary rule and multiple exceptions, should not imply that the system is static. Neither history nor logic suggests this. Both legislative and judicial movement have broadened existing exceptions and, with perhaps less frequency, created new ones. Illustrative of this trend are the decisions or legislative provisions (including court rules) that have enlarged the exceptions for business entries, statements of physical condition, and dying declarations. The same processes of cautious, incremental movement also have given shape to exceptions of more recent origin, such as those for present sense impressions, opinion surveys, and prior identifications.[93] Additionally, both legislatures and courts have

Federal Rules of Evidence, 1970 Utah L.Rev. 1; Hutchins & Slesinger, Some Observations on the Law of Evidence: Spontaneous Exclamations, 25 Colum.L.Rev. 432 (1928). Lempert & Saltzburg at 399–400 cite and comment upon the recent findings of Elizabeth Loftus and her associates, with special attention to the implications for the hearsay rule.

93. The exception for learned treatises, also comparatively recent, is mentioned in Ch. XII, § 106. See also Fed.R.Evid. 803(18). It should be noted that at least two jurisdictions have adopted an exception for statements of recent perception. See N.Mex.Stat. § 20–4–804(b)(2). West's Wis.Stat. Ann. § 908.045(2) provides that if

demonstrated inventive capacity by providing for the admissibility of needed hearsay evidence found sufficiently reliable to justify consideration by the factfinder, but which does not come within an established exception.[94]

Federal Rule 803(24), a carefully drawn "residual" or "catchall" exception to the hearsay rule, admits into evidence a probative statement, needed by the trier, when the "circumstantial guarantees of trustworthiness" are equivalent to the recognized exceptions. This Rule, which appears at the end of the exceptions grouped under Rule 803 (availability of declarant immaterial) and again at the end of the exceptions listed under Rule 804 (unavailability of declarant a condition of admissibility) provides:

> Other exceptions—A statement not specifically covered by any of the foregoing exceptions but having equivalent circumstantial guarantees of trustworthiness [is admissible], if the court determines that (A) the statement is offered as evidence of a material fact; (B) the statement is more probative on the point for which it is offered than any other evidence which the proponent can procure through reasonable efforts; and (C) the general purposes of these rules and the interests of justice will best be served by admission of the statement into evidence. However, a statement may not be admitted under this exception unless the proponent of it makes known to the adverse party sufficiently in

---

the declarant is unavailable there shall be a hearsay exception for a:
Statement of recent perception. —A statement not in response to the instigation of a person engaged in investigating, litigating, or settling a claim, which narrates, describes, or explains any event or condition recently perceived by the declarant, made in good faith, not in contemplation of pending or anticipated litigation in which he was interested, and while his recollection was clear.

94. See Mass.Gen.Laws Ann. Ch. 233, § 65 (admitting statements of a deceased person in civil actions if court finds declarations made in good faith upon personal knowledge); S.D. Code 30–15–7 (admitting hearsay in suits by or against personal representatives); Dallas County v. Commercial Union Assur. Co., 286 F.2d 388 (1961) (newspaper account of fire in courthouse admitted to show fact of fire where cause of structural damage was in dispute).

advance of trial or hearing to provide the adverse party with a fair opportunity to prepare to meet it, his intention to offer the statement and the particulars of it, including the name and address of the declarant.

Although it still is too soon to draw conclusions about how this Rule will fare in the hands of the judges, it already has received a fairly sympathetic reading from some courts of appeal.[95] Its salient feature is found in its frank recognition that no list of exceptions can account for the nuances or the endlessly varied contexts from which hearsay evidence may spring. Within the guidelines set forth in the Rule, a trial judge now can make a realistic appraisal of the variables that should determine admissibility. Thus, the Rule not only accommodates previously unencountered, unforeseen situations, but also helps courts identify circumstances in which the creation of a new exception might be justified. This latter usage provides a convenient bridge between past and future.

Any assessment of the future role of hearsay evidence, at least in criminal trials, must take account of the Constitution's Sixth Amendment guarantee to an accused of the right "to be confronted with the witnesses against him." [96] Although "the confrontation cases are in disarray and the policies to be served by the constitutional protection are far from clear," [97] certain conclusions may be drawn from the cases.

---

95. See, e. g., United States v. Leslie, 542 F.2d 285 (5th Cir. 1976) (requirements of 801(d) not applicable for prior inconsistent statement, under 803(24)); Muncie Aviation Corp. v. Party Doll Fleet, Inc., 519 F.2d 1178 (5th Cir. 1975) (evidence admitted despite the fact that some of requirements of 803(24) may not have been present). But see Arrow-Hart, Inc. v. Covert Hills, Inc., 71 F.R.D. 346 (E.D.Ky.1976) (803 (25) may not be used to circumvent foundation requirement for prior recorded testimony in 803(5)). For a careful, clause-by-clause application of the rule, see United States v. Carlson, 547 F.2d 1346 (8th Cir. 1976) (admitting grand jury testimony where witness refused to testify at trial for fear of reprisal).

96. This provision applies not only to the federal government but to the states as well. See Pointer v. Texas, 380 U.S. 400 (1965). The clause also can be read as guaranteeing the accused's right to be present at his own trial. See Illinois v. Allen, 397 U.S. 337 (1970).

97. S. Saltzburg & K. Redden, Federal Rules of Evidence Manual 600 (1977). A critical review of the

The confrontation clause never has been read so literally as to preclude generally the use of hearsay evidence in criminal trials. Indeed, the cases are replete with instances of hearsay statements admitted under the recognized exceptions.[98] It is fairly certain that there is no constitutional prohibition against either the substantive use of a prior extrajudicial declaration of a witness present at trial (at least where it clearly is shown that the prior statements were made) or, in cases of unavailability, against the use of prior testimony in circumstances in which the accused had an earlier opportunity to conduct a fair and full cross-examination.[99] Even admission against the accused of dying declarations apparently is permissible,[1] and most courts have turned aside confrontation clause challenges to such hearsay exceptions as declarations against interest,[2] business entries,[3] and party admissions by coconspirators.[4]

---

leading cases and a discussion of the conceptual framework underlying the confrontation clause may be found in Graham, The Right of Confrontation and the Hearsay Rule: Sir Walter Raleigh Loses Another One, 8 Crim.L.Bull. 99 (1972).

98. See McCormick, § 252, at 606 n. 10 for representative cases.

99. California v. Green, 399 U.S. 149 (1970); Mattox v. United States, 156 U.S. 237 (1895). See Barber v. Page, 390 U.S. 719 (1968), which contrary to the language in *Green* indicates that prior testimony at the preliminary hearing may not afford a defendant adequate opportunity to cross-examine because the issue at the preliminary hearing is limited to whether there is probable cause for a trial. See also Government of Virgin Islands v. Aquino, 378 F.2d 540, 549 (3d Cir. 1967).

1. Mattox v. United States, 156 U.S. 237 (1895), cited with approval in Pointer v. Texas, 380 U.S. 400, 407 (1965).

2. United States v. White, 553 F.2d 310 (2d Cir.), cert. denied 97 S.Ct. 2937 (1977).

3. United States v. Lipscomb, 435 F.2d 795 (5th Cir. 1971). See also Reed v. Beto, 343 F.2d 723 (5th Cir. 1965) (public records); State v. Finkley, 6 Wash.App. 278, 492 P.2d 222 (1972) (hospital's medical records). Contra, State v. Tims, 9 Ohio St.2d 136, 224 N.E.2d 348 (1967) (confrontation clause violated by use of business-hospital record).

4. Dutton v. Evans, 400 U.S. 74 (1970). Further, the confrontation clause does not extend to statements by persons whose declarations are not used to establish guilt at trial, such as witnesses before a grand jury, informers who provide information sufficient for probable cause to search, or probation officers who supply information relevant to sentencing. As

Nonetheless, the confrontation clause places limits, however uncertain, upon the freedom with which the prosecution may deny the accused adequate opportunity to cross-examine witnesses (including, in some circumstances, hearsay declarants) and the right to have adverse statements secured under oath and in the presence of the trier of fact. The Supreme Court apparently has rejected both of the most extreme readings of the confrontation clause.[5] Under one of these constructions, every hearsay declarant would be viewed as a witness against the accused and his presence at trial would be compelled constitutionally, thus blocking substantially all hearsay evidence. Under the opposite reading, the constitutional command would require merely a guarantee that evidence used to convict the accused be presented through trial witnesses. The source of the witness's information, while perhaps raising issues under an exclusionary rule of evidence such as the hearsay rule, would not present a constitutional problem.

In several cases, the Supreme Court has struck down under the confrontation clause evidence of inculpatory statements that the accused could not subject to meaningful cross-examination. Use of a transcript of prior testimony elicited from a witness during the accused's preliminary hearing at which the accused was not represented by counsel [6] was found constitutionally objectionable. Similarly rejected was improper "evidence" (although not formally admitted) of a prosecutor's use of the confession of the accused's codefendant: after the codefendant-witness invoked the fifth amendment and refused to testify, the prosecutor used the guise of refreshing the witness's recollection to read aloud the codefendant's earlier confession which implicated the accused.[7] In a third case, in which the ac-

---

one commentator notes, participants in the criminal process whose statements are not considered by a jury in connection with a determination of guilt or innocence are not "witnesses" against the accused as that term is used in the constitution. See Graham, supra note 97, at 125–29.

5. McCormick, § 252, at 607.

6. Pointer v. Texas, 380 U.S. 400 (1965). This case also holds that the confrontation clause is fully applicable to the states through the Fourteenth Amendment.

7. Douglas v. Alabama, 380 U.S. 415 (1965). Compare Barber v. Page,

cused did not take the stand, the use of a codefendant's confession which inculpated the accused was held to violate the latter's right of confrontation; [8] an instruction to the jury that it consider the confession only with regard to the codefendant's guilt was deemed ineffective. The Supreme Court also has indicated that the confrontation clause limits when a witness can be considered "unavailable" for purposes of a hearsay exception. In one case, state authorities who knew that a prosecution witness was in a federal penitentiary in another state made no attempt to secure his presence at trial. The Court held that the state denied the accused's right of confrontation when it used the witness's out-of-state custody as a ground for invoking the exception for prior recorded testimony.[9]

The Court has yet to clarify the reach of the confrontation clause, but reason suggests an analytical framework for future decisions. Like other constitutional provisions, the right of an accused "to be confronted with witnesses against him" should not be inflexible. Confrontation is a relative term to be given a functional meaning. Although the values to be protected by the confrontation clause are not altogether clear, the notion of confronting a witness implies a right to interrogate him effectively under oath and to bring him within the observation of the trier

---

390 U.S. 719 (1968). See supra note 99. In Parker v. Gladden, 385 U.S. 363 (1966), the Court found that a bailiff's secret remarks to the jury violated the accused's right to confront witnesses against him.

8. Bruton v. United States, 391 U.S. 123 (1968). But see Nelson v. O'Neil, 402 U.S. 622 (1971) (*Bruton* not controlling where co-defendant takes stand, denies inculpatory admission, and testifies favorably to accused); Harrington v. California, 395 U.S. 250 (1969) (*Bruton* violation can be harmless error; also *Bruton* may not apply when

codefendant takes the stand and admits statements).

9. Barber v. Page, 390 U.S. 719 (1968). But see Mancusi v. Stubbs, 408 U.S. 204, 211–13 (1971) (witness who had left country genuinely unavailable therefore defendant could not invoke Barber v. Page). See also California v. Green, 399 U.S. 149, 166–68 (1970) (admission at trial of statement taken from witness at preliminary hearing did not violate confrontation clause where accused had counsel and adequate opportunity to cross-examine at earlier proceeding).

of fact. At a minimum, it guarantees that the accused may effectively confront and cross-examine those who testify against him at trial.[10] Cross-examination may not be limited so as to significantly emasculate its effectiveness.[11] In all probability, the right of confrontation also ensures that an accused will not be convicted on the basis of statements by absent declarants that fall within no recognized exception to the hearsay rule. Thus, prosecutorial use at trial of the ex parte affidavit of an absent declarant to supply significant proof against the accused probably would violate his sixth amendment right to confrontation.

Beyond these situations, application of the confrontation clause should depend upon whether considerations of trustworthiness and adversarial fairness are satisfied. In ascertaining whether the confrontation of a witness at trial who merely presents documents [12] or who gives testimony which embodies the assertions of absent declarants satisfies the sixth amendment, at least three factors should be determinative: trustworthiness, the ease with which a declarant can be produced, and the importance of the evidence in question. If there is strong reason to distrust the reliability of the evidence, the preference for live testimony should be compelling. If the declarant reasonably can be produced, his courtroom presence should be demanded. In instances where the declarant is deceased or otherwise not available, the question whether the right of confrontation has been violated should depend on the degree of risk that the evidence will produce an erroneous finding. If the statements in question fall within a hearsay exception and thus have the imprimatur of judicial and legislative experience, this fact should weigh heavily in favor of a determination that the right to con-

---

10. The accused, however, can forfeit this right by disruptive conduct in the courtroom. Illinois v. Allen, 397 U.S. 337 (1970).

11. Davis v. Alaska, 415 U.S. 308 (1974) (accused must be permitted to show probationary status of juvenile witness against him); Smith v. Illinois, 390 U.S. 129 (1968) (accused must be allowed to ask a principal prosecution witness the latter's true name and address).

12. In some cases, where a document is self-authenticating, it will not be necessary to introduce it through a witness who attests to its genuineness. This fact, however, should not alter the analysis above.

frontation has been satisfied.[13] Finally, the significance of an accused's right to confront a witness should bear a direct relation to the significance of the evidence supplied by the witness. When this evidence is comparatively inconsequential, cross-examination of the in-court witness should be sufficient confrontation even though the source of the witness's testimony may be traced to an absent declarant.[14]

The foregoing analysis may fit as comfortably within a due process analysis as it does within the framework of the confrontation clause. Nonetheless, the Supreme Court already has embarked upon a course that accords the confrontation clause content beyond that found in the restrictive interpretation described earlier. A middle ground permitting ample flexibility to accommodate the growth of the hearsay rule seems consonant with the existing cases and highly desirable.

---

13. See Hoover v. Beto, 467 F.2d 516, 528–34 (5th Cir. 1972) (confession of principal admissible at accomplice's trial), cert. denied sub nom. Hoover v. Estelle, 409 U.S. 1086 (1972). But see Park v. Huff, 493 F.2d 923 (5th Cir. 1974) (confrontation clause violated by admission of co-conspirator's statements) rev'd en banc 506 F.2d 849, 860 (5th Cir. 1975) (no violation of confrontation clause), cert. denied 423 U.S. 824.

14. In Dutton v. Evans, 400 U.S. 74, 87–89 (1970) the Supreme Court noted that the hearsay evidence admitted against the accused was not "critical" or "devastating," especially in light of the other inculpatory evidence in the record. Although the significance of evidence which arguably violates the confrontation clause may be an important factor in determining if a constitutional violation has occurred, it would appear that a trial judge, faced with a timely constitutional objection, should reject even insignificant evidence if he thinks that it violates the accused's sixth amendment right.

CHAPTER VIII

IMPEACHMENT

§ 79. In General

The term "impeachment" is used loosely by the courts, but generally it refers to the introduction of evidence aimed at discrediting the testimony of a witness. In its broadest use, the term encompasses all evidence intended to cast doubt upon a witness's testimony, including evidence which calls into question the accuracy of his observation, his recollection, or the truthfulness of his testimony.[1] The cross-examiner may, for example, attempt to get a witness to concede that the latter was poorly situated to observe the event in question or that his memory has dimmed. Or the examiner may call other witnesses for the purpose of raising doubts about the credibility of the principal witness. These subsequent witnesses might testify, for example, that visibility was poor at the time of the occurrence in question or that the principal witness's faculties were impaired by intoxication or the use of drugs. The examiner also may seek to show, either through interrogation of the principal witness or through the use of other witnesses, that the background or possible motives of the principal witness suggest his mendacity. Finally, in its broadest use, "impeachment" includes the *contradiction* by one witness of another's testimony—that is, the use of a subsequent witness to give a contradictory account of the event about which the principal witness has testified.[2]

A more limited and technical use of the word "impeachment" refers to certain specific techniques designed to impugn a witness's credibility by revealing his tendency to distort or falsify his testimonial account of the facts. Impeachment in this nar-

---

1. Note that attacks on a witness's first-hand knowledge of an event or his ability to perceive, remember and relate can raise questions concerning his competence to testify at all. See Chap. IV, § 22.

2. See generally People v. Wilson, 254 Cal.App.2d 489, 492–95, 62 Cal. Rptr. 240, 242–44 (1967); People v. Pargo, 241 Cal.App.2d 594, 596, 601, 50 Cal.Rptr. 719, 720, 723 (1966); State v. Oswalt, 62 Wash. 2d 118, 381 P.2d 617 (1963).

row sense includes only discrediting evidence that aims primarily at "showing flaws in the witness," not evidence merely demonstrating some flaw or inaccuracy in his testimony.[3] Although the technique of impeachment by psychiatric evidence is generally included within this strict usage, opportunities to invoke this mode of impeachment are relatively infrequent.[4] The most commonly used techniques fall into three categories: (1) a revelation of bad character or dishonesty (shown by producing evidence of (a) a criminal conviction, (b) a prior dishonest act, or (c) bad character for truthfulness); (2) a showing of bias (by adducing evidence of hostility or favoritism); and (3) a demonstration of self-contradiction (by introducing evidence that the witness has made prior statements inconsistent with his present testimony). Unless otherwise noted, the term impeachment hereafter will refer only to this narrow usage.

§ 80. Impeachment of One's Own Witness

Determining who is permitted to impeach a witness presents a preliminary problem. For many years a rule has existed, until recently subject only to limited exceptions, that a party may not impeach his own witness. The origins of this prohibition remain uncertain, but it may have gained favor in the late 17th Century when adversary procedures began to replace inquisitorial methods of factfinding.[5] The right to call a witness was viewed as a special privilege, not to be abused by putting forth a witness and then attacking his credibility.[6] The rule against impeachment is embodied in the proposition, often repeated in the

---

3. Lempert & Saltzburg at 269.

4. The best known case is United States v. Hiss, 88 F.Supp. 559 (S.D.N.Y.1950). See also People v. Bastian, 330 Mich. 457, 47 N.W.2d 692 (1951).

5. See Ladd, Impeachment of One's Own Witness—New Developments, 4 U.Chi.L.Rev. 69, 70–74 (1936). But as noted in Maguire et al. at 423, this hypothesis is speculative.

6. Maguire et al. at 423. Another possible explanation for the origin of the rule against impeaching one's own witness is that it stems from the early ecclesiastical and English practice known variously as wager of law, oath swearing or compurgation. This involved purging or clearing the defendant by having witnesses testify that they believed he was telling the truth. Ibid. Here, of course, there was a strong identification between the defendant and his witness.

cases, that a party is "bound" by the testimony of his own witness. Although normally this means that impeachment is forbidden, the notion of a party being bound by his witnesses encompassed a complementary rule that had some support in the early cases: if a party presented a witness whose testimony was *unfavorable*, the points established in the testimony were conclusive against the proponent unless he could produce other witnesses whose testimony on these points was more favorable. So closely was a party identified with his witnesses that some courts held that he could not rely upon favorable evidence adduced during cross-examination of his adversary's witnesses to establish his claim or defense; [7] he had to produce his own witnesses to make out his case.

In modern lawsuits, where litigants have compulsory process and often must subpoena as a witness a stranger or hostile person, there is no justification for a rule forbidding impeachment of one's own witnesses. Nor is there justification for a rule that binds a party to his witnesses in the sense that his case depends exclusively upon their testimony. A party calls a particular witness because the latter has knowledge of relevant facts—not because he has an alliance or partnership with the party. Accordingly, the prohibition against impeachment and the concomitant rule limiting a party to his own witnesses understandably have been weakened or abandoned. [8] The rule that limits a party's favorable showing to the testimony of his witnesses has been generally repudiated. [9] The rule against impeaching one's own witness is now being abandoned—but with surprising

---

7. See, e. g., Behen v. St. Louis Transit Co., 186 Mo. 430, 85 S.W. 346 (1904).

8. Federal Rule 607 abandons entirely the rule against impeaching one's own witness. See In re Hayden's Estate, 174 Kan. 140, 254 P. 2d 813 (1953) (whether directed verdict proper is determined on basis of all favorable evidence including that elicited during cross-examination). In Virginia, however, there still is a rule that perhaps was spawned by the rule regarding the binding effect of testimony given by one's own witnesses. If a *party* testifies unequivocally to facts within his knowledge, he is bound by that testimony and cannot show by calling *other witnesses* (or by cross-examination) that the facts are more favorable than his testimony indicates. See Harris v. Harris, 211 Va. 459, 177 S.E.2d 534 (1970).

9. See, e. g., Bradford Audio Corp. v. Pious, 392 F.2d 67, 73 (2d Cir.

reluctance in some courts. Recently, a substantial number of jurisdictions has neutralized by statute or court rule the prohibition against a party impeaching his own witness.[10] Furthermore, as we shall see, the rule against impeachment gradually has lost much of its sting because of the creation of various exceptions. The invocation of one of these exceptions may be necessary where the party wishing to impeach has called the witness and the jurisdiction retains the rule against impeachment. But where the *court* has called the witness, which it will sometime do upon request of counsel, either party usually is free to impeach.[11]

An early exception to the prohibition against impeaching one's own witness was recognized where the law *requires* a party to call a witness.[12] For example, a statute or judicial rule might provide that a party must call the person who attested a will or other document in order to establish due execution.[13] Here, at least, the courts recognized that a party should be able to contest the credibility of a witness whom he was legally compelled to present. Practical as well as legal compulsion also should suspend the rule against impeachment, but only a few cases have adopted this broader approach.[14] However, jurisdictions increasingly have adopted (by court rule or statute) a second exception: when a party calls his adversary, some form of impeachment is allowable.[15]

A third exception is the "surprise doctrine," invoked when a party calling a witness is surprised by the latter's testimony;

1968); In re Hayden's Estate, supra note 8.

10. See, e. g., Fed.R.Evid. 607; West's Ann.Cal.Evid.Code § 785; Kan.Code of Civ.P. § 60–420; McCormick, § 38, at 77. See text accompanying notes 22–28, infra.

11. Lempert & Saltzburg at 271; Morgan at 63–64.

12. McCormick, § 38, at 77; Morgan at 63.

13. McCormick, § 38, at 77. In a criminal case, the prosecution may be required by statute or rule to call all witnesses who endorse the indictment. See People v. Connor, 295 Mich. 1, 294 N.W. 74 (1940); Morgan at 63.

14. Morgan at 63.

15. See McCormick, § 38, at 77; Ladd, Impeachment of One's Own Witness—New Developments, 4 U. Chi.L.Rev. 69, 77–78 (1936).

unexpected testimony entitles the party to impeach his witness by showing that the latter has made prior inconsistent statements. The theory is that the sponsoring party was deceived and should therefore be allowed to impeach the turncoat witness in an effort to lessen the damage to his case. The doctrine has been applied with varying degrees of strictness. A first requirement for its application is that the proponent demonstrate a basis for having believed that the witness would give favorable testimony. If the witness has given indications of unreliability or has not induced counsel reasonably to expect favorable testimony, the judge may find that the party calling the witness was forewarned and hence not genuinely surprised.[16] Further, under the traditional view, the witness's testimony must affirmatively be damaging: he must make a positive assertion adverse to a material part of the proponent's case.[17] Testimony that the witness can not remember usually will not justify impeachment.[18] But many courts, while not abandoning these requirements, have given the benefit of the doubt to the proponent on the question of whether he genuinely was surprised,[19] and have taken a realistic, practical view of what constitutes affirmative damage.[20]

---

16. See IIIA Wigmore § 904 (Chadbourn).

17. See Taylor v. Baltimore & Ohio R.R., 344 F.2d 281 (2d Cir.), cert. denied 382 U.S. 831 (1965); State v. Matlock, 65 Wash.2d 107, 396 P. 2d 164 (1964).

18. McCormick, § 38, at 76; III Wigmore, § 1043, at 1059–61 (Chadbourn). "The maximum legitimate effect of the impeaching testimony can never be more than the cancellation of the adverse answer by which the party is surprised." Kuhn v. United States, 24 F.2d 910, 913 (9th Cir.), cert. denied sub nom. Lee v. United States, 278 U.S. 605 (1928). The fear here, of course, is that when the witness is impeached by a prior inconsistent statement, the trier will use the prior statement as substantive evidence and thus violate the hearsay rule. See Ch. VI, § 52; Note, Prior Statements of One's Own Witness to Counteract Surprise Testimony: Hearsay and Impeachment Under the "Damage" Test, 62 Yale L.J. 650, 654 (1953).

19. Gaitan v. People, 167 Colo. 395, 447 P.2d 1001 (1969) (proponent knew witness was hostile and had not made inquiries of her that would have forewarned him of unfavorable testimony, but impeachment allowed); People v. Spinosa, 115 Cal.App.2d 659, 669–70, 252 P. 2d 409, 415 (1953) (witness gave contradictory versions prior to trial, but proponent entitled to rely on most recent account).

20. United States v. Cunningham, 446 F.2d 194 (2d Cir.), cert. denied

Without resorting to any of the foregoing exceptions to the rule against impeachment, counsel may by skillful examination of his own witness secure the desired testimony without crossing the forbidden line of impeachment. If the witness displays hostility or has an apparent lapse of memory, counsel usually may use leading questions.   He also may ask about prior inconsistent statements if he fairly can characterize his questions as an attempt to refresh his witness's recollection or to prompt the latter to correct an error in his testimony.[21] Finally, the examiner may use a prior writing (or other object) to "refresh" the witness's recollection.   None of these techniques is considered "impeachment" in the stricter sense in which that term is used.

In recent years, some jurisdictions either have granted the judge discretionary power to allow impeachment of a hostile witness or have abandoned altogether the proscription against impeaching one's own witness.[22] Notably, the Federal Rules of Evidence provide:

> The credibility of a witness may be attacked by any party, including the party calling him.[23]

In the commentary accompanying this provision, the Advisory Committee notes the unreality of the assumption that a party

---

404 U.S. 950 (1971) (witness who said at trial that he had seen defendant in the company of one identified as the robber "maybe [two or] three times" impeached by earlier statement that these two persons "hang around" together); People v. Le Beau, 39 Cal.2d 146, 245 P.2d 302 (1952) (denial of a fact that, if true, would help the state's case, sometimes can leave such a "damaging impression" that impeachment by state is justified).

21. See People v. Michaels, 335 Ill. 590, 167 N.E. 857 (1929); People v. Purtell, 243 N.Y. 273, 280–81, 153 N.E. 72, 74–75 (1926); Morgan at 64.

22. See, e. g., West's Ann.Cal.Evid. Code, § 785 (complete abrogation); Va. Code Ann. § 8.01–403 (judge's discretion). It should not be assumed that if the rule against impeachment of one's own witness is abandoned or modified any form of impeachment is permissible. There could be a limitation, such as that existing in Virginia, that the only allowable form of impeachment is showing prior inconsistent statements or some other method thought not to involve directly the use of evidence of bad character. See Smith v. Lohr, 204 Va. 331, 130 S.E.2d 433 (1963).

23. Fed.R.Evid. 607.

has unfettered liberty in selecting his witnesses.[24] The Federal
Rule makes a clean sweep of the old dogma by allowing the calling party to impeach by any of the techniques discussed in the
next section. Other reform statutes have not gone this far;
they allow impeachment of one's own witness only by prior inconsistent statements.[25]

The hesitancy of some jurisdictions to permit a party to use
any of the usual techniques to impeach his own witness apparently stems from a fear that this unlimited freedom might be
abused.[26] Impropriety might occur, for example, where the primary motivation for calling a witness identified with the opposing party is not to secure significant testimony, but rather to
impeach by a method (such as showing a prior conviction) that
directly reveals bad character or dishonesty.[27] Apprehension
concerning this abuse probably is unwarranted. Aside from the
fact that a party who undertakes this stratagem risks alienating
the trier of fact, the judge should have ample discretionary power to prevent improper impeachment.[28] Furthermore, if the witness's testimony is important to the outcome of the case, the opponent (or the court) probably will call him, in which event the
cross-examiner can impeach by any of the orthodox techniques
described below.

§ 81. Techniques of Impeachment: Character Traits Reflecting Mendacity

1. *Conviction of a Crime.* As an exception to the general
prohibition against the circumstantial use of character,[29] the

---

24. Adv.Comm.Note to Fed.R.Evid.
607.

25. See, e. g., Va.Code Ann. § 8.01–
403; see supra note 22. McCormick, § 38, at 76, describes the
English statutory precedents.

26. See Ladd, Impeachment of One's
Own Witness: New Developments,
4 U.Chi.L.Rev. 69, 80–86 (1936).

27. Impeachment by prior inconsistent statement does not necessarily

impugn character. See supra text
accompanying note 4.

28. See Waltz, The New Federal
Rules of Evidence 91 (2d ed. 1975).

29. The law always has displayed a
special concern for the truth of
courtroom testimony. Conditioning
devices, such as the oath and
cross-examination, are designed to
expose false statements. A witness
may be attacked by showing that

credibility of a witness may be challenged by showing that he has been convicted of a crime.[30]   The desired inference is that a person who commits a criminal offense is likely—or at least more likely than one who has not committed such an act—to give false testimony.   Disagreement, however, often occurs over what types of crimes indicate a propensity to falsify.   Does a conviction for manslaughter, for example, have probative force regarding credibility?   Some convictions, such as those for perjury [31] or fraud, yield strong circumstantial inferences relating to truth-telling.   Other offenses, however, such as manslaughter or reckless driving, have a tenuous link with credibility.[32]   Some courts have tried to solve this problem by resorting to amorphous verbal formulae.[33]   The most common are: crimes involving moral turpitude,[34] "crimen falsi," [35] and infamous crimes.[36] A plurality of courts, however, have reached a more practical

---

he has a bad character for truth and veracity. See infra § 81(3). Note that when prior convictions (§ 81(1)) and prior bad acts, (§ 81 (2)) are used to show a propensity to falsify, the relevant character trait is being shown by specific acts. This means of proof usually is disallowed when character is used circumstantially. See Ch. V, §§ 34, 36.

30. At common law, convictions of a felony or of a misdemeanor involving dishonesty (*crimen falsi*) rendered the convicted person incompetent as a witness. McCormick, § 43, at 84. Statutes negating the common-law prohibition typically provide that a conviction that would have rendered the witness incompetent may be shown to affect his credibility. See, e. g., Conn.Gen.Stat.Ann. § 52–145.

31. See Comment, 31 Ford.L.Rev. 797 (1963).

32. See, e. g., McIntosh v. Pittsburg R. Co., 432 Pa. 123, 247 A.2d 467 (1968) (pandering); State v. Russ, 122 Vt. 236, 167 A.2d 528 (1961) (traffic misdemeanor).   See also Annot., 20 A.L.R.2d 1217 (1951).

33. See McCormick, § 43, at 85–86, where statutes containing various formulae are set out and cases are cited. See also IIIA Wigmore §§ 923, 980 (Chadbourn); Slough, Impeachment of Witnesses: Common Law   Principles   and   Modern Trends, 34 Ind.L.J. 1, 22 (1958); Note, Admissibility of Prior Crimes Evidence to Impeach in Florida, 15 U.Fla.L.Rev. 220 (1962).

34. See, e. g., State v. Jenness, 143 Me. 380, 62 A.2d 867 (1948); McGee v. State, 207 Tenn. 431, 332 S.W.2d 507 (1960).

35. See, e. g., Commonwealth v. Kostan, 349 Pa. 560, 37 A.2d 606 (1944).

36. See Maguire et al. at 452. See generally IIIA Wigmore § 980 (Chadbourn).

accommodation: any conviction for a felony may be used to impeach, but a conviction for a misdemeanor may be used only if the illegal act involved dishonesty or a false statement.[37] Some jurisdictions modify this approach by restricting impeachment to felonies;[38] others allow proof of any conviction, no matter what its grade.[39] There also is lack of uniformity regarding the admissibility of juvenile adjudications[40] and the effect of probation or of the passage of a long period of time since the conviction was rendered.[41] It now is settled, however, that the Constitution forbids the use of a prior conviction obtained in violation of the right to counsel.[42]

The Federal Rule governing impeachment by prior conviction permits the use of any conviction—misdemeanor or felony—involving "dishonesty or a false statement."[43] Other convictions, however, may be used only if the underlying offense "was punishable by death or imprisonment in excess of one year . . . and the court determines that the probative value of admitting this evidence outweighs its prejudicial effect to the defendant. . . ."[44] Unfortunately, as noted below, the Rule so far has

37. See, e. g., D.C.Code § 14–305 (1973).

38. West's Ann.Cal.Evid.Code § 788.

39. 12 Okl.Stat.Ann. § 381. See Sullivan v. State, 333 P.2d 591 (Okl.Cr.1958). See also State v. Hurt, 49 N.J. 114, 228 A.2d 673 (1967).

40. Fed.R.Evid. 609(d) admits evidence of a juvenile conviction in a criminal case where (1) the juvenile witness is not the accused; (2) the offense would be admissible to attack the credibility of an adult; and (3) "the court is satisfied that admission in evidence is necessary for a fair determination of the issue of guilt or innocence." Most states totally bar evidence of a juvenile proceeding from other proceedings. I Wigmore § 196(3) contains an extensive list of such statutes.

41. Fed.R.Evid. 609(b) sets a 10-year period from the date of conviction or release from prison. After this period evidence of the conviction is admissible only if its probative value "substantially outweighs" its prejudicial effect, and the proponent provides advance written notice of his intent to use the evidence.

42. Loper v. Beto, 405 U.S. 473 (1972).

43. Fed.R.Evid. 609(a).

44. Fed.R.Evid. 609(a). The rule apparently reflects a special concern for "defendants" in a criminal context.

been read strictly so that the court may only consider the prejudicial effect to the criminal defendant and not to other parties.[45]

There is nearly general agreement concerning the evidentiary
means that may be used to prove a conviction: counsel may adduce the evidence during cross-examination by asking the witness to admit the fact of the conviction or he may introduce a
certified or exemplified copy of the prior criminal judgment.[46]
Neither of these means of proof consumes much time, and the
use of evidence of previous convictions usually poses only the
problem of assessing probative value and determining if probative worth is outweighed by prejudice. Courts usually disallow
detailed descriptions of the previous offense, confining counsel to
such essentials as the name of the crime, the time and place of
prosecution, and the punishment imposed.[47] Nor will courts allow the impeached witness to give an extended explanation or
time-consuming presentation of facts in mitigation of the conviction, although many courts permit a brief ameliorative
explanation.[48]

We already have seen that a criminal accused has the privilege of declining to testify.[49] But if he elects to take the stand,
he generally is subject to the usual rules governing the examination of witnesses, including the rules that allow the cross-examiner to engage in various kinds of impeachment. In most jurisdictions, an accused-witness may be impeached by evidence that
he has been convicted previously of crimes that reflect upon
credibility. This evidence is admitted solely to impugn credibility; in theory it may not be used to support the prejudicial inference that an accused-witness who has committed one or more
previous crimes is more likely to be guilty of the offense

45. See infra text accompanying
note 56.

46. In a few jurisdictions, proof is
limited to a copy of the criminal
judgment. McCormick, § 43, at 87.

47. McCormick, § 43, at 88. Recently, a federal court interpreted Federal Rule 609 as limiting the prosecutor's showing to the fact and

date of the conviction and the nature of the offense. United States
v. Tumblin, 551 F.2d 1001 (5th Cir.
1977).

48. McCormick, § 43, at 88–89.

49. See Ch. IV, § 31. See also Ch.
IX, § 92.

charged. Upon request, the judge will instruct the jury concerning the limited purpose for which the impeaching evidence may be considered. Nonetheless, the risk that such evidence may prejudice the jury has caused some jurisdictions to formulate protective rules when an accused takes the stand.[50] One approach, tried for a period of time in the District of Columbia, allows the trial judge discretion to reject evidence of prior convictions when he determines that its probative force is outweighed by the risk of prejudice or by the desirability of hearing the defendant's story free of the distraction of past crimes.[51] However, this balancing process creates uncertainty, disparity of practice among trial judges, and the encouragement of appeals.[52] Another protective method (applicable to all witnesses, but most helpful to the accused) is to narrow the kinds of convictions that will be allowed for impeachment purposes: only those convictions thought to have a strong bearing upon credibility are sanctioned.[53] A technique embodied in American Law Institute's

---

50. McCormick, § 43, at 89: "The accused, who has a 'record' but thinks he has a defense to the present crime, is thus placed in a grievous dilemma. If he stays off the stand, his silence alone will prompt the jury to believe him guilty. If he elects to testify, his 'record' becomes provable to impeach him, and this again is likely to doom his defense."

The risk of prejudice is highest where the prior crimes used to impeach are similar to the offense charged.

51. See Luck v. United States, 348 F.2d 763 (1965) and the attempt to explicate the Luck doctrine in Gordon v. United States, 383 F.2d 936 (1967), cert. denied 390 U.S. 1029 (1968). The applicable statute at the time of these cases was amended in 1970 and now provides for impeachment by evidence that the witness was convicted of an offense "punishable by death or imprisonment in excess of one year . . . or . . . involv[ing] dishonesty or false statement (regardless of punishment)." D.C. Code § 14–305 (1973). It is highly doubtful that the Luck doctrine survived the statutory change because the drafters intended to reject the doctrine. See Ladd & Carlson at 225. However, Federal Rule 609(a) embodies a discretionary approach similar to that announced in Luck. See generally People v. Montgomery, 47 Ill.2d 510, 516, 268 N.E. 2d 695, 698 (1971). See also Burg v. United States, 406 F.2d 235 (9th Cir. 1969); United States v. Palumbo, 401 F.2d 270 (2d Cir. 1968).

52. These and other criticisms are set forth in Ladd & Carlson at 224–225. For cases rejecting the approach, see Commonwealth v. West, 357 Mass. 245, 258 N.E.2d 22 (1970); State v. Hawthorne, 49 N. J. 130, 228 A.2d 682 (1967).

53. See IIIA Wigmore § 980 (Chadbourn).

Model Code of Evidence and an earlier version of the Uniform Rules is for the court to disallow an attack on the accused's credibility unless he first presents evidence supporting his truthfulness.[54] This is an unusual provision not only because it makes special provision for the accused, but also because it contravenes the traditional rule disallowing evidence in support of credibility unless the opponent (that is, the prosecutor) first has presented impeaching evidence.[55] For various reasons, none of these protective measures, particularly the last, has attracted a wide following.

The Federal Rules of Evidence give the trial judge discretionary power to reject evidence of prior convictions where he determines "that the probative value of admitting this evidence outweighs its prejudicial effect to the defendant," [56] but this discretion is available only if the prior conviction was not for a crime involving dishonesty or a false statement. Convictions for the latter classes of crime apparently are unconditionally admissible to impeach. Several aspects of the Rule cause difficulty. For example, what crimes involve "dishonesty" and thus come within the class of cases where the judge has no discretionary power —at least under Rule 609—to reject the evidence of conviction? The legislative history suggests strongly that the trial judge's discretion extends to all crimes except those in the nature of "crimen falsi," that is, those involving deceit, falsification, or untruthfulness.[57] A second difficulty arises because Rule 609

---

54. Model Code of Evidence 106(3); Uniform Rules of Evidence 21 (1953). See Kan.Stat.Ann. § 60–421. The new Uniform Rule follows Federal Rule 609. See Uniform Rules of Evidence 609 (1974). For a case applying the Model Code approach, see State v. Cantrell, 201 Kan. 182, 440 P.2d 580, cert. denied 393 U.S. 944 (1968). For a due process approach with a similar result, see State v. Santiago, 53 Hawaii 254, 492 P.2d 657 (1971). See also the discussion in United States v. Palumbo, 401 F.

2d 270, 272–73 (2d Cir. 1968), cert. denied 394 U.S. 947 (1969).

55. See infra § 85.

56. Fed.R.Evid. 609(a).

57. See the extensive opinion in United States v. Smith, 551 F.2d 348 (D.C. Cir. 1976). In United States v. Brashier, 548 F.2d 1315 (9th Cir. 1976), the court held that mail fraud was a crime involving "dishonesty, or false statement" within the meaning of Fed.R.Evid.

expressly singles out prejudice to the "defendant." The extent to which prior convictions may be excluded because of prejudice to the government or to a party to a civil case is unclear. Rule 403, discussed elsewhere,[58] allows the balancing of relevance with prejudice in all cases and grants the judge discretion to exclude evidence when prejudicial effect is the prevailing concern; this rule of general application arguably should apply in those situations where Rule 609 does not.[59] Finally, the question whether the probative value of a prior conviction outweighs prejudicial effect often is difficult to resolve, and inevitably gives rise to contrary positions among judges.[60]

The fact that the conferral upon the trial judge of discretionary power to reject evidence of a prior conviction creates inconsistencies in the administration of a rule generally allowing impeachment suggests the need for another solution. But it is not easy, nor perhaps is it wise, to eliminate discretion in the name of consistency. No rule absolute in its terms can take proper account of the variations from case to case. A possible approach, though not without its disadvantages, is to give careful attention to the question of what convictions bear a reasonable relationship to credibility, and then to adopt a single rule for all witnesses. Further, in instances where it appears necessary to protect a defendant (or some other party) the impeaching evidence can be limited, in the judge's discretion, to a showing only that the witness has been convicted of a felony on a certain date;[61] the offense need not be named unless the witness so

---

609(a). Other courts have given a broader meaning to the word "dishonesty." See, e. g., United States v. Bianco, 419 F.Supp. 507 (E.D. Pa.1976).

58. Ch. II, § 13.

59. S. Saltzburg & K. Redden, Federal Rules of Evidence Manual 350 (2d ed. 1977). The applicability of Rule 403 expressly was left an open question in several cases. See, e. g., United States v. Dixon, 547 F.2d 1079, 1083 n. 4 (9th Cir.

1976) (accused has right to impeach witness; discretionary exclusion under Rule 609 not allowed unless prejudice to criminal defendant may result).

60. See Annot., 67 A.L.R.3d 824, 853–89 (1975) and cases cited therein.

61. Cf. United States v. Tumblin, 551 F.2d 1001 (5th Cir. 1977) (details of prior conviction limited to conviction, date, and nature of offense).

desires.[62] This protective technique would be especially helpful when the offense used for impeaching an accused-witness is similar to the offense with which he is charged.

Some observers favor a rule that disallows the use of any prior conviction to impeach an accused. An absolute prohibition has not found acceptance, however, because of an unwillingness among courts and legislators to allow the accused to appear as a truthful person when his record of convictions, if made known to the jury, would cast serious doubt on his testimony. Thus, the tension between providing the jury with a full context for determining credibility and the consequent risk of undue prejudice remains the subject of a lively policy debate.

2. *Prior Bad Acts.* Suppose a witness once has committed an act that reflects unfavorably upon his truthfulness. We have seen that if his prior conduct led to a criminal conviction, that conviction may be shown to impeach his credibility.[63] But if there were no conviction,[64] can the act itself be proved? The courts divide on this question, but a majority now authorize impeachment by "prior bad acts."

---

62. There is obvious advantage in giving the defendant the option—exercised away from the jury—of allowing the disclosure of the offense: a felony conviction for a crime such as illegal wagering may arouse less jury antipathy than the unnamed "felony" or "crime."

63. See supra § 81(1).

64. In most instances, there will have been no prosecution for the prior act. Suppose, however, there has been a prosecution resulting in acquittal. May the prior act still be used to impeach? A trial judge exercising his discretion sometimes should disallow this inquiry, especially when the witness consistent-

ly has denied involvement in the prior act. See Lee v. United States, 368 F.2d 834, 836–37 (D.C. Cir. 1966). On the other hand, where a witness's statements are contradicted either by his contentions at the prior trial or by those aspects of the prior act that were shown clearly or uncontested, it would seem that inquiry about the prior act should be allowed. See Walder v. United States, 347 U.S. 62 (1954). Note, also, that the use of a prior bad act to impeach does not depend upon a showing of the act beyond a reasonable doubt. The standard is whether the cross-examiner in good faith believes the prior incident took place. See People v. Sorge, 301 N.Y. 198, 93 N.E. 2d 637 (1950).

Two difficulties attend this method of impeachment. First, there may be an issue of relevance because not all "bad" acts cast doubt on credibility. This, of course, is a familiar problem, the solution to which turns upon the general principle of relevance. Filing false statements on an application for a retail license clearly involves deceit. But engaging in drunken or disorderly conduct does not, and probably does not adversely reflect upon one's willingness to testify truthfully. A second problem—growing out of the practical aspects of trial administration—arises from the concern, generally shared by courts, that trials be neither unduly prolonged nor so conducted that the trier's attention is diverted from the principal issues in the case. In short, courts resist conducting a trial within a trial—that is, adjudicating the existence and circumstances of some distant act, which has relevance only because it brings into question the credibility of a witness.[65]

These considerations of relevance and distraction have caused some courts to prohibit any impeachment by prior bad acts.[66] Most jurisdictions, however, compromise by allowing impeachment by prior bad acts, but requiring that the examiner settle for such admissions or concessions as he can adduce during cross-examination.[67] He can not prove the prior bad act by additional or "extrinsic" evidence.[68] In theory, and usually in practice, the examiner may inquire only about acts that reflect upon credibility. Some courts, however, have taken a broad view of this requirement, permitting questions about acts such as assault with a weapon and performance of illegal abortions.[69]

---

65. See the discussion below of the collateral matter doctrine infra § 84. See also Ch. II, § 13.

66. McCormick, § 42, at 82–83.

67. Id. at 84. This statement implies that the cross-examiner is the counsel trying to impeach. In some instances, however, the attorney who called the witness may impeach. See supra § 80. But the principle of settling for the witness's answer would still apply.

68. See, e. g., United States v. Cluck, 544 F.2d 195 (5th Cir. 1976) (applying Fed.R.Evid. 608(b)); People v. McCormick, 303 N.Y. 403, 103 N.E.2d 529 (1952); McCormick, § 42, at 84. § 84, infra, deals in more detail with the use of extrinsic evidence.

69. See People v. Sorge, 301 N.Y. 198, 93 N.E.2d 637 (1950) and cases cited therein. See also Wright v. State, 243 Ark. 221, 419 S.W.2d 320 (1967), where the charge was rape

Of course, the examiner's cross-questions would be improper unless asked in good faith, based upon his reasonable belief that the witness had committed the prior act in question.[70] The Federal Rules of Evidence provide:

> Specific Instances of Conduct—Specific instances of conduct of a witness, for the purpose of attacking or supporting his credibility, other than conviction of crime . . . [which generally is allowed by Rule 609], may not be proved by extrinsic evidence. They may, however, in the discretion of the court, if probative of truthfulness or untruthfulness, be inquired into on cross-examination of the witness (1) concerning his character for truthfulness or untruthfulness, or (2) concerning the character for truthfulness or untruthfulness of another witness as to which character the witness being cross-examined has testified.[71]

This Rule generally accords with the precedents in those jurisdictions that permit impeachment by prior bad acts.[72] It emphasizes discretionary control by the trial judge, as do many of the decided cases.[73] The final clause of Rule 608(b) addresses the situation where a party who has presented one witness (the "principal" witness) offers another witness in support of the former's good character for truthfulness. In the limited instances in which this kind of evidence is permitted,[74] the char-

---

and the prior bad acts consisted of making indecent proposals to women.

70. Compare People v. Alamo, 23 N.Y.2d 630, 298 N.Y.S.2d 681, 246 N.E.2d 496, cert. denied 396 U.S. 879 (1969) with State v. Phillips, 240 N.C. 516, 82 S.E.2d 762 (1954). See also People v. Sorge, 301 N.Y. 198, 93 N.E.2d 637 (1950).

71. Fed.R.Evid. 608(b).

72. For discussion and a collection of the authorities, see IIIA Wigmore §§ 977–79 (Chadbourn).

73. See, e. g., Lehr v. Rogers, 16 Mich.App. 585, 168 N.W.2d 636 (1969); People v. Sorge, 301 N.Y. 198, 93 N.E.2d 637 (1950). Professor Morgan asserts that "In the United States the great majority of state court decisions make the discretion of the trial judge determinative." Morgan at 67.

74. See infra § 85; Ch. V, §§ 34–38.

acter witness may be asked about bad acts of the principal witness that the character witness should have taken into consideration.

3. *Bad Character Regarding Truth and Veracity.* As elsewhere indicated,[75] courts usually are reluctant to admit evidence of a party's character to support the inference that on a specific occasion he acted in accordance with the character traits shown. The credibility of witnesses, however, traditionally has been a subject of special concern for the courts; the outcome of many —if not most—trials is determined by which of the conflicting lines of testimony the trier believes. We already have observed that most courts admit evidence of prior conduct that reflects adversely upon a witness's honesty.[76] All courts agree that a witness may be impeached by evidence which speaks even more directly to his present character for truth and veracity: the impeaching party may offer witnesses who assert that based upon their knowledge of the principal witness, derived either from their familiarity with his reputation or (in some jurisdictions) their observations of his conduct, he has a bad character for truth and veracity. Traditionally, the courts have tried to provide the trier with a useful insight into the witness's character for truthfulness, while also attempting to minimize the burdens of delay and distraction caused by the introduction of secondary issues. Thus, the common law usually limits the type of evidence that may be provided by impeaching witnesses. Those who take the stand for the purpose of impugning the character of the principal witness are restricted to giving evidence of the latter's *bad reputation* for truth and veracity. Delay is minimized by limiting the evidence to conclusory statements about the witness's reputation and, concomitantly, by prohibiting proof of the underlying events that may have produced this disrepute.[77] Under this approach, if a witness, *W,* testifies for the plaintiff, de-

---

75. Ch. V, §§ 34–38.

76. The use of evidence of prior convictions and of prior bad acts also constitutes proof through character, although the opinions often do not make this clear. The prior conduct is used to infer a trait or propensity to falsify which is then used to infer that the witness gave false testimony.

77. See Ch. V, §§ 36, 38.

fense counsel can impeach W by calling another witness, X, to testify that W has a bad reputation for truth and veracity. As a predicate for his testimony, X must provide evidence that he is in a position to know about W's bad reputation. Hence, it usually is necessary that X testify he has resided or otherwise been present in the community in which W lives. Presumably, X's knowledge of W's bad reputation for truth and veracity is acquired from others who speak disparagingly about W. The intended inferences from this kind of evidence are clear: from W's unfavorable reputation, the trier can infer the existence of a mendacious trait, and then can infer that W is giving untruthful testimony.

In a mobile, urban society, the assumptions underlying impeachment by reputation are dubious at best. It may be doubted, for example, whether many persons who live and work in large urban centers have an established community reputation for traits of truth and veracity. Reacting to this problem, some courts have adjusted the traditional restrictions. A minority of jurisdictions allow impeachment by reputation if the impeaching witness has been present in an association or setting (such as a work environment) in which the principal witness may have established a reputation for truthfulness.[78] Other courts permit the impeaching witness, whatever the basis of his familiarity with the principal witness's reputation, to conclude his direct testimony by stating whether, based upon the reputation to which he has testified, he would believe the principal witness under oath.[79]

Increasingly, the mechanical repetition of a set formula by the reputation witness has been seen for what it usually is—a thinly

78. See McCormick, § 44, at 92–93; Morgan at 66–67; Annot., 112 A.L. R. 1020 (1938).

79. See, e. g., United States v. Walker, 313 F.2d 236, 239–41 (6th Cir. 1963), cert. denied 374 U.S. 807; Morgan at 66. Wigmore points out the inconsistency of purporting to restrict evidence to reputation yet allowing what amounts to a personal opinion of the impeaching witness. VII Wigmore, § 1985, at 159. For a case rejecting the question about belief under oath in circumstances where it was clear that the answer was based in part on personal opinion, see People v. Lehner, 326 Ill. 216, 157 N.E. 211 (1927).

disguised form of personal opinion. Consequently, in recent years there has been a decided shift toward permitting the impeaching witness to give his personal opinion of the veracity of the principal witness. The Federal Rules of Evidence state:

> Opinion and reputation evidence of character—The credibility of a witness may be attacked or supported by evidence in the form of opinion or reputation, but subject to these limitations: (1) the evidence may refer only to character for truthfulness or untruthfulness, and (2) evidence of truthful character is admissible only after the character of the witness for truthfulness has been attacked by opinion or reputation evidence or otherwise.[80]

This provision loosens the traditional restrictions, but does not go so far as to permit the impeaching (opinion) witness to describe, during direct examination, specific instances of conduct that reflect adversely upon the truth and veracity of the principal witness. The cross-examiner, however, may probe the basis of the opinion by inquiring about these specific events.[81]

§ 82. Techniques of Impeachment: Bias

The term "bias" denotes a variety of mental attitudes that may cause a witness to give false or misleading testimony.[82] In general, it signifies a witness's interest in the outcome of the case, including a friendly or hostile association with one of the parties that could induce him to color, distort, or falsify his testimony. The cross-examiner can expose any potential bias by showing the witness's relationship to the case, his financial interest in the outcome, or his association with one of the parties. For instance, the interrogator can attempt to demonstrate that a witness is related by blood or marriage to a party, employed by a party, has an economic stake in the outcome of the litigation, has a strong identification with an interest (such as nuclear de-

---

80. Fed.R.Evid. 608(a). See also Fed.R.Evid. 405(a).

81. Fed.R.Evid. 405(a).

82. See Maguire et al. at 440–444, which contains summaries of illustrative cases. See also Annot., 74 A.L.R. 1157 (1931).

velopment) involved in the litigation, or that he was promised immunity from prosecution or favored treatment in return for his testimony.[83]

Courts generally permit the impeaching party to prove bias either through cross-questions or by adducing extrinsic evidence, either from witnesses or documents.[84] However, if the cross-questions and answers adequately expose the basis of the bias, the judge can limit or prohibit further evidence.[85] Many jurisdictions require that as a prerequisite to the introduction of extrinsic evidence, counsel first must ask the witness about the circumstances underlying the alleged bias.[86] This requirement is justified on the grounds of fairness to the witness and efficient trial administration. The witness to be impeached has the first opportunity to give evidence regarding bias; furthermore, as noted above, his answers to cross-questions may be sufficiently complete to render extrinsic evidence unnecessary.

§ 83. Techniques of Impeachment: Prior Inconsistent Statements

A widely-recognized technique of impeachment consists of showing that the witness has made prior statements inconsistent

---

83. For a collection of illustrative cases, see IIIA Wigmore § 949 (Chadbourn).

84. See, e. g., United States v. Brown, 537 F.2d 438 (8th Cir. 1977); Kidd v. People, 97 Colo. 480, 51 P.2d 1020 (1935); Vassar v. Chicago, B. & O. R. R., 121 Neb. 140, 236 N.W. 189 (1931); Morgan at 70.

85. People v. Wilson, 254 Cal.App.2d 489, 62 Cal.Rptr. 240 (1967); State v. Roybal, 33 N.M. 540, 273 P. 919 (1928). Thornton v. Vonallmon, 456 S.W.2d 795, 798 (Mo.App.1970): "[w]here interest or bias is denied by the witness it may be shown by the testimony of others, and even when it is admitted the extent of the witness' bias and prejudice may be shown, though the trial court has considerable discretion as to how far the inquiry may be pursued in detail." See infra § 84 discussing the collateral matter doctrine and use of extrinsic evidence, and see infra § 83, note 87.

86. United States v. Hayutin, 398 F.2d 944 (2d Cir.), cert. denied 393 U.S. 961 (1968); Taylor v. State, 249 Ind. 238, 231 N.E.2d 507 (1967); People v. Payton, 72 Ill.App.2d 240, 218 N.E.2d 518 (1966). McCormick indicates that a majority of courts require this foundation. See McCormick, § 40, at 80; IIIA Wigmore § 953 (Chadbourn).

with his testimony at trial. A party entitled to impeach may
show the prior oral or written inconsistencies, but in presenting
his impeaching evidence he must take account of certain qualifications and restrictions. As we shall see, courts usually allow
impeaching counsel to *interrogate* a witness about a prior inconsistent statement even if the inconsistency relates only to an incidental of "collateral" matter. The theory in allowing these inquiries is that if the witness has rendered inconsistent statements about comparatively unimportant matters, his testimony
about more important events should be evaluated with special
care. But if the prior statement concerns only a collateral topic,
the interrogator must settle for such admissions of the prior inconsistency as he is able to adduce during cross-examination. If
the witness refuses to concede the existence of the earlier contradictory assertions, the court will not permit resort to extrinsic evidence.[87] The presentation of extrinsic evidence is thought
to be too costly in terms of time consumption and distraction.
On the other hand, if the prior statement involves a matter material to the elements of a claim or defense, the statement is not
considered collateral and extrinsic evidence may be introduced.

Care must be taken to comply with the rules requiring a foundation for impeachment by prior inconsistent statements. The
jurisdictions vary somewhat in the strictness of their demands
regarding an appropriate foundation. Considerations of fairness
to the witness and expedition of trials have led most courts to
require counsel to first ask the witness about the prior inconsistent statement and then to give him the opportunity to deny, affirm, or explain the earlier statement.[88] The witness presumably knows about the statement and can explain the earlier assertion. It seems fair that he should be given an immediate oppor-

---

87. See infra § 84, on the collateral
matter doctrine. Sometimes, however, a prior inconsistent statement
may show bias. In such a case,
extrinsic evidence should be permitted. See United States v. Harvey, 547 F.2d 720 (2d Cir. 1976).

88. A few jurisdictions, led by Massachusetts, do not require such a
foundation. See Tucker v. Welsh,
17 Mass. 160 (1821); IIIA Wigmore
§ 1028 (Chadbourn). Another approach is to invest the trial judge
with discretion to waive the foundation. See Giles v. Valentic, 355
Pa. 108, 49 A.2d 384 (1946) and cases cited therein.

tunity to respond to the examiner's charge of inconsistency, and his answers to cross-questions may eliminate the need for additional, extrinsic evidence. The courts demand that impeaching counsel's questions contain enough detail as to the circumstances surrounding the prior statement to enable the witness to identify the occasion and explain or deny the alleged inconsistency.[89] This requirement usually imposes upon counsel—often the cross-examiner—the duty of identifying the subject matter of the statement, the time and place of its utterance, and the person to whom it was made.

A minority of jurisdictions retain the Rule of Queen's [Caroline's] case [90] and impose an especially strict foundation requirement where the prior inconsistent statement is contained in a writing: the *first* step in laying the foundation for impeachment by a contradictory writing is presentation of the writing to the witness for his examination. Because this presentation precedes any question to the witness regarding whether he has made the writing or any statement within it, this preliminary procedure usually negates any chance of exposing a deceitful witness who otherwise might deny making an inconsistent statement. This early disclosure also affords the witness time to gather his thoughts and, sometimes, to explain away the inconsistency or lessen its effect.[91]

Even where the Rule of Queen's case has been abrogated, some courts display a penchant for excessive technicality when assessing the adequacy of the foundation required with respect to any

---

89. See Mead v. Scott, 256 Iowa 1285, 130 N.W.2d 641 (1964); Nichols v. Sefcik, 66 N.M. 449, 349 P. 2d 678 (1960). The requirement is defended in Osborne v. McEwan, 194 F.Supp. 117, 118–119 (D.D.C. 1961).

90. 2 Br. & B. 284, 129 Eng.Rep. 976 (C.P.1820). The doctrine of Queen's case is discussed in Ladd, Some Observations on Credibility: Impeachment of Witnesses, 52 Cornell L.Q. 239, 245–249 (1967).

Many jurisdictions have negated the rule, usually by legislation. See, e. g., West's Cal.Evid. Code § 768 (1966); Va. Code Ann. § 8.01–404 (1977); McCormick, § 28, at 56–57.

91. See McCormick, § 28, at 56: "While reading the [document or] letter the witness will be warned by what he sees not to deny it and can quickly weave a new web of explanation."

prior statement, whether written or oral.[92] They seemingly lose sight of the modest objectives that the rule requiring a foundation is designed to secure, namely, warning the witness that counsel has evidence of a prior contradictory assertion and giving the witness a fair opportunity to respond. To satisfy this purpose, mere specification of the subject matter of the prior inconsistency should be held sufficient if it enables the witness to identify and respond to the alleged inconsistent statement. Strict adherence to a particular formula is not needed because, as Wigmore notes, the identification of such circumstances as time, place, and persons present when the statement was made are means to the end of fairly apprising the witness.[93] As another example of rigid technicality, some courts impose the usual foundation requirement in instances when the witness to be impeached has not taken the stand, but is the source of admissible evidence because his deposition is introduced, his former testimony contained in transcript from another trial is admitted, or his admissible hearsay declarations are received.[94] Although fine distinctions can be drawn [95] among these situations where the "witness" is absent, at least it can be said that no foundation should be necessary where the individual sought to be impeached (1) never has been interrogated in a judicial setting (as usually is the case with the hearsay declarant [96]) or (2) even if subjected to some form of previous judicial interrogation, was not asked about the prior inconsistencies, either because they were unknown to the interrogator or because the inconsistencies were uttered after the interrogation.[97]

---

92. IIIA Wigmore §§ 1025–1029 (Chadbourn) contains an incisive discussion of the foundation requirement and also collects a host of examples.

93. See IIIA Wigmore, § 1029, at 1029 (Chadbourn).

94. See IIIA Wigmore §§ 1030–1035 (Chadbourn).

95. McCormick, § 37, at 73–74 presents a discriminating analysis.

96. The better cases support this view. See McCormick, § 37, at 74, and cases cited.

97. The authorities yield mixed results as to this proposition, but it appears sound. The admission of the inconsistency is desirable because it gives the trier a basis for careful evaluation of testimony that otherwise would stand unimpeached. For cases dealing with this problem, see IIIA Wigmore §§ 1031–32 (Chadbourn).

The usual foundation for a prior contradictory statement is not necessary when a *party* made the earlier inconsistent statement. Because the party admissions exception to the hearsay rule applies, the extra-judicial statement has independent value as substantive evidence of the facts asserted.[98] Thus, the statement is admissible even if the uttering party does not take the stand. This independent source of admissibility dispenses with the necessity of meeting the special foundation requirements that normally attend the use of prior inconsistent statements.[99]

In those cases where a witness to be impeached is entitled to an opportunity to deny or explain a prior inconsistency, the controlling considerations are fairness to the witness and to the litigants. Usually, efficient trial administration is served by affording the witness an opportunity during his adverse examination—before extrinsic evidence of the prior inconsistency is introduced—to answer the allegation that he has made a prior contradictory statement. His responses to cross-questions may render unnecessary the subsequent introduction of additional evidence. But while it generally is desirable that impeaching counsel inquire about alleged prior inconsistencies before introducing extrinsic evidence, in cases of excusable inadvertence little harm is done if evidence of the prior inconsistency is received and the witness is recalled to give his explanation. In instances where interrogation of the witness concerning the prior declaration is inconvenient or impossible, the earlier statement usually should be admitted unless special circumstances, such as a deliberate omission of the required foundation, justify a discretionary exclusion. It is significant that Rule 613(b) of the Federal Rules of Evidence incorporates a flexible approach to the foundation requirement:

> Extrinsic evidence of prior inconsistent statement of witness—Extrinsic evidence of a prior inconsistent statement by a witness is not admissible unless the witness is afforded an opportunity to explain or deny the same and

98. See Ch. VII, § 54.

99. State v. Mays, 65 Wash.2d 58, 395 P.2d 758 (1964), cert. denied 380 U.S. 953 (1965); Tuthill v. Alden, 239 Iowa 181, 30 N.W.2d 726 (1948); McCormick, § 37, at 74.

the opposite party is afforded an opportunity to interrogate him thereon, or the interests of justice otherwise require. This provision does not apply to admissions of a party-opponent   .   .   .   .[1]

Technicalities in addition to those associated with laying a
proper foundation can impede the use of evidence of a prior inconsistency. All courts agree that if a prior statement is received in evidence *to impeach*, it in fact must be *at variance* with
the testimony of the witness. Some courts, however, extend this
requirement beyond its common-sense purpose. In an Illinois
case, for example, a witness to an automobile accident stated at
trial that he saw several boys "crossing or attempting to cross"
the road. Earlier, the witness had asserted that the boys were
"trying to beat the traffic across" the highway. The court rejected a cross-question concerning this prior statement, holding
that the two statements were not inconsistent.[2] A problem of
determining inconsistency arises when the prior statement omits
a significant point included in the trial testimony. Does this
omission render the prior statement inconsistent? The cases
yield conflicting results.[3] Here, however, the controlling principle should be relevance: the judge should base his ruling upon
whether a reasonable jury could find the prior statement sufficiently at variance to cast doubt on the present testimony. If
the judge answers this question affirmatively, he should admit
the earlier assertion, leaving to the jury the decision whether to
discredit the witness.[4]

Another technical obstacle is the rule, applied by some courts,
that a prior inconsistency in the form of an opinion can not be
used to contradict testimonial "facts" given at trial. Under this
view, if a witness recites at trial that the driver stopped at the

---

1. Fed.R.Evid. 613(b). Rule 613(a)
    dispenses with the Rule of Queen's
    Case. See supra, text at note 90.

2. See Rogall v. Kischer, 1 Ill.App.
    3d 227, 273 N.E.2d 681 (1971).

3. See IIIA Wigmore § 1042 (Chad-
    bourn).

4. McCormick, § 34, at 68, states:
    "[s]eemingly the test should be,
    could the jury reasonably find that
    a witness who believed the truth of
    the facts testified to would have
    been unlikely to make a prior
    statement of this tenor?"

intersection (or if he gives other "facts" demonstrating careful conduct), it would be improper to impeach the witness by showing that previously he said "it was all the driver's fault." [5] The commentators, especially Wigmore and McCormick,[6] have argued convincingly against this misapplication of the opinion rule. That rule is inappropriate when applied to an out-of-court statement which, unlike trial testimony, is in final form and can not be rephrased. Hence, the opinion rule should not be raised as an artificial and obstructive limitation to the use of a prior inconsistent statement. Most recent cases have rejected the rule that prohibits contradiction by prior statements in opinion form.[7]

The foregoing discussion has focused upon the use of prior inconsistent statements to impeach a witness. But it will be recalled from an earlier chapter,[8] that under the orthodox view any statement not made from the stand in the present proceeding is hearsay if offered for its truth. Under this approach, a prior inconsistent statement is hearsay and can not be used for the truth of its assertion, unless, of course, it fits within a hearsay exception.[9] When no exception is applicable, the judge will instruct the jury that the prior inconsistent statement may be used solely for the limited purpose of evaluating the witness's trial testimony. This means that the trier may consider evidence that the witness has given more than one version of the same event, but only for the purpose of assessing the witness's

---

5. See Wolfe v. Madison Ave. Coach Co., 171 Misc. 707, 710, 13 N.Y.S.2d 741, 744 (1939) where the court acknowledges confusion in the cases but reasons that the impeaching evidence, despite its opinion form, still serves to discredit the witness and thus should be received. Cases are collected in Annot., 158 A.L.R. 820 (1945).

6. See IIIA Wigmore § 1041 (Chadbourn); McCormick, § 35, at 69–70.

7. See, e. g., Atlantic Greyhound Corp. v. Eddins, 177 F.2d 954 (4th Cir. 1949); Tigh v. College Park Realty Co., 149 Mont. 358, 427 P.2d 57 (1967). A very good discussion may be found in Crawford v. Commonwealth, 235 Ky. 368, 31 S.W.2d 618 (1930).

8. Ch. VI, § 52.

9. The exception for party admissions often applies because parties frequently take the stand. The application of any hearsay exception permits a prior statement to be used not only to impeach but also as proof of the point asserted in the earlier statement. See Ch. VI, § 52.

credibility. The arguments for and against this traditional restriction are set out elsewhere in this text.[10] Suffice it to say that recently a majority of jurisdictions, recognizing that many rules of evidence represent a practical accommodation of competing interests, have begun to permit the substantive use of a prior inconsistent statement.[11] Inasmuch as the witness who made the prior inconsistent assertion is on the stand and can be interrogated respecting both his present testimony and his prior statements, the hearsay dangers associated with the prior statement are significantly lessened.

§ 84. Prohibition Against Extrinsic Evidence on Collateral Matters

In the section dealing with prior bad acts,[12] we saw that in most jurisdictions impeaching counsel can inquire about past incidents casting doubt upon a witness's credibility, but must "settle" for such admissions as he can elicit during cross-examination. If the witness denies the past dishonest act, the examiner may not pursue the matter further by introducing extrinsic evidence to demonstrate the existence of the prior misdeed.

The prohibition against extrinsic evidence is not limited to impeachment by prior bad acts. It extends to any attempt to contradict testimony (including contradiction by a prior inconsistent statement) on an immaterial or "collateral" matter.[13] Although the cross-examiner has wide latitude in probing any point that may demonstrate a weakness or inaccuracy in the witness's testimony, he can not resort to extrinsic evidence which serves the sole purpose of contradicting the witness on a

---

10. Ch. VI, § 52.

11. The jurisdiction taking the lead in this reform is California. See West's Cal.Evid. Code § 1235. The Federal Rules of Evidence permit such substantive use only where the prior statement was made in an earlier trial or proceeding and the declarant spoke under oath and subject to the penalty of perjury. Fed.R.Evid. 801(d)(1).

12. Supra § 81(2).

13. The collateral matter doctrine applies to areas other than impeachment, but most often is applied there. The Federal Rules of Evidence abandon the doctrine in general, stating it expressly only in particular rules. See, e. g., Fed.R. Evid. 608(b) (no extrinsic evidence to show prior bad acts).

collateral point. Suppose, for example, a witness to an accident involving a corporate employee states that he is an officer of the corporation: the examiner could not show by extrinsic evidence that the witness held a position of lower rank. This limitation applies unless the witness's position is material (consequential) to a claim or defense, as it might be, for example, in a case where the issue is the authority of the witness to act for the corporation. In this latter instance, proof that the witness held a position of lesser authority would be admissible as substantive evidence, although it also would have an impeaching effect. Even in the case where the sole purpose of extrinsic evidence showing the witness's subordinate position is to contradict his assertion from the stand, there is a plausible argument supporting admissibility: if the examiner could introduce extrinsic evidence that the witness is only, say, the officer manager, the jury reasonably might conclude that one who misrepresents his employment status may be giving false testimony concerning the principal matter under construction. But the argument "falsus in uno, falsus in omnibus" (false in one, false in all) has generally been rejected by the courts. On balance, they have held, considerations of time and distraction militate against production of additional evidence on factual propositions that have no direct or circumstantial bearing on any element of a claim or defense.[14]

The rejection of extrinsic evidence pertaining to collateral topics usually is defensible. Even in the foregoing example, the application of the rule may be warranted. But the factual patterns with which the courts must deal seldom are clear cut, and determining what matters are collateral is not always easy.[15] The issue of what constitutes collateralness often surfaces in cases where counsel seeks to impeach a witness with extrinsic evidence that the witness has made a prior inconsistent statement. It also can arise when counsel seeks to demonstrate the inaccu-

---

14. It also is argued that the rule against collateral evidence serves to protect the witness from an unfair attack because he may not be prepared to present rebuttal extrinsic evidence on a remote point.

See IIIA Wigmore, § 1002, at 960 (Chadbourn).

15. Of course, the term itself gives little guidance and, as with many labels, sometimes serves as a substitute for careful analysis.

racy of a seemingly incidental part of a witness's testimony by producing another witness (or documentary evidence) intended to establish facts contradicting those to which the witness has testified. And, as we have seen, the rule against extrinsic evidence on collateral matters absolutely prohibits extrinsic evidence of prior bad acts.[16] Thus, the general prohibition against receiving extrinsic evidence on collateral matters affects admissibility frequently enough that counsel planning trial strategy must take account of this restriction and identify those evidentiary matters that are collateral.

The cases often hold a matter collateral unless it could be shown in evidence for some purpose other than impeachment or contradiction.[17] Although this statement sometimes is helpful, it can not be taken literally for, as we shall see, with certain of the impeachment techniques the courts freely admit extrinsic evidence even though its sole probative value is to discredit the witness. Furthermore, the rule for determining what matters are collateral can serve only as a general guide; usually the difference between a matter being material, as distinguished from being collateral, is one of degree and not kind.[18] A case decided by the Washington Supreme Court illustrates the extent to which the competing considerations involved in determining collateralness defy any mechanical test.[19] That case involved a prosecution for robbery that allegedly took place in Seattle on July 14, 1961. The defense was alibi, and the supporting witness, a restaurateur, testified that the accused, a regular patron, was in the witness's restaurant in Portland, Oregon on the night of the crime. On cross-examination, the witness stated, in response to a prosecution question, that he thought the accused

---

16. See supra § 81(2). When the only purpose of showing the prior bad act is to impeach the witness, extrinsic evidence is forbidden. But if the act has another probative purpose—as, for example, to show an element of the offense charged in the present trial—it is not within the rule forbidding extrinsic evidence.

17. See State v. Oswalt, 62 Wash.2d 118, 381 P.2d 617 (1963); Morgan at 76–77.

18. Ladd, Some Observations on Credibility: Impeachment of Witnesses, 52 Cornell L.Q. 239, 253 (1967).

19. State v. Oswalt, 62 Wash.2d 118, 381 P.2d 617 (1963).

had been in the Portland restaurant every day for the two months preceding the robbery. The prosecutor then sought to rebut this assertion with extrinsic evidence provided by a police officer that the accused was in Seattle on June 12, 1961 (one month before the alleged robbery) and for several days before that.

On appeal, the defendant contended that this rebuttal evidence was improper because it constituted impeachment by extrinsic evidence on a collateral point. The Washington Supreme Court agreed, holding that the challenged evidence had no purpose aside from the contradiction of the restaurateur because it failed to show that the accused was in Seattle on or near the date of the offense. The justices rejected as speculative the state's contention that evidence placing the accused in Seattle on June 12 had an independent purpose because his presence there gave rise to an inference that he was planning and preparing the crime that occurred a month later.[20]

Clearly the state could have tried to establish the defendant's presence in Seattle on the day of the offense. Perhaps the government could have shown his presence in that city a few days prior to the crime; certainly it could have done so had there been evidence of preparatory steps such as the acquisition of weapons or instrumentalities used in the offense. In the absence of evidence of planning and preparation, however, the case for admissibility grows weaker in proportion to the passage of time between the accused's presence in Seattle and the offense.

---

20. The only evidence of preparation was that the accused had spent several days in Seattle and had purchased a roll of adhesive tape. Although evidence of planning or preparation is admissible, it still must meet the general test of relevance, and its probative force must outweigh practical reasons for exclusion. Even assuming adhesive tape was used in the commission of the offense, the commonplace act of buying a roll of tape a month prior to the commission of the crime has only weak probative value to show preparation. The purchased article is one that most persons buy from time to time; further, absent additional evidence, it is erroneous to infer preparation from mere presence in the city where the offense took place, especially when that presence antedates the offense by a month and transportation facilities permit travel to the city in question in a short period of time.

A different line of argument, however, could support admission of the evidence of the defendant's presence in Seattle on June 12. The alibi was the major issue at trial, and the testimony of the restaurateur was critical. Arguably, any evidence that reflected upon the accuracy of his observation and memory is justified—at least the trial judge should have been given discretion to receive it. Unless there were some particular circumstance associated with July 14 (the day of the offense) that would cause the witness to remember the accused's presence on that date, it may be contended that the trier should have been allowed to evaluate the testimony concerning the critical day in light of evidence that the witness erred in his assertion that the defendant had been in his restaurant continuously for several months. This argument, of course, calls for a flexible application of the collateral evidence rule, suspending its prohibition in instances when the witness's testimony is very important to the outcome.

The essential point here is that shades of difference often are significant in a determination of what is collateral; rigid formulas are ineffective. Of course, even under the usual practice, a demonstration that the proffered evidence has relevance aside from its impeachment value always justifies admission. In close cases, however, it is important to consider whether the challenged evidence reflects indirectly upon testimony that goes to a central issue in the case. If it does, the case for admitting extrinsic evidence is stronger—at least where the matter falls in the shadowy area between what clearly is collateral and what clearly is consequential. Another factor that should be considered is whether or not the witness to be impeached asserts himself in unequivocal terms; if so, the jury may find the contradictory evidence especially useful in evaluating his testimony. Finally, it may be significant whether the (possibly) collateral point was raised first on direct or cross-examination. Where the direct examiner obtains the testimony upon which the "collateral" evidence casts doubt, it seems unfair to prohibit the cross-examiner from contradicting it,[21] at least where the direct

---

21. It may not be unfair, however, where the cross-examiner had ample opportunity to object to the testimony as irrelevant and could do so without causing the jury to react adversely.

examiner deliberately elicited the testimony that is the subject of the contradiction.

It is noteworthy that, except for prior bad acts, the courts generally have admitted extrinsic evidence even though its sole purpose is to impeach. Thus, extrinsic evidence has been admitted to show bias, bad character for truth and veracity, or to prove conviction of a crime. But extrinsic evidence of a prior inconsistent statement is permitted only if the subject matter of the inconsistency is consequential for reasons other than contradiction. It is not easy to reconcile these varying results. Perhaps evidence of a prior bad act or of a prior inconsistency relating to an incidental point lacks the probative force of the other impeachment techniques and fails to justify the delay and distraction associated with extrinsic evidence.

It also may be asked why courts always exclude extrinsic evidence of prior bad acts, but uniformly lift the ban when the bad act has resulted in a conviction. The explanation appears to be that a conviction provides the assurance that a high standard of proof was applied in determining that the bad act occurred. Further, because the only extrinsic evidence that can be introduced to establish the conviction is a certified copy of the judgment of the convicting court, a relatively brief time is spent in proving the impeaching fact.

§ 85. Accrediting the Witness (Rehabilitation)

The starting point for this discussion is the general principle that the credibility of a witness may not be supported in the absence of an impeaching attack. The justification for this restriction is in the assumption that most witnesses are conscientious and honest,[22] so that no reason exists for prolonging the trial by allowing supporting evidence of credibility when truthfulness is not called into question.[23] Further, admission of cer-

---

22. See Johnson v. State, 129 Wis. 146, 108 N.W. 55 (1906). The courts probably are endorsing a rule designed to keep evidence concerning credibility within manageable bounds. After all, it probably is the case that even those individuals who frequently engage in deceit or falsehood are truthful in the vast majority of instances.

23. Under the prevailing view credibility is not called into question simply because another witness

tain types of accrediting evidence, such as prior consistent statements, could motivate parties and witnesses to create favorable evidence, for example, by making a number of consistent pretrial statements.

The general rule against bolstering or accrediting, however, is not violated by incidental background information about a witness's employment or profession, even though this disclosure may carry the inference that the witness, because of his position of trust or responsibility, is probably honest and credible.[24] And even though the rule against bolstering usually operates to exclude prior consistent assertions,[25] some courts have admitted such statements in limited situations.[26] For example, on the theory that a prior out-of-court identification is at least as reliable as one subsequently made in the courtroom, a growing number of jurisdictions admit evidence of an earlier identification when the identifying witness is in the courtroom and available for cross-examination.[27] The admissibility of this evidence usually is analyzed under the hearsay rule, but its admission incidentally results in bolstering the credibility of the identifying witness [28]—at least where he is able to make an in-court identifi-

gives contradictory testimony. See United States v. Leggett, 312 F.2d 566 (4th Cir. 1962).

24. See, e. g., Elam v. State, 518 S. W.2d 367 (Tex.Cr.App.1975).

25. State v. Herrera, 236 Or. 1, 386 P.2d 448 (1963). See IV Wigmore § 1124 (Chadbourn).

26. The statements may also violate the hearsay rule. See Ch. VI, § 52.

27. Cases pro and con are collected in Annot., 71 A.L.R.2d 449 (1960). See also Ch. VI, § 52.

28. It is not always clear whether the admission of a prior identification constitutes substantive evidence that the person identified committed the act in question, or whether the court is admitting the evidence not for the "truth" of the prior identification but only to add assurances that the in-court identification is accurate. If the first use is allowed, the prior identification comes in as an exception to the hearsay rule. The second use purports to limit the evidence to an assessment of credibility, but it is doubtful the trier of fact can confine the evidence to such a restricted use. Of course, if only the second use is allowed and if the courtroom identification is so uncertain as to be insufficient to support a finding, the rule restricting the use of the prior identification to credibility has a determinative effect. See Ch. VI, § 52.

cation. Also, a sizable number of jurisdictions now receive evidence of a "fresh complaint" by a victim made promptly after the perpetration of a crime apt to be known only to victim and offender. The most frequent instance in which this evidence is approved is a rape case.[29] Some authorities extend the exception for prompt complaints to offenses such as attempted bribery or threatened arson.[30] There is a difference of opinion as to whether only the fact that a complaint was made can be shown or whether the details contained in the complaint also may be revealed.[31]

Attempts to accredit the witness most often occur after the witness has been impeached by one of the standard techniques discussed in this chapter. This process of supporting the witness following an attack on his credibility sometimes is referred to as rehabilitation. The most frequent problem that arises in this situation involves a determination of what kind of accrediting evidence rebuts the impeaching evidence. Note that evidence designed to rebut impeaching evidence can be directed either at *the impeaching facts themselves* or at *the inference of untruthfulness* that arises from the impeaching facts. Suppose, for example, that the impeaching evidence consists of evidence of a bad reputation for truth and veracity. Rebuttal evidence could consist of a showing that the principal witness enjoys a good reputation for these character traits.[32] The principal thrust of this rebuttal is directed toward the impeaching fact, that is, the witness's allegedly bad reputation. Assume, however, that the impeaching attack consists of evidence of a prior conviction and that in an effort to rehabilitate the witness, counsel offers evidence demonstrating that the witness has a good reputation for truth and veracity.[33] This rebuttal strikes

29. See McCormick, § 49, at 107; IV Wigmore §§ 1134–1140 (Chadbourn).

30. See IV Wigmore §§ 1141–44 (Chadbourn); Commonwealth v. Friedman, 193 Pa.Super. 640, 165 A.2d 678 (1960); State v. Slocinski, 89 N.H. 262, 197 A. 560 (1938).

31. See McCormick, § 49, at 107; IV Wigmore §§ 1134–1140 (Chadbourn).

32. See IV Wigmore § 1105 (Chadbourn). Of course, it also would be possible to impeach the impeaching witness thereby weakening or destroying the impeaching facts. See Morgan at 73–74.

33. Wigmore discusses this particular situation in some detail. IV Wigmore § 1106 (Chadbourn). See

not at the impeaching fact, but rather at the inference that the witness is untruthful.[34]

This second type of rebuttal, countering the inferences derived from the impeaching evidence, often generates issues of relevance.[35] If, for example, impeachment is by evidence of bad reputation for truthfulness, a rebuttal showing that the witness had made prior statements consistent with his testimony would have little or no probative force. The courts would reject it on the ground that because the witness also may have made false prior assertions, evidence of earlier consistencies has little value to rebut the inferences of untruthful testimony. A similar result should ensue where the witness is impeached on the ground of bias and the opponent seeks to accredit the witness with evidence of prior consistent statements. Unless these statements predate the alleged inception of the bias, they do not negate the impeaching evidence.

A difficult case is presented when impeachment is by prior inconsistent statements and the accrediting evidence consists of a showing of prior consistent statements—that is, out-of-court statements in accord with the testimony of the impeached witness. Here the courts split,[36] with the majority of decisions de-

---

also Gertz v. Fitchburg, R. R., 137 Mass. 77 (1884); McCormick, § 49, at 103–104 and notes 75 and 77.

34. Where the witness is impeached by a showing of bias, a demonstration of good reputation often is not received, especially where the bias does not flow from a questionable or corrupt motive but is rooted instead in family relationship or affection. See McCormick, § 49, at 104. The courts also divide on the issue of support by good reputation when impeachment has been by prior inconsistent statement. Id. See also IV Wigmore § 1108 (Chadbourn). It would appear that an especially strong argument can be made for rehabilitation evidence when the witness denies ever having made the prior inconsistent statement.

35. See supra note 34.

36. See Coltrane v. United States, 418 F.2d 1131 (D.C.Cir. 1969); Wofford Beach Hotel, Inc. v. Glass, 170 So.2d 62 (Fla.App.1964). Contra, Clere v. Commonwealth, 212 Va. 472, 184 S.E.2d 820 (1971) (admitting prior consistent statement). Fine distinctions and qualifications are drawn by some courts. For example, there are holdings that admissibility of the prior consistency is justified when the witness denies uttering the alleged earlier inconsistency and the supporting counsel has evidence of a prior consistency near in time to

nying admissibility by reasoning that even if evidence of the prior consistencies were received, the trier still would be left with inconsistent versions of the witness's story. Hence, the accrediting evidence fails to dissipate either the impeaching fact or its associated inference. An exception to the majority result is made where impeaching counsel directly or indirectly has charged the witness with recently fabricating his story or with falsifying or distorting his testimony because of some motive such as a financial interest in the outcome of the case or a promise of special leniency from the prosecutor. In these circumstances, a prior consistent statement *that predates* the alleged recent fabrication or the motive to falsify has sufficient probative value to be admitted because it tends to rebut the cross-examiner's charge of recent contrivance.[37]

NOTES

1. *Impeaching a Witness Called by Both Parties.* In a jurisdiction forbidding a party from impeaching his own witness, suppose the plaintiff calls *W* and, later in the case, the defendant also calls *W*. Can the plaintiff now impeach *W*? McCormick, § 38, at 77–78, indicates that the courts split but that the sensible solution is to allow either party to impeach the witness freely.

2. *Prior Conviction to Impeach.* Assume that in a prosecution for burglary, the accused takes the stand. The government then seeks to impeach him with evidence that he was convicted of illegal possession of intoxicating liquor. Admissible? Would a conviction for illegal sale of intoxicating liquor be treated differently? See State v. Jenness, 143 Me. 380, 62 A.2d 867 (1948). The problem, of course, is one of relevance.

3. *Plea of Nolo Contendere.* Sometimes a criminal accused enters a plea of nolo contendere. Under Fed.R.Evid. 410, evidence that such a plea was *offered or made* can not be entered against the pleader in another criminal action or in a civil suit for the purpose of establish-

---

the alleged self-contradiction. McCormick, § 49, at 106. The theory, of course, is that the prior consistency makes it less likely that the inconsistency was uttered.

37. People v. Coleman, 71 Cal.2d 1159, 80 Cal.Rptr. 920, 459 P.2d 248 (1969); People v. Singer, 300 N.Y. 120, 89 N.E.2d 710 (1949); Morgan at 74; IV Wigmore § 1128 (Chadbourn). See Fed.R.Evid. 801(d)(1) (B). See also People v. Gardineer, 2 Mich.App. 337, 139 N.W.2d 890 (1966) (consistent statement rejected because made after the bias existed).

ing guilt or liability. (In other words, a plea of nolo contendere will not be received as a party admission.) Furthermore, statements made in connection with the plea bargaining process are inadmissible in subsequent proceedings except where the statements are material to a subsequent prosecution for perjury or false statement and the statements were made "under oath, on the record, and in the presence of counsel." Fed.R.Evid. 410. This provision denies the use of such statements for impeachment purposes. But the conviction resulting from a nolo contendere plea *can be used* under Federal Rule 609 which allows impeachment by evidence of a prior crime. For reasons that remain obscure, the Advisory Committee removed a provision from 609(a) prohibiting such a use. See Weinstein & Berger, ¶ 609[01], at 609–54 to 55.

4. *Scientific and Medical Evidence of Credibility.* As noted in the text, one mode of impeachment is by the introduction of psychiatric evidence that the witness whose credibility is attacked suffers from a mental disease or disability that increases the likelihood of false statements. Such an impeachment technique was used by the defense in the prosecution of Alger Hiss. See United States v. Hiss, 88 F.Supp. 559 (S.D.N.Y.1950). Although psychiatric evidence bearing upon credibility generally is admissible, certain circumstances may justify the trial judge's rejection of this type of evidence. Some factors bearing upon admissibility are (1) the time involved in receiving the testimony; (2) the importance of the principal witness's testimony; (3) the nexus, according to medical authorities, between the mental condition alleged to exist and testimonial accuracy or truthfulness; and (4) whether there is reliable evidence corroborating the principal witness's testimony. Cases are collected in Maguire et al. at 475–77.

Science some day may provide us with a test of credibility that invariably detects conscious deception by the witness. The lie detector (polygraph) frequently is used by private persons (such as employers) and in criminal investigations, at least where the subject freely consents. But courts generally have rejected evidence of polygraph results. A typical case is People v. Leone, 25 N.Y.2d 511, 307 N.Y.S.2d 430, 225 N.E.2d 696 (1969). But see United States v. Ridling, 350 F. Supp. 90 (E.D.Mich.1972) (expert opinion based on polygraph admissible in perjury prosecution). Some courts admit evidence of lie detector tests where the parties have stipulated in advance that such evidence would be admissible. State v. Valdez, 91 Ariz. 274, 371 P.2d 894 (1962); Herman v. Eagle Star Ins. Co., 283 F.Supp. 33 (C.D.Cal. 1966), aff'd 396 F.2d 427 (9th Cir. 1968). See McCormick, § 207, at 507 and cases cited.

Normally, the results of the polygraph examination will be presented by the examiner who qualifies as an expert witness. By any measure, the test and its results have probative value to show

sincerity or insincerity. Resistance of the courts probably is rooted in the apprehension that the trier will be strongly inclined to
accept the results of the test even if it is made clear that the accuracy
rate is considerably short of perfect—probably around 80%. See Hor-
vath & Reid, The Reliability of Polygraph Examiner Diagnosis of
Truth and Deception, 62 J.Crim.L.C. & P.S. 276 (1971). There is,
however, some disagreement over the accuracy rate. Citations to the
experiments, statistics and argument are collected in McCormick, §
207, at 506. Much depends upon the skill and experience of the operator.

Various drugs have the effect of weakening or nullifying one's capacity to suppress his thoughts or to fabricate. These "truth serums," such as sodium pentothal, have been given a cool reception by
the courts. Statements made while under the influence of these drugs
usually have been rejected. See, e. g., People v. Myers, 35 Ill.2d 311,
331–33, 220 N.E.2d 297, 309–10 (1966). While there is serious doubt
whether the results of so-called narco-interrogation are reliable enough
to justify admission for the purpose of showing the truth of the subject's statements, a somewhat different issue is raised when a psychiatrist gives an expert opinion on such matters as sanity or the accused's state of mind and the opinion is based in whole or in part
upon responses elicited during a drug-induced state. Here, again, the
courts have shown resistance. See, e. g., Commonwealth v. Butler, 213
Pa.Super. 388, 247 A.2d 794 (1968); People v. Hiser, 267 Cal.App.2d
47, 72 Cal.Rptr. 906 (1968). These and other authorities and commentary may be found in Maguire et al. at 493–94. Hypnosis has been
treated similarly to truth serum. See McCormick, § 208, at 510. But
see State v. Jorgensen, 8 Or.App. 1, 492 P.2d 312 (1971) where the
trier is advised that the witness, who had suffered a memory loss, had
been successfully treated with a truth drug and hypnosis.

CHAPTER IX

PRIVILEGE

§ 86. Rationale and Characteristics

Privileged communications enjoy protection for a unique reason. As we have seen, the law of evidence generally seeks accuracy in factfinding by receiving relevant evidence thought to be reliable, while rejecting that thought to be insufficiently probative or trustworthy. But privileged communications, which by usual evidentiary standards may be highly probative as well as trustworthy are excluded because their disclosure is inimical to a principle or relationship (predominately non-evidentiary in nature) that society deems worthy of preserving and fostering. For example, the law confers upon the individual the constitutional privilege of not incriminating himself; it also accords a privileged status to confidential communications between attorney and client, husband and wife and between certain other communicants in special, private relationships. Quite often, the evidence that could be derived from these protected sources would be admissible if judged by the usual standards of probative value and trustworthiness.

The cost of evidentiary privileges is apparent, and it should not be borne with indifference. In the first place, conferral of a privilege results in the suppression of probative evidence and makes the trier decide factual issues without its benefit. Thus, one can question whether an evidentiary privilege is justified by citing the obvious ground that its application increases the probability that judicial disputes will be decided erroneously. In short, the privilege may not be worth its price. In the second place, the conferral of a privilege is grounded upon the assumption that its recognition significantly advances an interest, relationship, or principle that society considers a prevailing value. But whether recognition of the privilege actually results in advancing the protected interest is always open to question. That is, even if certain relationships, such as those of husband-wife or attorney-client, are worthy of the law's special protection, the privilege may not significantly foster the favored inter-

317

est. There might, for example, be substantial agreement that the law should promote the stability of marriage, yet there remains a serious question whether the conferral of a privilege covering confidential communications between spouses serves to encourage or stabilize marital ties.

A unique characteristic of privilege is that the right to assert the privilege, and thus cause the exclusion of privileged evidence, belongs to a person (or persons) vested with the interest or relationship protected by the privilege—the holder(s). The holder may be a party to litigation and thus conveniently situated to claim his privilege if he so wishes. But sometimes neither party-litigant is a holder; in this case, neither party has standing, in his own right, to object to the introduction of privileged evidence. The privilege thus is reserved for the holder, who may or may not wish to exercise it. Sometimes, however, a party or some other person is permitted to claim the privilege in a representative capacity on behalf of the absent holder. Such is always the case where express authorization to make the claim exists; the same is true where authorization, if not express, may clearly be implied, as where a lawyer, acting on behalf of a holder-client, invokes the attorney-client privilege. There also is authority in some jurisdictions allowing the judge, in the exercise of his discretion, to assert a privilege on behalf of an absent holder.[1]

Some interesting standing problems sometimes arise when information subject to a claim of privilege is offered at trial. If a party is the holder, the privilege can be waived if the holder-party himself offers the privileged evidence, or if an opposing party offers it against him and he fails to object.[2] Of course, if he does make a timely objection and the judge erroneously overrules it, the holder-objector may complain on appeal. Suppose, however, that the holder is not a party, and that evidence subject to a claim of privilege is erroneously admitted[3] against an

---

1. McCormick §§ 73, 83, 92.

2. Tillotson v. Boughner, 238 F. Supp. 621 (N.D.Ill.1965); Markwell v. Sykes, 173 Cal.App.2d 642, 343 P.2d 769 (1959); Pendleton v. Pen-

dleton, 103 Ohio App. 345, 145 N.E. 2d 485 (1957).

3. This could occur when the non-party-holder, or someone on his behalf, invokes his claim of privilege,

objecting party. Can the party against whom the evidence was admitted successfully complain on appeal? His appellate posture is not favorable: the evidence presumably is relevant and trustworthy, and the person whose rights have been violated by the incorrect ruling is not a party to the litigation but the holder of the privilege. Furthermore, even if the non-party-holder deserves some remedy, it is doubtful that reversal of the trial judgment is appropriate because that aids only the appellant. Consequently, the majority of the cases hold that a non-holder-party who has sustained an adverse trial judgment based in part upon evidence that properly was subject to someone else's claim of privilege can not prevail on appeal.[4] This result must be contrasted with a related, but distinct, appellate disposition. If the trial judge erroneously determines that proffered evidence is subject to a privilege (and thus excludes it), the party offering the evidence *may* complain.[5] It is of no consequence that the purported holder is an outsider: the offering party erroneously was denied the use of evidence not entitled to the special protection of privilege. His right to complain on appeal should not be foreclosed.

In the sections that follow, two privileged relationships are singled out for general discussion—those between attorney and client, and between husband and wife.[6] There follows an introductory discussion of the privilege against compulsory self-incrimination; additional privileges are mentioned in the notes at

---

but the court wrongly determines that the evidence is not within the ambit of privilege. For example, suppose a witness's testimony is properly subject to the claim of husband-wife privilege, but the holder is not a party to the action in which the witness takes the stand. Assume the holder—who might be the witness or his spouse —invokes the privilege, but the court erroneously determines that the privilege is inapplicable. As the text indicates, the losing party can not use this ruling as a basis for

gaining a reversal. Note, however, that if the holder refuses to divulge the privileged information and is cited for contempt, he can appeal this citation.

4. McCormick, § 73, at 153.

5. Id. at 152.

6. This selective treatment in part is a concession to limited space, but most of the problems common to other privileges are encountered in studying these two.

the end of the chapter. A general word of caution: care must be taken to examine statutory materials whenever a question of privilege is raised. Most privileges now are embodied in statutory provisions, although the spousal privilege covering confidential communications [7] and the attorney-client [8] privilege have long been recognized at common law. Also, it is important to recognize that privileges fostering confidential relationships prevent only the introduction of evidence designed to disclose *what a communicant said*. A litigant always is free to establish the facts discussed in the protected communication if he can do so by evidence independent of the privileged communication. For example, even though a husband's confidential statement to his wife that he negligently caused an automobile accident may be privileged, his culpability can be shown by other independent evidence, such as testimony from witnesses who observed the accident. Indeed, the husband may be called to the stand and examined fully about the accident; he can not, however, be made to disclose what he said to his wife—assuming, of course, that it comes within the husband-wife privilege.

§ 87. Spousal Privilege for Confidential Communications

This privilege protects confidential communications between spouses. It most often is justified on the ground that it promotes marital harmony. The theory usually invoked by courts is that the privilege encourages marital partners to share their most closely-guarded secrets and thoughts, thus adding an additional measure of intimacy and mutual support to the marriage. Serious doubt can be raised as to whether the evidentiary protection produces the supposed effect. To begin with, it may be safe to assume that many marital partners are unaware of the existence of the privilege. Generally, when a privilege is conferred a professional advisor (such as an attorney, doctor, or clergyman) is a party to the protected relationship. Such a person, of course, is likely to be aware of any privileges available to

---

7. McCormick, § 78, at 163.

8. Id., § 87, at 175. McCormick also discusses the roots of the attor-

ney-client privilege in Roman Law. Id.

himself or the person with whom he is conferring and can advise his confidant accordingly. But no professional or other person knowledgeable about privileged communications is a party to the protected husband-wife relationship. Furthermore, even assuming the marriage partners know about the privilege, one may ask whether its existence materially affects the flow of information between husband and wife. If there were no privilege and if the communicating spouses were aware of the absence of such protection, would marital communications be inhibited? Perhaps only in unusual circumstances, such as where a courtroom appearance was anticipated, would any chilling effect be found.[9]

Justification of the privilege, however, may be put on a different footing. There is much to be said for the notion that certain aspects of one's private life should be free from public disclosure. This especially is true in light of recent history, which has witnessed both diminished privacy in general and increased use of sophisticated electronic devices to collect and store information. The invasion of private marital communications is an indelicate and distasteful undertaking; it should not be sanctioned unless society's interest in disclosure is compelling.

McCormick argues that the marital privilege for confidential communications should "yield if the trial judge finds that the evidence of the communication is required in the due administration of justice."[10] Although this may accommodate fairly the competing interests involved, most legislatures and courts—perhaps doubting that such discretion would be wisely and evenly exercised—have made the privilege absolute.

---

9. McCormick, § 86, at 172–73; Hines, Privileged Testimony of Husband and Wife in California, 19 Calif.L.Rev. 390 (1931); Hutchins and Slesinger, Some Observations on the Law of Evidence: Family Relations, 13 Minn.L.Rev. 675 (1929). There might be a chilling effect in circumstances where the government focuses on a group or organization—such as draft resisters or the Communist party—even though no litigation is pending.

10. McCormick, § 86, at 174.

The privilege for marital communications extends to any *confidential* statement made *between spouses* during the existence of a legal marriage. In some jurisdictions, a broader construction of the privilege gives protection to the actions of one spouse in the presence of the other, at least where it reasonably can be inferred that the actor-spouse did not want his activity revealed.[11] Finally, there is some authority that the privilege attaches to facts or information that one spouse discovers, if it reasonably can be said that the discovery would not have been made except for the marital relationship.[12] The application of the privilege in this latter instance can not be justified on the theory that the privilege encourages communication, except in the unusual circumstance where the actor-spouse intended that the discovery be made. Whether the privilege nevertheless should apply because of society's distaste for public disclosure of private marital affairs is a question that is difficult to answer in the abstract. In an area such as this, a trial judge should be permitted to exercise discretion concerning the applicability of the privilege. He can take into account such matters as the importance of the testimony and the relationship of the spouses at the time of trial.

Although legislatures and courts differ somewhat on the scope of the privilege—that is, as to whether it extends beyond written or verbal communications—most authorities hold that the known presence of a third party when the spousal communication is made renders the privilege inapplicable for lack of confidentiality. This limiting principle recognizes the cost of conferring a privilege (namely, the suppression of relevant evidence) and indicates an unwillingness to extend protection beyond the

---

11. See People v. Sullivan, 42 Misc. 2d 1014, 249 N.Y.S.2d 589 (1964); People v. Daghita, 299 N.Y. 194, 86 N.E.2d 172 (1949); Menefee v. Commonwealth, 189 Va. 900, 55 S. E.2d 9 (1949). A different result should obtain where one spouse observes the other without the latter's knowledge. See People v. Sullivan, supra; Morgan at 98.

12. See McCormick, § 79, at 164; Morgan at 97–98. But see United States v. Smith, 533 F.2d 1077, 1079 (1976): "It is well settled that the communications to which the privilege applies have been limited to utterances or expressions intended by one spouse to convey a message to the other."

private husband-wife relationship.[13]   Thus, even where the third
party is a family member or is brought intentionally into the confidences of the spouses, the privilege generally does not apply.[14]
It also should be emphasized that the privilege does not attach unless the court finds from all of the surrounding circumstances that
the statements were intended to be imparted in confidence.
While courts probably tend to resolve doubts in favor of confidentiality, at least where the subject matter of the conversation
is not apt to be widely shared outside the marriage, this inclina-
tion usually does not extend to statements relating to business or
other matters likely to be openly discussed.[15]   Furthermore, subsequent revelations by one of the spouses may be influential in
causing the judge to find that no confidentiality was ever intended.   If, however, the court concludes that the statements were
intended to be confidential, a wrongful disclosure amounting to a
betrayal or breach of faith (as opposed to confirmation that no
confidence ever existed) does not destroy the privilege.[16]
Whether the privilege exists is a question for the judge.[17]

Several aspects of the privilege have disquieted the commentators.   Most jurisdictions hold that the privilege survives the ter-
mination of the marriage either by death or divorce.[18]   This extended protection appears to go beyond the fulfillment of any
reasonable policy underlying the privilege and represents an unwarranted obstacle to reliable factfinding.   In contrast, there is
co-existing authority that when a communication intended to be
private is overheard or intercepted by a third person, that per-

---

13.   Arguably, relationships such as
   parent-child are entitled to the protection of a privilege, but the
   courts have singled out the marriage relationship as the only family relationship deserving this special protection. Thus, if a husband
   admits privately to his wife that
   he committed the offense of shoplifting, the communication is privileged. A similar admission by a
   son to his mother is not. Can
   these disparate results be justified?

14.   Wolfle v. United States, 291 U.S.
   7 (1934); Gutridge v. State, 236
   Md. 514, 204 A.2d 557 (1964); Morgan at 98–99.

15.   McCormick, § 80, at 166–67.

16.   McCormick, § 82, at 168.

17.   Ch. X, § 97. See Id. § 98.

18.   McCormick, § 85, at 172.

son can give testimony revealing what was said by the marital partners.[19] Although seemingly prompted by a desire to minimize the suppression of relevant evidence, this latter result is questionable—at least in those instances in which spouses have taken reasonable precautions to preserve confidentiality. Indeed, recent authority suggests that placing the full burden of maintaining secrecy on the spouses is too great a demand, especially in light of modern communication devices (often involving other parties in the process of transmission) and technological advances in eavesdropping.[20] If the privilege is worth maintaining, it should not fail where the spouses have taken reasonable steps to ensure privacy. In the near future, there is likely to be a legislative and judicial shift to a position compatible with this proposition.[21]

The question often arises whether only the communicating spouse is the holder of the privilege. Wigmore felt that because the privilege was designed to foster marital communication, only the communicating spouse need be the holder.[22] This is the law in some jurisdictions.[23] In others, however, a statute or judicial decision makes both spouses holders.[24] This means that the party seeking to introduce a privileged statement must secure a waiver from both spouses or, in the case of a holder's death, from the successor in interest (usually the executor or administrator)

---

19. McCormick, § 82, at 167. The common law permitted eavesdroppers to testify as to the content of confidential communication based on two justifications: privileges should be strictly construed because they suppress relevant evidence and an individual truly concerned with confidentiality should take precautions to prevent eavesdroppers. R. Lempert & S. Saltzburg at 639–40 n. 39.

20. See Adv.Comm. Note to Proposed Fed.R.Evid. 503(b).

21. See generally McCormick, § 82, at 167–69.

22. 8 Wigmore § 2340(1) (McNaughton).

23. McCormick, § 83, at 169; see also Taylor v. Commonwealth, 302 S.W.2d 378 (Ky.App.1957); Louisell and Crippin, Evidentiary Privileges, 40 Minn.L.Rev. 413, 417 (1956).

24. Morgan at 101. See Martin v. State, 203 Miss. 187, 194, 33 So.2d 825, 827 (1948) (Griffith, J., specially concurring); People v. Sullivan, 42 Misc.2d 1014, 249 N.Y.S.2d 589 (1964).

of the deceased. In some situations the law will intercede and terminate the privilege; this occurs, for example, when one spouse is prosecuted for an offense against the other (or the children of either) or in certain civil actions, such as divorce, where the marital partners have assumed an antagonistic posture.[25]

§ 88. Privilege Under the Federal Rules of Evidence

When the Proposed Federal Rules of Evidence were considered and amended in Congress, the detailed provisions setting forth the various privileges were deleted. Congress replaced them with Rule 501, which provides that, unless there is a federal enactment to the contrary, privilege in the federal courts is to "be governed by the principles of the common law as they may be interpreted by the courts of the United States in the light of reason and experience." In civil actions where state law governs a claim or defense, as in diversity cases, the law of privilege in connection therewith is to be determined "in accordance with state law."

Commentators have suggested that although the specific, proposed federal rules for privilege were deleted they still remain persuasive evidence in the hands of a federal judge trying to interpret the common law in the light of "reason and experience." [26] The suggestion is cogent, especially because the United States Supreme Court had approved the proposed rules and

---

25. 8 Wigmore § 2338(9). The privilege also is lifted where one spouse is tried for a criminal offense and a confidential communication would tend to explicate him or at least reduce the grade of the offense. McCormick, § 84, at 171.

26. Waltz, The New Federal Rules of Evidence 47 (2d ed. 1975). The author discusses the deleted rules at 48–80. Judges who turn to the proposed rules for guidance, however, should not lose sight of the fact that in a few instances the proposed rules would have made significant changes in the common law. For example, the proposed rules do not recognize the privilege for confidential communication between husband and wife. Yet this privilege is firmly entrenched in the common law. See S. Saltzburg & K. Redden, Federal Rules of Evidence Manual 201 (2d ed. 1977).

Students of civil procedure may wish to ask whether Erie Railroad Co. v. Tompkins, 304 U.S. 64 (1938) and its progeny require that in diversity cases the federal courts must observe the state-created law of privilege.

transmitted them to Congress. Furthermore, the proposed rules governing privilege were not radical departures from existing law, but in general represented a careful selection from existing statutory provisions and judicial decisions.[26a]

§ 89. Spousal Privilege to Prevent Adverse Testimony in a Criminal Trial

More than half of the states recognize by statute the right of an accused spouse to prevent his (or her) marital partner from taking the stand against him in a criminal[27] proceeding. In a comparatively small number of jurisdictions, only the testifying spouse is the holder and thus entitled to invoke this privilege not to testify;[28] in others, both spouses are holders.[29] There is, of course, the possibility that the criminal proceeding will not be a trial but rather a grand jury hearing, in which case the accused spouse will not be present to claim the privilege. In this event, the testifying spouse should (if he or she is not the holder) be entitled to claim the privilege on behalf of the accused spouse.[30]

Testimony by a spouse called as a witness by the defense is unaffected by the privilege.[31] Further, once the testifying spouse takes the stand for the accused, the government can cross-examine him or her and, so it would seem, the scope of cross-examination will be in accordance with the usual rule for the jurisdiction.[32]

26a. But see supra note 26.

27. E. g., Va. Code Ann. § 19.2–271.2 (1977 Supp.). In a few jurisdictions, this right to prevent adverse testimony is extended to civil trials. See, e. g., West's Calif. Evid. Code § 971.

28. See, e. g., West's Calif.Evid. Code, § 970–71. Note that California gives the witness-spouse the privilege not to *testify against* a spouse (§ 970) and not to be *called as a witness* against a party-spouse (§ 971).

29. McCormick, § 66, at 145. Under existing federal decisional law, both spouses are holders. See Wyatt v. United States, 362 U.S. 525 (1960). See generally VIII Wigmore § 2241 (McNaughton).

30. See Proposed Fed.R.Evid. 505(b) and Adv.Comm.Note.

31. See Funk v. United States, 290 U.S. 371 (1933); N.C.Rev.Stat. § 8–57.

32. 8 Wigmore, § 2242, at 258 (McNaughton); N.C.Rev.Stat. § 8–57; Okla.Stat.Ann. 22, § 702. See Ch. IV, §§ 30–31.

But the witness may still be entitled to invoke the confidential communications privilege—at least the mere act of taking the stand does not waive this privilege. Note, also, that unlike the privilege protecting confidential communications, the privilege to render a spouse incompetent to testify exists when, and only when, the accused and the proposed witness are marital partners *at the time of trial*.[33] But if the accused and the person sought to be called by the prosecution are married at the time of trial, the privilege to decline to testify usually is not defeated on the ground that the events to which testimony is sought preceded the marriage.[34] The "incompetency privilege" does, however, in contrast to the confidential communications privilege, terminate with the dissolution of the marriage.[35]

The marital privilege to invoke testimonial incompetency is not without its critics. The privilege is difficult to justify where the witness-spouse desires to testify for the government but the accused prevents the witness from taking the stand. If the privilege is justified—as it is said to be—on the basis of marital preservation, it seems dubious that suppression of testimony is warranted when the relationship has reached the point that one partner is willing to disclose adverse facts. Such willingness is a persuasive indication that the marriage already has failed.[36]

---

33. Should the incompetency privilege be defeated if it appears that the marriage was a ploy to prevent testimony? It sometimes is held that the privilege still exists. See State v. Jaques, 256 N.W.2d 559 (S.D.1977). 8 Wigmore, § 2231, at 224 (McNaughton). Recently, federal courts seemed to have abandoned this view. See, e. g., United States v. Mathis, 559 F.2d 294 (5th Cir. 1977); United States v. Apodaca, 522 F.2d 568 (10th Cir. 1975). And no privilege exists if the marriage itself is part of the offense, e. g., in immigration fraud cases. See Lutwak v. United States, 344 U.S. 604 (1953), ignoring the validity of the marriage where the sole purpose of the spouses was to gain entry to the United States. The proposed Federal Rule 505(c)(2) would have resolved the difficulty of expedient marriages by limiting the incompetency privilege to matters occurring after the marriage. See Weinstein & Berger ¶ 505[01].

34. Lempert & Saltzburg at 680. But cf. Proposed Fed.R.Evid. 505(c)(2), denying the privilege where testimony concerns events which preceded the marriage.

35. See, e. g., United States v. Smith, 533 F.2d 1077 (8th Cir. 1976).

36. The counter-argument is that the willingness to testify may be a response to difficulties that are not

Arguably, if the privilege is to be conferred at all, the testifying spouse should be the holder—as is the rule in a distinct minority of jurisdictions.[37] Even in those jurisdictions, however, where the accused is the holder, there is no privilege when the crime charged is against the spouse or a child of one or both of the spouses.[38]

§ 90. The Attorney-Client Privilege: General Application

There is general recognition of a privilege preventing testimonial disclosure of a confidential communication between client and attorney made in connection with securing or rendering legal services. The client, whether a person or corporation, holds the privilege, although the attorney normally can invoke it on the client's behalf. As noted before, the confidential communication itself is protected, not the events that are its subject matter.[39] The privilege does not prevent disclosure by evidence of any relevant event acquired through the usual investigatory

---

irreconcilable but that would become so if adverse testimony were permitted in a criminal proceeding. See Hawkins v. United States, 358 U.S. 74, 77–78 (1958).

37. Query whether making the witness-spouse the holder encourages the prosecutor to exert unfair pressure upon him or her to secure his or her testimony.

38. McCormick, § 66, at 145. See N.C. Rev.Stat. § 8–57 (1969); Okla.Stat. Ann. 22 § 702 (1973). For an extensive analysis, see State v. Briley, 53 N.J. 498, 251 A.2d 442 (1969). Suppose the witness-spouse is a holder and the trial is for an offense against the holder-spouse. May he or she invoke the "incompetency privilege" and decline to testify? The usual result is to deny application of the privilege and compel the witness to take the stand. Denial of the privilege probably is justified by the possi-

bility that the accused spouse may exert coercive pressure upon the witness-spouse not to testify. Furthermore, once the government decides to go forward with the prosecution of an offense between spouses, it has determined that the disruptive effect of the prosecution upon the marriage is not the dominant consideration. Arguably, the additional disruption caused by compelling the spousal testimony should not be determinative. For a case suggesting that in trials for some offenses against the testifying spouse, he or she could invoke the incompetency privilege even though the accused spouse could not, see Wyatt v. United States, 362 U.S. 525 (1960) (In this Mann Act prosecution the Court relied on the legislative history of the Act to deny the witness-wife the right to invoke the privilege).

39. See supra § 86.

or discovery processes; it only prohibits use of attorney-client communications to prove the event. The purpose of the privilege is to encourage full and truthful statements by the client so that the attorney can give reliable advice and prepare the client's case on the basis of credible information.

Theoretically, the privilege applies only to the client's statements and not to those of the attorney. Practically, however, it is usually necessary to give privileged status to the statements of both attorney and client in order to protect fully the client's statements.[40] Furthermore, the nature of the attorney-client relationship makes it necessary to extend the privilege beyond statements made between attorney and client and to include statements made to and by certain third persons. Both participants, especially the attorney, often find it necessary to communicate through agents, assistants, or representatives (for example, a secretary, associate, accountant, or investigator). Thus, the statutes and cases generally make the privilege applicable to communications through agents or representatives of either attorney or client.[41] Where a client, for example, gives a message to a clerk to relay to the attorney, courts understandably treat the situation as if the client made the communication directly to the attorney. Likewise, if a client requests his physician to inform the former's legal representative of the client's mental or physical condition, the communication from the physician is usually within the attorney-client privilege.

Careful distinctions, however, should not be obscured by broad generalities concerning the applicability of the attorney-client privilege to communications through third-party representatives. Often a representative does not relay a communication from one principal to the other, but rather he communicates his own independent opinion based in part upon the principal's communication. A psychiatrist, for example, may listen to the client's communications and make a diagnostic communication to the attorney that represents, in large part at least, the psychiatrist's knowledge or opinion formed to a significant degree from state-

---

40. McCormick, § 89 at 183–84.

41. 8 Wigmore, § 2301, at 583 (McNaughton); West's Calif.Evid. Code §§ 951, 952 (1966).

ments made by the patient.[42] A physician performing a similar function would seem more removed from the privilege, because he often bases his conclusions substantially upon his objective findings rather than upon the client's communications.[43] Indeed, it is arguable that the doctors' statements in both of the foregoing instances constitute ordinary expert opinion and not a *communication by the client* in any meaningful sense.[44] Most courts have held, however, that the intermediary's communication is within the privilege because one of the principals to the privilege—often the client—is engaging a representative to make a communication of a specialized or technical nature that the principal, lacking the necessary expertise, cannot make himself.[45]

Application of the privilege to a second, but closely related, factual pattern (also different from communications relayed through an agent) extends incrementally the privilege even further from its original purpose of encouraging the client's full and candid disclosure. Some modern authority applies the privilege to communications between a lawyer and a representative, such as an accountant, investigator, or doctor, whom the lawyer engages not really to facilitate a communication from a principal, but rather to assist him in delivering legal services to the client.[46] For example, in instances where an attorney refers his client to a doctor for examination and evaluation, the physician's report

---

42. Psychiatric opinion often is included within the privilege, not on the ground that what the psychiatrist says is the client's communication, but on the ground that the psychiatrist is representing the lawyer in interpreting the client's condition. See text at n. 41 and United States ex rel. Edney v. Smith, 425 F.Supp. 1038, 1047–48 (E.D.N.Y.1976).

43. Courts, however, usually do not differentiate between psychiatrists and physicians with respect to the attorney-client privilege. Compare People v. Hilliker, 29 Mich.App.

543, 185 N.W.2d 831 (1971) (psychiatrist) with Lindsay v. Lipson, 367 Mich. 1, 116 N.W.2d 60 (1962) (physician).

44. See Friedenthal, Discovery and Use of Adverse Party's Expert Information, 14 Stan.L.Rev. 455, 462–69 (1962).

45. See, e. g., People v. Hilliker, 29 Mich.App. 543, 547–48, 185 N.W.2d 831, 833 (1971).

46. See Weinstein & Berger, ¶ 503(a)(3)[01]; Proposed Fed.R.Evid. 503 (b)(2).

to the attorney is within the privilege [47]—including, apparently, even those portions that originate from the physician's expertise or medical tests. This extension loses sight of the purpose of the privilege and expands its protection—which is absolute and can not be defeated even on a showing of a substantial need that can not be satisfied through other evidentiary sources—into an area which should be governed by other considerations, such as those underlying the work product rule.[48] Suppose, for example, an attorney engages an accountant to examine and analyze a client's preexisting financial records or a lawyer retains a chemist to analyze bloodstains or other foreign matter on clothing belonging to the client. Should the communications between the representative and the lawyer fall within the privilege? The statements of the accountant or chemist hardly can be said to be the client's communication. Because the rules prohibiting one adversary from discovering the work product of the other usually operate to conditionally shield these communications, the attorney-client privilege, which is absolute and permanent, should be restricted so as to apply only to such parts of the communication as reveal the client's communicative disclosures made in pursuit of legal services.[49]

---

47. The leading case is City and County of San Francisco v. Superior Court, 37 Cal.2d 227, 231 P.2d 26 (1951).

48. For a discussion of the work product rule in the federal system, see C. Wright, Law of Federal Courts, 405–16 (3d ed. 1976).

49. See generally Sachs v. Aluminum Co. of America, 167 F.2d 570 (6th Cir. 1948). Note that the proposed federal rule governing the attorney-client privilege, which was approved by the Supreme Court but rejected by Congress, would have extended the privilege to communications between the lawyer and his representative. See Proposed Fed.R.Evid. 503(b)(2) and (3). See also Adv.Comm. Note to Fed. R.Evid. 503(a)(3). As suggested in the text above, the privilege has even been extended to accountants retained by the attorney. See Weinstein & Berger, 503(a)(3)[01], at 24–26. This same problem could arise with respect to communications from a client's agent to the client. Note, however, that in some instances the disclosures of the agent's communications would indirectly reveal the client's communications. Of course, no communication—whether originating with the client or agent—should be protected unless it was made to facilitate the rendition of legal services.

To come within the privilege, written or oral communications whether directly between client and attorney or through an intermediary, must be made for the purpose of obtaining or rendering *legal* services.[50] The privilege does not extend to communications made in pursuit of business advice, nor to those made on the basis of friendship if only non-legal counseling is involved. Even these guidelines, however, often fail to delineate the reach of the privilege. Problems frequently arise because of the difficulty in identifying the motives of one who speaks with a lawyer; furthermore, several motives may operate simultaneously—a mixture, for example, of business and legal motives. There is some variance in the willingness of the courts to sustain the privilege in instances where the legal motivation for seeking advice is only one of several incentives.[51] Most authorities hold that the privilege applies only if the desire to acquire legal advice or services dominates over other reasons for making the communications.[52] This solution is compatible with the purpose of the privilege which, as we have seen, is to encourage confidences. To accomplish this purpose, the privilege need not, and should not, be raised with regard to statements that would have been made regardless of the (subordinate) desire to obtain legal services. Additionally, even where legal services are sought, the privilege will be denied if the court concludes from all surrounding circumstances that there is evidence sufficient to support the conclusion that the communication was to seek advice in furtherance of a future crime or fraud.[53]

Other problems lurk behind the seemingly simple facade of the attorney-client privilege. Suppose that the client is a corporation and that the communication is made by a corporate em-

---

50. 8 Wigmore §§ 2292, 2296 (McNaughton).

51. Illustrative cases are collected in 8 Wigmore, § 2296, at 567–68 (McNaughton).

52. See, e. g., Bernardi v. Community Hospital Ass'n, 166 Colo. 280, 295–96, 443 P.2d 708, 715–16 (1968);

Ballard v. Ballard, 296 S.W.2d 811 (Tex.Civ.App.1956); Weinstein & Berger, ¶ 503(a)(1)[01], at 21–22.

53. McCormick, § 95, at 200, noting that a requirement that the judge must actually find that the consultation was in furtherance of a crime or fraud would be unduly obstructive.

ployee to the attorney for the corporation. Depending on the context and one's view of the proper scope of the privilege, the statements of the employee could be either (1) communications from the corporate client and within the corporation's privilege, or (2) statements by an employee not authorized to speak for the corporate client (thus, essentially those of a witness) and not within the privilege. Because the corporation can speak only through individuals, the question may arise whether the corporation is making the communication. Clearly protected would be a communication from the corporate president to the attorney, in which the former seeks legal advice for the corporation. Clearly unprotected would be a statement by a non-management employee, made at his own initiative, revealing facts about an occurrence (for example, an accident) that may legally involve the corporate entity. The problem lies between these two extremes.

Some courts have formulated a "control-group" test that upholds the privilege only if the individual speaking to the attorney is vested by the corporation with authority both to *seek* legal advice and to *participate* significantly in the corporate response to the advice.[54] A somewhat broader test extends the privilege beyond the control group to embrace any communication by an employee involving his *corporate duties* and made *at the direction of* his corporate employer.[55] The latter test, which seems to be prevailing, yields possibilities for unduly extending the wall of privilege, especially since careful planning by counsel and corporate officials can increase the number of communications that stay within the protected area.

---

54. The leading case is City of Philadelphia v. Westinghouse Elec. Corp., 210 F.Supp. 483 (E.D.Pa. 1962).

55. See Harper & Row Publishers, Inc. v. Decker, 423 F.2d 487 (7th Cir. 1970). For another formulation see D. I. Chadbourne, Inc. v. Superior Court, 60 Cal.2d 723, 36 Cal.Rptr. 468, 388 P.2d 700 (1964).

A recent federal case, Diversified Industries, Inc. v. The Honorable James H. Meredith, 572 F.2d 596 (8th Cir. 1977) sets forth yet another variation. See also Simon, The Attorney-Client Privilege as Applied to Corporations, 65 Yale L.J. 953 (1956); Note, Attorney-Client Privilege for Corporate Clients: The Control Group Test, 84 Harv.L.Rev. 424 (1970).

§ 91. Attorney-Client Privilege: Special Problems of Waiver and Non-Applicability

Because the client holds the privilege, he can voluntarily relinquish or waive it. Waiver may, of course, take place expressly; it also may result from implication, as where the client voluntarily reveals the communication to a judicial or legislative body or to a person not within the group acting on behalf of the attorney or client.[56] In the corporate context especially, broad dissemination of attorney-client communications to personnel without a need to share the information may result in a waiver of the privilege (or else lead a court to conclude that no privilege ever attached because confidentiality was not intended).[57] A waiver also will be implied where the attorney and client become adverse parties and the dispute concerns a breach of duty by one or the other. This last rule is dictated by fairness, and is justified even though the client may assert that he intends no waiver.

Although the privilege generally survives the death of the client and passes to his personal representative [58] (a result of dubious wisdom), it is lifted in disputes between adverse persons who claim through the client. Thus, in a dispute between persons taking under the client's will and persons claiming property by intestacy, the privilege as to relevant communications between the deceased client and attorney is terminated.[59] Recent authority also ends the privilege in cases where the dispute is between one who claims by reason of an inter vivos transaction and one who claims by will or intestacy.[60]

Some difficulty occurs when two clients with a common interest seek legal assistance from the same attorney. Each client can invoke the privilege and protect his own statements from disclosure to third persons. But if subsequently the two clients

---

56. McCormick § 93.

57. Annot., 98 A.L.R.2d 241, 252–53 (1964).

58. 8 Wigmore, § 2323, at 630 (McNaughton).

59. McCormick, § 94, at 197–198.

60. McCormick, § 94, at 198; Proposed Fed.R.Evid. 503(d)(2).

become adversaries, the issue is posed as to what protection (if any) should be accorded the confidential communications made by each client to the attorney during the course of the joint representation.

For communications the clients made in each other's presence, a limited waiver (extending only to the other client and not to third persons) might be inferred: that is, the facts give rise to an inference that no confidentiality was intended as between the two clients. A more difficult problem is encountered with those communications made by one client to the attorney but communicated out of the presence of the other joint client. Circumstances may suggest, of course, that no confidentiality as between the two clients ever was intended because their interests and objectives are generally similar. In any event, fairness dictates that a waiver be implied by law no matter what the actual intention of the communicating client. If the clients seek joint representation and later become adversaries themselves, it does not seem fair to protect statements by one client that are pertinent to the matter of common interest simply because it was not made in the presence of the other. Further, where each client has made communications in the other's absence, the choice is either to protect the separate, private communications emanating from each client or to disclose the communications of each. In this setting, the general policy of promoting accurate fact-finding appears to outweigh the protection of statements made by the adversaries during a time when they were voluntary allies in a common cause. Thus, modern authority supports withholding the privilege from a communication made by a joint client, pertaining to the common interests of both clients, and offered in an action between them.[61]

---

61. Proposed Fed.R.Evid. 503(d)(5) uses essentially this language in limiting the application of the privilege. There is statutory support in West's Calif.Evid.Code § 962; N.J.Evid. Rule 26(2) in N.J.Stat. Ann. 2A:84A–20. See McCormick, § 91, at 189–90.

§ 92. The Privilege Against Self-Incrimination: Scope, Application, and Waiver

The fifth amendment to the United States Constitution [62] provides in part that "No person . . . shall be compelled in any criminal case to be a witness against himself." In Malloy v. Hogan,[63] decided in 1964, this provision was held applicable to the states through the command of the fourteenth amendment that a state shall not "deprive any person of life, liberty, or property without due process of law." Although "person" often is given a broad constitutional or statutory construction, in the present context it is more narrowly read: the privilege against self-incrimination is conferred only upon individuals. It is not available to a corporation, and it also is denied to an unincorporated entity, such as a labor union or a partnership, if the enterprise in question represents group interests as opposed to private or personal ones.[64] The constitutional proscription is designed to shield natural persons from sovereign compulsion to give testimony that might subject them to criminal liability; [65] this purpose generally can be achieved without extending the privilege to artificial entities that cannot, as such, be subjected to the same indignities or suffering as an individual.[66] A difficult case is presented when governmental compulsion is exerted to obtain incriminating communications that are attributable to a business group or entity, but the compulsion is resisted by an officer or agent of the enterprise on the ground that the group communications tend to incriminate him personally. Although an individual can not be compelled to give testimony concerning

---

62. For the history and policies behind the Fifth Amendment, see generally L. Levy, Origins of the Fifth Amendment (1968); Wigmore, §§ 2250–51 (McNaughton).

63. 378 U.S. 1 (1964).

64. Hale v. Henkel, 201 U.S. 43 (1906) (corporation); United States v. White, 322 U.S. 694 (1944) (labor union); Bellis v. United States, 417 U.S. 85 (1974) (partnership).

65. Compulsion need not consist of a direct, apparently enforceable order to speak, but can take a different form, such as a threat of job forfeiture if fifth amendment rights are claimed. See Garrity v. New Jersey, 385 U.S. 493 (1967). For a discussion of the policies and values underlying the privilege, see McCormick § 118. See also supra note 62.

66. McCormick, § 128, at 270.

his activities undertaken for the group that itself would incriminate him,[67] he can not bring within the privilege those communications of the entity (usually in the form of business records) that contain assertions or disclosures that incriminate him.[68] To hold otherwise would negate, as a practical matter, the principle that the privilege does not apply to collective enterprises,[69] for usually some individual within the association would claim that the entity's communications incriminate him personally.

Read literally, the constitutional language conferring the privilege against self-incrimination would apply only in criminal proceedings against the holder and, further, might be construed as protecting only incriminating statements that the government sought to elicit from the accused after he was sworn as a witness. But as we shall see, the language has received a sympathetic reading consistent with its underlying purpose of preventing the government from compelling an individual to make statements that contain incriminating assertions. To begin with, the privilege of the *accused* not to be a witness against himself has been construed to confer a right to remain off the witness stand—that is, the accused can not be called or sworn as a witness if he claims his privilege.[70] He thus is able completely to avoid interrogation in a criminal trial in which he is a named defendant. Furthermore, the prosecutor can not emasculate the privilege by forcing the accused to claim it in the jury's presence [71] or by commenting to the jury that the defendant refused to testify (thus inviting them to draw adverse inferences from his silence).[72]

---

67. Curcio v. United States, 354 U.S. 118, (1957).

68. United States v. White, 322 U.S. 694, 699–700 (1944).

69. Bellis v. United States, 417 U.S. 85, 89 (1974).

70. See 8 Wigmore, Evidence, § 2268, at 406 (McNaughton) and cases cited.

71. See, e. g., United States v. Housing Found. of Am., 176 F.2d 665, 666 (3d Cir. 1949); People v. Talle, 111 Cal.App.2d 650, 665–67, 245 P. 2d 633, 642–43 (1952).

72. Griffin v. California, 380 U.S. 609 (1965). Neither can the judge instruct the jury that adverse inferences are permissible. Ibid. See Grunewald v. United States, 353 U.S. 391 (1957) (improper to receive evidence that accused, who testified at trial, had invoked the fifth amendment before the grand jury).

case is presented where officials issue a subpoena to an individual, directing him to produce specified business records. Does his act of compliance fall within the protection of the fifth amendment because obedience amounts to an implied assertion by the respondent that the records produced are those called for in the subpoena? Although situations can be imagined in which mere production might constitute an implied, incriminating "communication," [78] in the vast majority of cases the act of gathering and submitting to the government those documents requested is not, standing alone, an incriminating assertion.[79] The respondent is not called upon to verify the truth of any incriminating *contents* that may be within the records produced; he only produces specified documents that were voluntarily prepared at an earlier time. Another difficult question, not yet definitively answered by the cases, is whether the fifth amendment protects the seizure of intimate private papers (such as a diary) even though the means of obtaining the material involves no element of prohibited compulsion. While the argument can be made that there is a zone of privacy into which governmental

---

78. In the unlikely circumstance that the respondent was required to produce such documents as he could verify were accurate as to their contents, the act of compliance would constitute an implied assertion that the documents produced were truthful. See Fisher v. United States, 425 U.S. 391, 413 (1976). Also, if a subpoena or other compulsory procedure required the respondent to aid the government in discovering whether certain documents ever existed at all, compliance might be deemed a violation of the self-incrimination of the fifth amendment. See Andresen v. Maryland, 427 U.S. 463, 473–74 (1976). It is likely, however, that a subpoena that is so general in its description of the documents desired that it runs afoul of the fifth amendment

would also lack the necessary specificity required by the fourth amendment.

79. The principal case is Fisher v. United States, 425 U.S. 391, 410–13 (1976). See also the comprehensive Note, Formalism, Legal Realism, and Constitutionally Protected Privacy Under the Fourth and Fifth Amendments, 90 Harv.L.Rev. 945, 979 (1977): "[I]t is difficult to imagine a case in which the accused's compliance with a subpoena would vouch for the truth of the contents produced and thus satisfy the implied authentication rationale . . . [of] *Fisher*." The Ninth Circuit has held that the mere production of business records is not testimonial. See United States v. Osborn, 561 F.2d 1334 (9th Cir. 1977).

intrusion will not be tolerated,[80] it is difficult to sustain this argument under a fifth amendment rationale. In recent years, the Supreme Court has broken away from the notion that the fifth amendment serves a privacy interest in addition to its prohibition against compulsion, and has resolved fifth amendment issues by asking whether coercive means were used to extract an incriminating communication.[81] The fact that a pre-existing, non-coerced communication is private in nature is probably not dispositive so long as it can be obtained and presented at trial without compelling the individual resisting disclosure to make incriminating statements.

The *third* situation in which the fifth amendment privilege is unavailable is the instance in which the danger of criminal liability has been removed, as, for example, where the claimant has already been convicted (or acquitted) of the act to be disclosed or where the prosecutor grants immunity from prosecution.[82] Grants of immunity sometimes are employed in criminal investigations and prosecutions. Although prosecutors often grant immunity from prosecution for the *transaction* to which the compelled testimony relates (transactional immunity), the constitution demands no broader immunity than a prohibition against *using the incriminating statements themselves* (use immunity), including any evidence derived therefrom, in a future

80. Early Supreme Court cases, starting with Boyd v. United States, 116 U.S. 616 (1886), pronounced that the fifth amendment shielded a person's private papers from seizure or production through either a search warrant or a subpoena. Subsequent cases have departed sharply from *Boyd* and have emasculated, if not in effect overruled, it. The cases are carefully reviewed in Note, Formalism, Legal Realism and Constitutionally Protected Privacy Under the Fourth and Fifth Amendments, supra note 79.

81. See Andresen v. Maryland, 427 U.S. 463 (1976); Fisher v. United States, 425 U.S. 391 (1976).

82. See McCormick, § 143, at 304. Statutory authority empowering the prosecutor to act is considered necessary in some jurisdictions. The federal immunity statute is found at 18 U.S.C.A. §§ 6001–6005. Other cases in which the privilege does not apply because there is no possibility of criminal liability include the expiration of the applicable statute of limitations and the pardon of the witness.

prosecution.[83] Thus, under the latter, more narrow grant of immunity, the person ordered to give incriminating testimony is not necessarily free of prosecution for the transaction to which his statements relate. The government still could initiate a criminal prosecution if sufficient evidence could be obtained without the use of the incriminating statements or evidentiary "fruits" derived therefrom.

Immunity granted by one sovereign within the United States (for example, a state) must be respected by another sovereign therein (for example, the federal government or another state), at least to the extent of prohibiting any use or derivative use ("fruits") of the incriminating statement by the nongranting jurisdiction.[84] The leading case of Murphy v. Waterfront Commission [85] held that a witness given a state grant of immunity may not refuse to testify on the ground that no federal immunity has been granted. The witness is protected against federal prosecutorial use of the state testimony by the fifth amendment. Dictum in *Murphy* indicates that a similar constitutional prohibition would apply where the federal government confers immunity and a state thereafter seeks to prosecute.[86] Presumably, the same result would obtain between two states.[87]

Waiver, a doctrine common to all privileges, sometimes operates to defeat one's claim to a right to remain silent. While waiver commonly is defined as the intentional relinquishment of a known right, we have seen (in the context of other privileges) that a waiver also may occur by implication even when it is doubtful that the holder intended to forfeit a right or privilege. In short, considerations of fairness or some other policy may in-

---

83. Kastigar v. United States, 406 U.S. 441 (1972).

84. If immunity granted by one sovereign—say a state—resulted in conferring *transactional* immunity in nongranting jurisdictions, a severe strain upon intergovernmental relations might result. For example, a state grant of immunity would prohibit any federal prosecutions concerning the transaction to which the compelled testimony related, even if the federal government had ample evidence to prosecute without reliance upon the compelled testimony.

85. 378 U.S. 52 (1964).

86. Id. at 78. See Reina v. United States, 364 U.S. 507 (1960).

87. R. Lempert & S. Saltzburg at 719.

fluence a court's decision concerning what actions constitute an implied waiver.

The extent of the waiver of the privilege against self-incrimination when the accused takes the stand and testifies provides a good example of the influence of these policies. Does the accused who takes the witness stand have a right either to limit generally the scope of adverse interrogation or to claim the privilege of an ordinary witness as to particular questions the response to which might be incriminating? Obviously, the accused's election to become a witness waives that branch of the privilege that shields him from giving any testimony. Beyond this, at a minimum the accused may be compelled to respond to cross-examination that tests the accuracy and truthfulness of his direct testimony. In short, he can not put forward favorable testimony and expect to successfully resist cross-questions that challenge that testimony or call for the disclosure of closely-related incriminating facts. Furthermore, support can be found for declaring a constitutional waiver of broader scope: when the accused testifies concerning the offense for which he is on trial he forfeits the privilege as to all facts relevant to that offense.[88] Some cases go beyond even this proposition and permit cross-examination concerning other offenses (in a multiple-count indictment) for which the accused is on trial, even though these other offenses were not the subject of his direct testimony.[89] Under either of these broader views, incriminating testimony can be compelled even if it does not relate to the direct testimony of the accused: the test is the relevance of the testimony to the present offense(s), and the fact that compelled testimony may have the effect of incriminating the accused as to the offense charged or some other offense is not determinative.[90] This broad waiver may prevent the accused from electing to testify but lim-

---

88. McCormick, § 132, at 278–79.

89. Id. at 280 discussing People v. Perez, 65 Cal.2d 615, 55 Cal.Rptr. 909, 422 P.2d 597 (1967).

90. However, the accused may still claim the privilege regarding an act for which he is not on trial when the prosecutor seeks to interrogate him as to this act for the purpose of impeaching the accused's testimony. McCormick, § 42, at 84. See also Ch. VIII, § 81 (2).

iting the risk of adverse consequences by planning his direct testimony so as to effect only a selective, limited waiver—as where the accused testifies solely on the subject of alibi and (under the limited view of waiver) waives his constitutional privilege only as to this subject.

Most cases, however, resolve the issue of the extent of the accused's waiver by holding that the testifying-accused waives the privilege against self-incrimination to a degree coextensive with the allowable scope of cross-examination.[91] An accused who takes the stand in a jurisdiction limiting the scope of cross-examination to matters probed on direct examination [92] waives his fifth amendment privilege only to the extent of the testimonial "coverage" normally permitted by the application of the rule governing permissible scope.[93] Some jurisdictions, of course, employ the rule of wide-open cross-examination that permits adverse interrogation on any relevant subject about which the witness has knowledge. In these jurisdictions an accused's waiver of fifth-amendment rights has its broadest reach, and cross-examination may extend to any subject relevant to the offense for which the accused is on trial.[94]

The waiver rule that depends upon the allowable scope of cross-examination has the dual appeal of predictability and symmetry with the non-constitutional rule governing scope; it raises troublesome questions, however, in the wake of Malloy v. Hogan.[95] That case imposes a federal standard governing the substance of the privilege. As McCormick points out, the rule limiting the permissible range of cross-examination traditionally has been subject to broad discretionary control by the trial

91. C. Wright & A. Miller, Federal Practice and Procedure, § 407, at 105 (1969).

92. See Ch. IV, § 30.

93. C. Wright & A. Miller, supra note 86 at 105.

94. Even in a jurisdiction that limits the scope of cross to that of direct, a broad direct examination results in an equally sweeping forfeiture of the privilege. See Johnson v. United States, 318 U.S. 189 (1943). But even sweeping testimony on direct does not waive the privilege regarding misconduct not mentioned during direct, the sole purpose of which is to impeach the testimony of the accused. McCormick, § 42, at 84.

95. 378 U.S. 1 (1964).

judge.[96] Such discretion is consistent with the purpose of the "scope rule" (which accommodates trial efficiency), but is not a proper means of governing a constitutional principle responsive to an entirely different set of values.[97] While the Supreme Court has yet to resolve definitively the problem of the extent of the accused's waiver,[98] a uniform standard for determining the forfeiture of the privilege against compulsory self-incrimination has much merit, particularly in light of *Malloy*. McCormick advances the possibility of extending the waiver no farther than necessary to provide a fair testing through cross-examination of the truth of the testimony given on direct.[99] Arguably, the government has no justification for a claim that the waiver should be more extensive than is necessary to enable the prosecutor to conduct a full and fair cross-examination of the accused's testimony.

This solution, however, is not without difficulties. It permits the accused to take the stand and, if he chooses, to confine his testimony to those portions of the case that can not be weakened or destroyed by cross-examination. Because he does not (under this proposal) forfeit fifth amendment protection as to those points not addressed in his direct testimony,[1] he insulates himself from cross-examination upon them. Presumably, he also can get an instruction that no adverse inferences may be drawn from his election to testify only as to part of the case. The argument supporting this instruction would be that the accused

---

96. McCormick, § 132, at 280.

97. Id.

98. The cases leave the extent of the accused's waiver upon taking the stand somewhat in doubt. Johnson v. United States, 318 U.S. 189, 195–96 (1943), stated that the prosecutor could question the accused about matters relevant to the crime charged. Justice Frankfurter later said the accused waives his privilege against self-incrimination to the extent of the rule as to scope of cross-examination. Brown v. United States, 356 U.S. 148 (1958). Still again, the Court re-cently has said that the defendant waives the privilege as to "matters reasonably related to the subject of his direct examination." McGautha v. California, 402 U.S. 183, 215 (1971). See also, United States v. Nobles, 422 U.S. 225, 240 (1975). See generally, C. Wright & A. Miller, Federal Practice and Procedure, § 407, at 103–04 (1969).

99. McCormick, § 132, at 281.

1. This statement assumes that fair testing of the direct testimony can be had without probing these other parts of the case.

who gives limited testimony should not be disadvantaged when compared with the accused who wholly declines to take the stand; in neither instance should a penalty attach to the exercise of a fifth amendment right. Whether these consequences accommodate the interests of both the government and the accused raises difficult questions about the values served by the privilege. Whatever the answer to this constitutional issue, however, it does seem clear that the extent of waiver should not be determined by the housekeeping rule that normally governs the scope of cross-examination.

The waiver doctrines applicable to the ordinary witness necessarily differ from those applicable to the accused. A witness compelled to take the stand and testify may invoke the fifth amendment selectively, declining to answer questions that require an incriminating response. If he does not claim his privilege, but rather knowingly elects to give an incriminating answer, he waives the privilege for that response. Further, once such a waiver occurs, the interrogator may be able to force disclosure of additional details or closely related information. The test appears to be whether further revelation significantly would add to the risk of prosecution. In a leading case, Rogers v. United States,[2] the witness voluntarily testified that, as an officer of the Communist Party, she once had possession of membership lists and party books. Claiming her fifth amendment privilege, she then declined to name the person to whom she had transferred these materials. The privilege was held unavailable: disclosure of her successor's identity posed no risk to her of incrimination beyond the information already revealed.

Two aspects of waiver apply uniformly to the accused and the ordinary witness. First, in jurisdictions that permit the cross-examiner to impeach a witness by inquiring into prior "bad acts"—incidents that cast doubt on credibility but that have not been the subject of a conviction[3]—it is settled that as to these acts the privilege against self-incrimination is not waived by the act of testifying.[4] The second aspect of waiver common to the

---

2. 340 U.S. 367 (1951).

3. See Ch. VIII, § 81(2).

4. As to the ordinary witness, there is no basis upon which to conclude a waiver has occurred But where

accused and an ordinary witness is the extent to which a waiver survives the proceeding in which it was given and operates to forfeit the privilege in a later inquiry. In general, the courts have rejected the extreme notions, on the one hand, of a permanent waiver applying to any subsequent proceeding and, on the other, a waiver applying only to the examination in which it occurs. As a starting point (subject to refinement), a waiver normally operates for the entire trial or other proceeding in which it was rendered.[5] At least one court has varied from this traditional position: in Ellis v. United States [6] the United States Court of Appeals for the District of Columbia ruled that a *nonindicted* witness voluntarily testifying to incriminating matter before a grand jury may not invoke the privilege to avoid a second disclosure at a criminal trial following the grand jury's indictment of other persons. Among other reasons advanced in support of the holding, the court suggested that the trial testimony did not substantially raise the risk of prosecution so long as the witness was not compelled to disclose incriminating matters that were unknown to the government.[7] Because the government obviously had access to the grand jury testimony, the compelled trial testimony posed little or no danger of additional incriminating matter.

---

the accused elects to take the stand, it has been argued that he forfeits protection from questions designed to test credibility. Wisely, the courts have rejected this argument, favoring instead the right of the accused to testify regarding the crime charged without the penalty of forced incriminations regarding separate events. See Coil v. United States, 343 F.2d 573 (8th Cir. 1965), cert. denied 382 U.S. 821; Fed.R.Evid. 608(b); McCormick, § 42, at 84.

5. McCormick, § 132, at 281.

6. 416 F.2d 791 (D.C.Cir. 1969).

7. The *Ellis* opinion in part is supported by cited passages from Professor McCormick. Interestingly, the second edition of McCormick on Evidence is critical of the decision. See McCormick, § 140, at 298–99. See also Saltzburg, Another Ground for Decision—Harmless Trial Court Errors, 47 Temple L.Q. 193, 221 (1974). The several arguments advanced in the *Ellis* opinion are (1) no additional danger of incrimination; (2) the government may have decided to prosecute on the basis of the witness's apparent willingness to testify; and (3) the privilege serves no useful function once it is voluntarily waived and possibly incriminating testimony is given. For a rebuttal, see supra McCormick.

§ 93. The Privilege Against Self-Incrimination: Special Application in Situations of Custodial Interrogation

Among the recurring constitutional issues before the Supreme Court, few surpass in importance or frequency of presentation the question of what protections should surround a criminal defendant's out-of-court admission or confession to police or other investigatory officials. Generally, "confession" means an admission of guilt, including details of the accused's perpetration of the crime in question, while "admission" denotes an inculpatory statement which falls short of a complete acknowledgment of guilt. The difference is unimportant in the present context, and the terms will be used interchangeably. Preliminarily, recall that the hearsay rule does not forbid the evidentiary use of the accused's extra-judicial inculpatory statements because such remarks constitute party admissions and as such are admitted into evidence either as an exception to the hearsay rule or, under the Federal Rules of Evidence, as nonhearsay. But the constitutional inquiry implicates other concerns, e. g., the guarantees of due process, the right to counsel,[8] and most importantly for our purposes, the prohibition against self-incrimination. This constitutional analysis usually is pursued in texts and courses devoted to criminal procedure or constitutional law. Consequently, what follows should be considered either a brief reminder or a bare introduction to a complex subject.

The judicial approach regarding the constitutional requirements governing criminal confessions initially developed along two lines: one based on the Supreme Court's review of confessions admitted in state criminal trials and the other based on the Court's review of confessions received in federal prosecutions. The differences in the Court's responses are now largely a matter of history, except for the enduring distinction that within the federal system the Supreme Court exercises an appellate supervisory power over lower federal courts and, by virtue of its place atop the national judicial hierarchy, may prescribe proce-

---

8. Miranda v. Arizona, 384 U.S. 436 (1966); Escobedo v Illinois, 378 U.S. 478 (1964). See generally McCormick §§ 130, 151–54. See also Id. at § 145 where the author raises doubts about classifying a confession as a party admission.

dural rules and standards that govern federal proceedings.[9] Because the Constitution does not command these rules, they are not binding upon the states. By contrast, the constitutional standards presently governing the admissibility of confessions in federal and state proceedings are uniform. For example, the incorporation of the fifth amendment privilege against self-incrimination into the fourtenth amendment in 1964 [10] makes the privilege directly applicable to the states and provides a single constitutional standard for the national and state sovereignties. The evolution of this standard is a fascinating chapter in constitutional history, the final pages of which are yet to be written by the United States Supreme Court.

In Brown v. Mississippi,[11] decided in 1936, the Supreme Court overturned, for the first time, a state conviction based upon an involuntary confession. It had been obtained after police had severly beaten the accused.[12] Decided almost thirty years before the incorporation of the fifth amendment privilege into the fourteenth, the Court based its holding on the due process clause of

---

9. In McNabb v. United States, 318 U.S. 332 (1942), the Court, citing a federal statute that entitled an arrested person to be brought before a judicial officer, held inadmissible statements obtained by federal agents during a period of unnecessary delay before presenting the suspect to a magistrate. This judicial officer performs such functions as advising the arrestee of his rights, inquiring into the need for a preliminary hearing, and setting bail. Later, in Mallory v. United States, 354 U.S. 449 (1957), the Court made it clear that a delay for *purposes of interrogation* was "unnecessary" within the meaning of Rule 5(a) of the Federal Rules of Criminal Procedure which, like the statute in *McNabb*, called for presentation without unnecessary delay. The so-called *McNabb-Mallory* Rule operated within the federal system and re-sulted in excluding statements obtained during the forbidden period of delay. In 1968 Congress intervened and prescribed that statements made within six hours of arrest should not be excluded on the sole ground of delay in bringing the arrestee before a judicial officer. See Title II of the Omnibus Crime Control and Safe Streets Act of 1968, 18 U.S.C.A. § 3501(c). Statements made after the six-hour period may also be admissible if the delay in presentation was reasonable. Id.

10. Malloy v. Hogan, 378 U.S. 1 (1964).

11. 297 U.S. 278 (1936).

12. The Court stated that the privilege against self-incrimination was not at issue in its holding. 297 U. S. at 285.

the fourteenth amendment. This clause was read as prohibiting state courts from basing a conviction upon evidence procured by state authorities through coercion.[13] The court's ruling was narrow, covering only the situation where physical abuse produced an involuntary confession of doubtful reliability that constituted the *sole* evidence of guilt. But subsequent rulings made it clear that coerced confessions would not be tolerated even where there was other evidence of guilt,[14] where coercion took a subtle form such as psychological pressure,[15] or where promises of favored treatment were given in return for a confession.[16] These post-*Brown* cases stressed that the probable unreliability of a coerced confession was not the only basis for its exclusion; other bases included the Court's unwillingness to tolerate improper police practices, its view that tactics designed to produce self-incrimination were incompatible with the Anglo-American adversarial system, and its desire to protect the values underlying the fifth amendment.[17] Thus the policies and values thought to underlie the fifth amendment privilege against self-incrimination greatly influenced the Court's determination of when activity by state—and for that matter federal—officials resulted in a violation of due process.[18]

---

13. Id. at 286.

14. Payne v. Arkansas, 356 U.S. 560 (1958).

15. Ashcraft v. Tennessee, 322 U.S. 143 (1944) (sustained interrogation over thirty-six hour period); see also Haynes v. Washington, 373 U.S. 503 (1963) (threat of continued incommunicado detention); Rogers v. Richmond, 365 U.S. 534 (1961) (police tell suspect his ill wife has been arrested for questioning).

16. See, e. g., Lynumn v. Illinois, 372 U.S. 528 (1963) (promise that cooperation would mean easier treatment coupled with threat that failure to comply would mean that conviction would result in loss of children). McCormick notes inconsistent results in cases where promises have been made. See McCormick, § 150, at 322–24.

17. See Blackburn v. Alabama, 361 U.S. 199 (1960); McCormick, § 148, at 315–316.

18. Recall that the fifth amendment privilege against self-incrimination had no direct applicability to the states until the decision in Malloy v. Hogan, 378 U.S. 1 (1964). See supra text at note 10. Until *Malloy* and subsequent cases, it was thought that the use of confessions in federal cases was governed by the due process clause of the fifth amendment. And that the existence of coercion was determined by assessing the same factors cited in reviewing state cases under the fourteenth amendment—although

Brown and its progeny required that a court determine the voluntariness of a confession, and thus its admissibility and use, by assessing all of the circumstances that attended the rendering of the confession. This "totality-of-the-circumstances" test took account of such variables as physical abuse, psychological pressures generated by substantial questioning or incommunicado detention, police artifice, the age and experience of the suspect, whether he had been advised of his right to remain silent, and whether he had been accorded a prompt hearing before a magistrate or other judicial officer.[19] Imprecision necessarily attended assessment of these and other variables, and the test predictably produced uncertainty and conflict among lower courts. It was not uncommon to find disagreement between state and federal judges reviewing the same confession, or between federal judges themselves.[20] Even the Supreme Court varied its inquiry, scrutinizing each of the circumstances in some cases,[21] while in others pronouncing the circumstances "inherently coercive" without undertaking any inquiry into the effect of each separate pressure upon the subject.[22]

Despite the vicissitudes of the totality-of-circumstances test, the cases decided by the Court kept moving toward more rigor-

---

the federal standard may have been more stringent. But in *Malloy*, the Court, citing Bram v. United States, 168 U.S. 532 (1897), declared that the federal standard was based upon the self-incrimination clause of the fifth amendment. Malloy v. Hogan, supra at 7. Henceforth, a single standard based upon the self-incrimination clause was to govern the courts of both sovereigns.

19. McCormick, § 149, at 318–319.

20. A case in point is Davis v. North Carolina, 384 U.S. 737 (1966). After Davis was convicted in the state trial court, he initiated appellate proceedings within the state system, where evidentiary admission of his admission was sus-

tained. See Davis v. North Carolina, 253 N.C. 86, 116 S.E.2d 365 (1960). Subsequently, Davis brought a collateral attack by filing a petition for habeas corpus in a federal district court. The use of the challenged confession was approved by the district court, 221 F.Supp. 494 (E.D.N.C.1963) and by a split court of appeals, 339 F.2d 770 (4th Cir. 1964), but the Supreme Court reversed. Davis v. North Carolina, supra.

21. See, e. g., Greenwald v. Wisconsin, 390 U.S. 519 (1968); Lynumn v. Illinois, 372 U.S. 528 (1963).

22. See Haynes v. Washington, 373 U.S. 503 (1963); Ashcraft v. Tennessee, 322 U.S. 143 (1944); McCormick, § 149, at 317–21.

ous control of state police and judicial practices.[23] In other areas of criminal procedure, the Court complemented this trend by ordering the states to exclude evidence derived from unlawful searches [24] and increasing its emphasis upon the accused's right to counsel.[25] The right to counsel was extended to pre-trial events (such as arraignment and pleading) whenever these events constituted a "critical stage" [26] in the criminal process. In one notable decision, Escobedo v. Illinois,[27] the court appeared to be edging toward a right to counsel during police interrogation. A divided court held that where a police investigation

> is no longer a general inquiry into an unsolved crime but has begun to focus on a particular suspect, the suspect has been taken into police custody, the police carry out a process of interrogations that lends itself to eliciting incriminating statements, the suspect has requested and been denied an opportunity to consult with his lawyer, and the police have not effectively warned him of his absolute constitutional right to remain silent, the accused has been denied "the Assistance of Counsel" in violation of the Sixth Amendment to the Constitution as "made obligatory upon the States by the Fourteenth Amendment" . . . and that no statement elicited by police during the interrogation may be used against him at a criminal trial.[28]

23. Compare, e. g., Brown v. Mississippi, 297 U.S. 278 (1936), with Haynes v. Washington, 373 U.S. 503 (1963).

24. Mapp v. Ohio, 367 U.S. 643 (1961).

25. Gideon v. Wainwright, 372 U.S. 335 (1963) (right to appointed counsel at trial of indigents in all serious cases); Douglas v. California, 372 U.S. 353 (1963) (right to appointed counsel exists through the first appeal of right).

26. See White v. Maryland, 373 U.S. 59 (1963) (initial appearance before judicial officer is critical when accused must enter plea and adverse effects flow from his election of plea); Hamilton v. Alabama, 368 U.S. 52 (1961) (arraignment is critical stage when certain defenses are lost if not raised during this procedure). The Court has subsequently characterized certain post-trial procedures as critical. See, e. g., Mempa v. Rhay, 389 U.S. 128 (1968) (probation revocation critical when this proceeding includes sentencing).

27. 378 U.S. 478 (1964).

28. Id. at 490–91.

Thus, pre-trial interrogation became a point of confluence where important rights, derived from several parts of the Constitution, merged to restrict police practices. *Escobedo* suggested the possibility that the right to counsel during interrogation would emerge in a future case as the most significant constitutional principle governing confessions.

That case turned out to be Miranda v. Arizona,[29] regarded as one of the most significant cases decided by the Supreme Court during this century. In *Miranda,* the Court abandoned the totality-of-circumstances test and set out specific procedural steps for all custodial interrogations.[30] Relying primarily upon the Fifth amendment right not to incriminate oneself (by then made directly applicable to the states through the Fourteenth amendment),[31] the Court found that, absent a waiver, the assistance of counsel during interrogation was necessary to vindicate this right. Then, in an unusual technique of constitutional adjudication, the Court prescribed an elaborate set of rules to govern interrogation by police when the suspect is "in custody . . . or otherwise deprived of his freedom of action in any significant way": [32]

> 1. Before questioning begins, the suspect must be clearly advised of his right to remain silent and he must be warned that anything he says can be used against him in court.
>
> 2. The suspect also must be told, prior to questioning, that he has the right to a lawyer's assistance before and during interrogation and that a lawyer will be appointed to assist him if he cannot afford to retain one.

---

29. 384 U.S. 436 (1966). For the British approach to the same problem, see Justice (British Section of the International Commission of Jurists), The Interrogation of Suspects (1967).

30. In Johnson v. New Jersey, 384 U.S. 719 (1966), the Court held that *Miranda* (as well as *Escobedo*) applied only to those cases coming to trial after the Court's decision.

31. Malloy v. Hogan, 378 U.S. 1 (1964).

32. Miranda v. Arizona, 384 U.S. 436, 478 (1966).

3. The suspect may exercise his right to remain silent or to engage counsel at any time prior to or during interrogation. If the suspect indicates that he wishes to remain silent, there can be no interrogation; if interrogation is in progress when he manifests his desire to remain silent, questioning must cease. Similarly, if the suspect indicates that he wants an attorney, there can be no further questioning until an attorney is present.

4. Unless the suspect is expressly and fully warned of his rights to silence and counsel and there is compliance with his decision, then no statement given by him can be used at trial to establish his guilt.

The Court declared that when a suspect makes an inculpatory statement in the absence of an attorney, "a heavy burden rests on the government to demonstrate that the defendant knowingly and intelligently waived his privilege against self-incrimination and his right to retained or appointed counsel." [33] Despite this seemingly direct language, lower courts have tended to find a waiver if the suspect makes statements after the police give the required warning.[34]

The *Miranda* opinion touched off a heated debate that continues today. Critics of the decision argue that it unnecessarily impedes law enforcement; proponents assert that the protective steps mandated by the Court are necessary to protect fundamental rights. Congress reacted by passing a statute that applies to the federal courts and purports to negate the *Miranda* ruling that proper warnings are prerequisites to admissibility.[35] Under the statutory approach, which reinstates a totality-of-circumstances test, a confession is admissible if voluntary. Failure of the police to warn the defendant of his rights or the absence of counsel during questioning are circumstances to be considered in

---

33. Id. at 475.

34. See, e. g., United States v. Pheaster, 544 F.2d 353, 368 (9th Cir. 1976). But see Brewer v. Williams, 430 U.S. 387, 401–06 (1977)

(finding no waiver under sixth amendment).

35. Omnibus Crime Control and Safe Streets Act of 1968, 18 U.S.C. A. § 3501.

determining voluntariness, but need not be conclusive. The constitutionality of the statute is doubtful.[36] Even though the *Miranda* court did leave the way open for Congress or the states to devise alternative means of protecting the custodial rights of the accused, it is difficult to read the *Miranda* opinion as sanctioning a return to the uncertain protection of the indefinite "totality" approach.

This is not to suggest the inviolability of the *Miranda* decision. The Supreme Court, reflecting the views of a changing membership,[37] already has restricted the reach of *Miranda*. In Harris v. New York,[38] the court held that statements made under circumstances violative of *Miranda* nonetheless could be used *to impeach the defendant* when he took the stand and gave testimony inconsistent with his earlier in-custody statements to police. The Court, four justices dissenting, distinguished *Miranda* on the ground that in that case the statements had been used by the state to establish guilt.[39] Ascribing to *Miranda* a primary purpose of preventing improper police conduct, the majority concluded that the *Miranda* rules had a sufficient deterrent effect on proscribed activity if tainted statements offered to establish guilt were excluded. To apply *Miranda* to evidence used to impeach credibility would allow perjurious testimony to go unchallenged because of improper investigatory procedures.[40]

---

36. Because federal authorities routinely give the warnings required by *Miranda*, the Supreme Court has not yet passed upon the constitutionality of the statute.

37. Of the nine justices presently composing the Court, only four participated in the *Miranda* decision; of these four, two dissented.

38. 401 U.S. 222 (1971).

39. 401 U.S. at 224–25. The controlling precedent was found to be Walder v. United States, 347 U.S. 62 (1954), a case in which the Court approved impeaching questions about a heroin capsule that had been illegally seized in connection with a narcotics offense other than the one charged. The government was seeking to impeach Walder's assertion, made during his direct examination, that he never in his life handled narcotics. For criticism of the Court's approach in *Harris*, see Dershowitz & Ely, Harris v. New York: Some Anxious Observations on the Candor and Logic of the Emerging Nixon Majority, 80 Yale L.J. 1198 (1971).

40. 401 U.S. at 225–26. But cf. Doyle v. Ohio, 426 U.S. 610 (1976) (barring use of silence by accused to impeach).

Issues still remain in applying *Miranda*, including (1) whether *Miranda* warnings must be given in cases of minor offenses [41] or to persons called to testify in grand jury proceedings;[42] (2) determining the point at which a suspect is "in custody" or otherwise restrained so that the *Miranda* rules become operative; [43] and, assuming custody exists (3) whether police activity such as confronting the suspect with physical evidence against him or with an adverse witness constitutes interrogation forbidden by *Miranda*.[44] Questions also exist as to when a waiver is effective, particularly when the waiver takes place after counsel's appointment, but in his absence.[45] While resolution of these problems, as well as others that might be posed, could restrict the scope of *Miranda*, these difficulties are not central to the current debate. The fundamental question is whether the *Miranda* ruling should be abandoned in favor of other protective measures. Curiously, those prosecutors, police, and other enforcement officials who voice the greatest dissatisfaction with *Miranda* should be its most forceful proponents because this decision adds certainty to the process of interrogation. If *Miranda* is followed—and adherence is comparatively easy—then statements secured from the accused are likely to be admissible in evidence.[46] Because there

---

41. Compare State v. Bliss, 238 A.2d 848 (Del.1968) and State v. Zucconi, 93 N.J.Super. 380, 226 A.2d 16 (1967) with Campbell v. Superior Ct., 106 Ariz. 542, 479 P.2d 685 (1971).

42. See, e. g., United States v. Wong, 431 U.S. 179 (1977); United States v. Mandujano, 425 U.S. 564 (1976).

43. McCormick, § 152, at 328–32. Cf. Beckwith v. United States, 425 U.S. 341 (1976) (questioning by I. R.S. not custodial).

44. Combs v. Commonwealth, 438 S. W.2d 82 (Ky.1969) (accused confronted with ballistics report, confession admissible because first in-formed of rights); McCormick, § 152, at 329–30.

45. See generally Brewer v. Williams, 430 U.S. 387, 401–403, 405, 406 (1977).

46. It is possible, but unlikely, that *Miranda* could be followed and yet, under all of the circumstances, a confession would be characterized as involuntary under the "totality" test. The likelihood of this occurrence is lessened by the clear admonition in the Court's *Miranda* opinion that a suspect always can change his mind and, after making some statements or waiving his right to counsel, reclaim his rights to silence and (or) the assistance of a lawyer. See Miranda v. Arizona, 384 U.S. 436, 475–76 (1966).

is yet no indication that *Miranda* procedures have diminished the number of confessions,[47] law enforcement officials perhaps are the ultimate beneficiaries of this landmark case.

NOTES

1. *Physician-Patient Privilege.* There are additional evidentiary privileges not treated in this chapter. Jurisdictional variations in the recognition and scope of these privileges make it essential that the practitioner avoid the assumption that a privilege long recognized in his state similarly applies in a sister state. The statutes must be carefully researched. Many jurisdictions, for example, have passed statutes protecting communications between patient and physician if the statements were reasonably necessary to enable the physician to render treatment. But this privilege does not receive universal recognition, and among jurisdictions according the privilege there are substantial variations in applicability and waiver. Typically, the privilege is confined to civil proceedings where public interest in full disclosure is not as great as in criminal trials. But even in the civil context, the privilege often is inapplicable where a court or public officer engages a doctor to conduct an examination; nor does it usually apply where the patient, who is the holder, puts his own physical condition in issue—as, for example, where he claims personal injuries. Under some of the statutes, a judge may negate the privilege when, in his judgment, the interest of justice so requires. See Va.Code Ann. § 8.-01–399. For a thorough and thoughtful discussion of the physician-patient privilege, see McCormick, §§ 98–105.

Should there be a separate privilege applicable to communications between psychotherapist and patient? The same rationale that supports the physician-patient privilege, the encouragement of the patient to reveal his condition, also serves as a justification for the psychotherapist-patient privilege. In the case of the psychotherapist, effective treatment in most cases largely depends upon the patient's willingness to talk freely. Thus, the need to ensure confidentiality is even more important. See Adv.Comm. Note to Prop.Fed.R.Evid. 504 (quoting Rept.No. 45, Group for the Advancement of Psychiatry 92 (1960)) and Slovenko, Psychiatry and a Second Look at the Medical Privilege, 6 Wayne L.Rev. 175 (1960). Accordingly, while some jurisdictions simply extend the physician-patient privilege to include psychotherapists, others have special provisions for the psychotherapist-patient privilege. See, e. g., Conn.Gen.Stat. § 52–146a (1966 Supp.). Note

---

47. Interrogations in New Haven: The Impact of *Miranda*, 76 Yale L.J. 1519, 1563–67, 1613 (1967).

that the proposed Federal Rules would have granted a privilege for psychotherapist-patient communications but not for physicians. Prop. Fed.R.Evid. 504. The drafters felt that most states that have the latter privilege have so riddled it with exceptions as to leave little, if any, basis for it. Adv.Comm. Note to Proposed Fed.R.Evid. 504. Suppose in the course of treatment the therapist learns that the patient has committed criminal offenses and is likely to repeat this conduct. What is the appropriate course of action? See generally Tarasoff v. Regents of University of California, 13 Cal.3d 177, 529 P.2d 553 (1974).

2. *Priest-Penitent Privilege.* A vast majority of the states recognize a clergyman-penitent privilege that shields statements made to a clergyman in his religious office. VIII Wigmore § 2395 (McNaughton). Again, however, care must be exercised in defining the limits of the privilege. Note that this privilege has no constitutional support. See In Re Moren, 564 F.2d 567 (D.C.C., 1977). Some statutes follow the pattern of Rule 29 of the 1953 Uniform Rules of Evidence and limit the privilege to statements that are the outgrowth of "enjoined religious discipline." McCormick notes, however, that more recent enactments protect against any disclosure that "would violate a sacred or moral trust." McCormick, § 77, at 158. See Unif.R.Evid. 505 (1974); Prop.Fed.R.Evid. 506.

3. *Journalist-Source Privilege.* A number of state legislatures have decided that confidential relationships between a journalist and his source should be protected. The result has been the passage of "shield laws" that vary from jurisdiction to jurisdiction but, basically, provide the newsman with immunity from forced disclosure of the identify of his source. See, e. g., West's Ann.Calif.Evid. Code § 1070. See generally Branzburg v. Hayes, 408 U.S. 665 (1972). The student might ask whether these statutes also should protect unpublished information obtained in confidence. Should the privilege belong to the reporter or to his informant, or both? Typically the journalist is the holder and thus can waive the privilege. Does the public interest in being informed by the press require that a reporter be prohibited from waiving his privilege without the consent of the informant?

4. *State Secrets.* The federal government is entitled to prevent the disclosure of military or state secrets if it can demonstrate a reasonable likelihood of danger to national security or of injury to international relations. This privilege is recognized in the leading case of United States v. Reynolds, 345 U.S. 1 (1953), where the Supreme Court considered, among other things, the kind of showing the government must make to invoke the privilege and the question of which governmental official should make this showing. Drawing on English and American precedents, the Court found the existence of the privilege in no doubt and went on to declare that the claim to privilege

should be advanced by the governmental department-head who had responsibility for the matter in question. The governmental officer must give the matter his "actual personal consideration," thereby assuring that the privilege will not be lightly invoked.

Once the privilege is claimed, the judge "must determine whether the circumstances are appropriate for the claim of privilege, and yet do so without forcing a disclosure of the very thing the privilege is designed to protect." 345 U.S. 1 at 7–8. The Court thought that the judge's role in resolving a claim to the privilege against self-incrimination provided a helpful analogy. In many cases the attending circumstances, including the statement of the department head, will indicate that exposure of the evidence in question poses a reasonable likelihood of danger to national interests. In such instances, the judge should not order an *in camera* examination. The Court, however, left open the possibility of inspection of the disputed evidence by the judge and also noted that the extensiveness of his probe would be influenced by the degree of need shown by the party seeking the evidence. In cases of high necessity, the judge should take extensive steps, if needed, to make certain the privilege applies. See also Prop.Fed.R.Evid. 509. For an analogous state statute, see West's Ann.Cal.Evid. Code § 1040. See also VIII Wigmore § 2378 (McNaughton).

Suppose an appropriate governmental unit resisting evidence makes a convincing showing of necessity so that the privilege clearly applies. If the government is a party to the action in which it invokes the privilege, may the judge take steps (such as striking a witness's testimony or finding against the government as to certain facts) to counterbalance the disadvantage suffered by the adverse party through loss of the privileged evidence? Clearly, strict measures, extending as far as dismissal, can be applied where the government invokes a claim of privilege in a criminal action in which it is the prosecuting party. Compensatory measures in civil cases also are appropriate where the government is a party and invokes the privilege, thereby denying the adversary access to material evidence. See McCormick, § 109, at 234. In a civil case, what difference, if any, does it make whether the government is a plaintiff or a defendant?

5. *Executive Privilege.* A privilege that has received an unusual degree of scholarly and judicial attention in recent years is that accorded the President to protect high-level communications in the Executive Department. The justification for the privilege rests upon the need to ensure frank expression and discussion among persons responsible for executive decisions. The separation of powers mandate raises concerns about the extent to which the judicial branch may probe the content of executive communications in order to ascertain if the claim to privilege is well taken. A related question is whether the privilege itself is absolute or whether it must give way where compet-

ing considerations are very strong. Recent scandals in the executive branch generated litigation over the existence and scope of executive privilege, culminating in *Nixon v. United States*, 418 U.S 683 (1974). The Supreme Court there found that the interests of accused Watergate conspirators in marshalling evidence in their defense outweighed the President's claim of privilege. Id. at 713. Litigants seeking governmental information should not overlook the Freedom of Information Act, 5 U.S.C.A. § 552, which provides that "any person" may request and obtain agency records covered by the Act. If necessary, the person seeking information may file a complaint in the federal district court and compel the agency to comply with the Act.

6. *Informer's Identity.* Both the federal and state governments often protect informers' information about criminal activity. This source would "dry up" if there were not some protection against disclosure of the names of the individuals supplying the information. The privilege not to disclose has several important exceptions, including one that applies when the informer's testimony is important to the accused in presenting his defense. See Roviaro v. United States, 353 U.S. 53 (1957). For a discussion of the privilege of national and state governments to refuse to name an informant, see Waltz, Criminal Evidence 258–266 (1975). See also McCormick, § 111, at 236–238 (1972).

CHAPTER X

THE ROLE OF JUDGE AND JURY:
A SUMMARY

§ 94. The Kinds of Factual Determinations Made by the Judge: In General

The allocation of function between judge and jury, as we have observed elsewhere,[1] cannot be dismissed with the generalization that the jury decides questions of fact and the judge decides questions of law. An irregular line drawn in light of historical judgments of each participant's particular strengths, divides the roles of these participants in the litigation process.

In the course of trial, the judge must make a variety of factual determinations regarding both the evidence as a whole and individual offers of proof. Different situations require the judge to apply dissimilar standards in these determinations, and in turn the judge's factual determinations have varying effects on the jury's role as the principal arbiter of factual questions. We already have encountered numerous instances in which the complementary roles of judge and jury were brought into clear relief: [2] Although the jury generally decides historic or adjudicative facts from the evidence as a whole, the judge first must determine whether the total evidence is *sufficient* to permit a reasonable jury to decide for either party; if a rational jury could reach but one conclusion, the judge directs a verdict.[3] Individual offers of proof place the judge in a different role. When proffered evidence is challenged as irrelevant he must determine whether, if believed by the jury, the evidence could increase the likelihood of a consequential factual proposition. But this role may be complicated by problems of conditional relevance: if evidence tends to show that X made certain representations that are relevant (consequential) only if X were acting as the defend-

---

1. Ch. 1, § 6.

2. See, e. g., Ch. I, § 6; Ch. II, §§ 10, 14; Ch. III, § 15; Ch. VII, § 56; note 2 at the conclusion of

Part B; §§ 72, 76; Ch. IX, text at note 73. See also note 2 at the conclusion of Ch. II.

3. Ch. III, § 15.

ant's agent, the judge must decide[4] whether there is sufficient evidence of the conditioning fact (the agency relationship) to permit a reasonable jury to find that the relation existed at the time X made the relevant statement. The jury, however, makes the final decision as to whether the relation did exist.

Distinctly different problems are encountered where the judge's ruling upon the application of a technical, exclusionary rule of evidence depends on the existence or nonexistence of certain facts:[5] a witness offered for the purpose of giving expert testimony is competent only if he has the requisite training or experience; a copy of a document offered to establish its terms is admissible only if the original is not available; an excited utterance is admissible as an exception to the hearsay rule only if the declarant spoke with the requisite mental state; a communication is privileged only if confidentiality was intended and the communication was between persons entitled to a privilege. In situations like these, the judge normally determines the existence of disputed facts upon which hinge the applicability of an exclusionary rule; furthermore he usually makes the *final decision* as to the existence of such preliminary facts, precluding any subsequent inquiry by the jury.

These varying roles of the judge in the factfinding process are grounded in a recognition of the judge's expertise and in the practical limitations of a lay jury's ability to deal with complex factual questions that interface with technical legal rules. In the following sections, we shall assess in detail the roles of judge and jury in dealing with questions of fact.

§ 95. The Judge's Role in Evaluating the Evidence as a Whole

When the judge determines whether the evidence *as a whole* justifies sending the case to the jury, his standard is whether or not the jury reasonably could find for *either* of the contending parties (put otherwise, whether the evidence favoring either party, if believed by the jury would justify its verdict for that

---

4. Ch. II, § 14.

5. See McCormick, § 53; Morgan at 40–45; note 2 at the conclusion of Ch. II.

party). If the evidence reasonably could lead to but one controlling factual conclusion, there is no role for the jury: its function is confined to the resolution of matters that *reasonably* are disputed. It follows that the party with the burden of persuasion —usually the plaintiff [6]—can place his case before the jury only if the evidence, taken as a whole, in support of his position justifies a finding in his favor by a preponderance of the evidence (or by whatever standard of proof is applicable). If the evidence is insufficient to justify such a finding, the judge should direct a verdict for the defendant. Similarly, if the plaintiff's evidence [7] is so convincing that no reasonable jury could find against him, the judge should direct a verdict in his favor.

Note that in administering the test for sufficiency, the judge prescribes only the outer limits of permissible jury action. Within its appropriate sphere of authority, the jury is empowered to make its own determination, finding only such facts as it chooses to believe exist. In sending a case to the jury for resolution, the judge leaves the jury free to evaluate any and all of the evidence before it. [8] Thus, even though the evidence supporting the plaintiff may be sufficient—*if believed and if accorded favorable inferences*—to justify a plaintiff's verdict, the jury is entitled to disbelieve the evidence or to decline to draw the possible inferences from it.

---

6. Sometimes, of course, the defendant bears the burden of persuasion as, for example, with affirmative defenses. See Ch. III, § 15. The prosecutor in a criminal case must establish the elements of the charged offense beyond a reasonable doubt and there can be no directed verdict in his favor. Id. at §§ 15, 16.

7. In some circumstances, the evidence favoring the party with the burden of persuasion may be so compelling that a reasonable jury could find only the existence of facts favoring the burdened party.

Real (including documentary) evidence is often helpful in establishing such a strong case.

8. The jury also has a second function in many cases: it characterizes the facts it chooses to believe in accordance with the controlling rule of substantive law. For example, in an action based upon negligence, the jury decides not only what the defendant did (i. e. his conduct) but also whether the defendant's action should be characterized as negligent. See Ch. 1, § 6.

§ 96. The Judge's Factual Determinations Regarding Individual Offers of Proof

In making a relevance determination after objection to a partic-ular offer of proof, the judge must scrutinize the proffered evi-dence and the proposition to which it is directed. The test of relevance, of course, is whether the proffered evidence tends to make the existence of a consequential proposition more probable than that proposition would be without the evidence.[9] If the judge finds that the proffered evidence could add to the likeli-hood of a consequential fact, he admits it (assuming it otherwise is not objectionable), but he leaves to the jury the final evalua-tion of that evidence. As we have seen, the jury is free to find the evidence false or discount it as being of little or no help in establishing the proposition it supports.

While the relevancy test applies to each proffered item of evidence, the more stringent sufficiency test applies only to certain offers of evidence.[10] Such offers occur when the rele-vance of proffered evidence is dependent upon the existence of a conditioning fact. Without the existence of the fact upon which relevance is conditioned, the proffered evidence is of no conse-quence in the case. Suppose, for example, that in a suit for breach of contract for sale of goods the plaintiff claims that X, as agent for the defendant, made certain representations warranting the quality of the goods. The defendant denies both the representa-tions and the agency of X. In an effort to prove the representa-tions, the plaintiff offers witnesses A, B, and C who will testify that X made similar representations of warranty to them re-garding the goods. This evidence passes the simple test of rele-vance: it tends to increase the probability that such representa-tions also were made to the plaintiff—and thus to support this *apparently* consequential proposition. But close observation re-veals that the relevance (or, strictly speaking, the consequential-ness or materiality)[11] of this evidence is conditioned upon a pre-

---

9. Ch. 2, § 10.

10. Ch. 2, § 14.

11. Materiality deals with whether a factual proposition has any legal

significance or, in the language of the Federal Rules, is "of conse-quence." See Ch. II, § 8.

liminary factual finding that X was acting as the defendant's agent, because (we assume) the defendant can not be held liable for the representations of a person not its agent. Thus, the plaintiff's use of evidence of X's representations depends upon his establishing the conditioning (or allied) fact that X was acting as defendant's agent. Other examples of conditional relevance are provided elsewhere.[12]

In situations involving conditional relevance, proper use of the proffered evidence depends upon the jury's finding of the existence of the allied (conditioning) fact upon which relevancy is premised. Therefore, in admitting the conditioned evidence the judge determines only that there is *sufficient* evidence of the allied or conditioning fact to permit a reasonable jury to find its existence.[13] The judge does *not make* a *conclusive* determination; the final responsibility for determining the existence of the conditioning fact is left to the jury.[14] So, in the above example, if the judge finds the evidence sufficient to support a reasonable belief that X was defendant's agent, he should admit the evidence of X's representations to A, B, and C.[15] The jury then should be instructed that if it finds that X was not defendant's agent, it should disregard the evidence of X's representations to others. This procedure should create no difficulty or confusion, because the jury readily can understand that if X was not acting for the defendant, the latter should not be liable for X's representations. It is apparent, of course, that since evidence of the conditioning fact and the evidence based upon it cannot be offered simultaneously, the proponent must choose which evidence to offer first. Although the final decision concerning the order of evidentiary presentation is made by the judge [16] (at least where there is an objection), he usually will

---

12. Ch. 2, § 14.

13. Fed.Rules Evid. 104(b) provides: Relevancy Conditioned on Fact —When the relevancy of evidence depends upon the fulfillment of a condition of fact, the court shall admit it upon, or subject to, the introduction of evidence sufficient to support a finding of the fulfillment of the condition.

14. Morgan at 39–40.

15. But see Ch. II, § 13.

16. Fed. Rules Evid. 104(b). Note that where documents are relevant only if authenticated, authentication is required *before* the document will be admitted. See Ch. XII, § 113.

approve the proponent's choice, provided the latter assures the judge that the "connecting evidence" will be forthcoming.

The judge also applies the sufficiency test in another situation involving an offer of proof. A general rule of evidence requires that a witness have first-hand knowledge of the matter about which he testifies.[17] Usually it is apparent from the witness's testimony that he had the opportunity to observe, and the adversary makes no issue of this point—although, as we have seen, the opponent frequently challenges the *accuracy* of observation. Occasionally, however, an opponent objects that since the witness did not observe the matter about which he testifies, his testimony should be either struck or disallowed. Although the role of the judge in responding to this objection has not often been discussed, the preferable procedure is for the judge to admit the testimony if he finds that the witness could have observed; that is, he need determine only that there is sufficient evidence for the jury reasonably to conclude that the witness has first-hand knowledge.[18] Again it is assumed that the jury can perform its proper role without difficulty. If the jury concludes that the witness did not have first-hand knowledge, it should—and probably will—disregard his testimony.

If the witness purports to be reporting what another person (the declarant) has said, the witness need have first-hand knowledge *only that the statements were made*, as opposed to first-hand knowledge of the events described in the statements. As to whether the absent declarant has first-hand knowledge of the events, the judge must determine from all of the circumstances whether the jury reasonably could find the declarant had an opportunity to observe. The problem of whether the declarant lacked first-hand knowledge usually is confronted after the evidence surmounts the barrier posed by the hearsay rule: ab-

---

17. See Fed.R.Evid. 602: "A witness may not testify as to a matter unless evidence is introduced sufficient to support a finding that he has personal knowledge . . . ." This rule, however, does not render inadmissible a party admission made by a party without personal knowledge of the event or condition about which he speaks. Ch. VII, note 3, at the conclusion of Part B.

18. McCormick, § 10, at 21.

sent an exception, this rule generally precludes evidence of the declarant's statement if offered to prove the truth of its content.[19] If an exception is applicable, the judge still must determine whether there is a reasonable basis for believing that the declarant had first-hand knowledge of the events described in his out-of-court declaration.

§ 97. The Judge's Role in Determining Competence and Applying Technical Exclusionary Rules

The law of evidence consists largely of a complex of rules that protect the integrity of the trial process or that otherwise serve policies that a jury of laymen is unlikely to understand or appreciate. Application of many of these rules turns upon the existence of certain facts. An example is provided by the rule that a witness's competence depends upon his ability to observe, remember, relate, and to appreciate his obligation to speak truthfully.[20] Issues of competence may arise with a very young witness or with one who suffers from a disabling mental defect. Arguably, the jury should make the final determination of competence, for presumably it could discount the witness's testimony in accordance with the disabilities that it concludes exist. Present authority, however, favors a conclusive resolution by the judge: [21] if he makes a negative determination, the testimony of the witness is disallowed, even if a reasonable jury could have believed the testimony. Likewise, the judge makes a conclusive determination when the credentials of a proffered expert witness are challenged.[22] The explanation for this placement of final responsibility in the judge may be that his training and experience enable him to make a more discriminating decision than can a lay jury. Courts also may be apprehensive that the jury would be unable to ignore the testimony of the challenged witness, even if, acting under instructions from the judge, it agreed that he technically was incompetent.[23]

---

19. Ch. VI, §§ 49–50.

20. Ch. IV, § 22.

21. See McCormick, § 53, at 121–122, § 70, at 149–50; Morgan at 41–42 points out some inconsistencies in the cases.

22. McCormick, § 53 at 122. See also Id. § 13, at 30–31.

23. Of course, if the judge finds the witness competent, opposing counsel still may assert (in closing argument) that the testimony was weak

The judge's role in the application of the technical exclusionary rules, such as those governing hearsay or privilege, remains to be considered. Suppose, for example, as to certain testimony a party or witness invokes the privilege for confidential communications between husband and wife; the opponent asserts that the couple was not married at the time of the communication. If this assertion is accurate, no privilege attaches. Assuming the evidence regarding marriage at the time of the communication is conflicting, the judge resolves conflict. Were this factual question allocated to the jury, several difficulties would arise. First, the judge would have to instruct the jury that if they believed the marriage existed at the time of the private communication, they should disregard the privileged statement. Such an instruction would place a difficult burden on the jury, especially if it had to perform a similar function with regard to every disputed fact conditioning a technical exclusionary rule. Second, it is doubtful whether a lay jury would be capable or desirous of ignoring a relevant communication simply because it passed between husband and wife. As McCormick notes, the exclusionary rules often are based upon long-term policies in which the jury has little or no interest.[24] Understandably, it would seem to a lay juror much more important to reach a "correct" verdict than to obey an exclusionary rule that forbids the use of probative evidence.

For these reasons, preliminary questions of fact governing the application of an exclusionary rule (other than relevancy or first-hand knowledge) normally are determined exclusively by the judge. His decision is final and is not subject to reversal by the jury. He decides, for example, if a dying declarant had a sense of impending death,[25] if an entry was made promptly in the normal course of business,[26] if there was the necessary state

---

or unreliable because of extreme youth, mental infirmity, lack of expertise, etc. As with other admitted evidence, the jury decides the degree of belief to which it is entitled.

24. McCormick, § 53, at 121.

25. See, e. g., Soles v. State, 97 Fla. 61, 119 So. 791 (1929).

26. See Eubanks v. Winn, 469 S.W. 2d 292 (Tex.Civ.App.1971).

of excitement to qualify a declaration as an excited utterance,[27] if a witness is unavailable (where unavailability is essential to the application of a hearsay exception),[28] or if an original document is unavailable so as to justify the admission of a copy under the best evidence rule.[29] Furthermore, in making these determinations the judge is "not bound by the rules of evidence except those with respect to privileges." [30]

Even though the judge makes a final determination concerning admissibility, the jury still determines how much, if any, probative value or "weight" to accord to the admitted evidence. Opposing counsel can argue that the evidence should be given little weight, but he may not argue to the jury that the nonexistence of one of the facts conditioning admissibility should preclude entirely the jury's consideration of the evidence. The judge already has made a conclusive determination as to the existence of these conditioning facts. Thus, in the context of one of the foregoing examples, it would be improper for counsel to contend before the jury that they should not even consider evidence of an excited utterance because they should find that it was not made under the influence of excitement or stress. Counsel had the opportunity to press this argument when the judge (usually out of the jury's hearing) was deciding the contested preliminary fact; having lost, he should not be allowed to

27. See, e. g., Wright v. Swann, 261 Or. 440, 493 P.2d 148 (1972).

28. See, e. g., Jackson v. State, 133 Neb. 786, 277 N.W. 92 (1938).

29. See, e. g., United States v. O'Connor, 433 F.2d 752 (1st Cir. 1970). The best evidence rule is discussed in Chapter XIII, § 116. Basically, it imposes upon the party who wishes to prove the terms of a writing the obligation of producing the original writing (if it is available), instead of proving the contents of the document by secondary evidence such as a copy or through oral testimony. See also Fed.R.Evid. 1008 (role of judge and jury as to documents); S. Saltzberg

& K. Redden, Federal Rules of Evidence Manual 700–02 (2d ed. 1977).

30. Fed.R.Evid. 104(a); McCormick, § 53, at 122 n. 91. At least this is the dominant and wiser view. McCormick, § 53, at 122 n. 91. The assumption is that the judge, experienced in the evaluation of evidence and aware of possible evidential infirmities, can properly weigh evidence that under the exclusionary rules would be inadmissible. Furthermore, in some situations practical necessity dictates that the judge consider "inadmissible" evidence. See Adv.Comm. Note to Fed.R.Evid. 104(a).

resurrect this contention. He can, of course, argue to the jury that they should disbelieve the utterance or give it little weight.

§ 98. Factual Determinations Necessary for the Application of an Evidentiary Rule: Special Situations

Several special circumstances introduce qualifications to the foregoing discussion or present situations that place a strain upon the usual distribution of judge-jury functions. In certain instances, a few jurisdictions vary the normal rule governing the allocation of responsibility for factual determinations that attend the application of an exclusionary rule. For example, although it now is settled that the judge determines for purposes of admissibility whether a confession is voluntary [31] (including whether the warnings required by Miranda v. Arizona [32] were given), several jurisdictions permit the jury to make a second determination as to whether a lack of voluntariness should preclude consideration of the confession. In these jurisdictions, the judge, who already has passed on the voluntariness question, instructs the jury that if they find that the confession was not voluntary, they should disregard it altogether. This instruction allows the jury to reject the same evidence that satisfied the judge and permits counsel to argue to the jury that they should find the confession involuntary and hence exclude it entirely from their consideration.[33]

---

31. In Jackson v. Denno, 378 U.S. 368 (1964), the Supreme Court held that a procedure that left to the jury the *sole* responsibility for determining voluntariness (in cases where a reasonable dispute existed) was a violation of the due process clause of the fourteenth amendment because this procedure did not adequately protect the substantive right of the accused not to be convicted on the basis of an involuntary confession.

32. 384 U.S. 436 (1966). See Ch. IX, § 93.

33. Because the jury always can consider the weight to be given a particular confession, it is appropriate in a case involving a contested confession for counsel to point to certain factors that might contribute to involuntariness (such as the youth of the accused) and to argue that these reduce the weight that should be accorded the confession. This generally accepted practice, however, is different from that of a few jurisdictions which permit the jury to find facts contrary to those found by the judge and completely disregard the confession, thereby, in effect, applying an exclusionary rule of evidence.

Another variation from the prevailing practice exists in some jurisdictions with regard to the dying declarations of a homicide victim. The principal preliminary fact governing the admissibility of a dying declaration is that the declarant spoke under the influence of a sense of impending death. Most jurisdictions make the judge responsible for resolving conclusively any factual dispute as to the declarant's state of mind. Under the majority view, this ends the matter insofar as argument about *admissibility* is concerned. But some jurisdictions preserve for the jury a factfinding function with regard to admissibility. The judge instructs the jury that should they find that the dying declaration was made without the required "settled, hopeless expectation of death," they should entirely disregard it.[34] Thus, despite the fact that the judge has determined that the requisite state of mind existed, counsel may urge the jury to find that it did not. A few jurisdictions appear to ignore altogether the orthodox view and hold that the judge makes only a sufficiency finding—that is, he determines only whether the evidence would support a reasonable dispute as to expected death. If the evidence is sufficient, the jury makes a final determination of the preliminary fact.[35]

None of these variant approaches merits continued support. The orthodox rule that assigns to the judge sole responsibility for preliminary facts governing an exclusionary rule is practical and expeditious. Further, it does not embroil the jury in the administration of evidentiary rules—a task it is ill-equipped to perform. McCormick doubts that these minority rules, apparently intended to aid the accused, actually have operated to his advantage,[36] for in a close case of admissibility, the judge may rule against the accused, knowing that the latter has a second chance to urge the inadmissibility of the contested evidence. Yet it is unlikely the jury will be receptive to such an argument,

---

34. McCormick, § 53, at 123 n. 92; Morgan at 269.

35. Supra note 34. This position presumably is prejudicial to the defendant because the jury is exposed to evidence that might be inadmissible.

36. McCormick, § 53, at 123.

or, if it is, that it will be able to disregard evidence it already has heard.

Aside from these minority deviations from the practice of the vast majority of courts, there are diverse practices of more widespread consequence. These diverse approaches result from special circumstances that call into question the usual procedure of conclusively assigning preliminary questions to the judge. The difficulties arise when a preliminary question of fact governing the application of an exclusionary rule coincides with an ultimate issue in the case. The point can be made in several contexts, but a case involving the spousal incompetency privilege not to testify against an accused spouse is illustrative. Suppose that the accused is prosecuted for bigamy resulting from a common-law marriage to X, followed by a ceremonial marriage to Y. The accused contends he was never married to X. When the state calls Y as a witness, the accused objects, invoking a statute that excuses a "spouse" from being called in a criminal proceeding to testify against a marital partner. Such a statute would be interpreted so that Y would not be considered a spouse if the accused already was married to X when he purported to marry Y. But whether the accused was married to X is an ultimate issue in the case; ordinarily this issue would be resolved by the jury. How should the judge discharge his function as the preliminary factfinder when the fact conditioning an exclusionary rule coincides with a disputed ultimate fact? At least two possibilities exist, each with some judicial support.

First, the judge could follow the usual practice and make a final determination of the preliminary evidentiary question. If he decides by a preponderance of the evidence that the accused never married X, he would sustain the objection to Y's testimony and presumably would thereafter grant the accused's motion for acquittal.[37] If he determines by a preponderance of the evidence

---

37. If the judge, using a more-probable-than-not standard, determines that the defendant and X never were married, it would be inconsistent to allow a jury finding, based upon a reasonable doubt standard, that the accused was guilty of bigamy because he first married X, and then purported to marry Y.

that the accused was married to X, he then would order Y to testify, but he would not disclose to the jury that he has found a preexisting common-law marriage between the accused and X. Counsel for the defendant would be free to argue to the jury that the accused should not be found guilty because he was never married to X.[38] The judge's undisclosed evidentiary ruling that the accused and X were married would not foreclose argument on the ultimate issue, which properly is within the jury's province. Note also that the judge's ruling is made on the basis of a preponderance of the evidence,[39] but that the jury, in order to convict, must find beyond a reasonable doubt that the accused and X were married. In sum, many courts find that the usual practice of allocating preliminary questions to the judge operates satisfactorily even in instances when the preliminary fact coincides with an ultimate fact. It is essential, however, that the judge not disclose to the jury his resolution of the preliminary fact when his determination is adverse to the accused.

A second practice, which has the support of Professor McCormick,[40] limits the judge to a finding of sufficiency. If the proponent (the prosecutor in the foregoing illustration) provides sufficient evidence to enable a reasonable jury using a preponderance-of-the-evidence standard to find the preliminary fact (that the accused and X were married), then the contested evidence is admitted. Insufficient evidence of this preliminary fact not only would result in excluding Y's testimony, but also would result in granting the defendant's motion for acquittal. As will be noted in the following discussion, this approach is subject to

---

38. Should the judge instruct the jury completely to disregard the evidence if the preliminary fact (the marriage of X and the accused) was not established? This would be confusing and unnecessary. If the jury found that the accused had not been married, then they would acquit the defendant.

39. Preliminary questions of fact are resolved in both criminal and civil trials by using a preponderance standard. This practice has been challenged when applied to confessions, but in Lego v. Twomey, 404 U.S. 477 (1972), a split Supreme Court sustained the use of the preponderance test. See generally Saltzburg, Standards of Proof and Preliminary Questions of Fact, 27 Stan.L.Rev. 271 (1975).

40. See McCormick, § 53, at 124.

the criticism that it offers insufficient protection for the accused.

Enormous confusion and diversity of practice have surrounded the introduction into evidence of a coconspirator's party admission in a case in which the substantive offense of conspiracy is charged. Before the coconspirator's statement can be admitted against the other alleged conspirators, there must be preliminary evidence, independent of the statement itself,[41] that (1) there was a conspiracy in which the declarant and the opponent(s) of the evidence were participants, and (2) the declaration in question was made in furtherance of the alleged conspiracy.[42] Thus, resolution of the preliminary factual issue requires that the judge determine the existence of a conspiracy, as well as who were its members, and in so doing to reach the ultimate issue in the case. It is not surprising that the courts have developed different approaches as to both the standard of probative force to be applied in assessing the independent evidence and the function of the judge in making the necessary factual determination.[43] One line of cases requires only a finding by the judge that the proponent has produced "prima facie" evidence of a conspiracy. Within this group of cases, the opinions are not always clear as to what measure of proof is prescribed by the term "prima facie." [44] What usually is meant is evidence sufficient to sustain a finding of conspiracy by a preponderance-

---

41. The admissibility of the coconspirator's statement depends upon a preliminary finding that there was a conspiracy. It would thus appear that the statement in question should not be considered in making the preliminary finding that conditions the admissibility of the statement. Such has been the law. See S. Saltzburg & K. Redden, Federal Rules of Evidence Manual 468 (2d ed. 1977). But in United States v. Petrozziello, 548 F.2d 20, 23 (2d Cir. 1977), the court, citing Fed.Rule Evid. 104(a), stated that the judge could consider all the evidence, including the statement in question, in deciding whether a conspiracy existed. Because the evidence admissible under the usual rules of exclusion was sufficient to establish the conspiracy, the court did not consider how a judge should proceed as to the disputed statement. 548 F.2d at 23 n. 2.

42. See Ch. VII, § 57.

43. Four different approaches are identified and thoughtfully discussed in S. Saltzburg & K. Redden, Federal Rules of Evidence Manual 462–68 (2d ed. 1977).

44. Id. at 462–63.

of-the-evidence standard.[45]　In any event, the judge screens the independent evidence to ensure its sufficiency and sometimes goes further by instructing the jury that they should not consider the statement of the coconspirator unless they first find from independent evidence that a conspiracy existed.[46]

Another line of cases requires that the judge make a factual determination from the independent evidence that there was a conspiracy.[47]　Here the judge does not, as under the first approach, *simply screen* the independent evidence to ensure that it is sufficient to justify a finding of conspiracy; the judge himself makes a determination whether the preliminary fact of a conspiracy exists.　Under this preferred practice, the judge employs the usual measure of proof for resolving preliminary questions of fact:　the preponderance-of-the-evidence standard.[48]　Further, he gives no instruction to the jury to make a preliminary factual determination before considering the coconspirator's declaration.　The judge simply instructs the jury that in order to convict the accused they must find beyond a reasonable doubt that a conspiracy existed and that the accused was a participant in it.

Although this area has seen much debate [49] and continues to be the source of conflicting opinions, both policy and sound prac-

---

45.　A leading case is Carbo v. United States, 314 F.2d 718 (9th Cir. 1963), cert. denied 377 U.S. 953 (1964).

46.　This instruction is very difficult for the jury to understand and follow.　To complicate matters, some courts erroneously charge the jury not to consider the coconspirator's statement unless they first find from the independent evidence that beyond a reasonable doubt there was a conspiracy.　S. Saltzburg & K. Redden, note 38 at 463–64.　If the jury makes this finding, the subsequent use of the declaration is unnecessary.

47.　See, e. g., United States v. Stanchich, 550 F.2d 1294 (2d Cir. 1977)

(judge must find conspiracy from a fair preponderance of the independent evidence).

48.　Some judges may be applying a higher standard of proof, but not confining the evidence they consider to the independent evidence.　For a careful analysis, see S. Saltzburg & K. Redden, Federal Rules of Evidence Manual, 462–68 (2d ed. 1977).

49.　See, e. g., Bergman, The Coconspirator's Exception: Defining the Standard of the Independent Evidence Test Under the New Federal Rules of Evidence, 5 Hofstra L. Rev. 99 (1976).

tice suggest that the judge should determine the preliminary fact using a preponderance standard. This provides more protection for the accused than mere screening to ensure that prima facie evidence of the conspiracy exists. The preponderance rule applies a more stringent test of admissibility and thereby protects the accused where only weak evidence of a conspiracy exists. Further, this approach also protects the accused by avoiding the confusion produced in some courts by instructing the jury that it must make a preliminary finding of conspiracy before it can consider the coconspirator's declarations. Because it is unlikely that a jury could either understand or follow such an instruction, it is equally unlikely that jury determination of a preliminary fact can afford significant protection against the improper use of evidence.

NOTES

1. *Concurrence of Preliminary and Ultimate Facts.* The coincidence of preliminary and ultimate fact can occur in various factual patterns in both criminal and civil settings. Suppose plaintiff sues defendant on the ground that the latter issued a surety bond that obligated him to guarantee the payment of debts of a certain third party who has defaulted. Plaintiff starts to testify as to the terms of the bond, whereupon defendant objects on the grounds of the best evidence rule. As discussed in Ch. XIII, § 116, in cases where the terms of a writing are to be proved, this rule requires the production of the original writing if it is available. The plaintiff contends that the bond was lost; defendant asserts that it never existed. Only if the original is unavailable is oral testimony acceptable. Availability normally is a preliminary question for the judge. But if the judge decides the question of loss, he also must resolve the question whether the bond existed, which is an ultimate issue in the case. Under the preferred practice, the judge would determine whether there was an original that now is unavailable. If he finds there was no original, he should direct a verdict for the defendant; if he determines there was an original that now is lost, he should allow testimony concerning the terms of the bond without revealing to the jury his finding as to its existence.

2. *Judge's Role: A Problem.* Assume that plaintiff sues defendant on the basis of fraudulent representations made with reference to certain timber land. The plaintiff testifies as to the alleged representations but on cross-examination is confronted with a letter, purportedly written by him, inconsistent with his testimony. A witness's prior inconsistent statements normally are admissible to impeach his testimo-

ny. In this case the statements, if made by the plaintiff, also constitute a party admission. The second page of the letter, containing the
signature, is missing. Plaintiff denies ever having written or seen
the letter and objects to its contents being revealed to the jury. How
should the judge proceed in resolving the problem of whether the evidence is admissible?

CHAPTER XI

OFFER OF PROOF AND OBJECTIONS

§ 99.   The Offer, Objection and Motion to Strike: In General

In a broad sense, every document proffered as evidence and every statement solicited from a witness on the stand is an offer of proof. But the term "offer of proof" most often is used to refer to the dual showing a proponent must make when the admissibility of his evidence is challenged. The offer includes (1) a presentation or description of the evidence he wishes to introduce, and (2) a statement of what he proposes to prove. The intended use of the evidence often is apparent from the trial context; if so, clarifying statements are unnecessary. But when evidence is challenged by an opponent's objection (or, as occasionally happens, by a question or objection from the judge [1]) the proponent must specify the nature and purpose of his proffered evidence.

A question to the witness may suffice as an offer of proof, if both the response sought and its intended purpose are clear. But if there is any doubt regarding the nature or purpose of the evidence sought, the proponent should specify, as part of the permanent trial record, exactly what evidence he seeks to adduce and the proposition to which it is directed. This he may accomplish either by summarizing the expected evidence himself or by questioning the witness (out of the jury's presence) and having the reporter record the answers. If the proponent offers a document or tangible object, he should explain for the record its purpose and ensure that the object—or at least an adequate description of it—becomes a part of the record. Although the offer often is made out of presence of the jury (and before only the judge, the court reporter, and opposing counsel), sometimes the interroga-

---

1. Failure of the opponent to object "does not of itself preclude the trial judge from excluding the [objectionable] evidence on his own motion if the witness is disqualified for want of capacity or the evidence is incompetent, and he considers that the interests of justice require the exclusion of the testimony."   McCormick, § 55, at 129.

tor's question to a witness, made in the regular course of interrogation and before the jury, is sufficient to constitute an offer. Furthermore, the proponent can often state for the record what he proposes to prove without any significant risk of wrongly influencing the jury, thus eliminating the need for excusing the jury or making the offer at the judge's bench, out of the jury's hearing.

By indicating the nature and purpose of the evidence, an offer of proof serves three related purposes. First, it enables the opponent to withdraw, refine, or restate his objection. Second, it allows the judge to make an intelligent, informed ruling on the admissibility of the evidence. Finally, it allows an appellate court to conduct an adequate, informed review of the trial court's ruling on admissibility, for the record will reveal what the proponent sought to prove and the evidence with which he intended to prove it.

The objection, like its counterpart the offer, should inform the adversary, the trial judge, and the appellate tribunal. Hence, it should indicate the basis of the objector's challenge to the proffered evidence. Sound trial administration and fairness to the proponent dictate that the objection should be made as soon as the alleged defect in the proffered evidence is perceived. Ideally, the objection will be made as soon as the question calling for improper evidence is asked (or as soon as an objectionable item is offered). But sometimes there is insufficient time to object, as where a witness answers quickly or gives an answer not responsive to the question. In circumstances where the evidentiary defect is not apparent until after the testimony has been received, a motion to strike the evidence is the proper remedy.[2]

Because offers and objections serve important informational functions, it is not surprising that the rules governing these devices encourage the offeror and objector to state their respective

---

2. Such a motion is appropriate, for instance, when evidence is admitted conditionally and it later becomes apparent the required conditions have not been fulfilled. See Ch. 2, § 14. The motion to strike, sometimes called an "after-objection," usually includes a request that the jury be instructed to disregard the inadmissible evidence.

positions as specifically as possible. This demand for specificity reflects the assumptions that counsel are familiar with the forthcoming evidence—presumably having had an opportunity to develop and study the available evidence—and that the judge, who does not have equal familiarity, is entitled to expect informed and clearly stated offers and objections. As we shall see, the specific rules governing offers and objections adversely affect the proponent or opponent who fails to take timely action that makes clear his position with regard to proffered evidence. Furthermore, these rules favor the trial judge by giving him "the benefit of the doubt" when his evidentiary rulings are brought into question before an appellate court.

§ 100. Offer of Proof: Proponent's Responsibilities

The requirement that an offeror make a showing of what evidence he seeks to adduce and what he intends to prove by this evidence not only advises the judge and opposing counsel of the proponent's claim of relevance, but also reveals whether the evidence is being offered for an admissible purpose. There are many instances, of course, where evidence, offered for an admissible purpose, would be inadmissible if offered for another purpose, and vice versa.[3]

The burden of selecting the purpose of the evidence falls, as it should, upon the proponent: if he chooses an improper purpose, he can not prevail on appeal by showing some other basis for admissibility.[4] The offer was accepted on its terms and the judge ruled accordingly. The proponent bears a similar responsibility when he offers evidence, such as documents or conversations, of which only a part is admissible. If he fails to offer only the admissible portions, he can not prevail on appeal after the judge has rejected the entire offer.[5] It is not the duty of the judge to screen the proposed evidence and discriminate between

---

3.   See Ch. 2, § 11 ; Ch. VI, § 50.

4.   See I Wigmore, § 17, at 320.

5.   Mucci v. LeMonte, 157 Conn. 566, 254 A.2d 879 (1969). See Mc-

Cormick, § 51, at 112: "If counsel offers both good and bad together and the judge rejects the entire offer, the offeror may not complain on appeal." See also I Wigmore, § 17, at 320.

the good and the bad, although in the give and take of trial, the judge may and probably should reveal his reason for rejecting the evidence so that the proponent might cure the defect by offering only the admissible portion.

§ 101.   Objection: Waiver and Appellate Review

If a party intending to complain about evidence admitted against him fails to enter a timely objection, he waives his right to protest [6]—save to urge an appellate court to deem the admission of the evidence so egregious that it constitutes plain error and justifies granting relief notwithstanding his failure to object.[7] Invocation of the plain error doctrine is often urged, but appellate courts are seldom obliging. It should be noted that in a minority of jurisdictions, the failure to take "exception" to the judge's adverse ruling on an objection also waives the right of appellate review of the judge's ruling. Recent thinking, however, rejects the ritual of "taking exception" as unnecessary and counterproductive.[8] Waiver also can occur where, after a party's objection to opposing evidence is sustained, he introduces through his own witness similar evidence of the same facts or transactions.[9] Note, however, that evidence admitted after an

---

6. See United States v. Jamerson, 549 F.2d 1263 (9th Cir. 1977), applying Fed.R.Evid. 103(a).

7. See People v. Humphreys, 24 Mich. App. 411, 180 N.W.2d 328 (1970) (alleged error in admitting pistol waived because no objection; however, prosecutor's improper remarks to jury constitutes plain error); McCormick, § 52, at 120; Fed.R.Evid. 103 which requires offers and objection nonetheless, specifies that the court will consider plain errors. Id. at 103(d). Cf. United States v. Musgrave, 444 F. 2d 755 (5th Cir. 1971) (judge's prejudicial comments to jury constituted plain error).

8. The objection itself makes it known that the objector believes the evidence inadmissible. Little is accomplished by the added expression "I take exception." Counsel, having made known his objection, should be permitted to wait until the full trial transcript is available for his review before deciding whether to appeal the point. Further, the accidental failure to take exception, which easily can occur in the heat of trial, will preclude appellate review of a meritorious complaint. See State v. Abbott, 36 N.J. 63, 75–79, 174 A.2d 881, 887–90 (1961).

9. See, e. g., United States v. Silvers, 374 F.2d 828 (7th Cir.), cert. denied 389 U.S. 888 (1967) where defense counsel objected to evidence that the accused had been in

objection is *overruled* may be rebutted or explained without waiving the right to challenge the court's ruling on appeal.[10]

Crucial at both trial and appellate levels is the specificity of the objection itself. Here again the responsibility is that of the moving party: his statement must be sufficiently specific for the judge and opposing counsel to know which of the many rules of evidence is invoked. If counsel simply states "I object,"—a so-called general objection—it is difficult for the trial judge to make an informed ruling. Accordingly, as we shall see, any ruling he does make likely will be upheld on appeal unless no possible ground supports his decision.[11] The rationale for favoring the judge at the expense of the objecting attorney is that the latter has had an opportunity to examine the available evidence through investigation and discovery procedures and to anticipate problems associated with the evidence; the trial judge, it is assumed, has had no comparable opportunity to familiarize himself with the evidence. Thus, the rule which gives the judge the benefit of any doubt is also designed to encourage objecting counsel to be specific. A specific objection also results in fairness to the proponent of the evidence, for it gives him the opportunity to restate his offer or to cure the deficiency in his proof by resort to other evidence. It can be seen that effective advocacy by the objector has the potential not only of securing a favorable ruling from the trial judge, but also of preserving the objector's appellate rights should the judge rule against him. Because the argument accompanying the objection becomes part of the record which the appellate court will review, it may help to support a

---

prison, but then made extensive use of the accused's prison background in an attempt to prove insanity. See also McCormick, § 55, at 128. The reported cases vary on the propriety of waiver. See I Wigmore, § 18, at 345. Perhaps the waiver doctrine is a convenient device in cases where the trial judgment clearly appears correct. An alternative appellate disposition is to hold that the evidence adduced by the objector ren-

dered the error of overruling his objection harmless.

10. See infra § 103.

11. Morgan at 47. An objection general in form ("I object") can function as a specific objection if it is clear that the judge and opposing counsel knew the specific (but unarticulated) ground upon which the objection was made. McCormick, § 52, at 115.

claim of error or to bolster the trial judge's ruling if favorable to the objector.

The familiar litany that evidence is "irrelevant, incompetent and immaterial" handly focuses the objection. There are many reasons why evidence might be incompetent (as when made so by rules of privilege, hearsay, or a dead man statute). By adding the words "irrelevant" and "immaterial," the objector at most has suggested that the evidence is not probative of the proposition to which it is directed or that it is directed toward a proposition not consequential. Thus the objector's trilogy can be viewed as no more educative of the court and the opponent than the general interjection "I object." McCormick suggests that the "three i's" do specify an objection based on the lack of probative force or materiality.[12] Many of the decided cases, however, support the view that this overworked rhetoric lodges only a general objection.

The specific rules governing a general objection are these: If a general objection *is overruled*, the objector rarely prevails on appeal. The appellate court will attribute to the trial judge the proper motive if any can be credited. There is an element of fair play in this attribution because the objector's failure to be specific has resulted in admission of the evidence and, at the same time, has failed to apprise the proponent of the specific defect. Thus, the latter has no meaningful opportunity or incentive to cure the infirmity or supply other evidence. Additionally, it is sometimes said to be unfair to upset the ruling below on argument presented for the first time on appeal. In any event, the general objector who sustains an unfavorable ruling from the trial judge is also likely to sustain an unfavorable appellate disposition. Only if there is no purpose or theory of admissibility to support the trial judge's ruling will it be overturned. It needs no emphasis that this is hardly the kind of appellate posture upon which careful counsel chooses to rely.

If the general objection *is sustained*, the protective appellate attitude toward the trial judge favors the objector. By charitably assuming that the judge had in mind all conceivable proper

12. McCormick, § 52, at 116.

grounds, the appellate court will uphold the ruling unless there is no basis for it whatsoever. Note that here the party appealing the judge's ruling will be the proponent of the evidence. He can increase his chances for success on appeal by making a careful offer of proof at trial. In the offer he should indicate clearly the purposes for which the evidence is offered, especially if it might be inadmissible for some purposes but not others. He also should request that the reason for the trial judge's ruling be indicated on the record, thereby perhaps exposing a specific erroneous basis.

Specific objections are governed by the following rules. The appellate disposition of the trial court's ruling on an opponent's *specific* objection—that is, where the opponent points out particular grounds—favors the judge only where the objector is wrong in his contention. If the opponent's specific objection *correctly* indicates the defect in the proffered evidence but the judge *erroneously overrules* his objection, the merits of the ruling will be reviewed on appeal. But the situation is different if the opponent of the evidence states an *erroneous* specific objection—that is, one based upon an untenable ground—which is *overruled*. Here, even if another ground would have called for exclusion of the evidence, (for example, if the objector based his objection on a claim of marital privilege, but the evidence actually was hearsay) the objector's posture on appeal is unfavorable.[13] The objector presented the trial judge with an invalid ground for excluding the evidence—an alleged defect which did not exist. Counsel's objection will be accepted on its terms on appeal, just as it was at trial: the appellate court will hold the trial judge acted correctly in overruling the erroneous objection —at least if there is any conceivable ground supporting admission. This result is consistent with the notion of party responsibility, and protects the trial judge who presumably recognized that the objection was without merit.

A more difficult question arises when the specific objector names an untenable ground and the judge *wrongly sustains* the

---

13. "If a specific objection is overruled, the ruling is correct if the defect specified does not exist even though the evidence is objectionable on other grounds." Morgan at 48. See McCormick, § 52, at 117.

objection although there is a valid, unnamed ground for exclusion. When the proponent of the evidence appeals, some appellate courts sustain the ruling of the trial judge on the theory that, although the reason was wrong, the result was correct.[14] There would seem to be little reason to retry the case merely to enter the proper reason for exclusion. But arguably this result is unfair to the proponent: if the proper basis for exclusion had been revealed, he might have been able to cure the defect [15] or present other, admissible evidence. For this reason, some courts, with the general approval of the commentators, reverse the ruling of the trial judge.[16]

Of course, one must study all of the foregoing rules with an awareness that evidentiary rulings, though erroneous, may be comparatively insignificant in their final effect on the final judgment. In such circumstances, the appellate court may deem the error harmless.

§ 102.   Offers of Proof and Objections under the Federal Rules of Evidence

Offers and objections are governed by Rule 103 of the Federal Rules of Evidence. The Rule codifies much of the common law, discussed previously. In order to predicate error upon a ruling of the trial judge admitting evidence, the party opposing the

---

14. See I Wigmore, § 18, at 342 n. 29. The leading case is Kansas City So. R. R. v. Jones, 241 U.S. 181 (1916). See also Eschbach v. Hurtt, 47 Md. 61, 65 (1877): the court "must determine . . . whether the testimony offered was admissible, and not whether a right or wrong reason was assigned for its rejection." Note that it is difficult to reconcile this language with the rule that if a specific objection based upon the wrong ground is *overruled,* the judge will be sustained on appeal even if a proper specific objection would have resulted in exclusion.

15. Suppose, for example, the true basis for exclusion were the best evidence rule. Were this known the proponent perhaps could lay the foundation for introducing a copy. See Ch. XIII, § 116.

16. See Bloodgood v. Lynch, 293 N. Y. 308, 56 N.E.2d 718 (1944); Larson v. Dougherty, 72 S.D. 43, 29 N. W.2d 383 (1947); Arcola v. Wilkinson, 233 Ill. 250, 84 N.E. 264 (1908); I Wigmore, § 18, at 342 n. 9; Morgan at 48.

evidence ordinarily must make a timely objection (or motion to strike) and set out his supporting ground.[17] A parallel requirement applies to a party who predicates error upon a ruling excluding evidence: he must ordinarily make an offer of proof in order to preserve his right to an appellate review on the merits. In either situation, the Rule allows the context of the situation to provide the required specificity; sound practice, however, usually dictates that the party against whom a trial ruling is made state plainly for the record the pertinent information regarding the admitted or excluded evidence.

Rule 103 also expressly vests the trial judge with discretion to manage the flow of information pertaining to the offer and objection. The Rule states that the court may direct that the offer be made in question and answer form. The court is also empowered to add statements pertaining to the character of the evidence, the form in which it is offered, the objections raised, and its ruling on the evidence. The Rule makes it clear that to the extent practicable, the court should take steps to prevent suggesting to the jury the content of inadmissible evidence. Normally the trial judge will implement this directive by using a side-bar conference or by excusing the jury. In general, the Federal Rule reflects the prevailing principle that the parties are primarily responsible for controlling the presentation and exclusion of evidence.[18]

§ 103. Curative Admissibility ("Open Door" Theory)

Should one party's introduction of improper evidence (that is, evidence violative of an exclusionary rule) justify a counterattack with improper evidence by the other party? Two limiting propositions should be stated at the outset. First, the use of improper evidence of a particular excludable *class* (for example, hearsay evidence or privileged evidence) does not justify the opponent's introduction, generally, of evidence from the same class:

---

17. United States v. Jamerson, 549 F.2d 1263 (9th Cir. 1977).

18. For an extensive treatment of Rule 103, see D. Louisell & C. Mueller, 1 Federal Evidence § 23 et seq. (1977). For more concise coverage, see S. Saltzburg & K. Redden, Federal Rules of Evidence Manual 18–35 (2d ed. 1977).

hearsay evidence on point A does not warrant the opponent's introduction of hearsay evidence on point B. The issue is whether the use of improper evidence on point A justifies the opponent's use of improper rebuttal evidence (regardless of class) *relevant to the same point.* Second, regardless of whether the opponent is entitled to introduce "inadmissible" evidence of his own, he always is entitled to attack by cross-examination the accuracy or reliability of his adversary's improper evidence. The problem involving a counterattack arises only when the party rebutting the improper evidence seeks to *introduce additional improper evidence,* not when he merely attempts by cross-examination or through the use of admissible evidence to reduce the probative force of the improper evidence that his opponent has produced.

Wigmore identified three views of the so-called doctrine of curative admissibility.[19] The first rejects the improper rebuttal evidence, the second admits it, and the third makes the result turn upon whether the rebuttal evidence is needed to remove prejudice caused by the initial incompetent evidence. In Wigmore's view, the variations in the cases largely are explained by the fact that whatever rule was chosen on appeal resulted in upholding the ruling of the trial judge.[20] McCormick, noting variations in the announced rules, offers valuable statements of what he believes are, or should be, controlling principles.[21] It should be added that direct or inferential case support probably can be found for any reasonable solution in this difficult and confused area.[22]

Suppose the proponent introduces evidence which violates the hearsay rule and the opponent enters a correct specific objection which the trial judge erroneously overrules. In theory, the op-

---

19. I Wigmore § 15.

20. I Wigmore, § 15, at 309. The author indicates that if the opponent duly objected, there was no need to admit improper rebuttal evidence because the opponent had a right to appeal the erroneous ruling. Thus, Wigmore would choose among the three rules only when there has been no objection. As noted later in the present text, a mere objection does not give sufficient protection.

21. McCormick, § 57, at 132–133.

22. A multitude of cases are collected in I Wigmore § 15; see also McCormick, § 57, at 132–133.

ponent is protected because he can appeal the ruling. But appeals are expensive, and there is a risk the appellate court will view the error as harmless. Further, a litigant wants to win at trial not only to improve his posture on appeal but also to gain an advantage in any post-trial negotiations to compromise or settle the suit and avoid an appeal. For these reasons, then, a litigant should be afforded an opportunity at trial [23] to counterbalance inadmissible evidence used against him.

If the rebuttal evidence is of the same class and origin as the admitted evidence, the rebuttal evidence likely will be admitted because the judge, consistent in his earlier ruling, will believe the rebuttal evidence proper. But what is the impact of this rebuttal evidence on the initial objection? One view results in a waiver of the rebutting party's earlier objection to this class of evidence: if he loses the verdict, he may not successfully complain on appeal. A preferable view is that the "improper" rebuttal does not effect a waiver because the rebuttal was necessitated by the original proponent. Under this view, however, the rebuttal evidence may make the original error harmless—a point which the trial judge can bear in mind when considering a motion for new trial and which the appellate court also can consider.[24]

Additional difficulties are introduced when the rebuttal evidence violates a different exclusionary rule than that violated by the original proponent. If the original proponent objects but the trial judge does *not exclude the rebuttal evidence,* the original proponent will complain on appeal. The appellate question should be whether the original improper evidence rendered the rebuttal evidence harmless error. A less desirable approach estops the original proponent from complaining because he started the sequence of erroneous admissions by "opening the door." [25] The harmless error approach has the flexibility to account for

---

23. Cf. McCormick, § 58, at 133.

24. See I Wigmore § 16, at 310–12 and cases cited therein for a discussion of the scope of judicial discretion at trial and on appeal. Wigmore appears to favor lodging in the trial judge discretion to apply waiver strictly, save where prejudice unfairly would result. Id. § 15, at 309.

25. See I Wigmore, § 15, at 309.

differences in prejudicial effect between the initial evidence and the rebuttal evidence. However, if the objection to rebuttal evidence which violates a different exclusionary rule than the original evidence *is sustained,* the offering (rebutting) party has no recourse other than to appeal the ruling which admitted that improper evidence.

When the initial proponent introduces improper evidence to which the opponent does not object, but subsequently the opponent offers improper rebuttal evidence to which the original proponent objects, does the action of the original proponent estop him from complaining about the rebuttal evidence? [26] The equities are close: the original proponent initiated the improper evidentiary course, but his opponent either chose not to object (even though, presumably, he could have blocked the improper evidence) or failed to see that the evidence was defective. This situation is best resolved by giving the trial judge discretion to admit or reject the evidence according to the degree of prejudice caused by the first improper evidence.[27] In most cases the decision of the trial court should not be disturbed on appeal.

NOTES

1. *No Necessity for Offer of Proof During Cross-Examination.* The requirements that normally attend an offer of proof usually are relaxed during cross-examination. McCormick, § 51, at 110. Presumably, the cross-examiner does not know what answer the witness will give. It would appear, however, that the cross-examiner could be required to show what he intends to prove by his question(s) if this is not apparent. However, this requirement has to be balanced against the disadvantage that might be caused the cross-examiner if he has to disclose his plan of attack or rebuttal. See generally Note, Appeal and Error—Excluded Evidence on Cross-examination—Reservation for Appeal, 33 N.C.L.Rev. 476 (1955).

---

26. See I Wigmore § 15, at 309. State v. Witham, 72 Me. 531, 535 (1881) appears to foreclose appeal by an original offeror whose improper evidence, admitted without objection, subsequently is rebutted by equally improper evidence. See also Meyers v. United States, 147 F.2d 663 (9th Cir. 1945).

27. This solution generally accords with that of Wigmore who maintains that the results in most of the decided cases support the action of the trial judge. See I Wigmore, § 15, at 309.

2. *Pretrial Objections to Evidence.* In certain instances, usually criminal cases in which it is claimed that evidence was obtained in violation of a constitutional principle (such as the prohibition against illegal searches and seizures or the ban against involuntary confessions), it is proper to object to the challenged evidence prior to trial. The procedural device for raising the objection is a motion to suppress the evidence. Such a motion normally requires a suppression hearing before the trial judge. This device, sometimes called a motion *in limine*, also may be used whenever highly prejudicial but allegedly inadmissible evidence is expected to be adduced at trial. See generally J. McElhaney, Effective Litigation 16–18 (1974).

3. *Waiver of Objection.* Suppose inadmissible evidence is offered by *P*, but *D* does not object and the evidence is admitted. Subsequently, for unrelated reasons there is a new trial on the same course of action. *P* again offers the improper evidence, but this time *D* objects. Did *D*'s failure to object at the first trial operate as a waiver in the second trial? See McCormick, § 52 at 114 indicating that objections based upon privilege or upon incompetency under the Dead Man's Statute are waived. See also I Wigmore, § 18, at 330.

4. *Objections: Tactical Considerations.* Knowing when to object is sometimes as important as knowing the correct ground. Often, for tactical reasons counsel will withhold an objection that could have been made. A consistent objector does not make a favorable impression upon the jury. Additionally, counsel may withhold an objection where admissibility is questionable because he thinks the topic introduced by his opponent's questions is one that he would like to pursue. Cf. § 103. See generally R. Keeton, Trial Tactics and Methods, Ch. IV, especially § 4.2.

CHAPTER XII

EXPERT TESTIMONY AND SCIENTIFIC EVIDENCE

§ 104. Role and Qualification of the Expert Witness

In an earlier chapter [1] we observed that there is a general restriction against receiving in evidence the opinion of a lay witness—at least, in circumstances where the opinion is not helpful to the trier of fact. By definition, however, an expert witness possesses knowledge and skill that distinguish him from ordinary witnesses. Presumably, he is in a position superior to the other trial participants, including the jury, to draw inferences and reach conclusions within his field of expertise. It follows that a witness who qualifies as an expert should be entitled to render opinions and conclusions within the area of his specialty. If he were not allowed to express his opinion, his testimony would not assist—and might confuse—the trier, for his only role would be to facilitate the admission of specialized information (facts and data) which was largely outside the grasp of the jury and from which they would be unable to draw rational inferences.

When one of the parties presents a witness to testify as an expert, the judge [2] must determine whether the proffered individual has the necessary qualifications. But there is a preliminary issue for resolution by the judge: he must decide whether the subject matter about which the expert will testify is sufficiently removed from common experience so that the trier will benefit from the assistance of a specialist. [3] When the subject concerns

---

1. Ch. IV, § 29.

2. Ch. X, § 97.

3. See McCormick, § 13, at 29–30; II Wigmore §§ 559–560. For a case finding the subject matter sufficiently within the grasp of lay persons, see Skelton v. Sinclair Refining Co., 375 P.2d 948 (Okla.1962) (architect proffered to testify as to safety of restrooms). In some instances, such as those involving an issue of mental competency, it may be possible to receive testimony from an expert and also from a

a technical aspect of such specialized fields as medicine, science, banking or photography, there is little question that the subject matter is largely beyond the mastery of an untrained person.[4] Even such matters as instruments or tools used by burglars[5] or the effect upon cattle of drinking salt water[6] have been deemed appropriate subjects for expert testimony. There is a division of authority, however, as to whether it is proper for an expert with experience in investigating automobile accidents to "reconstruct" an accident from the position of the debris or other clues;[7] disagreement also exists with regard to whether obscenity cases lend themselves to expert participation.[8] The Federal Rules of Evidence simply state:

> If scientific, technical, or other specialized knowledge will assist the trier of fact to understand the evidence or to determine a fact in issue, a witness qualified as an expert . . . may testify . . . .[9]

---

lay witness who has had an extended opportunity to observe.

4. For a general discussion containing various examples, see II Wigmore, §§ 559, 564–571.

5. State v. Oertel, 280 Mo. 129, 217 S.W. 64 (1919); but see Central Mutual Ins. Co. v. D. & B., Inc., 340 S.W.2d 525 (Tex.Civ.App.1960) rejecting testimony by an experienced burglar concerning how a professional outlaw would accomplish the robbery of a safe.

6. Manhattan Oil Co. v. Mosby, 72 F.2d 840 (8th Cir. 1934).

7. Compare Een v. Consolidated Freightways, 120 F.Supp. 289, aff'd 220 F.2d 82 (8th Cir. 1955) and Miller v. Pillsbury, 33 Ill.2d 514, 211 N.E.2d 733 (1965) with Housman v. Fiddyment, 421 S.W.2d 284 (Mo.1967) and Hagan Storm Fence Company v. Edwards, 245 Miss. 487, 148 So.2d 693 (1963). It may

make a difference whether there is eyewitness testimony available or whether scientific principles are used by the expert. See cases and discussion in Maguire et al. at 314–15.

8. See, generally, Frank, Obscenity: Some Problems of Values and the Use of Experts, 41 Wash.L.Rev. 631 (1966); Stern, Toward a Rationale for the Use of Expert Testimony in Obscenity Litigation, 20 Case W.Res.L.Rev. 527 (1969). See also McGaffey, A Realistic Look at Expert Witnesses in Obscenity Cases, 69 N.W.U.L.Rev. 218 (1974) in which the author discusses research which indicates experts have little effect in such value-oriented areas as obscenity.

9. Fed.R.Evid. 702. See Fernandez v. Chios Shipping Co., Ltd., 542 F. 2d 145 (2d Cir. 1976).

In determining *if the person proffered* has the necessary expertise to deal with the specialized subject matter, the judge considers education and experience. Either of these factors alone may suffice to qualify the witness, but typically both qualifications are present to some degree.[10] The determination is made with primary emphasis upon the qualifications the witness possesses when compared to lay or untrained persons. Hence, a general practitioner of medicine can qualify as an expert on a specialty within medicine (such as neurology or orthopedics) even though there are specialists who presumably are more knowledgeable within the restricted field.[11] It should be emphasized that considerable latitude is given to the trial judge in making his decision regarding expertise [12] and appellate reversals are infrequent.

§ 105. The Expert Witness: Direct Examination

The factfinder, of course, is always faced with the problems of determining what evidence to believe and what inferences to draw from the evidence. But the use and evaluation of expert testimony raises special difficulties for the trier. The first is determining exactly what facts underlie the expert opinion, and the second is deciding which, if any, of the specialized inferences or conclusions drawn by the expert should be accepted as true. The trier's task is made more difficult because the expert usually gives his testimony in an atmosphere of disputed facts and conflicting contentions. He testifies prior to the trier's deliberation and factfinding and usually before all of the evidence in the case is in. His opinion is necessarily based upon an underlying set of assumed facts, but these "facts" might be rejected by the trier as false or unproven. If the assumed facts are rejected, the opinion of the expert is weakened or destroyed. Therefore,

---

10. McCormick, § 13, at 30. Fed.R. Evid. 702 allows the witness to qualify by "Knowledge, skill, experience, training, or education. . . ."

11. Parker v. Gunther, 122 Vt. 68, 164 A.2d 152 (1960); see generally II Wigmore § 569.

12. II Wigmore § 561. Wigmore favors a rule that absolutely precludes appellate review. Id.

it is essential, as a first step, that there be some means by which the trier can identify what factual assumptions underlie the expert's opinion.

A simple example illustrates this point: A physician gives an opinion that his patient has contracted a certain disease. Two symptoms of the condition in question are persistent headaches and frequent nausea. The patient testifies that he has had these ill effects, but the opposing party offers conflicting evidence that challenges these assertions. It is important for the trier to know that the doctor's opinion was based at least in part upon the assumption that the patient experienced the symptoms. If the trier rejects all or part of the testimony of the patient, it will take this into account in determining the validity of the physician's opinion. Of course, the trier must still grapple with the question whether the doctor's conclusion might be valid despite the absence of some of the underlying facts; we shall take up this difficulty shortly.[13]

Identification of the evidentiary facts underlying an expert opinion may be relatively easy if one, or even several, of the witnesses who preceded the expert give all of the evidence upon which the expert bases his opinion. Counsel conducting direct examination of the expert can simply ask his witness to assume, for purposes of giving his opinion, that all of the facts to which the preceding witness(es) testified are true. Where the preceding testimony has not been long or involved, the trier is adaquately informed concerning the assumed facts underlying the opinion; the relative importance of these various facts is usually clarified during cross-examination. A similar convenience is realized where the expert himself supplies evidence of all of the underlying facts.[14] Complications arise, however, where evidence of the facts that underlie the opinion can be traced to numerous

---

13. See infra § 106.

14. In this situation, a few courts will permit the expert to express his opinion on the basis of personal knowledge of the facts without first setting out the facts. Development of the underlying facts occurs during the remainder of direct examination and on cross-examination. However, considerations of tactics usually dictate that the expert first give the underlying facts; by so doing his opinion is usually more persuasive.

witnesses and documents or when the one or two witnesses who supply the underlying facts give extensive testimony or appear to alter, qualify, or change their testimony during cross-examination. It then becomes necessary to use some other technique of identifying the supporting facts. The traditional technique for accomplishing this end is the use of a hypothetical question.[15] In the foregoing illustration, counsel might frame his question by saying "Assuming, Doctor, that the plaintiff [patient] has had persistent headaches over the period of the last two years, accompanied by frequent periods of nausea [and so forth], do you have an opinion, based upon reasonable medical certainty, as to the disease from which he is suffering?"[16] The central idea is to incorporate into the question the assumed, underlying facts so that the trier can understand the basis of the opinion. Yet, despite the apparent utility of the hypothetical question, it has been the subject of extensive discussion and growing dissatisfaction in recent years.[17]

One objection to the hypothetical question is that it is encumbered with technical requirements that ensnare the unwary and lead to excessive appeals.[18] Some courts, for example, insist that every fact in evidence that is relevant to the expert's opinion must be included within the hypothetical. There is an ancillary requirement, strictly imposed by some courts, that every fact alluded to must be supported by evidence in the record— that is, evidence actually introduced at trial. Reliance upon a presumably accurate hospital record that was not formally received into evidence would be improper even if it could have been introduced as a business entry. If any part of the opinion was based upon inadmissible hearsay, which of course could not be received into evidence absent consent or a waiver by the opposing party, then this improper basis invalidates the hypothetical.

---

15. McCormick, § 14, at 32.

16. For a complete example of a hypothetical question, see 6 Am.Jur. Proof of Facts 159–85 (1960).

17. See McCormick § 16; II Wigmore § 686.

18. For a case illustrating the pitfalls of the hypothetical question, see Ingram v. McCuiston, 261 N.C. 392, 134 S.E.2d 705 (1964). For a thoughtful article on expert testimony, see Ladd, Expert Testimony, 5 Vand.L.Rev. 414 (1952).

These technical demands, coupled with counsel's desire to phrase his hypothetical so as to broadly expose and emphasize his most favorable evidence, often leads to lengthy, slanted questions that are difficult for the jury to follow and understand. Furthermore, these burdensome inquiries frequently demand of the expert an artificial exactitude and definitiveness foreign to his accustomed training and methodology. The matter becomes increasingly complicated when sharp conflicts in the evidence make it necessary either on direct or cross-examination for the expert to render an opinion on various hypothetical factual groupings ("Would your opinion be the same if there were no headaches, but a low-grade fever?"). This series of varying factual assumptions increases the chance of jury misunderstanding and exaggerates even more the required precision with which the expert is to respond—for in most jurisdictions he is required to affirm that his opinion is within the bounds of reasonable medical certainty.

There is a growing movement away from the judicial rigidity associated with expert testimony and illustrated by the strict requirements surrounding the hypothetical question. The recent trend is toward a flexible procedure that gives the expert the freedom to testify other than in "opinion form," makes optional the hypothetical question, and abandons the exacting requirements that traditionally have required admissibility of all of the underlying facts. The Federal Rules of Evidence carry forward the reform momentum of some of the states.[19] Significantly, Rule 702 provides that an expert "may testify . . . in the form of an opinion or otherwise." This provision enables the expert to share his knowledge without the necessity of disclosing it in the form of an opinion. The purpose is to encourage the use of experts to explain scientific or other principles relevant to the case so that, in appropriate circumstances, the trier may apply them to the facts. In Rule 705, the federal draftsmen have made it clear that the use of the hypothetical question usually

---

19. See McCormick, § 17, at 37. Professor McCormick's careful and trenchant criticism of the hypothetical has been an influential factor in effecting change. See Rabata v. Dohner, 45 Wis.2d 111, 172 N.W.2d 409 (1969).

is optional. That rule specifies that an "expert may testify in terms of opinion or inference and give his reasons therefor without prior disclosure of the underlying facts or data, unless the court requires otherwise." No longer will it usually be necessary to bridle the expert (and the jury) with a long and detailed recitation of all of the assumed facts. These can be explored on cross-examination.[20] In another important reform provision, the federal rulemakers state:

> The facts or data in the particular case upon which an expert bases an opinion or inference may be those perceived by or made known to him at or before the hearing. If of a type reasonably relied upon by experts in the particular field in forming opinions or inferences upon the subject, the facts or data need not be admissible in evidence.[21]

Traditionally, an expert has gained his knowledge of the underlying facts (1) through *personal observation* of the matter in question (as where a doctor examines a patient), (2) *from attending trial* and perceiving the evidence presented or by taking the witness stand and listening to a hypothetical statement of the supporting evidence, or (3) by a combination of these means.[22] And, as we have seen, whatever the source of his factual knowledge, it has traditionally been critical that the expert's factual source be supported by admissible evidence. The quoted provision goes further by allowing the facts or data to be "made known . . . at or before the hearing" and by specifying that the "facts or data need not be admissible in evidence" if they are "of a type reasonably relied upon by experts in the particular field in forming opinions." This means that the expert is permitted to learn the facts prior to trial by means other than a personal examination or first-hand investigation and can utilize materials (such as reports of technicians, other specialists, or the

---

20. Fed.R.Evid. 705: "The expert may in any event be required to disclose the underlying facts or data on cross-examination."

21. Fed.R.Evid. 703.

22. See Adv.Comm.Note to Fed.R. Evid. 703.

reports or comments of professional observers) that are normally relied on in his field, even though these materials may not qualify for admission into evidence.

Finally, another significant provision of the Federal Rules negates a rule still found in some common-law jurisdictions.[23] The Federal Rules [24] make it clear that an expert (and a lay witness, as well) is free to give his opinion on an ultimate issue in the case. Of course, the opinion must assist the factfinder; the provision in the Rules does not clear the way for unnecessary expressions as to an ultimate matter that is beyond the expert's special competence.[25]

§ 106. The Expert Witness: Cross-Examination and Impeachment

The technique of cross-examining the expert differs somewhat depending upon which of the modes of direct examination discussed in the preceding section is used. For example, if the direct examiner does not ask a hypothetical question, the cross-examiner may need to identify more definitely the factual assumptions underlying the opinion; if the expert himself has supplied evidence of the underlying facts, the cross-examiner may wish to probe the accuracy of the expert's observation or memory.[26] There are several additional possibilities for testing or weakening the expert's opinion. The cross-examiner may ask the expert to assume different facts than those assumed during direct examination, and to state whether these new factual assumptions would alter his opinion. The interrogator may also probe the

---

23. See McCormick § 12. But many recent cases reject the "ultimate issue" rule, particularly where the challenged opinion comes from an expert as opposed to a lay witness.

24. See Fed.R.Evid. 704.

25. "The promulgation of Rule 704 [negating the ultimate issue rule] does not mean that witnesses will now be able to give testimony that involves nothing more than choosing up sides." J. Waltz, The New

Federal Rules of Evidence 112 (2d ed. 1975).

26. Sometimes, of course, the safest path for the adverse examiner is to waive his right of cross-examination. Since the expert is usually considerably more knowledgeable about his subject than the cross-examiner, he can sometimes embarrass his questioner or at least add strength to the opinion expressed during direct.

expert's education or experience, attempting to expose weaknesses that might discredit the soundness of the latter's opinion.[27]

Like other witnesses, the expert is subject to impeachment by any of the usual methods such as prior inconsistent statements, bad reputation for truthfulness, and so forth.[28] A commonly employed impeachment technique is to show that the expert is biased. For instance, the cross-examiner may prove that the expert is receiving a large fee to testify or that he always aligns himself with a particular point of view or with a particular kind of litigant, (such as the plaintiff in a personal injury suit). Furthermore, in many jurisdictions, the examiner may confront the expert witness with a text or other reference and, after extracting a concession that the work is recognized as a standard authority, point to passages that contradict the expert's opinion.[29] For example, if the expert has testified on direct that a "whiplash" injury is always manifested within several hours after the accident purportedly causing it, the examiner may impeach the expert by having the latter read from a learned treatise a passage that states that such manifestations can occur as long as a year after the accident.[30] As a tactical matter, however, the cross-examiner must be cautious lest the expert persuasively state why the passage is inapplicable to the present case or why its correctness is rejected by current professional thinking.

Note that although the text or other publication is ostensibly being used to discredit the expert witness, it is possible in some

---

27. In an extreme case, it might be possible to elicit facts that would render the witness unqualified as an expert. However, in the usual case, a challenge to the expert's qualification would take place before he had rendered his opinion.

28. See Ch. VIII, §§ 81–83. See, e. g., Scott v. Spanjer Bros., Inc., 298 F.2d 928 (2d Cir. 1962) (bias); Young v. Group Health Co-op of Puget Sound, 85 Wash.2d 332, 534 P.2d 1349 (1975) (prior inconsistent statement). See generally LeMere v. Goren, 233 Cal.App.2d 799, 43 Cal.Rptr. 898 (1965).

29. A few jurisdictions restrict this form of impeachment to circumstances in which the expert concedes that he relied upon the treatise. See Adv.Comm. Note to Fed. R.Evid. 803(18); Annot., 60 A.L. R.2d 77, 83–87 (1958).

30. See Ruth v. Fenchel, 21 N.J. 171, 121 A.2d 373 (1956).

jurisdictions to utilize the text as affirmative proof of its quoted content. This means of proof is available in those jurisdictions recognizing a hearsay exception for learned treatises. The Federal Rules provision is illustrative of this exception.[31]

§ 107. Scientific Proof

No attempt is made in this comparatively brief section to discuss comprehensively the various kinds of proof that might be termed "scientific." Instead, selected illustrations are provided and the general principles governing scientific proof are set forth. The adjective "scientific," as we broadly use it here, refers to evidence that draws its convincing force from some principle of science, mathematics, or the like. Typically, scientific evidence is presented by an expert witness who can explain data or test results and, if necessary, explain the scientific principles which are said to give the evidence its reliability.[32]

Occasionally, scientific evidence will establish conclusively the proposition to which it is directed, with the result that the factfinder will be prohibited from making a contrary finding. This conclusiveness is assured by instructing the trier to accept the scientifically established proposition as true or, in cases where the proposition is dispositive of the action, by concluding the trial through the use of a directed verdict or some other appropriate procedure.[33] Often, however, the scientific evidence will

---

31. Fed. Rule Evidence 803(18):

Learned Treatises.—To the extent called to the attention of an expert witness upon cross-examination or relied upon by him in direct examination, statements contained in published treatises, periodicals, or pamphlets . . . established as a reliable authority . . . [are admissible as an exception to the hearsay rule].

This exception to the hearsay rule is grounded on the assumption that the reliability of a standard work is likely to be high. Not only is the writer's reputation at stake, but, more importantly, the work is scrutinized and used by knowledgeable professionals in the field. See Adv.Com. Note to Fed.R.Evid. 803 (18). Note that the learned treatise exception also can be invoked during the direct examination of an expert and observe further that any qualified witness can be called to establish the treatise, etc., as a "reliability authority." Ibid.

32. As to expert testimony, see supra §§ 105–06. See also Ch. I, § 7, and note 33 immediately below.

33. Where the underlying scientific principles are well established, and hence subject to judicial notice, the

not be conclusive, but will serve only to increase the likelihood of the proposition toward which it is directed. In these cases, courts have displayed a resistance that is often justified, but in some instances appears out of step not only with science and technology, but also with rational judicial practice. Probably the greatest detriment to increased liberality in receiving scientific evidence is the apprehension that the factfinder, especially the jury, will be highly influenced by evidence that purports to bring the certainty of science or mathematics to the variables of human conduct. As we shall see, there can be a danger that the trier will exaggerate the reliability of scientific proof, and in some cases the courts wisely have rejected evidence that might be misleading.

In People v. Collins,[34] a case arising in California, the main issue was whether the accused couple, a Negro man and a Caucasian woman, were the persons who had committed the robbery offense in question. The couple was apprehended after the offense and at a place away from the scene of the crime. A witness for the state testified that a woman with blond hair and a ponytail ran from the scene and entered a yellow car driven by a Black male. He was described as having a beard and a mustache.

A mathematician then was called to the stand and asked to support the hypothesis that defendants were the assailants by applying the product rule of probability theory to the evidence of identification. Use of the product rule involves assessing the separate probability (expressed as a fraction) of the occurrence of each of a number of independent events and, then, because these events allegedly concurred, multiplying these individual probabilities. The product represents the probability of the *joint* occurrence of these separate events or characteristics. Thus, if the probability were 1 in 10 that a given automobile were yellow and 1 in 500 that an interracial couple were in the same car, the odds of such a couple being in a yellow car would be 1 in 5,000 (1/10 x 1/500). This result indicates that the couple apprehended was the same couple that committed the offense

---

witness need only be qualified to interpret accurately the evidence as, for example, where a police officer testifies to the results of us-

ing radar to detect the subject's vehicular speed.

34. 68 Cal.2d 319, 438 P.2d 33 (1968).

because of the comparatively remote chance that a similar couple was riding in a yellow car.

Already, a difficulty is apparent. How is it known that 1 out of 10 automobiles is yellow? Perhaps this statistic is available, but it would not be easy to obtain it. Furthermore, it is highly doubtful that there is a reliable statistic representing the chance that a car will be occupied by an interracial couple. Perhaps the chance of this separate event is as probable as 1 in 500 or as remote as 1 in 10,000. The point is that without a reliable probability, obtained by random sample or otherwise, for the happening of each of the component events represented in the product formula, the final product can not accurately reflect the actual chance of the joint occurrence. It is true that one can make arbitrary, but conservative assignments of probability [35] to each separate event and arrive at a product that supposedly understates the probability of all events concurring. Thus, conservatively, it might be assumed that the chance of a yellow car should be placed at ⅓ and that of an interracial couple occupying a car at ⅓ so that the chance of fortuitous concurrence is ⅑, or 1 in 9. But these assumptions are outside the province of reasonable certainty, and making calculations on the basis of such suppositions amounts to little more than simply taking a common-sense observation (it is unlikely that a given car will be yellow *and* contain an interracial couple) and giving it a mathematical expression.

There is yet another cautionary note to be sounded in the use of simple probability theory. The validity of the final product depends upon the *independence* of the separate events or characteristics. Suppose in the *Collins* case the following characteristics are said to have the probability noted:

	Probability
Interracial couple	1/500
Male with beard	1/10
Male with mustache	1/4

---

35. People v. Collins, supra note 34 involved an estimate of probabilities; so did State v. Sneed, 76 N. M. 349, 414 P.2d 858 (1966) in which an expert attempted to show by the product rule that suspect was the same person as the one who entered name, address and physical description in sales register.

Arguably, these last two events are not independent because many, perhaps even most, men with a beard also have a mustache. The danger lies in postulating as independent events those which in fact are related or dependent. By way of further example, suppose a murder weapon is known to be a .38 caliber handgun with five lands and grooves (ridges and depressions in the barrel). It might be a mistake to treat the number of lands and grooves as an independent factor. Even though, say, only one-fourth of all pistols have five lands and grooves, a high proportion of .38 caliber pistols may have this number.[36] If this is true, either the number of lands and grooves must be discarded as dependent or some adjustment in the mathematical formula must be made in order to take account of the dependency.

A final observation: The probability of the congruence of multiple, independent events *is built upon the assumption* that the independent events or characteristics exist. Suppose, for example, the separate events (or characteristics) in *Collins* were independent and suppose further that it were possible to assign an accurate probability to each event. A fatal defect in the accuracy of the conclusion based upon probability theory may still exist because there was a faulty observation of one or more of the separate events or characteristics. The woman assailant in fact may have had red hair instead of blonde; the man identified as Negro may have been an Indian, and so forth. Of these possibilities of mistaken perception (or faulty memory) the probability rule takes no account. To take an extreme example, suppose the eyewitness in *Collins* gave false testimony; in fact, the offense was committed by two Caucasian males. Obviously, the probability rule is of no help in reconstructing the historical facts, and it may endanger reliable factfinding. The tendency of the trier might be to focus upon the superficially persuasive mathematical odds and to lose sight of the significant point that the factual assumptions underlying the probabilities might be false or inaccurate. The Supreme Court of California stressed this danger in the *Collins* case, but it also rejected the statistical

---

36. See Louisell et al. at 70–72 where the problem is posed by excerpts from a closing argument.

proof on other grounds: there was no showing that the probability factors assigned to the separate characteristics were accurate and no showing that these characteristics were mutually independent.

An accepted means of proof utilizing statistics and principles of biology is using blood tests to establish identity. This technique can be useful in a variety of contexts. In its simplest form, it may only involve a showing that blood taken from clothing or elsewhere is the same type as, say, the defendant's blood. Since under one well-known classification there are four major blood groups (O, A, B, and AB) and the approximate percentage of persons falling within each group is established,[37] similarity of type can add force to the argument that the blood in question came from the alleged person. This contention is especially cogent where the group is comparatively rare: type AB is a good example for it is found in only 3% of the population.[38] Thus, if the victim (with say, type O blood) injures his assailant (AB blood) and the blood found at the scene of the crime matches the blood of the accused assailant, probative value is high. Even where a more commonly found blood group is involved—for example O, which is found in 45% of the population —similarity of blood type has probative value and is usually admitted into evidence for the purpose of establishing identity.[39]

---

37.   O – 45% of the population
     A – 42% of the population
     B – 10% of the population
     AB – 3% of the population

See Shanks v. State, 185 Md. 437, 45 A.2d 85 (1945) and, for a detailed explanation, see McCormick, § 211, at 517–519; 1 Wigmore § 165(b). As will be seen from the referenced texts, there are two other systems of grouping. These resulted from subsequent discoveries of additional characteristics of the human blood. The availability of three major systems yields additional opportunities to discriminate among blood groups.

38. See supra Note 37. The reader is reminded that other classifications exist. Ibid.

39. A leading American case is Shanks v. State, 185 Md. 437, 45 A.2d 85 (1945); see also United States v. Kearney, 420 F.2d 170 (D.C.Cir. 1969); Parson v. State, 222 A.2d 326, cert. denied 386 U.S. 935 (1966). For an English case where similarity of blood was apparently routinely admitted as increasing the probability of the asserted identity, see Mawaz Khan v. The Queen, 3 Weekly Law Reports 1275 (Privy Council, 1966).

This result is proper, especially since the trier should have no difficulty in understanding the evidence or in assigning to it an appropriate weight.

Evidence of blood group is also useful in resolving an issue of paternity. It is scientifically established that certain parental blood group combinations create an impossibility that the offspring can have blood of certain specified types. When the blood group(s) of the parents is known, these biological laws of heredity can be applied to limit the range of blood types that it is possible to find in an offspring. The most frequent use of these hereditary principles is in making determinations about whether a particular person (usually the putative father) is, or could be, the parent of the child in question. Information about the blood type of the child and that of one parent permits reliable conclusions about the possible blood type of the father. If, for example, the child's blood group is A and the mother's group is O, the father must be either A or AB; he can not be either B or O.[40]

It readily can be seen that it is scientifically possible to separate and exclude absolutely certain persons from those individuals who may be suspected of being the parent of the child in question. It is not surprising that evidence of blood grouping tests is always admissible when the results *preclude* the possibility that the defendant (or some other named person) is in fact the unknown parent. The principles of blood grouping are so widely recognized that it is not even necessary that an expert provide proof of the validity of the underlying principles; these can be the subject of judicial notice.[41] The expert can, if he wishes, briefly state the scientific principles and provide and interpret the test results. Is this evidence given a conclusive effect, or could there still be a civil or criminal judgment against the person who, under biological laws, could not be the parent? The better view, increasingly adopted in recent years, is that evidence establishing nonpaternity is conclusive if the blood-group-

40. See the table appearing in Greene, "Blood Will Tell," 1 Mercer L.Rev. 266, 268 (1950) and reprinted in McCormick, § 211, at 518.

41. See Ch. I, § 7.

ing tests were properly conducted. Any jury finding to the contrary can not stand.[42]

A difficulty arises when the test results do not exclude the alleged parent. May the party seeking to prove parentage introduce the results into evidence? The argument for admission is that since the putative parent is not within the excludable groups, his inclusion within one or more of the blood groups that could account for the child's blood type is probative that he is the parent. This contention is quite consistent with the general principle of relevance, which holds that evidence is relevant if it makes the proposition to which it is directed more likely than it would be in the absence of the evidence. The fact that the alleged parent is not within the excluded group adds to the probabilities that he is the father. In cases where the excluded blood groups constitute a high proportion of the general population, yet the putative parent is not excluded, probative force is significantly increased. But we have repeatedly observed that relevant evidence can be rejected if its probative value is substantially outweighed by such factors as unfair prejudice or misleading the jury. Nonetheless, it seems that the jury can properly assess the evidence that the charged party is within a group that could have produced the offspring. The danger of misleading the trier is reduced by revealing the percentages of the various

---

42. See Commonwealth v. D'Avella, 339 Mass. 642, 162 N.E.2d 19 (1959); Jordan v. Mace, 144 Me. 351, 69 A.2d 670 (1949); Commissioner of Welfare v. Costonie, 277 A.D. 90, 97 N.Y.S.2d 804 (1st Dept. 1950); Steiger v. Gray, 145 N.E.2d 162 (Ohio Juv.Ct. 1957). A famous case to the contrary involved the actor Charles Chaplin; see Berry v. Chaplin, 74 Cal.App.2d 652, 169 P.2d 442 (1950). As suggested in the text, the courts usually accord a conclusive effect by taking judicial notice of the undisputed validity of blood-grouping tests.

A more difficult question is presented in cases where a child is born in wedlock, but the husband seeks to show that he is not the father. The law favors legitimacy by raising a presumption that the husband is the father. Should this presumption be overcome by evidence of blood-test results that establish that the husband could not have been the father? McCormick points out that if the law ignores the reality, the husband is made answerable for a child that is not his and the true father escapes responsibility. See McCormick, § 211, at 521 and cases cited which admit the test results. If the tests are properly conducted, the results should be conclusive.

blood groups within the total population. Thus, it is curious, and seemingly indefensible, that the vast majority of cases [43] exclude test evidence that shows the alleged parent is within a blood group that makes his (or her) parentage possible.

The foregoing description of the use and admissibility of blood tests as evidence illustrates several points of general application in the field of scientific evidence. Whenever scientific evidence (as we broadly use that term here) is offered, the first inquiry is whether it adds to the likelihood of the proposition to which it is directed. This, of course, is the simple test of relevance. But with evidence of a technical nature, there is special concern: the trier might give undue weight to this evidence since it may appear to lend the certainty of an exact discipline to problematic factfinding. This concern is manifested in at least two cautionary judicial principles. First, there must be foundation evidence showing that the tests and procedures employed in adducing the scientific result were performed and followed in accordance with the accepted standards of the discipline in question.[44] Second, courts require a degree of recognition within the field or profession that the assumptions, principles or scientific laws that underlie the results are considered sound. In other words, among those who are knowledgeable in the field in question there must be acceptance of the validity and reliability of the evidence that is proffered for judicial use. At one point, the courts required

---

43. See the cases collected in 46 A. L.R.2d 1000, 1022 (1956). Rejection of this evidence often is justified as a matter of statutory interpretation. In many states, admission of test results which *exclude* paternity is also traced to a statutory provision (although it appears that a court would have inherent power to admit this evidence).

It is thus possible to conclude that since the statute only grants admissibility to results which preclude the possibility of paternity, results which do not exclude the charged party are inadmissible. Whether the legislature intended this result is a matter that can be pursued in the legislative history of the particular statute in question. Arguably, only a clear demonstration of the intended rejection of results showing the possibility of parenthood should overcome the usual judicial prerogative to admit relevant evidence that appears to fall within the area of admissibility.

44. See, e. g., State v. Baker, 56 Wash.2d 846, 355 P.2d 806 (1960) (setting out procedure to be used in breathalyzer test).

acceptance by those within the general field from which the evidence was developed.[45]   However, in recent years when highly developed specialties and sub-specialties have been burgeoning, it appears sufficient if experts in the particular narrow field of endeavor accord validity to the scientific basis of the evidence.[46] Sometimes the validity of a scientific principle is so widely and firmly established that it may be judicially noticed.[46a]

Observe, then, the various possibilities for rejecting scientific evidence.   The evidence might be refused because it is irrelevant, because probative value is overcome by a substantial possibility of jury confusion or misuse, because it was developed without following proper test procedures, or finally, because the validity of the evidence (even if proper procedures were used) has not been recognized within the field concerned.   If, on the other hand, the evidence is admitted it could be given either of two distinct effects: It could be considered conclusive as to the proposition to which it is directed or it could be given only such probative effect as the trier deems appropriate.   The important factor in the consideration whether the evidence should be conclusive is the extent to which those in the field accept as irrefutable the scientific conclusion in question.   Here the courts wisely await the development of a consensus within the general scientific community before denying to the trier the authority to reach a contrary conclusion.   Obviously, the greater impact of conclusiveness justifies a caution beyond that necessary when the evidence is admitted only for such probative effect as the trier determines to give it.

The use of radar for speed detection involves the application of several of the general rules governing the acceptability and use of scientific evidence.   It is now undisputed, and, hence, can

45.   This is the test set out in Frye v. United States, 293 F. 1013 (D.C. Cir. 1923).   See also Waltz, Criminal Evidence 321–22 (1975) where the *Frye* test is discussed.

46.   See J. Waltz, Criminal Evidence, supra note 45, at 322, citing People v. Williams, 164 Cal.2d Supp. 858, 331 P.2d 251 (1958) and Coppolina v. State, 223 So.2d 68 (Fla.App.) cert. denied 399 U.S. 927 (1968).

46a.   See Ch. I, § 7.

be judicially noticed, that the principles underlying radar are valid.[47] Thus, it is unnecessary to offer proof that a radio wave which strikes a moving object changes frequency in proportion to the speed of the object.[48] Of course, an officer or some other person must still provide a foundation covering such matters as the condition of the equipment, operative and record-keeping procedures, and identity of the offender's vehicle.[49] If this foundation testimony is not challenged, is the result of the radar test conclusive as to the driver's speed? This question is most frequently posed in criminal prosecutions for speeding where, by tradition if not by constitutional force, a verdict is not directed against the person charged.[50] Thus, the results of the radar measurement are not conclusive against the accused. In civil cases, however, it should be the rule that in the absence of a challenge to the foundation testimony, the test results are conclusive.

Even this concise treatment of scientific evidence would be truncated without some reference to comparatively new techniques and devices that are currently being proffered for judicial acceptance.[51] Neutron activation analysis (NAA) is a technique for the analysis, identification and comparison of physical evidence. Almost any substance can be subjected to this elaborate

47. See, e. g., People v. Magri, 3 N. Y.2d 562, 170 N.Y.S.2d 335, 147 N.E.2d 728 (1958); State v. Dantonio, 18 N.J. 570, 115 A.2d 35 (1955). For a brief treatment of judicial notice, see Ch. I, § 7. See generally McCormick § 328 et seq. McCormick elsewhere makes the point that state statutes often provide for judicial notice of the scientific principles underlying radar. McCormick, § 210, at 515.

48. For a description of the principle and operation of a radar unit, see J. Waltz Criminal Evidence 412–14 (1975); McCarter, Legal Aspects of Police Radar, 16 Clev.–Mar.L. Rev. 455 (1966).

49. See Waltz, supra note 48 at 414–15; Russell, Radar Speedometers in Court, 6 ABA Law Notes 69 (1970).

50. But the cases hold that the trier can find guilt beyond a reasonable doubt on the basis of the results of radar detection. See McCormick, § 210, at 515.

51. The polygraph (lie detector) is briefly treated in note 4 at the conclusion of Ch. VIII. The use and acceptability of truth serums is also mentioned.

and sophisticated process which can isolate and measure minute traces of an endless variety of materials such as gunpowder, narcotics, hair, alcohol, soil, rubber, etc.[52] The identification and quantitative analysis of the material in question are accomplished by measuring the gamma rays emitted after the sample has been irradiated by bombardment with neutrons in a nuclear reactor.[53] Although neutron activation analysis is expensive and requires complicated nuclear equipment, it appears exceedingly accurate in revealing most substances [54] and has yet another advantage: the material analyzed normally is not damaged and consequently can be preserved for other purposes such as courtroom exhibition. Several courts have given careful consideration to NAA and the developing attitude is one of receptivity.[55] For the near future, at least, a party intending to use NAA results as evidence should be prepared to offer one or more experts who will testify as to the validity of the process. Further, it is advisable, and apparently mandatory in a criminal case, to give the other party or the accused pretrial notice of the intended use of NAA test results.[56]

---

52. A good description of neutron activation analysis may be found in Waltz supra note 48 at 374–75. See also Note, Evidence—Admissibility of the Neutron Activation Analysis Test, 18 St. Louis U.L.J. 235 (1973).

53. Waltz supra note 48 at 375. For more details, consult Moenssens, Moses & Inbau, Scientific Evidence in Criminal Cases 389 et seq. (1973).

54. Difficulty is encountered in comparing blood samples. See State v. Stout, 478 S.W.2d 368 (Mo. 1972); Waltz supra note 48 at 376.

55. A leading case is United States v. Stifel, 433 F.2d 431 (6th Cir.), cert. denied 401 U.S. 994 (1970); see also State v. Coolidge, 109 N.H. 403, 260 A.2d 547 (1969), rev'd on other grounds 403 U.S. 443 (1971).

See generally Karjala, Evidentiary Uses of Neutron Activation Analysis, 59 Calif.L.Rev. 997 (1971). But see State v. Stout, 478 S.W.2d 368 (Mo. 1972) holding that NAA, although generally valid, is not sufficiently reliable to justify admission when employed to compare blood samples. Blood presents special problems, one of which is that certain trace elements in blood produce a disproportionate emission. See Waltz supra note 48 at 376.

56. Compare United States v. Kelly, 420 F.2d 26 (2d Cir. 1969) with United States v. Stifel, 433 F.2d 431 (6th Cir.), cert. denied 401 U.S. 994 (1970). *Stifel* indicates that the government must not only give notice, but must also give the financial assistance necessary to enable the accused to conduct his own tests.

Another technique that has recently gained the attention of courts and commentators is that of achieving voice identification through the use of an electromagnetic instrument called a spectrograph. This device is capable of producing graphic impressions ("voiceprints") of the human voice, taking account of such variables as frequency, volume and time intervals. If an identified voice sample is available, a voiceprint is made and it is then compared with the voiceprint of the unknown voice. Ten frequently used words (such as "and," "the," "I" and "you") normally serve as the basis of the comparative analysis. The theory underlying this means of identification is that human voices differ because of the number of variables involved in voice production. Speech involves the use of the various parts of the vocal cavities (throat, mouth, nose, and sinuses) which will vary in size and relationship from person to person. Voice production also utilizes the so-called "articulators" (soft palate, jaws, tongue, teeth and lips) which will be used differently among speakers.[57] The combination of differing physical characteristics and varying usage of the articulators is said to make it highly unlikely that any two voices are actually the same.[58]

The validity of the spectrographic technique of voice identification is subject to some dispute within the scientific community. Hence, it is not surprising that cases considering the admissibility of voiceprints reflect varying judicial attitudes. A 1970 New Jersey case rejected spectrographic evidence on the ground that at that time there was insufficient scientific acceptance of the validity and reliability of voiceprints as a means of identification.[59] However, several recent cases have reached a contrary result.[60] If voiceprints are received only after a comprehensive foundation and the jury is instructed that there is disagreement as to the reliability of this evidence, it would ap-

---

57. See Waltz supra note 48 at 391.

58. See Louisell 1170 where some sample voiceprints are reproduced.

59. State v. Cary, 56 N.J. 16, 264 A. 2d 209 (1970); see also People v. King, 266 Cal.App.2d 437, 72 Cal. Rptr. 478 (1968).

60. Worley v. State, 263 So.2d 613 (Fla.App.1972); State ex rel. Trimble v. Hedman, 291 Minn. 442, 192 N.W.2d 432 (1971); United States v. Raymond, 337 F.Supp. 641 (D.D. C.1971).

pear that spectrographic results can make a positive contribution
to factfinding. It is doubtful that the law should demand infalli-
bility of scientific results before granting admissibility; a wiser
course is to receive evidence that is generally reliable—at least
in those circumstances where the trier can be made aware of potential pitfalls and inaccuracies.

NOTES

1. *Fingerprints*. The use of fingerprints for the purpose of identification has long been accepted by the courts. The underlying biological principle is that the friction skin ridges, which make up the
fingerprint pattern, begin to form during fetal life and remain un-
changed until the skin decomposes after death. These patterns are
never duplicated in their minute details, not even on the fingers of a
single individual. Sweat pores in the skin ridges exude perspiration
and other bodily oils which leave an impression of the pattern whenever a smooth surface is touched. It is this impression which is
analyzed and used to match a person with the print. The scientific
principles underlying fingerprinting are judicially noticed. See generally II Wigmore § 414. For the history of fingerprinting, see
Hoover, The Role of Identification in Law Enforcement: An Historical
Adventure, 46 St.John's L.Rev. 613 (1972).

2. *Ballistics*. The scientific analysis of projectiles that are fired
from various kinds of arms yields important and admissible evidence
about the firearm used. See Annot., 26 A.L.R.2d 892 (1952). Variations in rifling, firing pins and even shell ejector mechanisms make
possible fine discriminations.

3. *Detection of Intoxication*. There are now several devices used
to determine, by chemical means, the subject's level of intoxication.
Measurements of the breath (by use of a "Breathalyzer") and of the
blood or urine can be used to indicate the approximate amount of
alcohol that has reached the brain. The legislatures have given extensive attention to this kind of evidence. Typically, the statutes
permit evidence of test results and prescribe what presumptions, if
any, shall arise from the findings. For example, a level of 0.05
percent (or less) of blood alcohol usually raises a presumption that
the subject was not under the influence of alcohol. On the other hand,
a finding of 0.10 percent (or more) usually creates a presumption
of intoxication. McCormick, § 209, at 511–512. See Generally Erwin,
Defending Drunk Driving Cases (3d ed. 1977).

4. *Detection of Narcotics Use*. The drug Nalline can be used
to detect the recent use of narcotics. When the drug is administered,

the eye pupils of a recent user dilate. The courts have been receptive to "nalline tests." See People v. Zavala, 239 Cal.App.2d 732, 49 Cal. Rptr. 129 (1966).

5. *Speed Detection.* The latest speed detection device for traffic control is called VASCAR (Visual Average Speed Computer and Recorder). It allows the subject's speed to be computed from a police car that is either moving or standing still. McCormick, states in § 210 at 516: "If [the use of VASCAR] . . . expands, it can be expected that admissibility problems will follow the patterns experienced with the radar speedometer: a period in which complete expert explanation is required, followed (if successful) by judicial notice of the underlying principles and general reliability of the system."

CHAPTER XIII

REAL EVIDENCE

§ 108. Real and Demonstrative Evidence: In General

The term "real evidence" generally refers to animate or inanimate physical things exhibited to the jury. Often, however, the term is used narrowly to refer only to tangible items (such as a weapon or a damaged mechanical part) originally involved in the litigated occurrence. The term "demonstrative evidence" often is employed to indicate those tangible items (such as maps, diagrams, or models) not directly involved in the litigated occurrence, but subsequently constructed or obtained by the parties to illustrate (demonstrate) their factual contentions or to help the jury understand the case. It has been suggested that although most real evidence itself has probative value, demonstrative evidence has none, being a mere visual or artificial aid designed to assist the trier in understanding the probative testimony or contentions of the parties.[1] The validity of this distinction is doubtful, at least if the term "probative value" denotes the tendency of evidence to make the existence of a fact more probable than it would be in the absence of the evidence.[2] In any event, this distinction often is ignored by the appellate opinions and, as we shall see, the use of both real and demonstrative evidence is conditioned upon criteria that reduce the risk of improperly influencing the trier.

In the following discussion, the term "real evidence," unless otherwise indicated, is used in its broadest sense to include any

---

1. See Smith v. Ohio Oil Co., 10 Ill. App.2d 67, 75, 134 N.E.2d 526, 530 (1956).

2. Whatever the technical limits of demonstrative evidence, practicing lawyers regard it as having probative force. See Belli, Demonstrative Evidence and the Adequate Award, 22 Miss.L.J. 284 (1951). See also III Wigmore, § 791, at 227 (Chadbourn), which states that a map or diagram used as part of a witness's testimony "*is evidence like any other part of the witness' utterance.*"

tangible thing ("res") exhibited to the jury. However, there is a distinction that should be grasped regarding the proper evidentiary foundation: When the exhibited item allegedly was involved in the occurrence or controversy in question (*original* real evidence), its admission is conditioned upon a showing by the proponent that the thing displayed is the *same* tangible that originally was involved.[3] But where the real evidence is used only demonstratively—that is to illustrate or clarify—its origin is not important:[4] what matters is whether the properties or characteristics of the item (map, model, or so forth) are sufficiently clear and accurate to assist, without misleading, the trier in understanding some aspect of the case.

When a party presents real evidence, its perceptible qualities can be ascertained by the trier without reliance on the testimonial capacities (observation, memory, and sincerity) of others.[5] Nonetheless, the use of real evidence also involves some reliance upon the foundation testimony establishing the origin or nature of the evidence. If the proponent fails to persuade the jury of the authenticity or accuracy of his real evidence, they may disregard it. In any event, the jury has the function of assessing the credibility of testimony relating to the imperceptible aspects of real evidence.

Finally, real evidence, like other forms of proof, can be used directly or circumstantially.[6] If an ultimate issue in a case rests on whether a certain antique is chipped and discolored, display of the item provides direct evidence of the defects.[7] But if the issue is the cause of the damage, the item is mere circumstantial proof generating an inference as to the cause of the defect. Likewise, the perceptible characteristics of a child (color of

3. See Higginbotham v. State, 262 Ala. 236, 240, 78 So.2d 637, 640 (1955); Isaacs v. National Bank of Commerce of Seattle, 50 Wash.2d 548, 551, 313 P.2d 684, 686 (1957); McCormick, § 212, at 527.

4. McCormick, § 212, at 528.

5. Morgan at 171. The leading article on the theoretical basis of real proof is Michael & Adler, Real Proof, 5 Vand.L.Rev. 344 (1952).

6. McCormick, § 212, at 526.

7. Cf. Woodward & Lothrop v. Heed, 44 A.2d 369 (D.C. Mun.Ct.App.1945).

eyes, skin, or hair, for example) are direct evidence of their nature, but circumstantial evidence that X is the father.[8]

§ 109. Real and Demonstrative Evidence: Conditions of Admissibility and Required Foundation

In order to be admissible, tangible evidence must provide the trier of fact with some knowledge or understanding it lacked before viewing the thing presented.[9] Further, the insights gained must be material to the controversy being tried. This is a familiar theme. Relevant evidence makes the consequential proposition to which it is directed more likely that it would be without the evidence; often, however, courts relax even this undemanding standard when dealing with real evidence. Although real evidence sometimes can have very high probative force—as, for example, where it is used as direct proof of an ultimate issue [10]—it also may serve only to illustrate or explain testimony directed to the background or setting of the litigated transaction. In this latter circumstance the probative force of the real evidence is marginal at best, but courts nonetheless admit it unless it has a potential for causing confusion or delay. Perhaps it may be generalized that courts consider real evidence "relevant" if it either increases the probability of consequential proposition *or* assists the trier in understanding the case.

All evidence, of course, is subject to the objection that its probative weight is outweighed by prejudice, distraction, confusion, or undue delay. With real evidence this balancing test most often is required when the proffered item likely will inspire a sharp emotional response such as pity, repugnance, or resent-

8. See Lohsen v. Lawson, 106 Vt. 481, 174 A. 861 (1934); McCormick, § 212, at 526.

9. See McAndrews v. Leonard, 99 Vt. 512, 134 A. 710 (1926) where one question presented on appeal was whether the trier could gain useful knowledge from touching a depression (caused by a fracture) in the plaintiff's skull. This case and other pertinent cases and comments may be found in Maguire et al. at 95–113.

10. If there were an issue whether a person were scarred or dismembered and that person were presented to the trier, the probative force would be obvious. See McCormick, § 212, at 526.

ment. Nonetheless, when the evidence displays a condition that is in issue the courts almost always will admit it.[11] And even where probative force is comparatively weak, the tendency still is toward admission: such things as a plaintiff's preserved knee cap,[12] decedent's blood-stained clothing,[13] and pictures of a deceased victim of a crime [14] all have been admitted. Because the trial judge has considerable discretion in balancing the worth of real evidence against its negative aspects, reversals of his rulings are relatively rare.[15]

The proponent of real evidence must provide a proper foundation, a process variously referred to as identification or authentication. This generally consists of having one or more witnesses describe the item, supply information about its origin, and, if needed, provide such additional testimony as is required to show

---

11. Lanford v. People, 159 Colo. 36, 409 P.2d 829 (1966) (motion picture of allegedly intoxicated driver); Darling v. Charleston Comm. Mem. Hosp., 50 Ill.App.2d 253, 200 N.E.2d 149 (1964) (stump of amputated leg); Olson v. Tyner, 219 Iowa 251, 257 N.W. 538 (1934) (shriveled arm). See McCormick, § 212, at 526, especially notes 15 and 22. See also Slattery v. Marra Bros., 186 F.2d 134, 138 (2d Cir. 1951).

12. Russell v. Coffman, 237 Ark. 778, 376 S.W.2d 269 (1964) (physician used severed knee cap to demonstrate nature of injury and reason for surgery). But see Harper v. Bolton, 239 S.C. 541, 124 S.E.2d 54 (1962) (admission of removed eye was error because it was conceded plaintiff lost her eye in the accident). These cases and others are cited and summarized in Maguire et al. at 126–131.

13. Wilson v. State, 247 Ind. 680, 221 N.E.2d 347 (1966); see also Wimberley v. Patterson, 75 N.J. Super. 584, 183 A.2d 691 (1962) (wrongful death action based on

shooting; while refusing to hold that the trial court abused its discretion in rejecting the clothing the court noted that the apparel might have assisted the jury in determining the degree of the decedent's visibility).

14. Wilson v. State, 247 Ind. 680, 221 N.E.2d 347 (1966); Napier v. Commonwealth, 426 S.W.2d 121 (Ky.Ct.App.1968); IV Wigmore, § 1157, at 340–50 n. 3. But see State v. Poe, 21 Utah 2d 113, 441 P.2d 512 (1968). In People v. Burns, 109 Cal. App.2d 524, 241 P.2d 308 (1952) the court held that the trial judge abused his discretion in admitting photographs of deceased taken after an autopsy; probative value, in the court's view, was low or nonexistent and the potential for prejudice quite high.

15. See, e. g., State v. Bucanis, 26 N. J. 45, 138 A.2d 739 (1958); Wimberley v. Patterson, 75 N.J. Super. 584, 183 A.2d 691 (1962); Smith v. Ohio Oil Co., 10 Ill.App.2d 67, 134 N.E.2d 526 (1956).

that the item is relevant. Where the evidence is "original" in the sense that it played a part in the controversy, identification entails a showing that the thing offered is the *same item* involved in the litigated transaction[16]—for example that the proffered rifle is the weapon used by the defendant or the proffered ring is the one that was falsely claimed to be a diamond. It will be seen immediately that this logical condition requiring that the origin of the thing be shown is a function of the principle of relevance—more specifically of conditional relevance.[17] The weapon or the ring is not helpful unless it is the one involved in the parties' conduct. Observe, however, that where the evidence only is demonstrative, authentication involves having a witness identify the proffered item—for example, as the map of a certain region or a model of the human skeleton—or provide such brief additional explanation as is necessary for the trier to understand what is exhibited. The origin of the res is not important.

There is an additional requirement—again based upon relevance—that must be satisfied during identification, and it too varies with whether or not the real evidence is original. With original evidence, the proponent should elicit testimony that the relevant quality or condition of the proffered thing *has not changed substantially* since the time of its involvement in the controversy.[18] The basic principle of relevance, which demands probative force but weighs this against countervailing practical considerations, requires this showing.[19] If the item has been substantially altered, its probative value is reduced or negated and it may mislead or confuse the jury. On the other hand, if the proffered thing is not original but rather is demonstrative, the proponent need show only that the proffered item is a fair representation of what it purports to be.[20] For example, if a map or a model

---

16. See supra note 3.

17. See Ch. II, § 14.

18. Anderson v. Berg, 202 Kan. 659, 451 P.2d 248 (1969); McElfresh v. Commonwealth, 243 S.W.2d 497 (Ky.App.1951); McCormick, § 212, at 527.

19. See Ch. II, §§ 11–13.

20. See III Wigmore, § 793, at 239 (Chadbourn); McCormick, § 212, at 528, 529.

is used it should be sufficiently accurate in all pertinent respects so as not to mislead the trier of fact.

There is some uncertainty about the proper role of the judge in determinations of identification. In most instances he performs only a screening function: if a reasonable jury could find that the object is what its proponent claims, the real evidence will be admitted. But real evidence, which appeals directly to the visual sense, can sometimes have a telling probative impact upon the jury.[21] Thus in certain instances where there is a danger that the jury might be misled, the judge may himself determine if authentication is satisfactory. In such cases, he is treating the real evidence as raising an issue of competence and not as simply raising an issue of conditional relevance. Although the governing rules are not always clear, the judge sometimes— at least in common-law jurisdictions—assumes a fact-finding role where scientific evidence is offered or, as we shall see shortly, where there is a question involving a chain of custody.[22] In these instances he is demanding more than simply a prima facie evidentiary foundation that, *if believed by the jury*, would entitle it reasonably to find the elements of identification.

In any event, when the foundation is complete, the proffered thing should be formally introduced into evidence. This invariably is the practice with original evidence, but some jurisdictions do not require that demonstrative evidence be introduced into the record.[23] This relaxation of the usual requirement of having a complete trial record seems ill-advised because it leads to uncertainty at the appellate review stage.[24]

As the foregoing suggests, the general principles governing the introduction of real evidence are relatively simple. Practical

---

21. Weinstein & Berger, ¶ 901(a)[01], at 17: "Real proof often has enormous apparent probative force because the lay trier may lose sight of the fact that its connection to a party may depend upon the credibility of an authenticating witness."

22. See infra note 31 and accompanying text.

23. McCormick, § 213, at 529.

24. See Crocker v. Lee, 261 Ala. 439, 74 So.2d 429 (1954); Radetsky v. Leonard, 145 Colo. 358, 358 P.2d 1014 (1961); McCormick, § 213, at 529.

complications, however, often arise in the case of original real evidence when the proffered res has no distinguishing characteristic, or when, even though such a characteristic exists, the witness is unable to recall having observed this characteristic. The practical problem posed is this: How shall the proponent fulfill that requirement of identification which demands that there be foundation evidence that the proffered item is the same one involved in the controversy? The difficulty can arise with any kind of original evidence—for example, a weapon, a bottle, or a piece of rope; its resolution is found in establishing a *chain of custody,* through the testimony of successive custodians, that substantially eliminates the possibility the proffered item is not the original res. Identification through a chain of custody usually is necessary where a sample (such as blood, semen, or clothing particles) is collected and subjected to scientific tests. Typically, the specimen passes through the custody of several persons: the police, for example, give the sample to a technician, who delivers it to an expert who, after conducting tests, places the sample in the prosecutor's safekeeping. The evidentiary foundation must show that the original item was the thing tested, that it is the same as the thing now offered, and that the test results reported in court were derived from analysis of the sample.[25] Again, the solution lies in the testimony of the various custodians,[26] perhaps supplemented by business entries [27] that help to substantiate authenticity.

There is some variation in the degree of certainty required when a chain of custody is used to fulfill the requirement of

25. See Brewer v. United States, 353 F.2d 260 (8th Cir. 1965). It is customary to introduce into evidence the sample. Introduction of the sample, however, would not appear essential, at least if the evidence shows that the original evidence was analyzed and the results produced in court were derived from the test. If, however, loss or destruction of the sample prevented the other party from challenging the test because of his inability to conduct his own analysis, a more difficult problem arises. The resolution should turn upon whether there is a reasonable possibility that further testing and testimony would produce different results.

26. See, e. g., Eisentrager v. State, 79 Nev. 38, 45, 378 P.2d 526, 530–531 (1963). See also Lestico v. Kuehner, 204 Minn. 125, 283 N.W. 122 (1938) (no chain of custody necessary when a witness can identify the object).

27. See note 27 on page 421.

identification. If tracing an item by its chain of custody is tested by the principle of conditional relevance, the chain adequately
should be forged if the evidence accounting for the item is *sufficient* to allow a reasonable jury to conclude that the offered res
is the original.[28] Presumably, if the trier concluded that an
item other than the original had been introduced, it would ignore the evidence because it readily would see that a false or
substituted thing had no probative force.[29] Yet some cases,
most commonly criminal, appear to require that the evidence of
custody render it *reasonably certain* that the original evidence
has been traced accurately.[30] This more rigorous requirement
arguably is justified by the seriousness of a criminal proceeding
and by the obligation of the government to adopt standard,
trustworthy procedures for safeguarding evidence. An added
safeguard—now employed by many courts—is to require that
the judge [31] determine preliminarily that this standard has been
satisfied before admitting the real evidence. In this regard, he
departs from his usual role of screening the foundation for sufficiency.

Against the foregoing considerations must be weighed the
jury's probable competence to deal with an issue of authenticity.
It should also be noted that the recorded cases contain many examples of unnecessarily formalistic application of the "reasonably certain" standard, resulting in the exclusion of evidence that

---

27. See Wheeler v. United States,
211 F.2d 19 (D.C.Cir.1953), cert.
denied 347 U.S. 1019 (1954).

28. Fed.R.Evid. 901 appears to have
adopted this standard. But see
text and discussion infra at note 33.

29. This statement assumes that the
proponent did not provide an alternative foundation by supplying evidence that, even if the proffered
item were not the original, it had
the same relevant characteristic.

30. See Eisentrager v. State, 79 Nev.
38, 45, 378 P.2d 526, 530–531 (1963).

McCormick states that the chain
must "render it improbable that
the original item has either been
exchanged with another or been
contaminated or tampered with."
McCormick, § 212, at 528.

31. This is a departure from the
usual rule of conditional relevancy
that requires simply that the judge
pass upon whether the jury could
reasonably find that the evidence
was that which its proponent
claims it to be. See Ch. II, § 14;
Ch. X, § 96, infra § 113.

in all likelihood was reliable.[32]   Thus, there may be justification for Federal Rule of Evidence 901(a) which provides that authentication or identification requires only a showing *sufficient* to support a jury finding that the item offered is what it purports to be.[33]   It states:

> The requirement of authentication or identification as a condition precedent to admissibility is satisfied by evidence sufficient to support a finding that the matter in question is what its proponent claims.

It appears that once the proponent supplies evidence sufficient to support a finding of genuineness, the question of proper identification always becomes a jury issue.   This accords with existing common law with regard to most items of real evidence.   As noted earlier, however, there is some judicial support for having the judge first determine issues involving chain of custody and, occasionally, those regarding the proper foundation for scientific evidence.[34]   Some of the cases—particularly many of those involving scientific evidence—may be thought of not principally as instances of the judge ruling upon identification, but rather as examples of the judge exercising his power to exclude evidence that may be misleading or prejudicial.[35]   In other cases, how-

---

32.   See, e. g., Robinson v. Commonwealth, 212 Va. 136, 183 S.E.2d 179 (1971).

33.   5 Weinstein & Berger, ¶ 901(a) [01] (1975), at 15.   But see S. Saltzburg & K. Redden, Federal Rules of Evidence Manual 641–45 (2 ed. 1977).

34.   But the cases are in disarray. Compare Brewer v. United States, 353 F.2d 260 (1965) (judge must determine if physical object such as marijuana that is connected with commission of crime is in substantially the same condition at time of trial as when seized) with State v. Baker, 56 Wash.2d 846, 355 P.2d 806 (1960) (state must produce prima facie evidence of proper foundation for admitting results of breathalyzer test).   See also Yecny v. Eclipse Fuel Eng. Co., 210 Cal. App.2d 192, 26 Cal.Rptr. 402 (1963) (whether conditions of experiment sufficiently similar to actual conditions of explosion to be probative is question for jury; judge screens).

35.   This would arguably be the rationale underlying a judge's rejection of results of a psychological test for sanity or his rejection of a tape recording that he determined was not made under reliable conditions.   See S. Saltzburg & K. Redden, Federal Rules of Evidence Manual, 641–45 (2 ed. 1977).

ever, the judge is preempting the jury and finding conclusively that the thing offered is not satisfactorily shown to be the original. The extent to which Rule 901 nullifies these protective practices is not altogether clear,[36] but its language indicates that in all cases questions of identification or authentication are conditional relevance issues for the jury. However, the trial judge still has power under Rule 403 to exclude probative evidence that raises substantial dangers of prejudice or of misleading the jury.

§ 110. Pictorial Evidence: Photographs, X-rays, and Motion Pictures

Accuracy of reproduction usually is important when pictorial evidence is presented to the trier. It always is required that the proponent of photographic evidence establish that the pertinent parts of the picture are a reasonably accurate representation of the subject pictured. This general requirement may be satisfied in various ways, depending upon the particular kind of photographic evidence. Identification of a still picture or snapshot is complete if a witness (not necessarily the photographer) has observed the subject and testifies that the picture is an accurate reproduction.[37] This same means of identification usually suffices in cases where a moving picture is offered,[38] but some cases —particularly the older ones—require a more elaborate method of identification, including testimony about the conditions and technical aspects of taking, processing, and showing the film.[39] Despite the fact that this more detailed showing somewhat reduces the risk of distortion, it would appear unnecessary where

---

36. One of the few discussions of the problem is found in S. Saltzburg & K. Redden, supra note 35, at 241–45. For a recent case involving authentication of a writing, but interpreting Fed.R.Evid. 901 as requiring only "prima facie" evidence, see United States v. Goichman, 547 F.2d 778 (3rd Cir. 1976).

37. United States v. Valdes, 417 F. 2d 335, 338 (2d Cir. 1969), cert. denied 399 U.S. 912 (1970); State ex rel. State Highway Commission v. Eilers, 406 S.W.2d 567, 570 (Mo. 1966); McCormick, § 214, at 530–531.

38. The more recent cases so hold. See United States v. Richardson, 562 F.2d 476 (7th Cir. 1977); McCormick, § 214, at 533.

39. McCormick, § 214, at 533.

a witness who has viewed the scene or event portrayed states that the reproduction is accurate.

Sometimes photographic evidence may be identified by reliance upon basic principles of photography strengthened by assurances that the equipment used and the procedures followed were proper.[40] This always is the case with x-rays, and is also the case with photographs or motion pictures in circumstances where no witness can verify the accuracy of the depiction of the subject.[41] X-rays, for example, may be introduced upon an evidentiary foundation establishing that the x-ray equipment was an acceptable type, in proper working order, that a qualified operator using correct procedures took the picture, and that the x-ray film (plate) offered depicts the subject in question.[42] In addition, because most x-ray photographs require interpretation in order to be understood by the trier, it usually becomes necessary to show that the individual "reading" the x-ray is a qualified expert. In practice, however, a lengthy process of identification during trial proceedings often is unnecessary; issues of authentication usually are settled at pre-trial conference or by stipulation. Furthermore, unless there is reason to doubt the accuracy of the X-ray picture, the testifying expert usually assumes that the written record on the plate is accurate and proceeds to interpret the picture.[43]

The better-reasoned decisions support the proposition that photographs are "substantive evidence" in the sense that photographic evidence alone can support a finding by the trier. Sur-

---

40. See, e. g., Ferguson v. Commonwealth, 212 Va. 745, 187 S.E.2d 189 (1972) ("Regiscope" pictures of accused's bad check and identification papers); Sisk v. State, 236 Md. 589, 204 A.2d 684 (1964) (Ibid.). See Fed.R.Evid. 901(b)(9); McCormick, § 214, at 531–32.

41. See supra note 40; McCormick, § 214, at 532.

42. See Waltz, Criminal Evidence 369 (1975). Case authorities are collected in Annot., 5 A.L.R.3d 303 (1966).

43. See Maguire et al. at 160 n. 1; Fed.R.Evid. 703 (allowing expert to base his opinion on facts "of a type reasonably relied upon by experts in the particular field. . .") Cf. Fed.R.Evid. 901(b)(9), indicating by way of illustration that the requirement of identification can be satisfied by describing a process or system that produces an accurate result.

prisingly, substantial contrary authority can be found to the effect that photographs are merely illustrative of a witness's testimony and, as such, have no independent probative effect.[44] McCormick correctly describes this limitation as groundless, and given contemporary society's increasing use of photographic techniques in a wide variety of areas, it is difficult to believe that this restriction will persist.[45]

§ 111. Experiments

The result of a carefully conducted experiment often can assist the factfinder. For example, an experiment may demonstrate the unlikelihood or impossibility that certain testimonial assertions are true [46] or that the factual hypothesis of one of the parties is invalid.[47] Conversely, of course, experimental evidence can help establish the correctness of testimonial assertions or of a factual hypothesis.[48]

The principal requirement for admissibility is that the experiment be conducted under conditions substantially similar to

---

44. McCormick, § 214, at 531.

45. Ibid. Suppose an accused, while burglarizing a commercial establishment at night, is photographed by an automatic camera. If there is no eyewitness, would the prosecution fail even if the pictures showed beyond a reasonable doubt that the accused had perpetrated the act? See supra note 40.

46. E. g., Brown v. State, 74 Tex. Cr.R. 356, 169 S.W. 437 (1913) (experiment to show that murderer's position could not have been where accused claimed it was).

47. Cheetham v. Union R. R. Co., 26 R.I. 279, 58 A. 881 (1904) (demonstration that speed was not cause of derailment of electric car); Davis v. State, 51 Neb. 301, 70 N.W. 984 (1897) (experiment demonstrates,

contrary to defendant's contention, that it was possible to remove certain part of railroad track in a short time).

48. People v. Spencer, 58 Cal.App. 197, 208 P. 380 (1922) (test conducted to show scream was audible at place witness said he heard it). See McCormick, §§ 202, 215, at 484–485, 536, where cases are collected that demonstrate the varying uses of experimental evidence. In one interesting case, described in Comment, Experimental Evidence, 34 Ill. Law Rev. 206, 210–211 (1939), a magician was used to show that a money bag used by banking institutions could be opened and resealed without leaving traces of the tampering. Because of the time required for this feat, it was possible to ascertain who the custodian was at the time of the actual loss of funds.

those existing when the contested event occurred.[49] This requirement follows from considerations of relevance; therefore, as with other problems of relevance, the counterweights to admissibility (such as distraction, delay, and prejudice) must be considered. Predictably, the trial judge's decision whether to admit the experimental evidence is likely to be upheld on appeal.[50]

Occasionally, the thrusts and parries of the adversaries will permit relaxation of the usual requirement that an experiment must be performed under substantially similar conditions. This is not to suggest that an irrelevant experiment is permitted, but only that the nature of the parties' assertions may make the exact duplication of conditions unnecessary. Thus, where one party asserted that it was impossible for a driver to control an automobile with a disabled suspension system, it was held proper to demonstrate otherwise, even though the experiment involved another driver who traversed different terrain in another automobile equipped with the same type of suspension system.[51]

Courts have approved experiments conducted both in and out of the courtroom.[52] When the experiment is conducted as part of the trial proceedings, the factors of delay and distraction from the principal issues take on added proportions.[53] On the other hand, an out-of-court experiment, even if less consumptive of judicial time, often involves more difficulty in ensuring that the test was fairly conducted. This problem becomes most acute where the adversary is unaware of the experiment until presentation of the results at trial. If lack of notice denied the opposing party an opportunity to ensure the fairness and validity of

---

49. Ramseyer v. General Motors Corp., 417 F.2d 859, 864 (8th Cir. 1969); Thomas v. Chicago Transit Authority, 115 Ill.App.2d 476, 253 N.E.2d 492 (1969).

50. Ramseyer v. General Motors Corp., 417 F.2d 859, 864 (8th Cir. 1969).

51. Chambers v. Silver, 103 Cal. App.2d 633, 230 P.2d 146 (1951).

See McCormick, § 202, at 486, citing *Chambers* and other cases; Comment, Experimental Evidence, 34 Ill.L.Rev. 206, 207–208 (1939).

52. Cases are collected in Maguire et al. 143–54.

53. McCormick, § 215, at 536.

the experiment, exclusion from evidence of the test results seems appropriate.[54]

§ 112. Writings and Other Recordations: In General

Writings are subject to the general requirement of identification or authentication; traditionally, the latter term has been used most frequently when discussing writings. Because writings, unlike most chattels, directly display recorded information the process of authentication is slightly different. Generally, the relevance of a writing depends upon its authorship, so that the proponent of the writing must, *as a condition preceding admission*, provide an evidentiary basis sufficient for the trier to conclude that the writing came from the source claimed. For example, where a document is signed, the proponent usually must provide evidence sufficient for a reasonable trier to conclude that the writing in fact was signed by the person whose name appears on the document. Of course, written materials are not always signed; in these instances, the proponent must offer preliminary evidence that allows the factfinder to conclude that the document came from the source claimed. The justification for the requirement of authentication, and in particular the requirement that proof of authorship always precede the introduction of the writing, will be discussed in the next section. Suffice it to say that the law of evidence always has treated writings with special care.

A second instance of such careful treatment is the so-called "best evidence" or "original documents" rule. Frequently, a liti-

---

54. See McCormick, § 202, at 487. He notes that the present law does not impose as a condition of admissibility the giving of notice and the opportunity of the adversary to be present. Perhaps this is because a careful and thorough cross-examination often can expose any unfairness in the conduct of the experiment. One difficulty with a routine requirement that the adversary be present at the experiment is that the proponent may hesitate to attempt the test if he is uncertain of the results. One possible solution is to require the proponent of test results to give notice to his adversary after the experiment, but prior to trial. This notice should give the pertinent details of the experiment and should be served in ample time to allow the opponent to draft interrogatories asking about the experiment, or to conduct his own test.

gated issue turns upon the contents or terms of a writing, making it important that the evidence of the writing be reliable. It could be maintained that writings should be treated like other evidence, leaving to the parties the free choice of what material they produce to prove the content or terms of a writing. Under such an approach, a party who relied only on testimony to prove the contents of a writing when there was no apparent reason why he could not produce the writing itself would presumably suffer in his efforts to persuade the jury. Nonetheless, for reasons explained later, the law of evidence imposes a rule of preference: the original document is preferred whenever a party seeks to prove the terms of a writing; secondary evidence (such as copies or testimony) generally is inadmissible if the original is available.   The best evidence rule originally applied exclusively to writings. In recent years, however, there has been a tendency to extend it to other kinds of permanent recordation such as tape recordings and, in certain instances, photographs. In its modern form—illustrated by Federal Rules of Evidence 1002 and 1003—the best evidence rule is modified to give due recognition to the accuracy of modern means of producing copies.

It should be stressed that the obstacles encountered in satisfying the requirements of authentication and best evidence often are more apparent than real. By means of requests for admissions, stipulations, or other agreements reached before or during trial, the opposing lawyers often reach practical accommodations that obviate the need for courtroom compliance with the evidentiary requirements pertaining to documentary evidence.

§ 113. Authentication: In General

The requirement of authentication can be viewed simply as a function of the principle of relevance: a writing must be linked to its source by sufficient evidence whenever the relevance of the written matter depends upon its source. Evidence of a written contractual acceptance, for example, will be irrelevant (immaterial) unless it came from the defendant now charged with contractual breach; an acceptance not traceable to the defendant will not support his liability. In most circumstances where (as in this example) there is a problem of conditional relevance —that is, the relevance of proffered evidence depends upon the existence of some preliminary fact—the judge can, in his discretion, admit the proffered evidence. His admission is conditioned upon a subsequent presentation of evidence of the allied or conditioning fact, so as to make it reasonable for the jury to find this underlying fact.[55] This option regarding the order of presentation is not usually available with writings (or other tangibles). The general practice in all jurisdictions is to require that before a writing is admitted, there must be sufficient evidence of authorship to enable a reasonable factfinder to conclude that the writing is genuine or, put otherwise, that it is what the proponent claims it to be. Note, however, that in jury trials, the judge need not decide himself that the writing is genuine, but he must, as a condition of admission, conclude that the evidence of authorship is sufficient for the jury so to find. However, even if the proponent meets this preliminary condition of admissibility (authentication), the final determination of authenticity rests with the jury. If the jury finds that the document did not come from the source claimed, it should disregard the writing.

Authentication may be properly seen as a logical application of the general principle of conditional relevance. If it were only this, however, and no more, the exacting demands of some of the cases would be unexplainable. Additional purposes of authentication are said to be the prevention of fraud and of mistaken attribution of a writing to one who, by coincidence, has the same name as the author.[56] Whether authentication effectively serves either of these purposes is doubtful, but the belief that it does accounts for the stringent standard applied when courts are asked to determine whether evidence of authorship is sufficient to link the writing with its purported source. This standard is based upon the premise that the mere appearance of a signature, standing alone, is not sufficient evidence of authorship. Thus, in order to satisfy the judge that there exists sufficient evidence of authorship to permit a jury finding, the proponent of a writing usually must offer some evidence *in addition* to

---

55. See Ch. II, § 14; Ch. X, § 96.   56. See McCormick, § 218, at 544.

the appearance of a signature or other written recital of the source.

The net effect of this requirement is to make the standard of sufficiency more exacting where writings are concerned.[57] Indeed, some of the earlier cases aberrantly carried the concept of sufficiency to extremes.[58] Although recent cases and evidence codes maintain the basic principle that authentication requires evidence in addition to a mere recital of source within the writing, this requirement is not applied to some types of writings such as newspapers, government publications, and documents from a public depository. Even where the principle applies, there is an increasingly liberal attitude concerning what evidence beyond a recital on the face of the proffered document is sufficient to establish genuineness. As we shall see, such additional evidence, standing alone, need not meet high standards of probativeness.

§ 114.   Authentication by Evidence Extrinsic to the Writing

The requirement of authentication can be satisfied by producing either direct or circumstantial evidence extrinsic to the proffered document. Direct evidence of genuineness can consist of testimony by the author or by a witness who saw the proffered

57. Supra note 56. As McCormick points out, in both business and social affairs, it is customary and seemingly quite reasonable, to rely upon the writing itself as accurately divulging its source. McCormick, § 218, at 544.

58. The cases most frequently cited are Mancari v. Frank P. Smith, Inc., 114 F.2d 834 (D.C.Cir. 1940) holding that newspaper advertising circular containing defendant's name and advertising the shoes he sold did not provide a sufficient basis to attribute the writing to defendant, and Keegan v. Green Giant Co., 150 Me. 283, 110 A.2d 599 (1954) holding the label on a can of peas insufficient to support a finding that the writing (label) was published by the defendant, Green Giant. Without this evidence, the plaintiff could not establish that the peas came from the defendant and hence a directed verdict was entered in favor of Green Giant. These cases are usually reprinted or summarized in the leading casebooks. See, e. g., Maguire et al. at 174–78. Clearly, the holding in *Green Giant* is rejected by Fed.R. Evid. 902(7). *Mancari*, too, appears to have been cast aside by the rulemakers. See Fed.R.Evid. 901(b)(4), 902(6); Weinstein & Berger, ¶ 902 (6)[01], at 27.

writing made or signed.[59] A witness familiar with the handwriting in question also can testify that the proffered document is genuine.[60] The reliability of this mode of authentication is suspect [61] and the leniency of the courts in routinely approving it can not be reconciled with other circumstances in which courts, purportedly applying the normal standard for authentication, make greater demands of the proponent.[62]

Circumstantial evidence of genuineness also can take a variety of forms. For example, the handwriting of the proffered document may be compared by the jury (or by an expert) to exemplars that are found to be genuine [63] or distinctive characteristics of the appearance or contents of a document may be shown in support of a finding that the signature or recital of authorship is genuine.[64] Authentication by reference to communica-

---

59. McCormick, § 219, at 545.

60. Apple v. Commonwealth, 296 S. W.2d 717 (Ky.1956); Hershberger v. Hershberger, 345 Pa. 439, 443, 29 A.2d 95, 98 (1942); McCormick, § 221, at 547. One could view the form of proof as circumstantial because the witness is comparing what he sees with what he remembers and infers from the similarities that the proffered writing is genuine. Nonetheless, the trier is not required to make inferences. See Ch. II, § 9.

61. Very limited familiarity often is held to qualify the witness to assert that the writing is genuine. State v. Bond, 12 Idaho 424, 86 P. 43 (1906) (witness had seen person write "several" times). See McCormick, § 221, at 547. Professor Inbau has conducted an experiment strongly indicating that authentication by one familiar with the handwriting in question is unreliable. See Inbau, Lay Witness Identification of Handwriting (An Experiment), 34 Ill.L.Rev. 433 (1939).

62. See supra note 58.

63. This is an area where the competence of a lay jury overlaps that of an expert. Although a handwriting expert is entitled to give his professional opinion based upon a comparison of the sample with the contested writing, the jury also is held competent to compare genuine exhibits with the one in dispute. See Tracy, The Introduction of Documentary Evidence, 24 Iowa L.Rev. 436, 445 (1939). Some courts require the judge to make a final determination that the specimens used for comparison themselves are genuine. See, e. g., University of Illinois v. Spalding, 71 N.H. 163, 51 A. 731 (1901). The Federal Rules, however, require only that there be sufficient evidence that the samples are genuine. See Fed.R.Evid. 901(b)(3).

64. McFarland v. McFarland, 176 Pa.Super. 342, 345, 107 A.2d 615, 616 (1954) (writing style of author); Fed.R.Evid. 901(b)(4).

tive content occurs when the document in question reveals information likely to be known only to the purported author.[65] Similarly, the proponent may authenticate by showing that the questioned writing is a *reply* to an earlier writing addressed to the
purported author. For example, if *A* writes to *B* inquiring
about a loan and *B*'s reply directly or indirectly makes reference
to *A*'s letter, *B*'s writing can be authenticated by first introducing acceptable proof of the content of *A*'s letter and then
showing the responsive terms of the document allegedly written by *B*.[66] Another means of providing circumstantial evidence of authentication is to introduce evidence of the process or
system that produced the questioned writing and then to show
the accuracy of that system. A writing produced by a computer, for example, could be authenticated by this means. Finally,
to this nonexhaustive list can be added the ancient documents
rule: a document that is sufficiently aged (usually 30 or more
years),[67] regular on its face, and found in a place (or in a person's custody) where it likely would be located were it genuine,
can be admitted without further authentication. These requirements for admitting aged documents perhaps provide a modest
check against fraud because (1) the visible signs raise no suspi-
cions, (2) it is rather unlikely that a fraudulent document will
go undetected for such a long period, and (3) it is unlikely that
someone would falsify a document if the erroneous entries would
not have an operative effect for many years thereafter. Whatever the validity of these assumptions, however, the ancient documents rule practically accommodates the recognized difficulty
of finding authenticating witnesses after the lapse of a long peri-

65. People v. Adams, 162 Mich. 371,
127 N.W. 354 (1910) (letter discloses
knowledge of a conversation and
was mailed in city where purported
writer said he would be); Abbott
v. McAlóon, 70 Me. 98 (1879)
(knowledge of oral agreement concerning sale of certain goods).

66. See Anstine v. McWilliams, 24
Wash.2d 230, 163 P.2d 816 (1945).
It is presumed that *B* received *A*'s
initiating letter and, where necessary, it also is presumed that *B*
(who signed as business agent) had
authority to act. Ibid. See also
Ch. III, §§ 16–17.

67. The common-law rule required
that the document be 30 or more
years of age. McCormick, § 223, at
549. The Federal Rules of Evidence reduce this period to 20 or
more years. Fed.R.Evid. 901(b)(8).

od of time. It should be emphasized that the ancient documents rule here discussed is a means of proving authorship or authenticity. Introducing documentary assertions often raises a hearsay difficulty,[68] although many jurisdictions have created an exception to the hearsay rule for ancient documents.[69]

§ 115. Self-Authentication

The preceding section focused upon accepted methods of meeting the requirement of authentication by producing evidence extrinsic to the proffered writing. In a number of situations, usually specified by statute,[70] a document can be authenticated from within its four corners, that is, in specified instances, the face of the document is sufficient proof of authenticity to justify its admission. Documents so classified often are said to be "self-authenticating" or "prima facie genuine" and, as such, entitled to admission into evidence. Any dispute as to the authenticity of these documents, of course, will be resolved by the trier.

Analytically, the process of self-authentication normally involves an assertion on the face of the document that it is genuine,[71] coupled with an indication (such as an official seal or stamp) that the asserter is the official duly authorized to certify authenticity. Typically, the official will be a notary public or the public custodian of the writing in question. Acknowledged bills of exchange or instruments of conveyance frequently are authenticated on their face. Documents in the custody of a public official, such as tax returns, wills, licenses and court judgments, usually are admitted on the basis of a written certification executed by the public custodian. Many states have passed

---

68. This difficulty is encountered when the assertions in the document are entered for their truth. See Ch. VI, §§ 49–50. Proof of the contents of a document also may raise problems associated with privileged communications. See Ch. IX.

69. See, e. g., Fed.R.Evid. 803(16) (twenty-year standard).

70. There also is a common-law rule providing for the "self-authentication" of public documents. See Lembeck v. United States Shipping Board Emergency Fleet Corp., 9 F. 2d 558, 559 (2d Cir. 1925). See also Annot., 70 A.L.R.2d 1227 (1960).

71. This assertion, which is accepted for its truth, constitutes an exception to the hearsay rule. See V Wigmore § 1677.

laws that permit legislative enactments to be admitted into evidence if the printed material containing the statutes purports to have been printed or published by a sovereign.[72] Finally, the Federal Rules of Evidence extend the concept of self-authentication beyond its traditional boundaries to include such writings as newspapers and trade inscriptions.[73]

§ 116. The Best Evidence Rule

We have noted that the rule requiring the production of the original document applies only when the proponent is attempting to prove the contents or terms of a writing. The original is preferred because its use eliminates the risk of mistranscriptions or testimonial misstatements of what the document said; inspection of the original also reduces somewhat the chance of undetected tampering.[74] Note that sometimes a writing recites or records a perceivable event or condition such as a marriage (marriage certificate), payment of money (receipt), or the utterance of certain words (transcript). Here, the proponent wishing to prove the underlying event may proceed in either of two ways: he may (1) offer the testimony of an observer, or (2) offer the writing that records or recites the event. The first approach does not involve the best evidence rule because the proponent is not attempting to prove the terms of a writing, but merely is presenting evidence of an event perceived by a witness. It makes no difference that the occurrence of the event is recited in a writing that was made subsequent to its occurrence, for the writing does not, so far as legal rules of proof are concerned, "erase" or supplant the preceding event. Of course, if the proponent chooses to make his proof by use of a writing, the best evidence rule must be satisfied. There are, moreover, some instances where the law prescribes that a writing has the effect of subsuming, so to speak, any prior events. In these situations, illustrated by a deed, a written contract, or a judgment, the law regards the transaction as "essentially written" and the proponent must make his proof by the writing if it is available.[75]

---

72. See V Wigmore § 1677; Mc-
Cormick, § 228, at 557.

73. See Fed.R.Evid. 902.

74. McCormick, § 231, at 561.

75. McCormick, § 233, at 563.

The courts are in general accord with the foregoing analysis, although there has been some tendency in criminal cases to prefer a written, signed confession over the testimony of a person claiming to have heard an oral confession.[76] Perhaps this preference can be justified as a protective measure, but analytically the proponent does not seek to prove the terms of a writing; therefore his choice should affect only the weight of his evidence.

Where there are several writings, application of the best evidence rule requires a determination of which one (or ones) constitutes an original. Preliminarily, it should be noted that parties can create *multiple* originals: if copies (such as carbons or photostatic reproductions) of a contract, will, or other agreement are duly executed (signed), the parties have manifested their intention to accord equal status to all of the identical writings regardless of their mechanical characteristics. Beyond this, reference to the substantive law is often necessary to determine what constitutes an "original" for purposes of the best evidence rule. Suppose, for example, a defendant types an original of a libelous document; he then makes a photostatic copy, but he publishes only the latter. The copy is the operative document under the substantive law and, as such, constitutes the original with respect to the best evidence rule. A similar analysis should be employed with regard to telegrams. If *D* writes out a contractual offer at the telegraph office and the terms of the offer then are embodied in a telegram, the telegram is the original—assuming the telegraph company is acting as *D*'s agent. This result turns not upon which writing was created first, but rather upon which document has an operative legal effect.[77] In addition to the problems created by certain substantive legal doctrines, modern technology often blurs the line between an original and a copy. For instance, data can be entered and stored in a computer or similar device and then, upon command, returned

---

76. Id. at 564–65. The leading case to the contrary is Meyers v. United States, 171 F.2d 800 (D.C.Cir. 1948), cert. denied 336 U.S. 912 (1949), where a split court held that in a trial for subornation of perjury the prior transcribed testimony of a witness could be proved by oral testimony of one who overheard it.

77. See McCormick § 235.

in printed form. All such printouts should be considered originals, and this characterization appears to have been accepted by the courts.[78] The term "duplicate or multiple original" often is used to describe these documents of equal evidentiary status.

Once an original has been identified, it should be produced if feasible, assuming the proponent seeks to prove its terms. Unexecuted photographic copies of the original are considered secondary evidence and, quite obviously, oral testimony purporting to give the terms of the original falls into the same category. Unexecuted carbon copies probably should stand on the same footing as photographic copies, but some authorities treat a carbon as a duplicate original.[79]

It might be asked whether there is any longer a need for the best evidence rule, given the reliability of modern means of reproduction. Because of technological accuracy, it is difficult to base one's choice between the original and a copy (as opposed to one's choice between the original and verbal testimony) on the ground that the copy lacks reliability because it more likely contains accidental inaccuracies or omissions. Perhaps the rule preferring the original can be justified on the ground that as between the original and a copy, the former is more likely to yield clues to tampering or fraud.[80]

The Federal Rules of Evidence strike a balance which preserves a preference for the original and at the same time gives due recognition to the accuracy of copies produced by modern means. Rule 1002 provides that "To prove the content of a writing, recording, or photograph, the original . . . is required, except as otherwise provided. . . ." Rule 1003, however, states that "A duplicate is admissible to the same ex

---

78. McCormick, § 236, at 569. See also Federal Union Surety Co. v. Indiana Lumber & Mfg. Co., 176 Ind. 328, 95 N.E. 1104 (1911) (three printed slips made by a device called an autographic register are held triplicate originals).

79. See, e. g., Davis, Agent v. Williams Brothers Const. Co., 207 Ky.

404, 269 S.W. 289 (1925); Annot., 65 A.L.R.2d 342 (1959). It could be argued that carbon copies are more reliable than photographic copies because tampering can be more easily detected in the former.

80. McCormick, § 231, at 561. See supra note 79.

tent as an original unless (1) a genuine question is raised as to the authenticity of the original or (2) in the circumstances it would be unfair to admit the duplicate in lieu of the original." [81] Thus, the federal draftsmen adopted a middle ground between rejection of the best evidence principle and adherence to its traditional formulation. Another feature of the Federal Rules is noteworthy: the application of the best evidence rule extends beyond writings to include sound recordings and photographs.[82] This enlargement of the rule can be traced to similar extensions in several of the states,[83] and it should not be viewed as a far-reaching change.

The original of a sound recording usually is the initial recording, and the original of a photograph is the "negative or any print therefrom." [84] In most cases the proponent would offer these "originals" even without the force of a rule.[85] With regard to still and moving pictures, proof of the photographic contents is not necessary very often. Commonly, photographic evidence is admitted as a graphic representation of a scene or subject that a testifying witness has observed. This illustrative use of photographic evidence does not involve proving the contents of the picture but rather is an attempt to establish the scene itself by testimony.[86] But if no witness has observed the pictured scene or event (as in the case of an x-ray or where an automatic cam-

---

81. As an example of a circumstance of unfairness, consider a situation where the copy reveals only a portion of the original and there is a reasonable possibility that the remainder would modify the duplicated excerpts or provide other relevant information. See Weinstein & Berger ¶ 1003 [03] where this and other examples of unfairness are cited.

82. Fed.R.Evid. 1002.

83. People v. King, 101 Cal.App.2d 500, 225 P.2d 950 (1950) (recording); Cellamare v. Third Ave. Transit Corp., 273 A.D. 260, 77 N. Y.S.2d 91 (1948) (x-rays); Annot.,

62 A.L.R.2d 686, 689; West's Ann. Cal.Evid.Code § 250.

84. Fed.R.Evid. 1001(3).

85. For a case in which a "copy" of a tape was admitted along with the original (which contained excessive background noise), see United States v. Madda, 345 F.2d 400 (7th Cir. 1965); see also McGuire v. State, 200 Md. 601, 92 A.2d 582 (1952) (written transcript of tape admitted because accurate playback of tape not practical).

86. See Paradis, The Celluloid Witness, 37 U.Colo.L.Rev. 235, 249–251 (1965).

era photographs a litigated event), or a photograph is alleged to be libelous, obscene, violative of a copyright or of one's privacy, the photographic contents are in issue and the best evidence rule applies.[87]

Federal or state statutory provisions sometimes modify the usual application of the best evidence rule. Congress, for example, has enacted a statute allowing photographic reproduction of tax returns and certain Treasury documents.[88] State and federal statutes permitting copies of public records are common,[89] as are provisions that apply to regularly kept business records.[90] If no exception to the best evidence rule can be discovered, then care should be taken to determine what circumstances will excuse production of the original.

If the original is lost or destroyed (excepting bad faith destruction by the proponent himself) production is excused.[91] The same result occurs where the original is difficult or impossible to obtain,[92] or where the original is in the hands of the opponent and, after due notice, he fails to produce it.[93]

Finally, the careful practitioner should ascertain if the jurisdiction in question prefers a particular kind of *secondary* evidence. Many courts extend the principle of the best evidence rule and thus give it an operative effect even after production of the original has been excused. The most common extension to secondary evidence is to require a copy (when available) in lieu

---

87. See S. Saltzburg & K. Redden, Federal Rules of Evidence Manual 676 (2d ed. 1977); Adv.Comm.Note to Fed.R.Evid. 1002.

88. 26 U.S.C.A. § 7513.

89. See McCormick § 240. There also is a common-law rule allowing copies of public documents. Id. at 574, n.9.

90. The Uniform Photographic Copies of Business and Public Records as Evidence Act has been adopted by a large number of states. See 9A U.L.A. 117 (1967 Supp.). A fed-

eral statute has similar provisions. See 28 U.S.C.A. § 1732(b).

91. McCormick, § 237, at 570; Fed. R.Evid 1004(1).

92. McCormick, § 238, at 571–572; Fed.R.Evid. 1004(2).

93. McCormick, § 239, at 572–574; Fed.R.Evid. 1004(3). If the proponent wants the original, he should use an appropriate discovery device, such as a request to produce documents or a subpoena *duces tecum*, to obtain it.

of oral testimony purporting to give the terms of the original.[94] But the Federal Rules of Evidence contain no provision for "classes" of secondary evidence.[95] Usually, the self-interest of the proponent will operate to place before the trier the most reliable secondary evidence.

NOTES

1. *Jury's Use of Real Evidence.* By force of tradition or in some instances, statute, the jury usually is permitted to take to the jury room tangible exhibits (including writings) admitted into evidence. This general practice, however, is subject to the trial judge's discretionary modification unless a court rule or statute provides otherwise. When a writing serves as a substitute for testimony, as in the case of depositions and recorded recollection, the prevailing practice is to disallow inspection in the jury room. The reason is that the "written testimony" may be given undue emphasis in relation to the oral testimony presented during trial. Should the written confession of an accused be withheld from jury-room inspection? McCormick notes in § 217, at 540, that such confessions, even though testimonial in nature, usually are made available to the jury during their deliberations. What, if anything, justifies this practice?

2. *Authentication of Telephone Calls.* Telephonic communications, although obviously not writings, present a problem of authentication similar to that presented by written evidence. If a witness testifies that he recognized the voice of the speaker, the requirement of authentication is fulfilled. Even in the absence of voice recognition, the witness can authenticate the speaker's voice by showing that he (the witness) called the number assigned to the speaker by the telephone company and that during the conversation the speaker identified himself. Cf. Benson v. Commonwealth, 190 Va. 744, 750, 58 S.E.2d 312, 314 (1950). Furthermore, if the number is a business number and the answering speaker purports to act for the company called, it will be presumed that the speaker was "clothed with authority to transact the business conducted." Korch v. Indemnity Ins. Co., 329 Ill.App. 96, 102, 67 N.E.2d 298, 301 (1946). In the absence of voice recognition, a difficult problem can arise when the speaker calls the witness and

---

94. This probably is the majority position. See Baroda State Bank v. Peck, 235 Mich. 542, 209 N.W. 827 (1926); McCormick, § 241, at 575–576.

95. If the proponent, under the operation of Fed.R.Evid. 1002 and 1003, is required to produce the original, but production of the original is excused under the provisions of Fed.R.Evid. 1004, then any probative secondary evidence may be used. See Adv.Comm. Note to Fed.R.Evid. 1004.

then identifies himself. This identification, standing alone, is insufficient to authenticate the speaker's voice. Other clues, however, such as the revelation of facts likely to be known only to the speaker, may supply the needed link. See Sunray Sanitation, Inc. v. Pet, Inc., 249 Ark. 703, 461 S.W.2d 110 (1970); McCormick, § 226, at 554.

3. *Judge's Role.* The reader is reminded that with regard to authentication of writings, the judge usually ensures only that the evidence is sufficient for a jury finding of authenticity. However, preliminary factual questions attending the application of the best evidence rule—such as whether the original has been lost—normally are resolved with finality by the judge. See Ch. X, §§ 96–97 and note 1 at the conclusion of the chapter.

APPENDIX
RULES OF EVIDENCE
FOR
UNITED STATES COURTS
AND MAGISTRATES

Effective July 1, 1975

As Amended Through July 1, 1978

TABLE OF CONTENTS

Article VIII. Hearsay:
Rule

801. Definitions:
    (a) Statement
    (b) Declarant
    (c) Hearsay
    (d) Statements which are not hearsay:
        (1) Prior statement by witness
        (2) Admission by party-opponent

802. Hearsay rule

803. Hearsay exceptions; availability of declarant immaterial:
    (1) Present sense impression
    (2) Excited utterance
    (3) Then existing mental, emotional, or physical condition
    (4) Statements for purposes of medical diagnosis or treatment
    (5) Recorded recollection
    (6) Records of regularly conducted activity
    (7) Absence of entry in records kept in accordance with the provisions of paragraph (6)
    (8) Public records and reports
    (9) Records of vital statistics
    (10) Absence of public record or entry
    (11) Records of religious organizations
    (12) Marriage, baptismal, and similar certificates
    (13) Family records
    (14) Records of documents affecting an interest in property
    (15) Statements in documents affecting an interest in property
    (16) Statements in ancient documents
    (17) Market reports, commercial publications
    (18) Learned treatises
    (19) Reputation concerning personal or family history
    (20) Reputation concerning boundaries or general history
    (21) Reputation as to character
    (22) Judgment of previous conviction
    (23) Judgment as to personal, family, or general history, or boundaries
    (24) Other exceptions

804. Hearsay exceptions; declarant unavailable:
    (a) Definition of unavailability
    (b) Hearsay exceptions:
        (1) Former testimony
        (2) Statement under belief of impending death
        (3) Statement against interest
        (4) Statement of personal or family history
        (5) Other exceptions

RULES OF EVIDENCE

FOR

UNITED STATES COURTS
AND MAGISTRATES

Effective July 1, 1975

As Amended Through July 1, 1978

ARTICLE I.   GENERAL PROVISIONS

Rule 101.

SCOPE

These rules govern proceedings in the courts of the United States and before United States magistrates, to the extent and with the exceptions stated in Rule 1101.

Rule 102.

PURPOSE AND CONSTRUCTION

These rules shall be construed to secure fairness in administration, elimination of unjustifiable expense and delay, and promotion of growth and development of the law of evidence to the end that the truth may be ascertained and proceedings justly determined.

Rule 103.

RULINGS ON EVIDENCE

(a) Effect of erroneous ruling. Error may not be predicated upon a ruling which admits or excludes evidence unless a substantial right of the party is affected, and

(1) *Objection.* In case the ruling is one admitting evidence a timely objection or motion to strike appears of record, stating the specific ground of objection, if the specific ground was not apparent from the context; or

(2) *Offer of proof.* In case the ruling is one excluding evidence, the substance of the evidence was made known to the judge by offer or was apparent from the context within which questions were asked.

(b) Record of offer and ruling. The court may add any other or further statement which shows the character of the evidence, the form in which it was offered, the objection made, and the ruling thereon. It may direct the making of an offer in question and answer form.

(c) Hearing of jury. In jury cases, proceedings shall be conducted, to the extent practicable, so as to prevent inadmissible evidence from being suggested to the jury by any means, such as making statements or offers of proof or asking questions in the hearing of the jury.

(d) Plain error. Nothing in this rule precludes taking notice of plain errors affecting substantial rights although they were not brought to the attention of the court.

Rule 104.

PRELIMINARY QUESTIONS

(a) Questions of admissibility generally. Preliminary questions concerning the qualification of a person to be a witness, the existence of a privilege, or the admissibility of evidence shall be determined by the court, subject to the provisions of subdivision (b). In making its determination it is not bound by the rules of evidence except those with respect to privileges.

(b) Relevancy conditioned on fact. When the relevancy of evidence depends upon the fulfillment of a condition of fact, the judge shall admit it upon, or subject to, the introduction of evidence sufficient to support a finding of the fulfillment of the condition.

(c) **Hearing of jury.** Hearings on the admissibility of confessions shall in all cases be conducted out of the hearing of the jury. Hearings on other preliminary matters shall be so conducted when the interests of justice require or, when an accused is a witness, if he so requests.

(d) **Testimony by accused.** The accused does not, by testifying upon a preliminary matter, subject himself to cross-examination as to other issues in the case.

(e) **Weight and credibility.** This rule does not limit the right of a party to introduce before the jury evidence relevant to weight or credibility.

Rule 105.

LIMITED ADMISSIBILITY

When evidence which is admissible as to one party or for one purpose but not admissible as to another party or for another purpose is admitted, the court, upon request, shall restrict the evidence to its proper scope and instruct the jury accordingly.

Rule 106.

REMAINDER OF OR RELATED WRITINGS OR RECORDED STATEMENTS

When a writing or recorded statement or part thereof is introduced by a party, an adverse party may require him at that time to introduce any other part or any other writing or recorded statement which ought in fairness to be considered contemporaneously with it.

ARTICLE II. JUDICIAL NOTICE

Rule 201.

JUDICIAL NOTICE OF ADJUDICATIVE FACTS

(a) **Scope of rule.** This rule governs only judicial notice of adjudicative facts.

(b) **Kinds of facts.** A judicially noticed fact must be one not subject to reasonable dispute in that it is either (1) generally known within the territorial jurisdiction of the trial court or (2) capable of accurate and ready determination by resort to sources whose accuracy cannot reasonably be questioned.

(c) When discretionary. A court may take judicial notice, whether requested or not.

(d) When mandatory. A court shall take judicial notice if requested by a party and supplied with the necessary information.

(e) Opportunity to be heard. A party is entitled upon timely request to an opportunity to be heard as to the propriety of taking judicial notice and the tenor of the matter noticed. In the absence of prior notification, the request may be made after judicial notice has been taken.

(f) Time of taking notice. Judicial notice may be taken at any stage of the proceeding.

(g) Instructing jury. In a civil action or proceeding, the court shall instruct the jury to accept as conclusive any fact judicially noticed. In a criminal case, the court shall instruct the jury that it may, but is not required to, accept as conclusive any fact judicially noticed.

ARTICLE III.   PRESUMPTIONS IN CIVIL ACTIONS AND PROCEEDINGS

Rule 301.

PRESUMPTIONS IN GENERAL IN CIVIL ACTIONS AND PROCEEDINGS

In all civil actions and proceedings not otherwise provided for by Act of Congress or by these rules, a presumption imposes on the party against whom it is directed the burden of going forward with evidence to rebut or meet the presumption, but does not shift to such party the burden of proof in the sense of the risk of nonpersuasion, which remains throughout the trial upon the party on whom it was originally cast.

Rule 302.

APPLICABILITY OF STATE LAW IN CIVIL ACTIONS AND PROCEEDINGS

In civil actions and proceedings, the effect of a presumption respecting a fact which is an element of a claim or defense as to which state law supplies the rule of decision is determined in accordance with state law.

ARTICLE IV. RELEVANCY AND ITS LIMITS

Rule 401.

DEFINITION OF "RELEVANT EVIDENCE"

"Relevant evidence" means evidence having any tendency to make the existence of any fact that is of consequence to the determination of the action more probable or less probable than it would be without the evidence.

Rule 402.

RELEVANT EVIDENCE GENERALLY ADMISSIBLE; IRRELEVANT EVIDENCE INADMISSIBLE

All relevant evidence is admissible, except as otherwise provided by the Constitution of the United States, by Act of Congress, by these rules, or by other rules prescribed by the Supreme Court pursuant to statutory authority. Evidence which is not relevant is not admissible.

Rule 403.

EXCLUSION OF RELEVANT EVIDENCE ON GROUNDS OF PREJUDICE, CONFUSION, OR WASTE OF TIME

Although relevant, evidence may be excluded if its probative value is substantially outweighed by the danger of unfair prejudice, confusion of the issues, or misleading the jury, or by considerations of undue delay, waste of time, or needless presentation of cumulative evidence.

Rule 404.

CHARACTER EVIDENCE NOT ADMISSIBLE TO PROVE CONDUCT; EXCEPTIONS; OTHER CRIMES

(a) **Character evidence generally.** Evidence of a person's character or a trait of his character is not admissible for the purpose of proving that he acted in conformity therewith on a particular occasion, except:

(1) *Character of accused.* Evidence of a pertinent trait of his character offered by an accused, or by the prosecution to rebut the same;

(2) *Character of victim.* Evidence of a pertinent trait of character of the victim of the crime offered by an accused, or by the prosecution to rebut the same, or evidence of a character trait of peacefulness of the victim offered by the prosecution in a homicide case to rebut evidence that the victim was the first aggressor;

(3) *Character of witness.* Evidence of the character of a witness, as provided in Rules 607, 608, and 609.

(b) **Other crimes, wrongs, or acts.** Evidence of other crimes, wrongs, or acts is not admissible to prove the character of a person in order to show that he acted in conformity therewith. It may, however, be admissible for other purposes, such as proof of motive, opportunity, intent, preparation, plan, knowledge, identity, or absence of mistake or accident.

Rule 405.

METHODS OF PROVING CHARACTER

(a) **Reputation or opinion.** In all cases in which evidence of character or a trait of character of a person is admissible, proof may be made by testimony as to reputation or by testimony in the form of an opinion. On cross-examination, inquiry is allowable into relevant specific instances of conduct.

(b) **Specific instances of conduct.** In cases in which character or a trait of character of a person is an essential element of a charge, claim, or defense, proof may also be made of specific instances of his conduct.

Rule 406.

HABIT; ROUTINE PRACTICE

Evidence of the habit of a person or of the routine practice of an organization, whether corroborated or not and regardless of the presence of eyewitnesses, is relevant to prove that the conduct of the person or organization on a particular occasion was in conformity with the habit or routine practice.

Rule 407.

SUBSEQUENT REMEDIAL MEASURES

When, after an event, measures are taken which, if taken previously, would have made the event less likely to occur, evidence of the subsequent measures is not admissible to prove negligence or culpable conduct in connection with the event. This rule does not require the exclusion of evidence of subsequent measures when offered for another purpose, such as proving ownership, control, or feasibility of precautionary measures, if controverted, or impeachment.

Rule 408.

COMPROMISE AND OFFERS TO COMPROMISE

Evidence of (1) furnishing or offering or promising to furnish, or (2) accepting or offering or promising to accept, a valuable consideration in compromising or attempting to compromise a claim which was disputed as to either validity or amount, is not admissible to prove liability for or invalidity of the claim or its amount. Evidence of conduct or statements made in compromise negotiations is likewise not admissible. This rule does not require the exclusion of any evidence otherwise discoverable merely because it is presented in the course of compromise negotiations. This rule also does not require exclusion when the evidence is offered for another purpose, such as proving bias or prejudice of a witness, negativing a contention of undue delay, or proving an effort to obstruct a criminal investigation or prosecution.

Rule 409.

PAYMENT OF MEDICAL AND SIMILAR EXPENSES

Evidence of furnishing or offering or promising to pay medical, hospital, or similar expenses occasioned by an injury is not admissible to prove liability for the injury.

Rule 410.

INADMISSIBILITY OF PLEAS, OFFERS OF PLEAS, AND RELATED STATEMENTS

Except as otherwise provided in this rule, evidence of a plea of guilty, later withdrawn, or a plea of nolo contendere, or of an offer to plead guilty or nolo contendere to the crime charged or any other crime, or of statements made in connection with, and relevant to, any of the foregoing pleas or offers, is not admissible in any civil or criminal proceeding against the person who made the plea or offer. However, evidence of a statement made in connection with, and relevant to, a plea of guilty, later withdrawn, a plea of nolo contendere, or an offer to plead guilty or nolo contendere to the crime charged or any other crime, is admissible in a criminal proceeding for perjury or false statement if the statement was made by the defendant under oath, on the record, and in the presence of counsel.
As amended Dec. 12, 1975.

Rule 411.

LIABILITY INSURANCE

Evidence that a person was or was not insured against liability is not admissible upon the issue whether he acted negligently or otherwise wrongfully. This rule does not require the exclusion of evidence of insurance against liability when offered for another purpose, such as proof of agency, ownership, or control, or bias or prejudice of a witness.

ARTICLE V. PRIVILEGES

Rule 501.

GENERAL RULE

Except as otherwise required by the Constitution of the United States or provided by Act of Congress or in rules prescribed by the Supreme Court pursuant to statutory authority, the privilege of a witness, person, government, State, or political subdivision thereof shall be governed by the principles of the common law as they may be interpreted by the courts of the United States in the light of reason and experience. However, in civil actions and proceedings, with respect to an element of a claim or defense as to which State law supplies the rule of decision, the privilege of a witness, person, government, State, or political subdivision thereof shall be determined in accordance with State law.

ARTICLE VI. WITNESSES

Rule 601.

GENERAL RULE OF COMPETENCY

Every person is competent to be a witness except as otherwise provided in these rules. However, in civil actions and proceedings, with respect to an element of a claim or defense as to which State law supplies the rule of decision, the competency of a witness shall be determined in accordance with State law.

Rule 602.

LACK OF PERSONAL KNOWLEDGE

A witness may not testify to a matter unless evidence is introduced sufficient to support a finding that he has personal knowledge of the matter. Evidence to prove personal knowledge may, but need not, consist of the testimony of the witness himself. This rule is subject to the provisions of Rule 703, relating to opinion testimony by expert witnesses.

Rule 603.

OATH OR AFFIRMATION

Before testifying, every witness shall be required to declare that he will testify truthfully, by oath or affirmation administered in a form calculated to awaken his conscience and impress his mind with his duty to do so.

Rule 604.

INTERPRETERS

An interpreter is subject to the provisions of these rules relating to qualification as an expert and the administration of an oath or affirmation that he will make a true translation.

Rule 605.

COMPETENCY OF JUDGE AS WITNESS

The judge presiding at the trial may not testify in that trial as a witness. No objection need be made in order to preserve the point.

Rule 606.

COMPETENCY OF JUROR AS WITNESS

(a) At the trial. A member of the jury may not testify as a witness before that jury in the trial of the case in which he is sitting as a juror. If he is called so to testify, the opposing party shall be afforded an opportunity to object out of the presence of the jury.

(b) Inquiry into validity of verdict or indictment. Upon an inquiry into the validity of a verdict or indictment, a juror may not testify as to any matter or statement occurring during the course of the jury's deliberations or to the effect of anything upon his or any other juror's mind or emotions as influencing him to assent to or dissent from the verdict or indictment or concerning his mental processes in connection therewith, except that a juror may testify on the question whether extraneous prejudicial information was improperly brought to the jury's attention or whether any outside influence was improperly brought to bear upon any juror. Nor may his affidavit or evidence of any statement by him concerning a matter about which he would be precluded from testifying be received for these purposes.

Rule 607.

WHO MAY IMPEACH

The credibility of a witness may be attacked by any party, including the party calling him.

Rule 608.

EVIDENCE OF CHARACTER AND CONDUCT OF WITNESS

(a) Opinion and reputation evidence of character. The credibility of a witness may be attacked or supported by evidence in the form of opinion or reputation, but subject to these limitations: (1) the evidence may refer only to character for truthfulness or untruthfulness, and (2) evidence of truthful character is admissible only after the character of the witness for truthfulness has been attacked by opinion or reputation evidence or otherwise.

(b) Specific instances of conduct. Specific instances of the conduct of a witness, for the purpose of attacking or supporting his credibility, other than conviction of crime as provided in Rule 609, may not be proved by extrinsic evidence. They may, however, in the discretion of the court, if probative of truthfulness or untruthfulness, be inquired into on cross-examination of the witness (1) concerning his character for truthfulness or untruthfulness, or (2) concerning the character for truthfulness or untruthfulness of another witness as to which character the witness being cross-examined has testified.

The giving of testimony, whether by an accused or by any other witness, does not operate as a waiver of his privilege against self-incrimination when examined with respect to matters which relate only to credibility.

Rule 609.

IMPEACHMENT BY EVIDENCE OF CONVICTION OF CRIME

(a) General rule. For the purpose of attacking the credibility of a witness, evidence that he has been convicted of a crime ιall be admitted if elicited from him or established by public record during cross-examination but only if the crime (1) was punishable by death or imprisonment in excess of one year under the law under which he was convicted, and the court determines that the probative value of admitting this evidence outweighs its prejudicial effect to the defendant, or (2) involved dishonesty or false statement, regardless of the punishment.

(b) **Time limit.** Evidence of a conviction under this rule is not admissible if a period of more than ten years has elapsed since the date of the conviction or of the release of the witness from the confinement imposed for that conviction, whichever is the later date, unless the court determines, in the interests of justice, that the probative value of the conviction supported by specific facts and circumstances substantially outweighs its prejudicial effect. However, evidence of a conviction more than 10 years old as calculated herein, is not admissible unless the proponent gives to the adverse party sufficient advance written notice of intent to use such evidence to provide the adverse party with a fair opportunity to contest the use of such evidence.

(c) **Effect of pardon, annulment, or certificate of rehabilitation.** Evidence of a conviction is not admissible under this rule if (1) the conviction has been the subject of a pardon, annulment, certificate of rehabilitation, or other equivalent procedure based on a finding of the rehabilitation of the person convicted, and that person has not been convicted of a subsequent crime which was punishable by death or imprisonment in excess of one year, or (2) the conviction has been the subject of a pardon, annulment, or other equivalent procedure based on a finding of innocence.

(d) **Juvenile adjudications.** Evidence of juvenile adjudications is generally not admissible under this rule. The court may, however, in a criminal case allow evidence of a juvenile adjudication of a witness other than the accused if conviction of the offense would be admissible to attack the credibility of an adult and the court is satisfied that admission in evidence is necessary for a fair determination of the issue of guilt or innocence.

(e) **Pendency of appeal.** The pendency of an appeal therefrom does not render evidence of a conviction inadmissible. Evidence of the pendency of an appeal is admissible.

Rule 610.

RELIGIOUS BELIEFS OR OPINIONS

Evidence of the beliefs or opinions of a witness on matters of religion is not admissible for the purpose of showing that by reason of their nature his credibility is impaired or enhanced.

Rule 611.

MODE AND ORDER OF INTERROGATION AND PRESENTATION

(a) Control by court. The court shall exercise reasonable control over the mode and order of interrogating witnesses and presenting evidence so as to (1) make the interrogation and presentation effective for the ascertainment of the truth, (2) avoid needless consumption of time, and (3) protect witnesses from harassment or undue embarrassment.

(b) Scope of cross-examination. Cross-examination should be limited to the subject matter of the direct examination and matters affecting the credibility of the witness. The court may, in the exercise of discretion, permit inquiry into additional matters as if on direct examination.

(c) Leading questions. Leading questions should not be used on the direct examination of a witness except as may be necessary to develop his testimony. Ordinarily leading questions should be permitted on cross-examination. When a party calls a hostile witness, an adverse party, or a witness identified with an adverse party, interrogation may be by leading questions.

Rule 612.

WRITING USED TO REFRESH MEMORY

Except as otherwise provided in criminal proceedings by section 3500 of title 18, United States Code, if a witness uses a writing to refresh his memory for the purpose of testifying, either—

(1) while testifying, or

(2) before testifying, if the court in its discretion determines it is necessary in the interests of justice,

an adverse party is entitled to have the writing produced at the hearing, to inspect it, to cross-examine the witness thereon, and ɔ introduce in evidence those portions which relate to the testimony of the witness. If it is claimed that the writing contains matters not related to the subject matter of the testimony the court shall examine the writing in camera, excise any portions not so related, and order delivery of the remainder to the party entitled thereto. Any portion withheld over objections shall be preserved and made available to the appellate court in the event of an appeal. If a writing is not produced or delivered pursuant to order under this rule, the court shall make any order justice requires, except that in criminal cases when the prosecution elects not to comply, the order shall be one striking the testimony or, if the court in its discretion determines that the interests of justice so require, declaring a mistrial.

Rule 613.

PRIOR STATEMENTS OF WITNESSES

(a) **Examining witness concerning prior statement.** In examining a witness concerning a prior statement made by him, whether written or not, the statement need not be shown nor its contents disclosed to him at that time, but on request the same shall be shown or disclosed to opposing counsel.

(b) **Extrinsic evidence of prior inconsistent statement of witness.** Extrinsic evidence of a prior inconsistent statement by a witness is not admissible unless the witness is afforded an opportunity to explain or deny the same and the opposite party is afforded an opportunity to interrogate him thereon, or the interests of justice otherwise require. This provision does not apply to admissions of a party-opponent as defined in Rule 801 (d) (2).

Rule 614.

CALLING AND INTERROGATION OF WITNESSES BY COURT

(a) **Calling by court.** The court may, on its own motion or at the suggestion of a party, call witnesses, and all parties are entitled to cross-examine witnesses thus called.

(b) **Interrogation by court.** The court may interrogate witnesses, whether called by itself or by a party.

(c) **Objections.** Objections to the calling of witnesses by the court or to interrogation by it may be made at the time or at the next available opportunity when the jury is not present.

Rule 615.

EXCLUSION OF WITNESSES

At the request of a party the court shall order witnesses excluded so that they cannot hear the testimony of other witnesses, and it may make the order of its own motion. This rule does not authorize exclusion of (1) a party who is a natural person, or (2) an officer or employee of a party which is not a natural person designated as its representative by its attorney, or (3) a person whose presence is shown by a party to be essential to the presentation of his cause.

ARTICLE VII.   OPINIONS AND EXPERT TESTIMONY

Rule 701.

OPINION TESTIMONY BY LAY WITNESSES

If the witness is not testifying as an expert, his testimony in the form of opinions or inferences is limited to those opinions or inferences which are (a) rationally based on the perception of the witness and (b) helpful to a clear understanding of his testimony or the determination of a fact in issue.

Rule 702.

TESTIMONY BY EXPERTS

If scientific, technical, or other specialized knowledge will assist the trier of fact to understand the evidence or to determine a fact in issue, a witness qualified as an expert by knowledge, skill, experience, training, or education, may testify thereto in the form of an opinion or otherwise.

Rule 703.

BASES OF OPINION TESTIMONY BY EXPERTS

The facts or data in the particular case upon which an expert bases an opinion or inference may be those perceived by or made known to him at or before the hearing. If of a type reasonably relied upon by experts in the particular field in forming opinions or inferences upon the subject, the facts or data need not be admissible in evidence.

Rule 704.

OPINION ON ULTIMATE ISSUE

Testimony in the form of an opinion or inference otherwise admissible is not objectionable because it embraces an ultimate issue to be decided by the trier of fact.

Rule 705.

DISCLOSURE OF FACTS OR DATA UNDERLYING EXPERT OPINION

The expert may testify in terms of opinion or inference and give his reasons therefor without prior disclosure of the underlying facts or data, unless the judge requires otherwise. The expert may in any event be required to disclose the underlying facts or data on cross-examination.

Rule 706.

COURT APPOINTED EXPERTS

(a) Appointment. The court may on its own motion or on the motion of any party enter an order to show cause why expert witnesses should not be appointed, and may request the parties to submit nominations. The court may appoint any expert witnesses agreed upon by the parties, and may appoint witnesses of his own selection. An expert witness shall not be appointed by the court unless he consents to act. A witness so appointed shall be informed of his duties by the court in writing, a copy of which shall be filed with the clerk, or at a conference in which the parties shall have opportunity to participate. A witness so appointed shall advise the parties of his findings, if any; his deposition may be taken by any party; and he may be called to testify by the court or any party. He shall be subject to cross-examination by each party, including a party calling him as a witness.

(b) Compensation. Expert witnesses so appointed are entitled to reasonable compensation in whatever sum the court may allow. The compensation thus fixed is payable from funds which may be provided by law in criminal cases and civil actions and proceedings involving just compensation under the Fifth Amendment. In other civil actions and proceedings the compensation shall be paid by the parties in such proportion and at such time as the court directs, and thereafter charged in like manner as other costs.

(c) **Disclosure of appointment.** In the exercise of its discretion, the court may authorize disclosure to the jury of the fact that the court appointed the expert witness.

(d) **Parties' experts of own selection.** Nothing in this rule limits the parties in calling expert witnesses of their own selection.

ARTICLE VIII. HEARSAY

Rule 801.

DEFINITIONS

The following definitions apply under this Article:

(a) **Statement.** A "statement" is (1) an oral or written assertion or (2) nonverbal conduct of a person, if it is intended by him as an assertion.

(b) **Declarant.** A "declarant" is a person who makes a statement.

(c) **Hearsay.** "Hearsay" is a statement, other than one made by the declarant while testifying at the trial or hearing, offered in evidence to prove the truth of the matter asserted.

(d) **Statements which are not hearsay.** A statement is not hearsay if—

(1) *Prior statement by witness.* The declarant testifies at the trial or hearing and is subject to cross-examination concerning the statement, and the statement is (A) inconsistent with his testimony, and was given under oath subject to the penalty of perjury at a trial, hearing, or other proceeding, or in a deposition, or (B) consistent with his testimony and is offered to rebut an express or implied charge against him of recent fabrication or improper influence or motive, or (C) one of identification of a person made after perceiving him; or

(2) *Admission by party-opponent.* The statement is offered against a party and is (A) his own statement, in either his in-

ual or a representative capacity or (B) a statement of
ich he has manifested his adoption or belief in its truth, or
(C) a statement by a person authorized by him to make a statement concerning the subject, or (D) a statement by his agent
or servant concerning a matter within the scope of his agency
or employment, made during the existence of the relationship,
or (E) a statement by a co-conspirator of a party during the
course and in furtherance of the conspiracy.
As amended Oct. 16, 1975, eff. Oct. 31, 1975.

Rule 802.

HEARSAY RULE

Hearsay is not admissible except as provided by these rules or
by other rules prescribed by the Supreme Court pursuant to statutory authority or by Act of Congress.

Rule 803.

HEARSAY EXCEPTIONS: AVAILABILITY OF DECLARANT IMMATERIAL

The following are not excluded by the hearsay rule, even
though the declarant is available as a witness:

(1) Present sense impression. A statement describing or explaining an event or condition made while the declarant was
perceiving the event or condition, or immediately thereafter.

(2) Excited utterance. A statement relating to a startling
event or condition made while the declarant was under the stress
of excitement caused by the event or condition.

(3) Then existing mental, emotional, or physical condition.
A statement of the declarant's then existing state of mind, emo-
tion, sensation, or physical condition (such as intent, plan, motive, design, mental feeling, pain, and bodily health), but not
including a statement of memory or belief to prove the fact remembered or believed unless it relates to the execution, revocation, identification, or terms of declarant's will.

**(4) Statements for purposes of medical diagnosis or treat-
ment.** Statements made for purposes of medical diagnosis or
treatment and describing medical history, or past or present
symptoms, pain, or sensations, or the inception or general character of the cause or external source thereof insofar as reasonably pertinent to diagnosis or treatment.

(5) Recorded recollection. A memorandum or record concerning a matter about which a witness once had knowledge but now has insufficient recollection to enable him to testify fully and accurately, shown to have been made or adopted by the witness when the matter was fresh in his memory and to reflect that knowledge correctly. If admitted, the memorandum or record may be read into evidence but may not itself be received as an exhibit unless offered by an adverse party.

(6) Records of regularly conducted activity. A memorandum, report, record, or data compilation, in any form, of acts, events, conditions, opinions, or diagnoses, made at or near the time by, or from information transmitted by, a person with knowledge, if kept in the course of a regularly conducted business activity, and if it was the regular practice of that business activity to make the memorandum, report, record, or data compilation, all as shown by the testimony of the custodian or other qualified witness, unless the source of information or the method or circumstances of preparation indicate lack of trustworthiness. The term "business" as used in this paragraph includes business, institution, association, profession, occupation, and calling of every kind, whether or not conducted for profit.

(7) Absence of entry in records kept in accordance with the provisions of paragraph (6). Evidence that a matter is not included in the memoranda reports, records, or data compilations, in any form, kept in accordance with the provisions of paragraph (6), to prove the nonoccurrence or nonexistence of the matter, if the matter was of a kind of which a memorandum, report, record, or data compilation was regularly made and preserved, unless the sources of information or other circumstances indicate lack of trustworthiness.

(8) Public records and reports. Records, reports, statements, or data compilations, in any form, of public offices or agencies, setting forth (A) the activities of the office or agency, or (B) matters observed pursuant to duty imposed by law as to which matters there was a duty to report, excluding, however, in criminal cases matters observed by police officers and other law enforcement personnel, or (C) in civil actions and proceedings and against the Government in criminal cases, factual findings resulting from an investigation made pursuant to authority granted by law, unless the sources of information or other circumstances indicate lack of trustworthiness.

Records of vital statistics. Records or data compilations, any form, of births, fetal deaths, deaths, or marriages, if the report thereof was made to a public office pursuant to requirements of law.

(10) Absence of public record or entry. To prove the absence of a record, report, statement, or data compilation, in any form, or the nonoccurrence or nonexistence of a matter of which a record, report, statement, or data compilation, in any form, was regularly made and preserved by a public office or agency, evidence in the form of a certification in accordance with Rule 902, or testimony, that diligent search failed to disclose the record, report, statement, or data compilation, or entry.

(11) Records of religious organizations. Statements of births, marriages, divorces, deaths, legitimacy, ancestry, relationship by blood or marriage, or other similar facts of personal or family history, contained in a regularly kept record of a religious organization.

(12) Marriage, baptismal, and similar certificates. Statements of fact contained in a certificate that the maker performed a marriage or other ceremony or administered a sacrament, made by a clergyman, public official, or other person authorized by the rules or practices of a religious organization or by law to perform the act certified, and purporting to have been issued at the time of the act or within a reasonable time thereafter.

(13) Family records. Statements of fact concerning personal or family history contained in family Bibles, genealogies, charts, engravings on rings, inscription on family portraits, engravings on urns, crypts, or tombstones, or the like.

(14) Records of documents affecting an interest in property. The record of a document purporting to establish or affect an interest in property, as proof of the content of the original recorded document and its execution and delivery by each person by whom it purports to have been executed, if the record is a record of a public office and an applicable statute authorized the recording of documents of that kind in that office.

(15) Statements in documents affecting an interest in property. A statement contained in a document purporting to establish or affect an interest in property if the matter stated was relevant to the purpose of the document, unless dealings with the property since the document was made have been inconsistent with the truth of the statement or the purport of the document.

(16) Statements in ancient documents. Statements in a document in existence 20 years or more whose authenticity is established.

(17) Market reports, commercial publications. Market quotations, tabulations, lists, directories, or other published compilations, generally used and relied upon by the public or by persons in particular occupations.

(18) Learned treatises. To the extent called to the attention of an expert witness upon cross-examination or relied upon by him in direct examination, statements contained in published treatises, periodicals, or pamphlets on a subject of history, medicine, or other science or art, established as a reliable authority by the testimony or admission of the witness or by other expert testimony or by judicial notice. If admitted, the statements may be read into evidence but may not be received as exhibits.

(19) Reputation concerning personal or family history. Reputation among members of his family by blood, adoption, or marriage, or among his associates, or in the community, concerning a person's birth, adoption, marriage, divorce, death, legitimacy, relationship by blood, adoption, or marriage, ancestry, or other similar fact of his personal or family history.

(20) Reputation concerning boundaries or general history. Reputation in a community, arising before the controversy, as to boundaries of or customs affecting lands in the community, and reputation as to events of general history important to the community or state or nation in which located.

(21) Reputation as to character. Reputation of a person's character among his associates or in the community.

(22) Judgment of previous conviction. Evidence of a final judgment, entered after a trial or upon a plea of guilty (but not upon a plea of *nolo contendere*), adjudging a person guilty of a crime punishable by death or imprisonment in excess of one year, to prove any fact essential to sustain the judgment, but not including, when offered by the government in a criminal prosecution for purposes other than impeachment, judgments against persons other than the accused. The pendency of an appeal may be shown but does not affect admissibility.

Judgment as to personal, family, or general history, or **~~daries~~.** Judgments as proof of matters of personal, family general history, or boundaries, essential to the judgment, if the same would be provable by evidence of reputation.

(24) Other exceptions. A statement not specifically covered by any of the foregoing exceptions but having equivalent circumstantial guarantees of trustworthiness, if the court determines that (A) the statement is offered as evidence of a material fact; (B) the statement is more probative on the point for which it is offered than any other evidence which the proponent can procure through reasonable efforts; and (C) the general purposes of these rules and the interests of justice will best be served by admission of the statement into evidence. However, a statement may not be admitted under this exception unless the proponent of it makes known to the adverse party sufficiently in advance of the trial or hearing to provide the adverse party with a fair opportunity to prepare to meet it, his intention to offer the statement and the particulars of it, including the name and address of the declarant.

Rule 804.

HEARSAY EXCEPTIONS; DECLARANT UNAVAILABLE

(a) Definition of unavailability. "Unavailability as a witness" includes situations in which the declarant:

(1) Is exempted by ruling of the court on the ground of privilege from testifying concerning the subject matter of his statement; or

(2) Persists in refusing to testify concerning the subject matter of his statement despite an order of the court to do so; or

(3) Testifies to a lack of memory of the subject matter of his statement; or

(4) Is unable to be present or to testify at the hearing because of death or then existing physical or mental illness or infirmity; or

(5) Is absent from the hearing and the proponent of his statement has been unable to procure his attendance (or in the case of a hearsay exception under subdivision (b)(2), (3), or (4), his attendance or testimony) by process or other reasonable means.

A declarant is not unavailable as a witness if his exemption, refusal, claim of lack of memory, inability, or absence is due to the procurement or wrongdoing of the proponent of his statement for the purpose of preventing the witness from attending or testifying.

(b) **Hearsay exceptions.** The following are not excluded by the hearsay rule if the declarant is unavailable as a witness:

(1) *Former testimony.* Testimony given as a witness at another hearing of the same or a different proceeding, or in a deposition taken in compliance with law in the course of the same or another proceeding, if the party against whom the testimony is now offered, or, in a civil action or proceeding, a predecessor in interest, had an opportunity and similar motive to develop the testimony by direct, cross, or redirect examination.

(2) *Statement under belief of impending death.* In a prosecution for homicide or in a civil action or proceeding, a statement made by a declarant while believing that his death was imminent, concerning the cause or circumstances of what he believed to be his impending death.

(3) *Statement against interest.* A statement which was at the time of its making so far contrary to the declarant's pecuniary or proprietary interest, or so far tended to subject him to civil or criminal liability, or to render invalid a claim by him against another, that a reasonable man in his position would not have made the statement unless he believed it to be true. A statement tending to expose the declarant to criminal liability and offered to exculpate the accused is not admissible unless corroborating circumstances clearly indicate the trustworthiness of the statement.

(4) *Statement of personal or family history.* (A) A statement concerning the declarant's own birth, adoption, marriage, divorce, legitimacy, relationship by blood, adoption, or marriage, ancestry, or other similar fact of personal or family history, even though declarant had no means of acquiring personal knowledge of the matter stated; or (B) a statement concerning the foregoing matters, and death also, of another person, if the declarant was related to the other by blood, adoption, or marriage or was so intimately associated with the other's family as to be likely to have accurate information concerning the matter declared.

(5) *Other exceptions.* A statement not specifically covered by any of the foregoing exceptions but having equivalent circumstantial guarantees of trustworthiness, if the court determines that (A) the statement is offered as evidence of a material fact; (B) the statement is more probative on the point for which it is offered than any other evidence which the proponent can procure through reasonable efforts; and (C) the general purposes of these rules and the interests of justice will best be served by admission of the statement into evidence. However, a statement may not be admitted under this exception unless the proponent of it makes known to the adverse party sufficiently in advance of the trial or hearing to provide the adverse party with a fair opportunity to prepare to meet it, his intention to offer the statement and the particulars of it, including the name and address of the declarant.

Rule 805.

HEARSAY WITHIN HEARSAY

Hearsay included within hearsay is not excluded under the hearsay rule if each part of the combined statements conforms with an exception to the hearsay rule provided in these rules.

Rule 806.

ATTACKING AND SUPPORTING CREDIBILITY OF DECLARANT

When a hearsay statement, or a statement defined in Rule 801 (d) (2), (C), (D), or (E), has been admitted in evidence, the credibility of the declarant may be attacked, and if attacked may be supported, by any evidence which would be admissible for those purposes if declarant had testified as a witness. Evidence of a statement or conduct by the declarant at any time, inconsistent with his hearsay statement, is not subject to any requirement that he may have been afforded an opportunity to deny or explain. If the party against whom a hearsay statement has been admitted calls the declarant as a witness, the party is entitled to examine him on the statement as if under cross-examination.

ARTICLE IX. AUTHENTICATION AND IDENTIFICATION

Rule 901.

REQUIREMENT OF AUTHENTICATION OR IDENTIFICATION

(a) General provision. The requirement of authentication or identification as a condition precedent to admissibility is satisfied by evidence sufficient to support a finding that the matter in question is what its proponent claims.

(b) Illustrations. By way of illustration only, and not by way of limitation, the following are examples of authentication or identification conforming with the requirements of this rule:

(1) Testimony of witness with knowledge. Testimony that a matter is what it is claimed to be.

(2) Nonexpert opinion on handwriting. Nonexpert opinion as to the genuineness of handwriting, based upon familiarity not acquired for purposes of the litigation.

(3) Comparison by trier or expert witness. Comparison by the trier of fact or by expert witnesses with specimens which have been authenticated.

(4) Distinctive characteristics and the like. Appearance, contents, substance, internal patterns, or other distinctive characteristics, taken in conjunction with circumstances.

(5) Voice identification. Identification of a voice, whether heard firsthand or through mechanical or electronic transmission or recording, by opinion based upon hearing the voice at any time under circumstances connecting it with the alleged speaker.

(6) Telephone conversations. Telephone conversations, by evidence that a call was made to the number assigned at the time by the telephone company to a particular person or business, if (A) in the case of a person, circumstances, including self-identification, show the person answering to be the one called, or (B) in the case of a business, the call was made to a place of business and the conversation related to business reasonably transacted over the telephone.

(7) Public records or reports. Evidence that a writing authorized by law to be recorded or filed and in fact recorded or filed in a public office, or a purported public record, report, state-

ment, or data compilation, in any form, is from the public office where items of this nature are kept.

(8) Ancient documents or data compilation. Evidence that a document or data compilation, in any form, (A) is in such condition as to create no suspicion concerning its authenticity, (B) was in a place where it, if authentic, would likely be, and (C) has been in existence 20 years or more at the time it is offered.

(9) Process or system. Evidence describing a process or system used to produce a result and showing that the process or system produces an accurate result.

(10) Methods provided by statute or rule. Any method of authentication or identification provided by Act of Congress or by other rules prescribed by the Supreme Court pursuant to statutory authority.

Rule 902.

SELF-AUTHENTICATION

Extrinsic evidence of authenticity as a condition precedent to admissibility is not required with respect to the following:

(1) Domestic public documents under seal. A document bearing a seal purporting to be that of the United States, or of any state, district, commonwealth, territory, or insular possession thereof, or the Panama Canal Zone, or the Trust Territory of the Pacific Islands, or of a political subdivision, department, officer, or agency thereof, and a signature purporting to be an attestation or execution.

(2) Domestic public documents not under seal. A document purporting to bear the signature in his official capacity of an officer or employee of any entity included in paragraph (1) hereof, having no seal, if a public officer having a seal and having official duties in the district or political subdivision of the officer or employee certifies under seal that the signer has the official capacity and that the signature is genuine.

(3) Foreign public documents. A document purporting to be executed or attested in his official capacity by a person authorized by the laws of a foreign country to make the execution or attestation, and accompanied by a final certification as to the genuineness of the signature and official position (A) of the executing or attesting person, or (B) of any foreign official whose certificate of genuineness of signature and official position relates to the execution or attestation or is in a chain of certificates of genuineness of signature and official position relating to the execution or attestation. A final certification may be made by a secretary of embassy or legation, consul general, consul, vice consul, or consular agent of the United States, or a diplomatic or consular official of the foreign country assigned or accredited to the United States. If reasonable opportunity has been given to all parties to investigate the authenticity and accuracy of official documents, the court may, for good cause shown, order that they be treated as presumptively authentic without final certification or permit them to be evidenced by an attested summary with or without final certification.

(4) Certified copies of public records. A copy of an official record or report or entry therein, or of a document authorized by law to be recorded or filed and actually recorded or filed in a public office, including data compilations in any form, certified as correct by the custodian or other person authorized to make the certification, by certificate complying with paragraph (1), (2), or (3) of this Rule or complying with any Act of Congress or rule prescribed by the Supreme Court pursuant to statutory authority.

(5) Official publications. Books, pamphlets, or other publications purporting to be issued by public authority.

(6) Newspapers and periodicals. Printed materials purporting to be newspapers or periodicals.

(7) Trade inscriptions and the like. Inscriptions, signs, tags, or labels purporting to have been affixed in the course of business and indicating ownership, control, or origin.

(8) Acknowledged documents. Documents accompanied by a certificate of acknowledgment executed in the manner provided by law by a notary public or other officer authorized by law to take acknowledgments.

(9) Commercial paper and related documents. Commercial paper, signatures thereon, and documents relating thereto to the extent provided by general commercial law.

(10) Presumptions under acts of Congress. Any signature, document, or other matter declared by Act of Congress to be presumptively or prima facie genuine or authentic.

Rule 903.

SUBSCRIBING WITNESS' TESTIMONY UNNECESSARY

The testimony of a subscribing witness is not necessary to authenticate a writing unless required by the laws of the jurisdiction whose laws govern the validity of the writing.

ARTICLE X. CONTENTS OF WRITINGS, RECORDINGS, AND PHOTOGRAPHS

Rule 1001.

DEFINITIONS

For purposes of this article the following definitions are applicable.

(1) Writings and recordings. "Writings" and "recordings" consist of letters, words, or numbers, or their equivalent, set down by handwriting, typewriting, printing, photostating, photographing, magnetic impulse, mechanical or electronic recording, or other form of data compilation.

(2) Photographs. "Photographs" include still photographs, X-ray films, and motion pictures.

(3) Original. An "original" of a writing or recording is the writing or recording itself or any counterpart intended to have the same effect by a person executing or issuing it. An "original" of a photograph includes the negative or any print therefrom. If data are stored in a computer or similar device, any printout or other output readable by sight, shown to reflect the data accurately, is an "original."

(4) Duplicate. A "duplicate" is a counterpart produced by the same impression as the original, or from the same matrix, or by means of photography, including enlargements and miniatures, or by mechanical or electronic re-recording, or by chemical reproduction, or by other equivalent techniques which accurately reproduces the original.

Rule 1002.

REQUIREMENT OF ORIGINAL

To prove the content of a writing, recording, or photograph, the original writing, recording, or photograph is required, except as otherwise provided in these rules or by Act of Congress.

Rule 1003.

ADMISSIBILITY OF DUPLICATES

A duplicate is admissible to the same extent as an original unless (1) a genuine question is raised as to the authenticity of the original or (2) in the circumstances it would be unfair to admit the duplicate in lieu of the original.

Rule 1004.

ADMISSIBILITY OF OTHER EVIDENCE OF CONTENTS

The original is not required, and other evidence of the contents of a writing, recording, or photograph is admissible if—

(1) Originals lost or destroyed. All originals are lost or have been destroyed, unless the proponent lost or destroyed them in bad faith; or

(2) Original not obtainable. No original can be obtained by any available judicial process or procedure; or

(3) Original in possession of opponent. At a time when an original was under the control of the party against whom offered, he was put on notice, by the pleadings or otherwise, that the contents would be a subject of proof at the hearing, and he does not produce the original at the hearing; or

(4) Collateral matters. The writing, recording, or photograph is not closely related to a controlling issue.

Rule 1005.

PUBLIC RECORDS

The contents of an official record, or of a document authorized to be recorded or filed and actually recorded or filed, including data compilations in any form, if otherwise admissible, may be proved by copy, certified as correct in accordance with Rule 902 or testified to be correct by a witness who has compared it with the original. If a copy which complies with the foregoing cannot be obtained by the exercise of reasonable diligence, then other evidence of the contents may be given.

Rule 1006.

SUMMARIES

The contents of voluminous writings, recordings, or photographs which cannot conveniently be examined in court may be presented in the form of a chart, summary, or calculation. The originals, or duplicates, shall be made available for examination or copying, or both, by other parties at reasonable time and place. The court may order that they be produced in court.

Rule 1007.

TESTIMONY OR WRITTEN ADMISSION OF PARTY

Contents of writings, recordings, or photographs may be proved by the testimony or deposition of the party against whom offered or by his written admission, without accounting for the nonproduction of the original.

Rule 1008.

FUNCTIONS OF COURT AND JURY

When the admissibility of other evidence of contents of writings, recordings, or photographs under these rules depends upon the fulfillment of a condition of fact, the question whether the condition has been fulfilled is ordinarily for the court to determine in accordance with the provisions of Rule 104. However, when an issue is raised (a) whether the asserted writing ever existed, or (b) whether another writing, recording, or photograph produced at the trial is the original, or (c) whether other evidence of contents correctly reflects the contents, the issue is for the trier of fact to determine as in the case of other issues of fact.

ARTICLE XI. MISCELLANEOUS RULES

Rule 1101.

APPLICABILITY OF RULES

(a) Courts and magistrates. These rules apply to the United States district courts, the District Court of Guam, the District Court of the Virgin Islands, the District Court for the District of the Canal Zone, the United States courts of appeals, the Court of Claims, and to United States magistrates, in the actions, cases, and proceedings and to the extent hereinafter set forth. The terms "judge" and "court" in these rules include United States magistrates, referees in bankruptcy, and commissioners of the Court of Claims.

(b) Proceedings generally. These rules apply generally to civil actions and proceedings, including admiralty and maritime cases, to criminal cases and proceedings, to contempt proceedings except those in which the court may act summarily, and to proceedings and cases under the Bankruptcy Act.

(c) Rule of privilege. The rule with respect to privileges applies at all stages of all actions, cases, and proceedings.

(d) Rules inapplicable. The rules (other than with respect to privileges) do not apply in the following situations:

(1) *Preliminary questions of fact.* The determination of questions of fact preliminary to admissibility of evidence when the issue is to be determined by the court under rule 104.

(2) *Grand jury.* Proceedings before grand juries.

(3) *Miscellaneous proceedings.* Proceedings for extradition or rendition; preliminary examinations in criminal cases; sentencing, or granting or revoking probation; issuance of warrants for arrest, criminal summonses, and search warrants; and proceedings with respect to release on bail or otherwise.

(e) Rules applicable in part. In the following proceedings these rules apply to the extent that matters of evidence are not provided for in the statutes which govern procedure therein or in other rules prescribed by the Supreme Court pursuant to statutory authority; the trial of minor and petty offenses by United States magistrates; review of agency actions when the facts are subject to trial de novo under section 706(2)(F) of title 5, United States Code; review of orders of the Secretary of Agriculture under section 2 of the Act entitled "An Act to authorize association of producers of agricultural products" approved February 18, 1922 (7 U.S.C. 292), and under sections 6 and 7(c) of the Perishable Agricultural Commodities Act, 1930 (7 U.S.C. 499f, 499g(c)); naturalization and revocation of naturalization under sections 310–318 of the Immigration and Nationality Act (8 U.S.C. 1421–1429); prize proceedings in admiralty under sections 7651–7681 of title 10, United States Code; review of orders of the Secretary of the Interior under section 2 of the Act entitled "An Act authorizing associations of producers of aquatic products" approved June 25, 1931 (15 U.S.C. 522); review of orders of petroleum control boards under section 5 of the Act entitled "An Act to regulate interstate and foreign commerce in petroleum and its products by prohibiting the shipment in such commerce of petroleum and its products produced in violation of State law, and for other purposes", approved February 22, 1935 (15 U.S.C. 715d); actions for fines, penalties, or forfeitures under part V of title IV of the Tariff Act of 1930 (19 U.S.C. 1581–1624), or under the Anti-Smuggling Act (19 U.S.C. 1701–1711); criminal libel for condemnation, exclusion of imports, or other proceedings under the Federal Food, Drug, and Cosmetic Act (21 U.S.C. 301–392); disputes between seamen under sections 4079, 4080, and 4081 of the Revised Statutes (22 U.S.C. 256–258; habeas corpus under sections 2241–2254 of title 28, United States Code; motions to vacate, set aside or correct sentence under section 2255 of title 28, United States Code; actions for penalties for refusal to transport destitute seamen under section 4578 of the Revised Statutes (46 U.S.C. 679); actions against the United States under the Act entitled "An Act authorizing suits against the United States in admiralty for damage caused by and salvage service rendered to public vessels belonging to the United States, and for other purposes", approved March 3, 1925 (46 U.S.C. 781–790), as implemented by section 7730 of title 10, United States Code.

Rule 1102.

AMENDMENTS

Amendments to the Federal Rules of Evidence may be made as provided in section 2076 of title 28 of the United States Code.

Rule 1103.

TITLE

These rules may be known and cited as the Federal Rules of Evidence.

INDEX

MEDICAL EXPENSES
Paid by potential defendant, 154.

MEMORY
Competency, 65.
Recorded past recollection, 83–84, 231–234.
Testing through cross-examination, 81, 159–160, 189.

MENTAL STATE
See Hearsay Exceptions, Mental condition; Hearsay Rule, Statements revealing state of mind.

MILITARY AND STATE SECRETS
See Privileges, State secrets.

MISLEADING QUESTION
See Form of Questions.

MODELS
Demonstrative evidence, 415.
Foundation, 417–418.

MOTION IN LIMINE
When used, 390.

MOTION PICTURES
Authentication, 423–424.
Whether substantive evidence, 424–425.

MOTION TO STRIKE
Purpose, 379.
Time of making, 379.

MULTIPLE PROBATIVE VALUE
Basic principle, 27–28.
Illustration, 165–166.

NARCO–INTERROGATION
See "Truth Serums"

NEWSMEN
See Privileges, Journalist-source.

NOLO CONTENDERE
Admission, 314–315.
Impeachment, 315.

NOTICE
Evidence of prior crime, 143 n. 28.
Of intent to take judicial notice, 13.
Residual exception to hearsay rule, 372–373.
To produce original document, 438.

OATH OR AFFIRMATION
Competency of witness, 65.
Former testimony, 252.
Prior statements outside hearsay rule, 186–187.

OBJECTIONS
Generally, 379–380, 381–390.
Appeal, 381
Curative admissibility, 386–389.
Exceptions, 381.
Exclusion by judge without, 6.
Former testimony, 255–256.
General, 382–384.
Harmless error, 385.
Motion to strike, 379.
Narrative testimony, 71.
"Opening the door," 386–389.
Plain error, 381.
Pretrial, 390.
Rationale, 382.
Specific, 382–385.
Tactics, 390.
Time of making, 379, 390.
Waiver, 318, 381–382, 390.

OFFER OF PROOF
Generally, 378–379, 380–381, 385–386, 389.
Cross-examination, 389.
General offer, 380–381.
Meaning of term, 378.
Necessity of, 378.
Purposes, 379–380.
Real evidence and documents, 378.
Techniques, 378–379.

OFFICIAL WRITTEN STATEMENTS
See Hearsay Exceptions, Public records.

OPENING AND CLOSING ARGUMENT
Nature and limitations, 69–70, 96–87.
Sequence, 97–98.

"OPENING THE DOOR"
See Curative Admissibility ("Opening the Door").

OPINIONS
See also Expert Witness.
Generally, 84–89, 99, 111–112, 296–297.